P9-DYO-533

REDEMPTION
FROM
ADDICTION

The Eleven Powers and The Eleven Arts

Gerard "Jerry" Egan

authorHOUSE®

AuthorHouse™
1663 Liberty Drive
Bloomington, IN 47403
www.authorhouse.com
Phone: 1-800-839-8640

© 2011 Gerard "Jerry" Egan. All rights reserved.

No part of this book may be reproduced, stored in a retrieval system, or
transmitted by any means without the written permission of the author.

First published by AuthorHouse   12/20/2011

ISBN: 978-1-4678-3443-8 (sc)
ISBN: 978-1-4678-3442-1 (hc)
ISBN: 978-1-4678-3441-4 (e)

Library of Congress Control Number: 2011960083

Printed in the United States of America

Cover photography and interior photographs by Kellie Riess of Re-image photo.com.

Author's photo on back cover is credited to James Greene Photography of Delray Beach, Florida

This book is printed on acid-free paper.

Because of the dynamic nature of the Internet, any web addresses or links contained in
this book may have changed since publication and may no longer be valid. The views
expressed in this work are solely those of the author and do not necessarily reflect the
views of the publisher, and the publisher hereby disclaims any responsibility for them.

ACC LIBRARY SERVICES AUSTIN, TX

The Eleven Powers and The Eleven Arts

CONTENTS

Acknowledgements

Almost three years ago a very special and gifted man with the extraordinary vision of building an organization that would change the lives of addicts and alcoholics—freeing them from their madness and relieving the suffering of their families and loved ones—invited me and many of his staff to hear and participate in a Life Changing weekend. He recognized the awesome benefit of bringing his staff, or what I prefer to call our Team, to an event that would create the passion that would equal his own, and align his vision with the force and power of his carefully selected Team to bring forth the combined creativity that would be essential to manifest his dream and turn it from a "Possibility into a Probability!"

This special and very gifted man enabled me to learn from an equally extraordinarily special and very gifted man (Anthony Robbins) who is well known for his ability in his seminars to "Unleash the Power that is Within" us. This book is a direct result of the power, insight, creativity, perseverance, and deep faith of especially those two extraordinary men; but also all the people that I began to see and view in ways I was totally blind—till that Life Changing weekend!

For many years I have been deeply privileged to work within the "Palm Partners" organization and to witness the phenomenal growth of Dr. Harrigan's, Dr. Murdorf's and Dr. Beley's dream! Today "Palm Partners" is a formidable force and power that not only absolutely "Frees the Addicts and Alcoholics from their Madness and relieves the Misery and Suffering of Families and Significant others!" But provides vital long term services such as all levels of Coaching—Life, Recovery and Family Coaching; Opportunities for the newly recovering person to enter into Certificate Earning Education and College courses with transferable credits towards Bachelor's and Masters Degrees; providing the missing and essential recovery ingredient—the path to self esteem and true self value through self empowerment! The recovering person will be propelled into a compelling vision of not only a spectacular new view of themselves but the ability to choose their future destiny!

This extraordinarily imaginative team of which I am deeply proud of being a member has been establishing a uniquely innovative as well as ingenious methodology to truly produce a "Change For Life."

LONG OVER DUE?

—BUT—

"ALL THINGS HAPPEN IN GOD'S TIME"—

WHICH MEANS THIS IS THE EXACT PERFECT TIME!

ADDICTS, ALCOHOLICS, AND THEIR FAMILY MEMBERS
MADE THIS BOOK POSSIBLE!
AND I THANK YOU, AND DEEPLY APPRECIATE AND LOVE
EVERY ONE OF YOU!

This book is dedicated to every addict and alcoholic or family member that has Pushed me, Prodded me and enthusiastically encouraged me for a tangible book that they could own and study due to the fact that for over 25 years they have repeatedly told me and informed me that the ideas, observations and suggestions I have discussed with them—they have never heard.

It is very awkward to speak highly about myself and in fact somewhat if not majorly embarrassing but until someone reads this book and written comments are given—I can only relate that every therapy group that I have conducted and every single person I have ever spoken to—have been pleasantly shocked and surprised at my insights and understanding of their or their loved ones condition.

The greatest complement I have ever been paid was at least 20 years ago when an addict stated to me in a large group session the following:

"You make things so clear to us—that even Ray Charles could see it!!
(For those of you who are not that old—Ray Charles was
one of the greatest singers and musicians of all time—just
look him up on the Internet!)

By the way he was totally BLIND!

I KNOW—I FORGOT?

Lots of People—Family and Friends

BUT!

MY BEST FRIEND that I have been married to for over 40 years and have known for 44 years is Dolores and without this very truly loving and courageous woman I would have died long ago of my own Madness that she has successfully kept locked in the attic of our lives.

In 1973 in April she requested, "It is my birthday—will you please see a psychologist that is the only present I want!" Dr. Eddy whom I owe my entire life to—worked with me for two and a half years and launched me into college—when I met him I barely had a high school diploma and was barely alive! He said, "You need to get an education so that it will give you the right to do what you do so well, and that is helping other people!"

This has enabled "Jerry" to function unhampered by his Madness and to be privileged to touch and change literally thousands of lives (Hopefully thousands but it may have been hundreds and possibly a thousand—but who was counting and who REALLY knows.) What I do know is that Dolores stood by me while I abandoned her for hundreds of hours to write this book! "DEE? You should never of bought me the Mac—that I said I would never use!"

My special thanks to my older daughter "Dawn" who tirelessly believed in this project and had full faith that this work could be written and completed. Dawn and her husband Ulises then literally relentlessly "HOUNDED" me into making this book possible—She would constantly remind me to "WRITE" and would challenge my "Good Intentions" and remind me to turn it from a "Possibility into a Probability!" Her husband Ulises read some of the more difficult "concepts" and helped reassure me that as bizarre as they sounded—"they did in fact make some sense—in fact common sense!"

It should be especially noted that Kellie Riess of Re-Image Photo is my daughter and she is a professional photographer who lives with her husband Ralph and Scarlett in Hawaii where she took all the awesome photos for this book and her work is "SECOND TO NONE!" She has been a major inspiration for me to help me truly believe that this book was absolutely needed and necessary and would in fact help many of God's children and their families who are suffering from the devastating condition of addiction!

People sometimes would say they have a calling—it is at this time that I am writing this "Appreciation" which is part of the final pages of this book—that I am hoping and truly believing that—This work was inspired by God and that is quite a testament from one who was confused, baffled and bewildered at this God concept—but I have to be the first to admit—Although I wrote this entire volume without assistance from anyone—everyone of His Children made it possible!!

FOREWORD

At the time of this writing I was convinced that the book that you are about to read; had already been written, and all I had to do was rediscover it page by page from some cosmic dimension that some people and I would prefer to call God. As in the book Alcoholics Anonymous, I will be describing and suggesting controversial concepts and ideas, and it is NOT my intention to excite or create a forum for discussion; it is my desire AND ONLY my desire to provide other paths to recovery.

AA and NA have only reached a very small segment of alcoholics and addicts as indicated by the simple fact that there are 18 million alcoholics and 5 million addicts, which means that the combined memberships of both AA and NA would indicate that only about 10% of all addicts and alcoholics, find an effective solution through 12 Step programs. (See official membership estimates at the end of the Introduction.) Although AA and NA combined has helped millions it has failed to help many millions more. Due to this pitiful low percentage, other methods and routes to recovery must be found to help the remaining 21 million addicts and alcoholics still stuck in their madness!

New ideas must be embraced and honestly explored. I have been painfully aware of how there has been a tendency for alcoholics and addicts to see themselves somewhat uniquely different from each other and to address this major disconnect, I felt compelled that any time and every time there appears a quote in this book, that is just about alcoholism, or one just about addiction or the addict; I have taken the liberty to add "and addiction" or "addict" to all phrases and quotes that omit "addict." I will state "the alcoholic *and the addict*," or I will state "alcoholism *and addiction*," or "The addict *and alcoholic* must…" To preserve the integrity of the quote I will show this modification by italicizing my additions as seen in the above examples.

In addition to this I have exercised my right of authorship to write this book and to use a style that varies font sizes as well as using a particular Case and punctuation in which I typed specific words for maximum impact! My English professor would give me a <u>FAILING</u> Grade for "SUCH" atrocities, Blasphemy and ("TOTAL") disregard for the "LAW" at least according to Harbrace! (for those not acquainted with Harbrace in 1976, when I was a college student, it was the end all standard of writing the "KINGS ENGLISH."

In addition it should be noted that although there is only very minimal use of adult language it was carefully selected and considered in order to effectively maximize significant concepts—some readers may find it objectionable but this book is about addiction and was written to empower the addict and alcoholic and to use words with lesser impact would be to dilute and weaken the very Powers that are discussed and presented.

ANOTHERWORD

There are awesome and powerful creative forces that can be fully tapped; that will absolutely unleash our dreams and hopes transforming them into a desired reality.

OR

These same forces will send us into the deepest darkest Hell we have ever known!

Many contemporary philosophers and motivation specialists discuss the nature of this creative force, which can transform anyone's dreams into realities or what I refer to as turning "Possibilities into Probabilities."

"If a person fails to understand that they have a huge responsibility to take full possession and control of this great creative power, then that failure to take this responsibility will always lead to these forces taking control of the person in an undesirable, destructive and potentially deadly manner."

"All addictions are a manifestation caused by the poor or improper use of these forces and powers!"

"Any addict or alcoholic who day dreams and night dreams about the substances they used and focuses on memories of the feelings they experienced under the influence, are summoning this power to provide what they long for and desire—which is to get high or drunk again!"

"If the person fails to challenge these feelings and memories, then their...

"Subconscious through some powerful and unknown force converts and transforms their thoughts into a manifested reality."

"In other words opportunities and temptations to use will present themselves as a direct result of failing to take control of these forces or misusing their power!"

Since thoughts are things then the intense passion of thinking and talking about drug and alcohol use, assure that the opportunity to drink and use drugs will materialize. In other words addicts and alcoholics have mastered the principles of success and use those very same concepts to assure their own failure and destruction!

The purpose of this book is to alert the addict and alcoholic of the dynamics that undermine their efforts to recover and to provide methods to create the necessary desire and actions that will absolutely enable them to change their life.

By forcing yourself to do what you don't want to do enables you to gain hold of and grasp these powerful forces and turn them in the direction of success instead of failure!

Make sure you are growing and cultivating the right kinds of seeds. Attend the seeds of a recovery lifestyle and you will reap great riches in every area of your life. Cultivate the wrong seeds of an addictive lifestyle, then watch every dream, hope, desire, promise, vision and aspiration be slowly choked and shattered!

"The very laws that govern the ability for anyone to accomplish anything in their lives for their GOOD;

are the very same laws that also govern the ability to accomplish anything BAD in their lives!"

"The Law of Attraction does not know right from wrong—it works for the greater good of a person or if used improperly will absolutely destroy that same person! It is no different than Nuclear Power—if properly used it provides the greatest HEAVENLY gifts, such as electricity and nuclear medicine. If improperly used it creates the greatest dread and literally HELL on earth!

This book will give you the essential Eleven Powers and Eleven Arts that will enable you to Change your life. The use of these Powers and Arts will enable you to take full control of not only your addiction, but provide endless opportunities to have an entire new Destiny!! Teach yourself and learn to direct the awesome creative forces within you and learn to turn your "Possibilities into Probabilities!"

Before you begin to even start reading the following Introduction it is very important if not helpful to read and review Chapter 12 titled "Definitions Determine Direction." It will be through this understanding that many of my ideas and proposals may be viewed in a better context and hopefully you the reader will be more receptive to accept.

Now after a careful review of these actual definitions that are being utilized to clarify abstract concepts described through out this book; you should be able to begin to ascertain that the views of this author have, if not a solid foundation for further discussion; then certainly at least my ideas need to be given some consideration; especially when there are no current answers for the still suffering 21 million addicts and alcoholics that have not found the power or willingness to end their madness!

INTRODUCTION

It should be noted that this introduction was the first idea that this author wrote. The need to write this book arose from my first discovery, which is that as I approach the age of 60 my time remaining on the earth is much shorter than the time I have already spent on the earth. As a result of this discovery I decided that there are numerous ideas, thoughts and suggestions that I need to share with others, who are like me suffering from a condition referred to as "addiction." It should be noted of the three things that I hope to share, which are my thoughts, suggestions and ideas; "suggestions" is the most important of these things. It will be though the willingness to follow these suggestions that I hope, and wish to set you free from the madness of addiction.

After all Bill Wilson, cofounder of Alcoholics Anonymous, wrote on page 34 in his "Twelve Steps and Twelve Traditions," book that "willingness is the key" in fact he implied that there was "only one key and that is the key of willingness" but is that the only key?

> "What does a person do when there is no "WILLINGNESS" to follow these or any other suggestions? Are they then DOOMED, and is there no salvation, no hope, no chance of staying sober and clean, no way to disrupt their destructive destiny?"

Fortunately I was one of those people and I found that "willingness" is not the only key, and in fact "WILLINGNESS IS NOT NECESSARY"- what is necessary is intense passion, and every addict and alcoholic have a huge abundance of intense love or hate or both for the substances or things that they do. It is a recognized fact that anytime an addict or an alcoholic are sharing an experience that occurred while under the influence they usually do so in a loud and vivacious (lively, cheerful, energetic) manner.

"WILLINGNESS IS _NOT_ THE _ONLY_ KEY."

"WILLINGNESS IS _NOT_ NECESSARY-

"WHAT _IS_ NECESSARY _IS_ INTENSE PASSION."

Bill Wilson was absolutely right in the Third Step when he wrote, "A beginning, even the smallest, is all that is needed." But while he was referring to willingness being the only key, and the need to use it as in his quote "Cut away the self will that has always blocked the entry of God-or, if you like, a Higher Power, into our lives." I propose that there are other Keys that will enable a "beginning, even the smallest" and keys that create and produce the power to change one's life, even if there is a natural resistance to doing so.

According to AA it is necessary to have willingness, and I believe that due to this premise; this is one of the main reasons AA has not reached the great majority of those in need. My personal experience and professional experience with alcoholism and addiction, as well as recovery and relapse, all seem to indicate that most alcoholics remain unwilling, and therefore continuously fail in any attempt to recover. The reason they seem to fail to learn from past mistakes, and seem to have the inability to make any significant permanent changes in their attitudes and behaviors, is due to their natural tendency to be resistant, rebellious and oppositional. By using these intense negative feelings and behaviors I will guide you to master the "Eleven Powers and Eleven Arts" that will provide you a "Redemption from Addiction."

"Most addicts and alcoholics are plagued with the inability to develop enough willingness to change their attitudes and behaviors."

It is therefore this author's intention to demonstrate multiple effective solutions that do not require any willingness at all. It may seem like a contradiction, that if a person takes action or changes their behavior, attitudes or beliefs, that this required willingness; but this may not be exactly true.

"Ability to change behavior does not necessarily hinge upon desire or willingness."

I believe that many substance abusers that could have been saved have perished, due to they could not develop strong enough desire, and could not accept the concept of needing God in their lives, and these two things are essential for success in AA or any 12-Step program. This lack of faith or desire would then be blamed on the person being to arrogant or not being able to develop enough honesty to recognize they have no choice, but to believe in God, and through that belief, develop the necessary desire to change their behaviors.

Their resistance many times was not due to arrogance, but due to severe injury or disappointment and having the belief that God, was somehow responsible and could have intervened. If willingness to "Turn my will and my life over to God as I understand him" is the only key, then it is obvious that there are many more addicts and alcoholics who cannot, or will not believe in any kind or type of deity; then there are those who are "willing."

Due to this fact, we must be creative enough to find words and language that is absolutely friendly, and nonthreatening or offensive that will enable these rebellious, resistant addicts, and alcoholics freedom from the madness of their addictions. It will be by developing the "Power of Spirituality" through the "Art of Giving" that will enable the addict or alcoholic to find a strong healthy faith or spirituality.

> "It is everyone's moral responsibility to be open and receptive to new and controversial concepts, ideas and suggestions, that can provide hope for the helpless and help for the hopeless."

Your opinion and my opinion does not count, what counts is that we as a society must find new and effective technology that will save the lives, and the sanity of what has been up till this time the "unreachable and the unteachable." Since this very unfortunate majority of addicts and alcoholics do not have the ability or capacity to develop desire, none-the-less strong desire to change their lives, which is due to either a loss of faith or trust in God, or religious principles or just simply due to the fact, that most are immature, and manifest their lack of development by being oppositional defiant and rebellious.

> "Regardless of any situation it should be noted that while willingness and desire are necessary to change attitudes; they are <u>ABSOLUTELY</u> not required to change behavior."

A change in behavior occurs when a person either willingly desires to make a change, or despite having no willingness and no desire; they make the change anyway. They do something differently regardless of how their emotions may be influencing them. It should be further noted that when someone does something differently, the action taken has nothing to do with desire or willingness, as clearly demonstrated in the following.

> "Everyone has forced himself or herself to do something they were not willing to do. Has not everyone gotten up on some mornings and absolutely did not want to go to

work; did not feel like getting out of bed; but they did, and they went to work, and they were absolutely not willing, nor had any desire to do so, and yet they took the action of getting up and leaving the house."

It is a matter of making a decision and taking an action and this has nothing to do with willingness nor desire, and when a person takes any consistent action, even the smallest action taken regularly and daily will always result in huge changes in their future! It appears that in order to take an action you must have desire, and if you have strong desire you will take strong actions; but if there is no strong desire, then how does a person find the power to change their behaviors. Despite a lack of desire, a person has the ability to envision a drug and alcohol free future that will give them the power to move towards it!!

In other words desire can be cultivated through the use of strong visualizations. More will be presented regarding the powerful benefit and need to develop the ability to visualize in the chapter "Visualizing Victory." The force behind creating desire where there is no desire is by understanding and grasping the "Power of Positive Pressure" through the "Art of Controlling Click." The following is an example of an EXTREME dream or visualization.

"See yourself waking up in the morning full of energy and excitement. With strong enthusiasm about all the things you are going to achieve today. Having even greater desire to meet every challenge that arises throughout the day, driven by a clearly defined sense of purpose and strong confidence in your ability to manage any situation, without the need or desire to ingest alcohol or drugs."

You can expand upon this vision challenge by letting your imagination and dreams run absolutely wild!

"Allow yourself to envision waking up in the morning next to the most desirable, special and most wonderful person that is equally enthusiastic, confident, sensitive, and unselfish. That special person deeply cares about you and everyone else in a mature and loving manner.

Now develop this even further seeing yourself living in a luxury home with giant large rooms, beautifully decorated by a very talented interior decorator. Greeting the maid[s] and staff that absolutely take care of the home and surrounding property. Expand the dream to including two hundred acres or two thousand acres with perfect white fences with horse stables if you desire. Drive in a luxury automobile fully equipped with every known gadget and device.

See yourself running a large company with employees who are appreciative, and all are in a position in which they have opportunity to learn, grow and improve their own status or position in life. Having the privilege and opportunity to help others to live more fulfilling lives. Having a private airplane in order to be more effective and efficient in this challenge. On a daily basis have the passion to try and do new things and activities. All with never a thought, desire or passing interest in the use of alcohol or drugs!

Although this may seem to be "pie in the sky", as well as an absurd fantasy, it should be noted that people from the beginning of time have envisioned fantastic unbelievable things in their lives. Their passion and desire was directly created from the envisioned experience, and this absolutely fulfilled their dreams beyond their wildest expectations.

The list of these extreme dreamers is endless. In the chapter "Visualizing Victory" I will introduce to you some of these extreme dreamers, but for now here is just a few who achieved incredible success despite the fact they had dropped out of high school or never attended college.

Halle Berry is an Oscar-winning actress who never went to college. Instead, she moved to Chicago immediately after high school to become a model and actress. She ranked #66 on Forbes' Celebrity 100 in 2006 and reportedly made $16 million that year. Berry is also a spokeswoman for Revlon cosmetics and was able to command a higher advertising fee after winning an Academy Award.

Michael Dell, the founder and CEO of Dell, Inc., dropped out of college at 19. He first started his computer company in his college dorm room, later using company's earnings and family loans to expand. In 2008, Forbes ranked Michael Dell #11 in its 400 Richest Americans. As of 2009, he has an estimated net worth of $12.3 billion.

Henry Ford never graduated high school, but went on to start one of the largest automobile manufacturing companies in the world, Ford Motor Company. He's also credited as being the first auto manufacturer to use assembly line technology, which completely revolutionized the way cars were produced. The assembly line allowed Ford to sell cars at a lower price but make higher profits because sales volumes continually increased. Time magazine called Ford one of the most influential people of the 20th century.

Bill Gates, a college dropout, has been named the richest person in the world by Forbes magazine 27 times. Bill Gates, who was 10 points away from a perfect score on the SAT, enrolled at Harvard College in 1973 only to take a leave of absence two years later to form a partnership with classmate Paul Allen. The partnership became known as Microsoft. In 2007, Bill Gates received an honorary doctorate degree from Harvard University. In 2009, Forbes reports Gates' net worth at $40 billion.

Andrew Jackson, is most known for being the 6th president of the United States, but he was also a military governor, Army commander, an attorney, and a congressman – all without ever going to college.

Rachel Ray hasn't had any formal culinary training, including college, but has several cooking shows on the Food Network, a talk show on NBC, several New York Times bestselling cookbooks, and her own magazine. She got her start teaching cooking classes to customers at Cowan & Lobel, a gourmet market in Albany, New York. The classes showed customers how to cook meals in 30 minutes or less. In 2008, Forbes.com ranked Rachel Ray #76 in Celebrity 100, reporting her earnings at $18 million a year.

John D. Rockefeller Sr., a high school dropout, became the first American billionaire and is said to be the richest man in history.

He founded Standard Oil, the first multinational corporation, in 1870.

Steven Spielberg, is a movie director and producer. Spielberg was denied acceptance to film school and dropped out of California State University in Long Beach. He co-founded DreamWorks, a major film studio that's produced several of the highest grossing movie hits and Academy award winning films. Spielberg ranked #205 on Forbes 2009 list of world billionaires with a net worth of $3 billion. He was later granted an honorary degree by USC in 1994.

Mark Zuckerberg, founder of the social networking site Facebook #785 in the World's Billionaires ranks #321 on Forbes' list of 400 richest Americans. Born in 1984, Mark had an estimated net worth of $1.5 billion in 2008 and is the youngest person ever to appear on one of Forbes' billionaire lists. He developed Facebook one year on summer vacation after borrowing money from Paypal's co-founder Peter Theil. In 2008, Microsoft paid $240 million for 1.6% share of Facebook, leading us to believe the site is worth $15 billion.

"And quite obviously NOT having a college degree was NOT an obstacle! All they had and all they needed was their Extreme Dream and the passionate Faith to fulfill that dream! Passionate Faith drives Dreams not Willingness!"

The Bible states that "all things are possible for those who believe in God," but for those who wrestle with having a belief in God, this concept is difficult to conceive. For the disillusioned or doubtful the concept of God can be more easily accepted and appreciated by viewing GOD as an acronym, which stands for Good Orderly Direction, and every addict needs good orderly direction.

"It should be clear that every addict needs GOD (Good Orderly Direction) and they need to follow it regardless of whether they have any willingness or the desire to do so."

In 1979 I was the focus of an intervention and my use of substances was interrupted and fortunately for me that interruption has lasted for over 31 years. For most of those years I was not willing to make many significant changes, but what drove me and motivated me to make the few changes, that allowed me to stay sober and clean was not willingness.

> "I had no interest or desire to be clean and sober, and in fact what drove me to make those few necessary changes was the fact I was STUCK IN AN INTENSE EMOTIONAL STATE that no willpower and no level of desperation could relieve. On a daily basis I felt bored beyond imagination or like a seething volcano ready to erupt at any moment!"

If you also are finding being clean and sober beyond difficult and in fact agonizing, then there is hope, and the great news of this book is that if you are the resistant type as I was; it is not necessary to change everything in your life as AA and NA and all the Twelve Step Programs propose. The destructive force inside me was my tendency to be rebellious and oppositional and just plain and simply stated I had no Good Orderly Direction.

In regards to helping the hopeless and giving hope to the helpless, will require some creativity. After all I am about to turn your mind inside out, for after all Bill Wilson the cofounder of Alcoholics Anonymous, and the author of the book by the same name, was of course right, when he wrote, "The main problem of the alcoholic is centered in his mind rather than his body."

This book will take you through a very novel approach that will enable the addict or alcoholic to identify the beliefs and issues that are deep inside. Once these beliefs get to the outside they can be carefully examined, and then the person may decide what they want to keep, and what they may want to discard. It is by understanding and implementing the "Power of Resisting the Resistance" through the "Art of Self Defiance" that enables the ability of "Turning Resistance into Resolution;" that the problem that is centered in the mind can be better resolved!

This is radically different than being told that the only way to recover is, "you must change everything in your life." With the behavioral and language technology detailed in this book the addict and alcoholic will be fully empowered. The most novel thing that this book demonstrates is that the addict or alcoholic does not have to admit powerlessness, nor have any willingness at all; but in fact they will be taught how to harness their own power through learning and applying the "Eleven Powers and Eleven Arts" described through out this book.

The book Alcoholics Anonymous states in the Chapter titled "To The

Agnostic" on page 45. "Lack of power was our dilemma and we had to find a power greater than ourselves."

> "It is the purpose of this book to help the powerless addict and alcoholic to end their madness, and to find "Eleven" other "Essential Powers" and teach the "Art" and effective methods to keep them alive long enough; until they can finally develop the capability to surrender to a "Higher Power," that they cannot initially accept nor believe in at the current time!"

It is neither my intention nor desire to create any controversy regarding this proposal. This proposal is only for the addict or alcoholic that cannot or will not try to accept or believe in anything. Since they believe in nothing they cannot be forced to believe, and therefore some other key must be found. Since willingness will not work for most addicts and alcoholics, some other positive path must to be established.

By just taking some simple actions, by implementing some Good Orderly Direction, your life is guaranteed to change and you will recover, even if you have no desire or willingness or interest in sobriety. One way to try to understand how it is possible to make this change can be found in what Napoleon Hill, had referred to in his book "Think and Grow Rich," as the "Law of Attraction"-which simply means that what we desire with strong emotion we will manifest in our lives.

This should be of significant importance to the addict or alcoholic, who must come to the realization that they have a tendency to frequently, if not constantly, obsess on the need or hope that they can safely use alcohol or drugs, despite all the previous facts that would indicate the contrary. Since the "Law of Attraction" does not differentiate between good desires or bad desires, and just works mechanically to manifest what is desired or dreamed; the addict or alcoholic needs to be aware how this law is a driving force behind their repeated failures to recover, and therefore they must take control of this powerful force. More will be explained in the chapter that describes the " The Power of Positive Pressure through the "Art of Controlling Click" that shows a step by step method to create strong desires, when none were previously present.

> "It is a well known and accepted fact that "willingness" is not a natural state or drive in alcoholics, but defiance and rebelliousness is…"

Therefore it just makes more sense to use what comes natural, than to try to create an unnatural desire or attitude. By utilizing the addict's natural tendency for rebelliousness and defiance, we can flip it around, and direct the negative energy in a very positive manner back towards the addict or alcoholic. This book will teach and guide people to challenge themselves and to challenge their own impulsive tendencies. They will learn the "Power of Resisting Resistance" through the "Art of Self Defiance."

"It is great fun to challenge yourself and to defy the odds-what do you have to lose?"

"After all what is easier to do—change a personality or act naturally?"

There are many ideas, suggestions and recommendations within these pages describing methods to accomplish this.

There is one more concept we need to understand, if we are going to learn to manage or control the emotional impulses that have been directing our bad decisions, and dictating our wrong actions. We need to be very aware that what we focus on, verbally and non-verbally, and especially what we say to ourselves, and the way we move our body all contribute and control what we emotionally experience as well as our emotional impulses.

"What we emotionally experience is perceived to be our reality."

Since we can change our emotions though the guaranteed techniques described throughout this book, then we can absolutely set ourselves free from whatever limiting beliefs we have or ever have had regarding our ability to not only achieve sobriety, but a lifestyle, only previously dreamed about.

The "Power of Imagination" unleashed through the "Art of Visualization," will give you the ability to clearly set yourself free to create, and design your life in any manner that you have ever dreamed.

Another technique discussed in this book will be the use of "Spin," and that is when entire meanings and experiences are transformed just by choosing different words, to describe or express a view or a situation. The chapter on "Eganisms" will absolutely have your head "Spinning" in the right directions!

Whenever anything happens to us we are always trying to make sense of it. We then assign a meaning to that event, and anytime we assign a meaning to an event we automatically create an accompanying emotion.

The assigned meaning occurs through a process in which words we say to ourselves or words others have said to us create that emotion which is experienced. Many times that emotion is actually unnecessary and unwanted.

By using the "Power of Spin through the "Art of the Second Thought" will enable the person to make rapid changes to free themselves of this unwanted "emotional baggage!" Some people believe that they are powerless to change their feelings associated to a past trauma and need to realize that the trauma was not the problem but the meaning they assigned to it!

> "Even though a past event can never be changed, the meaning can always be easily changed, by utilizing the "Art of the Second Thought" through engaging the "Power of Spin and that will automatically change the unwanted and unnecessary "emotional attachment."

You will absolutely learn that by taking control of the way you breathe, or the way you move your body, and what you choose to focus on, all will absolutely work to change your past, present and future. By using the "Power of Breath" through the "Art of Breath Management" you will gain the ability to almost instantly change any unpleasant feelings, emotions, sensation or moods!

> "Your past can never be the problem; simply due to the __ABSOLUTE__ fact that it no longer exists!"

The past is not stored away in some file cabinet, where you frequently or infrequently open the draw to study and review it. No the past is the past, and the fact that it is the past, means you have absolutely survived it. It is the residual memories of the past that haunt you not the events of the past.

Past events can never be changed, but the impact they have had upon you can absolutely be changed, by changing the meaning we assigned to it. If and when we choose to open that file cabinet draw and we smell or feel something disturbing, it can be changed immediately by simply changing the way we breathe, or the way we move our body and the facial expressions or other gestures we make. All these techniques will be described through out this book.

Words are power, and whether they are used willingly or with or without desire, this book will empower anyone with information and understanding that when specific words are simply acknowledged, and implemented they will enable a person to be free of any behavior they have not been willing to change or had no desire to change. The "Power of Transformational Communication" through the "Art of Word Selection" will give you the insight and ability to manage the emotional impact of almost anything that happens to you!

> "Once again I want to reiterate that "willingness" is not the key. Yes it is a key for some and in fact for the very few, as measured by the statistics of membership in AA and NA. (See the official A.A. membership estimates at the end of this Introduction.) It is very unfortunate that this key, this key of willingness, is not available to the great majority of those suffering from addictions."

To accept these views may be both challenging and controversial; but I will back up all my proposals through just simple common sense as well as the use of the dictionary. In the Foreword of this book I emphasized that it will be helpful if not in fact necessary to FIRST read the chapter titled "Definitions Determine Direction."

It is in that chapter I will educate the reader into understanding, believing and therefore implementing these concepts into their lives. If you are feeling offended or affronted by these views please read or reread the "Definitions Determine Direction" chapter before continuing, and then just consult a dictionary and you will find the argument that, "Willingness is not necessary to take an action" is indisputable.

> "My dream and hope is that the information contained in these pages will free the addict and alcoholic from their madness, and relieve the agony and suffering of their families and loved ones."

It is totally to this purpose and cause I have dedicated my life. For over twenty-five years addicts and their families have asked me "Do you have a book- you should write a book-I have never heard the things you have said."

"This book is in response to those long overdue requests.

At last I believe there is absolute "Hope for the Helpless and Help for the Hopeless."

Alcoholics Anonymous and the 2010 survey of estimates of A.A. Groups and Members

Estimated A.A. Membership and Group Information	
Groups in U.S.	56,694
Members in U.S	1,264,716
Groups in Canada	4,887
Members in Canada	94,163
Groups Overseas	52,600
Members Overseas	704,266
Internationalists Groups	3
Groups in Correctional Facilities (U.S./Canada)	1,589
Members in Correctional Facilities	39,731
Lone Members	157
Total Members:	2,103,033
Total Groups:	115,773

Because A.A. has never attempted to keep formal membership lists, it is extremely difficult to obtain completely accurate figures on total membership at any given time. Some local groups are not listed with the U.S./Canada General Service Office. Others do not provide membership data, thus are not recorded on the G.S.O. computer records. The membership figures listed below are based on reports to the General Service Office as of January 1, 2010, plus an average allowance for groups that have not reported their membership. There is no practical way of counting members who are not affiliated with a local group.

My search on the Internet for a similar Census breakdown for Narcotics Anonymous was not available, however they do have very complex statistics of membership characteristics based on 2009 International Convention Survey completed by almost 12,000 members. Unfortunately there is no estimate of total membership. It should be noted that if you note in the first chapter "Awakening Awareness" it is estimated there are approximately 5,000,000 addicts and 18,000,000 alcoholics in the United States!

Chapter One

Awakening Awareness

The following statistics are alarming and frightening and evidence that past traditional attempts and approaches to resolve the addictions dilemma have not adequately resolved this predicament.

"The following data reveals the devastating impacts of addiction to every man woman and child and preborn. A review of these startling facts should sober up anyone who is wrestling with the decision of whether to seek help for himself, or herself, or someone they love."

"Please take action against the addictions whether you want to or not; don't wait to have "willingness" nor desire just immediately begin to implement the suggestions in this book. Take action now-Don't delay –Don't be part of these statistics!!"

All material appearing in this report is on the Internet in the public domain and may be reproduced or copied without permission from the Substance Abuse and Mental Health Services Administration. Substance Abuse and Mental Health Services Administration, Office of Applied Studies (2008). The following is the results from the 2007 National Survey on Drug Use and Health: National Findings (NSDUH Series H-34, DHHS Publication No. SMA 08-4343). Rockville, MD.

This report presents the first information from the 2007 National Survey on Drug Use and Health (NSDUH), an annual survey sponsored by the Substance Abuse and Mental Health Services Administration (SAMHSA). The survey is the primary source of information on the use of illicit drugs, alcohol, and tobacco in the civilian, noninstitutionalized population of the

1

United States aged 12 years old or older. The survey interviews approximately 67,500 persons each year. Unless otherwise noted, all comparisons in this report described using terms such as "increased," "decreased," or "more than" are statistically significant at the .05 level.

- Approximately 43 percent of the population has a family member who is an alcoholic.
- People who are addicted to alcohol are twice as likely to be divorced than those who don't have this type of addiction.
- 76 million people grew up with an alcoholic parent or married someone with an alcohol problem.
- Overall 23 million people are addicted to some type of substance. (It is possible to have multiple addictions at the same time.) Of these people, the majority (18 million) are addicted to alcohol.
- Almost three times as many men as women are problem drinkers.

Alcohol and Children

- Fetal Alcohol Syndrome causes mental retardation, hyperactivity and slow growth in children and it is 100% preventable.
- Alcohol use among teens has been linked to learning problems, motor vehicle accidents and violent behavior including date rape.
- It is a leading cause of death for young people.
- Over 11, 000 teens in the United States try using alcohol for the first time every day.
- More than four million underage young people drink alcohol in any given month and almost one-third of them (31.5 percent) reported that they had consumed five or more drinks in a single sitting within the previous 30 days.
- Almost three times as many men as women are problem drinkers.
- The earlier young people begin drinking, the more likely they will have problems in school including poor academic performance and attendance issues.
- As they become adults, they are more likely to be involved in violent acts and other kinds of criminal behavior.
- A child who begins drinking alcohol in his or her mid-teens (age 15) is four times more likely to become an alcoholic than a person who had his or her first drink at the age of 21.

- Alcohol-related car accidents are the number one killer of teens.
- Alcohol also plays a role in the next three leading causes of death among young people, which are homicide, suicide and drowning.

Alcoholism Costs

- Between 25 and 40 percent of all hospital beds in the United States are being used to treat health conditions that are related to alcohol consumption.
- Alcohol abuse statistics tell us that untreated addiction costs the U.S. $400 billion per year.
- Children of alcoholics tend to spend more time in the hospital.
- Alcohol-related problems that are not treated account for about $186 billion in costs to businesses as well as the health care and justice systems.
- When underage teens decide to drink, it costs the health care system approximately $3.7 billion per year to treat those injured in motor vehicle accidents and suicide attempts.
- When teens choose to consume alcohol, the total cost to society is about $52.8 billion.

Alcoholism Statistics

- Untreated addiction is more expensive than three of the nation's top 10 killers. And it is four times more expensive than cancer, which is $96.1 billion a year.
- Every American adult pays nearly $1,000 per year for the damages of addiction.
- Shortfalls in productivity and employment among individuals with alcohol or other drug-related problems cost the American economy $80.9 billion in 1992, of which $66.7 billion is attributed to alcohol and $14.2 billion to other drugs.

Alcoholism Statistics for Children and Youth

- More than nine million children live with a parent dependent on alcohol.
- 62% of high school seniors report that they have been drunk.

- Fetal Alcohol Syndrome is the leading known cause of mental retardation – and the most preventable of all birth defects.
- Alcohol abuse statistics tell us that alcohol use by minors is estimated to cost $58 billion per year. This includes traffic crashes, violent crime, burns, drowning, alcohol poisonings, suicide attempts, and treatment.
- A survey of female college students found a significant relationship between the amount of alcohol the women reported drinking each week and their experiences of sexual victimization.
- Alcoholism statistics tell us that <u>between 700,000 to a million Americans receive alcohol dependency treatment on any given day.</u>
- Women comprise 34% of the Alcoholics Anonymous membership.
- Surveys indicate that up to 11 percent of elderly patients admitted to hospitals exhibit symptoms of alcohol dependence, as do 20 percent of elderly patients in psychiatric wards.
- Between 20 and 30 per cent of male psychiatric admissions are alcohol dependent or have alcohol-related problems.

Alcoholism and Work

- In 1995, productivity losses due to alcohol were estimated to be $119 billion.
- Up to 47% of industrial injuries can be linked to alcohol consumption and alcohol dependence.
- Post accident testing of railroad employees in 1990 showed alcoholism statistics at 3.2 for those who tested positive for alcohol or other prohibited drugs.
- Alcohol-related job performance problems are caused not only by on-the-job drinking but also by heavy drinking outside of work.

Alcoholism Statistics on Fatalities and Violence

- Alcohol contributes to 100,000 deaths annually, making it the third leading cause of preventable mortality in the US.
- 40 percent of all traffic fatalities are alcohol related.
- Between 48% and 64% of people who die in fires have blood alcohol levels indicating intoxication.
- Alcohol has been involved in violence caused by 86 percent of

homicide offenders, 37 percent of assault offenders, 60 percent of sexual offenders, 57 percent of men and 27 percent of women involved in marital violence, and 13 percent of child abusers.

- Based on victim reports, each year 183,000 (37%) rapes and sexual assaults involve alcohol use by the offender, as do just over 197,000 (15%) robberies, about 661,000 (27%) aggravated assaults, and nearly 1.7 million (25%) simple assaults.
- Studies of suicide victims in the general population show that about 20% of such suicide victims are alcohol dependent.
- One-quarter of all emergency room admissions, one-third of all suicides, and more than half of all homicides and incidents of domestic violence are alcohol-related.

Illicit Drug Use

- In 2007, an estimated 19.9 million Americans aged 12 or older were current (past month) illicit drug users, meaning they had used an illicit drug during the month prior to the survey interview. This estimate represents 8.0 percent of the population aged 12 years old or older. Illicit drugs include marijuana/hashish, cocaine (including crack), heroin, hallucinogens, inhalants, or prescription-type psychotherapeutics used nonmedically.
- The rate of current illicit drug use among persons aged 12 or older in 2007 (8.0 percent) was similar to the rate in 2006 (8.3 percent).
- Marijuana was the most commonly used illicit drug (14.4 million past month users). Among persons aged 12 or older, the rate of past month marijuana use in 2007 (5.8 percent) was similar to the rate in 2006 (6.0 percent).
- In 2007, there were 2.1 million current cocaine users aged 12 or older, comprising 0.8 percent of the population. These estimates were similar to the number and rate in 2006 (2.4 million or 1.0 percent).
- Hallucinogens were used in the past month by 1.0 million persons (0.4 percent) aged 12 or older in 2007, including 503,000 (0.2 percent) who had used Ecstasy. These estimates were similar to the corresponding estimates for 2006.
- There were 6.9 million (2.8 percent) persons aged 12 or older who used prescription-type psychotherapeutic drugs nonmedically in the past month. Of these, 5.2 million used pain relievers, the same as the number in 2006.

- In 2007, there were an estimated 529,000 current users of methamphetamine aged 12 or older (0.2 percent of the population). These estimates were not significantly different from the estimates for 2006 (731,000 or 0.3 percent).
- Among youths aged 12 to 17, the current illicit drug use rate remained stable from 2006 (9.8 percent) to 2007 (9.5 percent). Between 2002 and 2007, youth rates declined significantly for illicit drugs in general (from 11.6 to 9.5 percent) and for marijuana, cocaine, hallucinogens, LSD, Ecstasy, prescription-type drugs used nonmedically, pain relievers, stimulants, methamphetamine, and the use of illicit drugs other than marijuana.
- The rate of current marijuana use among youths aged 12 to 17 declined from 8.2 percent in 2002 to 6.7 percent in 2007. The rate decreased for both males (from 9.1 to 7.5 percent) and females (from 7.2 to 5.8 percent).
- Among young adults aged 18 to 25, there were decreases from 2006 to 2007 in the rate of current use of several drugs, including cocaine (from 2.2 to 1.7 percent), Ecstasy (from 1.0 to 0.7 percent), stimulants (from 1.4 to 1.1 percent), methamphetamine (from 0.6 to 0.4 percent), and illicit drugs other than marijuana (from 8.9 to 8.1 percent).
- From 2002 to 2007, there was an increase among young adults aged 18 to 25 in the rate of current use of prescription pain relievers, from 4.1 to 4.6 percent. There were decreases in the use of hallucinogens (from 1.9 to 1.5 percent), Ecstasy (from 1.1 to 0.7 percent), and methamphetamine (from 0.6 to 0.4 percent).
- Among those aged 50 to 54, the rate of past month illicit drug use increased from 3.4 percent in 2002 to 5.7 percent in 2007. Among those aged 55 to 59, current illicit drug use showed an increase from 1.9 percent in 2002 to 4.1 percent in 2007. These trends may partially reflect the aging into these age groups of the baby boom cohort, whose lifetime rates of illicit drug use are higher than those of older cohorts.
- Among persons aged 12 or older who used pain relievers nonmedically in the past 12 months, 56.5 percent reported that the source of the drug the most recent time they used was from a friend or relative for free. Another 18.1 percent reported they got the drug from just one doctor. Only 4.1 percent got the pain relievers from a drug dealer or other stranger, and 0.5 percent reported buying the drug on the Internet. Among those who

reported getting the pain reliever from a friend or relative for free, 81.0 percent reported in a follow-up question that the friend or relative had obtained the drugs from just one doctor.

- Among unemployed adults aged 18 or older in 2007, 18.3 percent were current illicit drug users, which was higher than the 8.4 percent of those employed full time and 10.1 percent of those employed part time. However, most illicit drug users were employed. Of the 17.4 million current illicit drug users aged 18 or older in 2007, 13.1 million (75.3 percent) were employed either full or part time.

- In 2007, there were 9.9 million persons aged 12 or older who reported driving under the influence of illicit drugs during the past year. This corresponds to 4.0 percent of the population aged 12 or older, similar to the rate in 2006 (4.2 percent), but lower than the rate in 2002 (4.7 percent). In 2007, the rate was highest among young adults aged 18 to 25 (12.5 percent).

Alcohol Use

- Slightly more than half of Americans aged 12 or older reported being current drinkers of alcohol in the 2007 survey (51.1 percent). This translates to an estimated 126.8 million people, which was similar to the 2006 estimate of 125.3 million people (50.9 percent).

- More than one fifth (23.3 percent) of persons aged 12 or older participated in binge drinking (having five or more drinks on the same occasion on at least 1 day in the 30 days prior to the survey) in 2007. This translates to about 57.8 million people, similar to the estimate in 2006.

- In 2007, heavy drinking was reported by 6.9 percent of the population aged 12 or older, or 17.0 million people. This rate was the same as the rate of heavy drinking in 2006. Heavy drinking is defined as binge drinking on at least 5 days in the past 30 days.

- In 2007, among young adults aged 18 to 25, the rate of binge drinking was 41.8 percent, and the rate of heavy drinking was 14.7 percent. These rates were similar to the rates in 2006.

- The rate of current alcohol use among youths aged 12 to 17 was 15.9 percent in 2007. Youth binge and heavy drinking rates were 9.7 and 2.3 percent, respectively. These rates were essentially the same as the 2006 rates.

7

- Past month and binge drinking rates among underage persons (aged 12 to 20) have remained essentially unchanged since 2002. In 2007, about 10.7 million persons aged 12 to 20 (27.9 percent of this age group) reported drinking alcohol in the past month. Approximately 7.2 million (18.6 percent) were binge drinkers, and 2.3 million (6.0 percent) were heavy drinkers.
- Among persons aged 12 to 20, past month alcohol use rates in 2007 were 16.8 percent among Asians, 18.3 percent among blacks, 24.7 percent among Hispanics, 26.2 percent among those reporting two or more races, 28.3 percent among American Indians or Alaska Natives, and 32.0 percent among whites.
- In 2007, 56.3 percent of current drinkers aged 12 to 20 reported that their last use of alcohol in the past month occurred in someone else's home, and 29.4 percent reported that it had occurred in their own home. About one third (30.2 percent) paid for the alcohol the last time they drank, including 8.2 percent who purchased the alcohol themselves and 21.8 percent who gave money to someone else to purchase it. Among those who did not pay for the alcohol they last drank, 37.2 percent got it from an unrelated person aged 21 or older, 20.7 percent from another person under 21 years of age, and 19.5 percent got it from a parent, guardian, or other adult family member.
- In 2007, an estimated 12.7 percent of persons aged 12 or older drove under the influence of alcohol at least once in the past year. This percentage has decreased since 2002, when it was 14.2 percent. From 2006 to 2007, the rate of driving under the influence of alcohol among persons aged 18 to 25 decreased from 24.4 to 22.8 percent.

"I hope you took the time to carefully and not just briefly study these statistics"—

"But if you didn't! Here is an alarming review of the impacts and damage done by alcohol and drugs…"

- It is the leading cause of death for young people.
- Alcohol-related car accidents are the number one killer of teens.
- Alcohol also plays a role in the next three leading causes of

death among young people, which are homicide, suicide and drowning.

- Fetal Alcoholism Syndrome causes mental retardation, hyperactivity and slow growth in children and it is 100% preventable.
- Alcohol abuse statistics tell us that untreated addiction costs the U.S. $400 billion per year.
- Untreated addiction is more expensive than three of the nation's top 10 killers. And it is four times more expensive than cancer, which is $96.1 billion a year.
- Alcoholism statistics tell us that between 700,000 to a million Americans receive alcohol dependency treatment on any given day.
- Up to 47% of industrial injuries can be linked to alcohol consumption and alcohol dependence.
- One-quarter of all emergency room admissions.
- One-third of all suicides, and more than half of all homicides and incidents of domestic violence are alcohol-related.
- 40 percent of all traffic fatalities are alcohol related.
- Between 48% and 64% of people who die in fires have blood alcohol levels indicating intoxication.
- Alcohol has been involved in 86 percent of homicide offenders.
- 37 percent of assault offenders.
- 60 percent of sexual offenders,
- 57 percent of men and 27 percent of women involved in marital violence.
- 13 percent of child abusers.
- 183,000 (37%) rapes and sexual assaults involve alcohol use by the offender.
- 197,000 (15%) robberies.
- 661,000 (27%) aggravated assaults.
- 1.7 million (25%) simple assaults
- 19.9 million Americans aged 12 or older were current (past month) illicit drug users,

A brief review of the above statistics should now have "Awakened Awareness" and alerted anyone who is concerned about addiction that efforts to address this problem are not succeeding, to the degree that is necessary. This may be clearly observed in the fact that the overall estimate of addicts and alcoholics receiving help through the 12 step programs is approximately a little over 2 million people. Since there are approximately 23,000,000 people who are considered addicted to a mood altering substance...

"It is unfortunately very clear that AA, and NA have only been able to address a small splinter group of addicts and alcoholics."

Once again this book is dedicated and committed to reaching the majority of those affected by and directly involved with the above statistics. "Those that cannot or will not or are absolutely incapable of having now; or as some may believe ever have the willingness to change their behaviors." For those people we must develop effective methods that are outside the understanding and scope of how 12-step programs operate.

One last thought regarding this. This author has no issue with any 12-step program and in fact has been a member for over 31 years. It is this writer's contention that the requirements of membership in these 12-step programs as simple as they may be "To admit and announce that you're are an alcoholic or addict" at this time seems to have excluded the great majority of those suffering from all addictions. Once again it needs to be repeated. It is everyone's moral responsibility to be open and receptive to new and controversial concepts, ideas and suggestions that can provide hope for the helpless and help for the hopeless.

"Too many times while we are waiting for someone to become "willing" they suffer incredible consequences and many will die. It is to this dilemma that this book is dedicated to all those that cannot and may never become willing; none the less surrender. The ideas I propose may seem bizarre and extraordinary, but I have witnessed their power during the years of my practice. Addicts have said to me "I never knew all I had to do was stop doing what I wanted to do, and do what I don't want to do, and I would recover. Anyone can turn resistance into resolution and...

—" STOP THE MADNESS"—

Chapter Two

Stop The Madness

As one of those who were unwilling, I would like to return to my own experience to demonstrate the powerful forces that can be harnessed to create changes. Even when we are reluctant to change or even when we are deeply resistant to want to change. I was suffering from intense emotional states that drove me and pushed me, and forced me to do many things in recovery that I did not want to do. Those minimal actions that I took that changed me, without the willingness to change, I now call the "The Eleven Arts and the Eleven Powers." These are the forces that change resistance into resolution and they were not motivated by willingness, but rather by pure desperation.

> "I had to find a way to get these intense emotional monkeys off my back and I was absolutely unwilling to take suggestions."

To demonstrate the depth and severity of my own resistance I will share with you how I asked my second sponsor to sponsor me. I was having a particularly difficult day since I had just chased a building inspector off the roof of a house I was reroofing. The building inspector began to point out work defects and I grabbed my utility knife and started slashing the roofing paper; since he insisted on inspecting what was underneath. It was at that time he became fearful or disgusted with my behavior, and walked off the job, stating that he was not coming back. For those who are not acquainted with the law; without the building inspector's approval I could not complete the roof replacement.

Due to my uncontrolled anger, I caused a major problem that would take some time to resolve, so I did what we in AA are told, and that is, "No matter what-even if your ass falls off- put it in a bag and take it to a meeting with you." It was at that meeting someone named Bob P told me that I needed to ask Dave F, to sponsor me, and it was emphasized "He is probably the only one that can help you as bad as you are." I took this advice, and spoke to David and told him I needed a sponsor. He said, "I have been waiting for over a year for you to ask me or at least someone."

It was then that I proved beyond a shadow of doubt that some of us are sicker than others, and I am one of the sickest ones, as clearly demonstrated by what I said to David. When I asked him to sponsor me- no let me correct that statement; when I told him "I have to have a sponsor I then informed him loudly and clearly that "I need a sponsor, but I am telling you now- I am not going to do anything you tell me- so can you help me." He was momentarily perplexed but stated "Let's talk tomorrow at lunch and see."

We met for lunch the following day and he emphasized to me that "You need to make COMMITMENTS." I told him I do what I can and he strongly confronted me that "Doing what I can" was totally unacceptable, and he once again firmly and assertively uttered "Jerry what COMMITMENTS are you willing to make for your recovery!" I once again adamantly and loudly expressed "I go to meetings when I can and I do what I can—I told you that—what do you want from me?" He then strongly verbalized in an almost disgusted tone of voice—"What COMMITMENTS are you willing to make! I don't want to hear that you try to go to meetings—I want to hear that you are specifically committed to attend a certain meeting at a certain time!"

It was at this point I found myself becoming extremely pressured and that pushed me over the edge. While he was leaning over the table and pointing his finger in my face—almost screaming "What COMMITMENTS are you willing to make Jerry!" He was saying this at the precise moment that I was starting to crush saltine crackers into my chicken noodle soup—But instead of going in the soup—I threw them in his face!

I know it now but I absolutely did not know it then—What he was introducing me into is what I now call the "Power of Commitment" through the "Art of Accountability." In a latter chapter I will discuss this in much more detail!

If it was not so sad that I was that resistant; the scene at the restaurant table would have been hilarious. The cracker crumbs were all over his beautiful manicured white mustache and falling from his silver—white hair onto the table like a bad case of dandruff!

Without missing a beat he rapidly brushed the cracker crumbs from his eyes and eyebrows and leaned even closer to me and this time he did scream; "Jerry what COMMITMENTS are you willing to make for your recovery!"

From my above history it is vivid and clear that there was no willingness, but there was intense overwhelming desperation, and emotional pain that had to be released. If I did not get it vented, I felt like I would kill myself or someone else. The driving force inside me was not willingness-it was anger, frustration, hate, confusion, fear, mistrust, bewilderment and cynicism. It was pure unfiltered desperation without a shred of willingness. I know now that I was able to use these negative feelings and emotions to stay sober for most of those 30 years.

> "Everyday there was a driving obsession to find a moment of peace, but an intense resistance to take any of the actions that others promised would create that inner peace."

Despite tremendous hardship leading to such great desperation, that I asked a man to sponsor me, but I still could not force myself to take suggestions or follow his recommendations. The few things that I did do set me free, but those things were done under duress and protest and absolutely with no willingness.

> "The great news I want the reader to know is that "you can stop the madness of using destructive substances, even when you don't want to, by just simply turning these intense emotional negative passions upside down and inside out. Despite the confusion, stop hating yourself, the world and the people in it."

> "End the mistrust, arguing and fighting and debating with everyone including yourself as well as God, if you believe in God, and learn to tap and utilize all this intense destructive passionate energy, and learn to use it in excitingly new, incredibly challenging, creative and positive ways."

Since I am an addict and alcoholic, I have a PECULIAR view about many things that others do not have to struggle with. For instance most people do not have to wrestle with the question of whether drinking and using drugs is stupid, reckless and costly; especially after having suffered major alcohol or drug related problems or being diagnosed with a substance abuse or dependency disorder.

Common sense would and should dictate to an addict, that drugs and alcohol, and in fact all mood-altering substances are extremely dangerous, and should be avoided at all cost. Most people can drink a drink or even do some drugs, maintain their perspective and stop or control their use. They do not suffer serious consequences that could destroy their life.

> "It is helpful to understand that in the event of some serious or even minor incident or consequence due to drinking or drug use; most people would immediately change their behaviors to avoid the risk of any potential repetition of that problem."

> "They have no trouble with the recognition that they have suffered consequences, and the best protection from the risk of a repetition of these troubles, is to refrain from any further use of alcohol or drugs."

> "However the addict or alcoholic are unable, and in fact incapable of seeing things so clearly."

Addicts and alcoholics have PECULIAR perceptions that blur, and distort situations, and events that occur in their lives. It is this TWISTING of perceptions that leads the addict or alcoholic into a potential lifetime battle, with their inability for clear recognition of the need for complete and total abstinence. They are obsessed with the belief that "Somehow, some way, and some day I can use and get away." They focus on the false belief that they will be able to control not only their consumption of substances, but also control the circumstances around their substance use, so they can use or drink safely without any serious consequences.

> "An alcoholic, and for some other people that are addicted to or use certain addictive drugs, may at times experience some partial or total loss of memory. Now you would think, that after having what can only be described as a terrifying experience, any normal person would take immediate action to prevent ever having a reoccurrence."

> "You would believe that the fear would cause the person

to be willing to do anything, to prevent any possibility of a repetition of that event."

For the uninitiated an alcohol related "Blackout" may be defined as a period of time in which total or partial amnesia occurs as a result of drinking alcohol or consuming certain drugs in certain quantities or combinations.

"With most people, when drinking alcoholic beverages results in an alcohol related Blackout they immediately become aware that drinking alcohol is becoming problematic, and immediately stop or modify their drinking or using behavior; due to the deep dread they feel from losing complete control of their life for those few moments."

"Yes they in fact lost control over those moments because they will never remember what they said or did during the Blackout period."

The person in the Blackout will have no memory or just partial memory. This means that the next day, it will virtually be impossible for that individual to recall what they said or what they did. This is a condition in which permanent memory loss has occurred, and no matter how memorable the day or night should have been, there is no recording in the brain or memory of the events in the mind of this individual.

"It should be emphasized that there are documented cases in which an individual has suffered Blackouts that lasted for days. It should be obvious how troubling and problematic this condition should be to the drinking individual."

They may have said lovely things that were deeply passionate and full of love or vicious and hateful hurtful things; but either way they will have absolutely no memory of what had transpired. Discovering that you have been in a total or partial state of amnesia should immediately result in a strong desire, and clear commitment to stop drinking or use of drugs. At least that is the way non-alcoholic and non-addicts react.

"To continue the use of substances following a sentinel event such as a Blackout is sheer madness. It is in fact proof of insanity or may be described as someone suffering from a condition I refer to as having "Peculiar Perceptions."

The suffering caused by a Blackout is well known to the drinker's family and friends who may have taken the blunt of the offensive behaviors, and accordingly so would want an explanation or at the very least an apology. Since the drinker has no way to recall the events, they are reluctant to acknowledge any wrongdoing.

Many times the drinker will deny any transgressions, or they will attempt to manipulate the offended person into believing it was their fault. This manipulation is motivated by fear and the need to convince the other person as well as themselves, that it was that person's fault. It reduces their fear and anxiety to believe or rationalize that the offended person provoked the unmentionable and inappropriate behavior.

"The drinker cannot bear the fact that they acted inappropriately, and that alcohol or that the use of drugs was somehow responsible."

If they were able to clearly see the connection between bad behaviors, and the consumption of alcoholic beverages, this would logically lead to a decision to abstain from any further use of these substances. Early on in the developing history of the addict or alcoholic, the consumption of alcohol and or drugs is deemed as being too high on the drinkers priority list, to ever consider giving it up. They resist due to what they perceive as "some simple misunderstandings," or in fact, they believe that the people confronting them, had actually provoked the incident, and they are "Just really exaggerating how bad it was."

These TWISTED and PECULIAR perceptions are the essence of something that the drinker has to develop before they can be referred to as a person who is an alcoholic or addict. This "something" is identified as "denial." Therefore despite everyone around the drinker knowing that drinking is a bad thing.

"The drinker develops the false belief that alcohol or drugs are not the problem, but the way others interact with him or her when they drink is what is problematic, but not the substance use."

When the drinking person begins to frequently minimize problems, and consequences or begins to blame others to reduce their own sense of guilt, regret and shame, they are in the midst of developing "Denial." Once this process begins it can lead to incredibly tragic events in the drinker's lives and all to whom they come in contact with.

It is this denial that blocks or interferes with a person's ability to develop willingness to see the reality of a Blackout, and its destructive actions, as well as potential destructive power. Despite this Denial, a person can still make significant changes in their behaviors and activities that will allow them to change without willingness.

Now once again it appears to be contradictory, regarding how it is possible for a person to change when they are not willing to change. The fact is that "willingness" has nothing to do with whether people can change or not.

"The controversial concepts I utilize will be carefully defended and explained by the use of dictionary definitions in the chapter, "Definitions Determine Direction" and it will become quite clear that there are no contradictions."

The importance of being very open minded, as well as receptive to these radical ideas and concepts can be clearly found in the following Blackout incidents.

One of the most traumatic examples of Blackout behaviors this author has witnessed is the damage and harm a man did to his family and himself when he sexually molested his young daughter during an alcoholic Blackout. The severity of this cannot be measured. This loving father had literally committed a despicable and heinous felony crime; but far worse in that moment of insanity his daughter suffered a brutality, and her entire life will never be the same.

The man in all high probability permanently destroyed the relationship he had with not only his daughter; but his entire family, not to mention the guilt, shame and horror he will have to live with for the rest of his life. How could this horrific situation have occurred and how could have it been prevented? No one should have to suffer so horribly through such innocent ignorance and resistance.

First and foremost it must be accepted that any person who is experiencing memory loss or confusion after drinking or drugging needs to understand.

"They are now afflicted with a condition in which they have loss total control of their mental faculties, and during those times they are capable of absolutely any action or behavior. This includes the greatest good or the darkest evil, and it is not possible to predict which one it will be."

Therefore the best and only way to avoid potential serious consequences, when a person begins to notice memory failure after drinking or using drugs is to without hesitation, follow this suggestion.

"When memory loss begins.

Permanently lose the alcohol and drugs simply put"

"Stop the Madness."

Please note that a person does not have to have any kind of willingness to "lose the alcohol or stop their drug abuse." All they need is an intense passionate emotion that is so painful that they stop doing what they were doing. This preventive action is not motivated by willingness, but by "fear, confusion, anger, frustration and or bewilderment.

The key that turns resistance into effective resolution happens when a person becomes aware of the risks and potential dangers as well as the consequences of their continued use of substances. It is through this awareness they develop a painful understanding that they must immediately stop any use of mood altering substances.

"Unfortunately due to their PECULIAR perceptions connecting the event with the potential risk and danger rarely ever occurs in the early history of an addict or alcoholic."

When a person gives up their right to ingest drugs or alcohol, it means they have to accept that they never again will experience that very special feeling that drugs and alcohol create. They will have to come to terms with the fact that they never again will have that incredible and unexplainable event happen when drugs and alcohol slam into the brain. Those substances explode into the most fantastic and extraordinary experiences in not only the mind, but they also cause exciting sensations and stimulations throughout the body. They will never again be able to take total control of their feelings and bend or twist them into an incredible and indescribable pleasurable state.

The above description utilizing very powerful and pleasing words to describe the drinkers or users experience, were chosen to alert the non addict or non alcoholic of what is at stake when a person is forced to choose to use or not use a mood altering substance. In this manner I hope to impart some insight of what the addict and alcoholic have to give up for the rest of their lives, and why they resist. I did this purposely to instill a deeper understanding why it is almost virtually impossible for an addict or alcoholic to just "quit" nonetheless to become "willing."

This resistance to quit is due to the fact that drugs and alcohol produce one of the most powerful mental, emotional, as well as physical encounters a human being can experience. When a person has to quit using or drinking, they will definitely experience a significant amount of intense sadness and grief.

This grief translates itself into an outward expression of passionate resistance against the suggestion or need to stop using substances. When someone has to give up something they enjoy or even love; there is no eagerness or willingness attached to that need or decision. In fact there is an intense emotional resistance to making the change, and it is this passionate energy that provides the key and not willingness.

> "There is power in all emotions and willingness certainly
> has motivational power, but there is even greater power
> in the feelings of resistance because this feeling stacks
> upon itself many other intense emotions."

A minimum list of those feelings are rebellion, anger, frustration, determination, disgust, confusion, bewilderment, hate, perplexity, puzzlement and paradoxically the notion of strong willpower. Please note that willpower has no relation to the concept of willingness. In fact...

> "...it is the natural occurring emotion of willpower that

> will be tapped to help the addict or alcoholic to recover
> even when they don't want to."

The fact that a person can force himself or herself to do something should never be confused with the notion of willingness, as I will demonstrate in the chapter "Definition Determines Direction" that presents an overview of the dictionary definitions of these concepts.

> "Therefore the message I will continue to scream out in
> this book is that willingness is not required for change
> to occur."

Chapter Three

Resisting Resistance

The first of the essential Eleven Powers and Eleven Arts is: The "Power of Resisting Resistance" through the "Art of Self Defiance" which enables the addict or alcoholic to absolutely know that they can act now and act immediately to "STOP THE MADNESS," they do not have to wait to become willing or develop willingness to change; all they have to do is turn their intense resistance into a rewarding resolution. The following chapter will describe in detail the concept of "Resisting Resistance."

"Resisting Resistance produces a new direction and a new destiny. Do not wait for the next serious consequence, and regret before you begin to implement this concept. If you fail to act on this suggestion, then this failure may bury you."

As it did to the man in the following story, which hopefully may convince you to decide sooner, rather than later-to act now and act immediately.

There was a career soldier who during an alcoholic Blackout was arrested, and when he awoke or came to from his previous night of drunkenness, he found himself in a jail cell. Through his years in the military, waking up in jail with no memory of what offence he had committed was nothing new to him. His only concern was that this might lead to the loss of some rank, since this too had happened before.

While he sat in the jail cell and waited for someone to inform him when he could leave, his only real feeling was that he was very disappointed in himself. When the guard finally came over he was glad to see a familiar face, and it was somehow reassuring. The look on his guard's friends face alarmed him, and he knew this situation was different, than the ones that occurred numerous times before. "You killed someone last night-they are saying you murdered another guy last night—another soldier."

He was convicted and spent the next fifteen years in a federal prison. His career in the service was over. The lives of his victim's family will never be the same. His victim will never have the life he should, and deserved to have lived. He will live with the burden of guilt, and regret for something he will never be able to remember that he did. All because of drinking alcohol and believing that "a Blackout is no big thing-everybody gets Blackouts. —"I always Blackout, when drinking too much."

This should have been the end of his drinking, and so it was for a while. He became active in AA in the federal prison system, and in fact when he was released he went to work in the mental health field. He did great work with other alcoholics and addicts, but one day he just could not help himself when he was out with his esteemed colleagues. They were drinking and celebrating and he felt left out. So he ordered a rum and coke.

This was his first taste of alcohol in over twenty years, and I hope it was really good for him, since he paid an incalculable price for that drink—his military career, fifteen years of his freedom and not to mention the blood of an innocent man, as well as that man's family was not costly enough to convince him, to remain permanently abstinent.

My intention is not to make you willing or teach you willingness. The focus here is to alert you to the great benefit of tapping your power of resistance, and tapping your strong willpower, for failure to do this could result in a similar story about you.

> "He drank again due to the stupid emotional experience that he was feeling left out, and because he could not resist this stupid emotional state he started drinking again. Drinking was not his problem, but it was his solution to the awkward emotions of feeling left out. So the real problem was his inability to manage a stupid feeling, and instead of resisting that feeling, he let that feeling manage him."

Despite how tragic this story is, there have been numerous jokes developed regarding Blackouts that completely minimize the potential threats and consequences of losing all control of your faculties. It is jokes and attitudes like the following that contribute to the deepening of a person's denial.

Two very old classical jokes told in AA meetings currently, and in years past demonstrate the complexity as well as the severity of a Blackout, as seen in the following: "How do you know if a person has an allergy to alcohol? They break out in spots—New York, Cincinnati, Buffalo, Miami or California."

Another joke relates to "When I drink, sometimes when I come to, I don't know where I am, and so I immediately get a newspaper as soon as I am able, and I check what city I am in as I look for today's date."

Although the searching for a newspaper to identify location is certainly now obsolete with the advent of the Internet, cell phones, and other electronic media; it does not change the fact that an addict or alcoholic on a frequent basis, wakes up either in a bed (their own, or somebody else's), on the floor (their house or somebody else's), in an alley, in a car (their own or somebody else's), or in the snow, and they do not have the vaguest idea or memory of how they got there.

The terrifying truth that is the foundation for these jokes is that the person has been moving through time and space, sometimes just for a few minutes and other times literally for days at a time, and has no memory of recent events. In fact, quite literally for the rest of their lives, they will never have any recall of what they did or did not do during the Blackout period.

"Blackouts are nothing to laugh at or to be ignored, but
need to be literally seen as a life threatening event, that
needs immediate corrective attention."

When non-alcoholic people drink, and they experience a Blackout or some level of amnesia for even a few minutes this immediately grabs their attention. As a direct result of this awareness they modify their use and consumption. In the event that a second alcohol related Blackout should occur, they usually then choose to thereafter stay abstinent.

"Once again, as soon as memory loss is detected after
a drinking episode, it is time to quit drinking, and
commit to total permanent abstinence, even if you don't
want to!

It is helpful to understand that in the event of some serious or even minor incident or consequence due to drinking or drug use; most people would immediately change their behaviors to avoid the risk of any potential repetition of that problem. They have no trouble with the recognition that they have suffered consequences, and the best protection from a reoccurrence is to refrain from any further use of alcohol or drugs. It is very unfortunate that the addict or alcoholic does not see things so clearly. We must always remember that addicts and alcoholics have PECULIAR perceptions, that blur and distort situations or events that occur in their lives.

It is this TWISTING of perceptions that leads the addict or alcoholic into a potential lifetime battle with their inability for clear recognition of the need for complete and total abstinence.

> "It becomes immediately clear that for most alcoholics and drug addicts "pain and suffering " does not create a restraining force against the continued destructive use of mood altering substances."

Since it never comes natural for an addict or alcoholic to just stop using drugs or alcohol, due to some embarrassment or lost moments of time; the person must learn that they can rarely control what they think and feel but they can always control the way they act.

Whereas any normal person would immediately be too fearful to pick up a drink or a drug after a very traumatic event has occurred, due to their use of mood altering substances; the alcoholic or addict is too fearful to stop using the destructive substances. The normal person develops immediate WILLINGNESS to make changes; whereas the addict makes immediate EXCUSES, and creates elaborate ALLIBIS, and willingness to change never forms no matter how great the need or necessity. Instead of surrender the alcoholic becomes spiteful, and vindictive towards anyone who tries to make them see the connection between drinking or being high. They fail to perceive that the latest crisis in their lives has directly resulted from their substance use.

Despite the fact that they may hurt and alienate their family, friends, loved ones and even face times in jail or prison; they still place high value on the substances that are costing them everything worthwhile in life.

> "It seems that the more costly their continued use is, the more they value its continued use."

Due to these very TWISTED and PECULIAR perceptions, the only solution is to teach a person how to use their resistance to stop their drug or alcohol use, as a means to stopping the use. This may seem quite a bizarre proposal, but through resistance training it is not only possible, but also highly probable that change will occur.

"Resisting Resistance" outlines a method to learn as well as utilize, which has nothing to do with willingness, as much as it has to do with learning how to effectively use resistance, in a manner of Self-Defiance.

"The implementation of Self-Defiance results in strong Self-Reliance."

Just as military aircraft that weigh thousands of tons are able to lift off and fly; resistance and defiance can be utilized to bring down denial. The way an airplane is able to leave the ground is not so much through great power and thrust; but by the way the wing is shaped and engineered. The shape, which is an airfoil, allows for a change in air pressure above the wing to be reduced, thus the higher pressure under the wing lifts it up. When you take this principle of the airfoil design and turn it completely upside down, and place it on the front and back of a racecar the principle is the same, but it works backwards. This results in reducing the air pressure under the airfoil. The effect is to cause the car to be forced and held to the ground at speeds near, and above two hundred miles per hour.

It is following this principle that I propose to take the concepts of defiance as well as resistance, and teach you to flip them upside down so you can get a completely different result. The direct effect of this will change your life whether you want to change it or not. Instead of lifting you up and away from recovery, I will show you how to utilize that rebellious and defiant energy to push yourself down into recovery, by not changing or transforming the attitude, but by simply turning it upside down. But first it is necessary to gain some understanding and insight into why people return to substance use, abuse, thus resulting again in dependency.

Why is it that so many people work so sincerely hard to change their lives, and when they reach a point of success so many will tend to fail. What we need to understand is that all the actions that a person takes, is directly based on how much value they assign to the goal or the action. Their sense of value is directly dependent upon the strength of the feeling they experience; which is determined by the belief they have regarding how they should feel, once the action is taken and or completed.

"Many people in recovery will sincerely try very hard and despite all their intense effort, they will fail or will <u>believe</u> that they have failed."

To gain more understanding of how this occurs it will be helpful to review the following case history. We will refer to the person(s) as Michael or Michelle.

Michelle or Michael are addicts or alcoholics who have entered into early recovery. Early recovery is defined as a period of time from the completion of detox up until and sometimes in fact many times beyond 12 months. Most addicts or alcoholics would believe that being clean and sober from 6 to 12 months should guarantee that they would feel positive and satisfied as well as comfortable and stable.

Now Michelle or Michael are people who understood the importance of not only taking suggestions, but also following them with strong desire and passion. They followed the recommendations to attend 90 meetings in 90 days as well as selecting a sponsor early in the process, and finding the appropriate male or female sponsor that required them to make a phone call on a daily basis and to discuss how their day went, as well as what feelings they experienced. Their sponsors also were strong believers that a person in early recovery needed to stay focused and fully committed.

To facilitate their willingness the sponsor gave frequent reading and written assignments and reviewed them on a weekly basis. Now Michelle and Michael believed what they had heard when they began to attend the 12 step programs of either AA or NA. They observed in the meetings that many people spoke about how they became "happy joyous and free" and had achieved this by being willing to listen and follow simple suggestions and directions. In the meetings they noticed that the members that attended had achieved high levels of peace and through the committed actions they took, led them into having extraordinary and desirable changes in their thoughts, feelings and emotions.

> "In the beginning Michael and Michelle had much hope and passion and had a strong "Belief" that if they did all the things that they heard and saw others doing, that they too would experience those same tremendously great feelings and rewards."

Therefore every day Michael or Michelle followed almost every suggestion and recommendation. They were very disciplined to call their sponsor on a daily basis and to honestly discuss the issues that they were experiencing. They worked hard to complete the assignments and they honestly discussed their feelings, insights, frustrations, hope and beliefs.

After three to six months of following the program recommendations, they began to experience some dissatisfaction and disillusionment. These negative emotions initially were not that noticeable, but they began to intensify until it became an extreme chore, to even take the simple actions that they had found initially were so easy to do. Their disillusionment and their frustration intensified and eventually led to a reduction, and then the complete abandonment and elimination of most, if not all the actions that they had been taking.

What really needs to be emphasized here is that during this time, they began to make very measurable progress, in several areas of their lives. For the first time they had been able to maintain strong disciplines in many areas of functioning.

They both were able to reconcile much of the trouble that had developed within their families. They found jobs that they initially felt were interesting and challenging. They actually enjoyed the work they were doing. Both maintained active regular employment and involvement in their local gym. Their sponsor and recovery friends provided great excitement, enthusiasm, spirituality, as well as support.

As you can see Michelle and Michael had worked very hard and had gained great rewards and benefits as a direct result of maintaining strong discipline and commitment in following and completing the recovery recommendations. They also followed the suggestions of the people they had met in AA or NA. Yet nonetheless despite the fact that they had achieved great goals they still relapsed.

"Despite the fact that they were making significant and measurable progress in most of the areas of functioning; they did not feel that they were making any progress at all."

It is not just Michael or Michelle that have experienced this phenomenon in which measurable progress can be clearly observed by others and yet the person feels that it's just not worth continuing with the disciplines that they had previously been following. It is very common to hear such terms as "I got bored" or "I just did not get what I had expected after all this work" or "Things were just not coming as fast as I wanted."

"It becomes obvious that expectations based on mistaken beliefs lay the foundations for failure"

Michael and Michelle believed that after a certain period of time they should experience a very specific feeling that was demonstrated to them through the observation of other people in recovery; and when they did not experience this feeling they became extremely disillusioned.

"They had the mistaken belief that if they had done

all the work exactly as it was recommended and being suggested, that it was guaranteed that they would feel better after a certain period of time."

Now you may recall in the beginning of this chapter it was indicated that many people fail or they have the "belief" that they have failed. Herein lies the answer to the riddle of how a person can be living in a very positive and responsible manner, but that person does not feel happy or successful. In fact when asked why a person will destroy everything they worked so hard to build-the response is usually "I just was not happy and it didn't seem worthwhile to continue" or "Yes my life was going good, and great things were happening, but something still felt terribly wrong" or "I just wanted to feel high again and I believed that I could handle it."

It may be helpful to recognize that the measure of the person's success is solely based on their personal "beliefs." Despite all the objective facts and truths that would indicate that they were living positively, successfully as well as productively; if their feelings did not match their personal beliefs, they may fail to recognize, what they HAD in fact achieved.

"Something that needs to be further understood is the fact that many times the person in recovery will not experience an expected positive or powerful emotional feeling, when they engage in right and healthy actions. This results in the person losing hope or trust regarding the actions they were taking or were told to do."

It should be clearly noted that no recovering person should evaluate whether they are succeeding based upon an expected emotional return. In other words just because the person does the right things does not necessarily mean they will feel right. This results in the twisted and disillusioned experience in which the person believes that they have failed; simply because they did not experience the feelings that they believed they should have had, as a result of doing the right things and living right.

Beliefs are the driving force that provides a clear sense of direction of whether actions being taken are leading to achieving levels of expectation.

"Since most recovering people have lived their lives based on believing that their feelings <u>must</u> match their actions; if they don't experience the emotional expectation that they believe is associated to an action, then they may mistakenly believe that it was the wrong action."

As Michael and Michelle's story indicates that despite achieving great things in their recovery, they quit because they didn't feel the emotions that they believed they should have had as a direct result of taking the actions and achieving their goals.

Very simply put, the dilemma that is experienced occurs when despite engaging in specific behaviors and activities that the person believes should lead to joy and happiness, instead they experience restlessness, irritability and discontent. These negative emotions then lead to a loss in their faith and belief that by taking these actions they could change their lives.

The addict or alcoholic must learn to pay particular attention to the fact that despite the absence of the expected emotional reward, they have accomplished many good things and that the lack of an expected emotional reward does not negate those achievements. The huge mistake that most addicts and alcoholics make happens in the area of expectation and beliefs. They must learn how to manage their beliefs and expectations so that they know that they are successful, even when they don't feel successful. They need to learn to pay close attention to the absolute fact that a feeling can never invalidate the progress or accomplishment of a goal or a task and to learn to celebrate success regardless of how they feel!

"Happiness needs to be more dependent on the facts rather than the feelings, because feelings "lie" and they tend to make you "believe" the "lie." You begin to believe that success is based on an emotion rather than an accomplishment."

The recovering person unfortunately "invalidates" their hard work and accomplishments due to the "belief" that success is based on an associated feeling, that they expect to feel when an action is taken or completed. They must stop allowing their feelings and emotions to dictate their actions and causing them to discount and invalidate recovery achievements and to falsely validate "feelings and emotions that are out right lies."

Many times mistaken "Beliefs" cheat and steal from a person and deceive them and betrays them—Beliefs many times control feelings and depending on the belief; we experience an accompanying feeling.

"You must immediately begin the process of changing

31

your belief system so you can experience the fantastic
feelings and emotions that you absolutely deserve when
you are living a clean and serene sober life."

We need now to take control of our faulty belief systems and replace them
with healthy and powerful ones. Values and beliefs are the source of knowing
whether we have succeeded or we have failed. Throughout our lives we have
given labels and levels to those things that we perceive have given us pain
or pleasure. To understand this is to recognize that how we develop values,
will be specifically determined by the feelings that we experience regarding,
what is perceived as a pleasant experience or a painful one. The way in which
we evaluate what the meaning of "success" is, will determine very different
specific directions in which we take our lives.

"By believing that success must be accompanied by a
feeling of successfulness, people can mistakenly believe
that they have failed simply because the feeling that
they expected—failed to materialize."

"It is necessary for the addict and alcoholic to begin the
process of measuring their progress objectively through
the actions that they take, and to avoid the trap of
expecting a specific emotional return or reward for the
actions taken."

When you change the way you define what "success" means, you
completely change the direction of your life, because it changes what you
focus on and this creates a completely different result. In other words instead
of feeling disappointed and disillusioned with your recovery actions and
efforts; you will know that you have succeeded, and will be able to notice the
success for what it is, and not for the feeling that is felt or not felt.

The associations to pain and pleasure literally govern our destiny. If you
have linked pain to something you will try to avoid it; even though you are
engaged in successful recovery actions that are resulting in very positive
changes in your life, if you associate pain or feel a lack of pleasure you will
abandon these efforts.

"Now as strange as it seems if you link pleasure to
something, then you will do almost anything to acquire

it, even if it means giving up recovery due to the mistaken belief that recovery seems too painful, and the return to addiction seems more desirable and rewarding."

When we are in a peak state of emotion things can mistakenly get linked together such as developing strong resistant and negative emotions with our recovering actions and efforts. This happens due to the fact that living in a recovery lifestyle, or attempting to do so, causes much stress and frustration at times. There is much pressure when a person feels forced or obligated to attend meetings, or calling others on the phone, or any of the numerous other actions that have been perceived and believed to be necessary to maintain abstinence.

"After a period of time the pressure of having to force yourself to take and do the right things eventually becomes associated with anger, disillusionment and frustration; especially when no matter what the person does they do not experience satisfaction or happiness."

Because the recovery actions they are taking are causing suffering, they begin to believe and perceive that all those actions {recovery focused actions} are too painful to continue. This then results in a reduction of motivation to continue with those activities. These negative feelings that cause recovery failure must be addressed and changed.

Since it is clear that beliefs determine whether we feel successful or not, then by changing the belief we change the feelings; therefore you need to create, and use new more empowering beliefs that will improve and strengthen your chances for a long lasting recovery. It is through this process, that the faulty associations of pain that unfortunately got linked to recovery actions that led to the abandonment of those actions can now be corrected. We have to change those negative associations. We need to replace them with the positive feelings and associations that we want and expect.

"It is through the process of daily and frequent repetition of new powerful beliefs that will enable us to create new associations for our successful actions taken. These new beliefs will lead to a great sense of appreciation of what has in fact been accomplished, rather than disillusionment and frustration.

Through this process, you will learn that not only is
it possible to change the way you feel by changing the
beliefs you have, it is also possible to change the way you
feel by simply changing the way you act."

The following is an exercise to enable you to take full control over your
beliefs. By practicing speaking them out loud frequently, everywhere and
anywhere you will be able to incorporate these desired new powerful beliefs.
This will enable you to successfully make the emotional shifts and changes
necessary for your recovery. It should be noted that making out loud statements
eventually becomes habitual and this is not only something that you come to
desire, but something that will also automatically lead to great pleasure and
joy. This process is presented in much greater detail in the end of the chapter
titled "Visualizing Victory."

Each morning you MUST ask yourself these questions OUT LOUD
because that is the fastest most powerful way to change your focus; which
is the way to change your emotions and feelings. The way we feel at any one
time is based on questions that we are either consciously, but even more so
unconsciously or subconsciously asking ourselves.

"By taking conscious control of the questions that we
ask will enable us to change our focus instantly and
thereby create the feelings and emotions that we desire
the most."

Since the primary driving force behind the use of mood altering drugs is
the fact that they absolutely guarantee a change in the way we feel; we must
develop the ability to accomplish this without the reliance on mood altering
substances.

Questions to ask at least daily:

1. "What Am I Excited About In My Life Right Now?" "What
   about that makes me excited?" "How Does That Make Me
   Feel?"
2. "What Am I Happy About In My Life Right Now?" "What
   About That Makes Me Happy?" "How Does That Make Me
   Feel?"
3. "What Am I Proud About In My Life Right Now?" "What Is It
   That Makes Me Proud?" "How Does That Make Me Feel?"

4. "What Am I Enjoying Most In My Life Right Now?" "What Is It That Is So Enjoyable?" "How Does That Make Me Feel?"

5. "What Am I Committed To Right Now?" "What About That Makes Me Committed?" "How Does Being Committed Make Me Feel Right Now?"

6. "What Am I Grateful For In My Life Right Now?" How Does It Make Me Feel –To Be Grateful Right Now?"

7. "Who Do I Love Right Now And Who Loves Me Right Now?" "How Does That Make Me Feel To Love and be Loved Right Now?"

8. "Do I Have A Choice To Change Any State Or Focus I Experience?" "How Fast Can It Change?" "How Does That Make Me Feel When I Can Choose To Change Things Instantly?"

9. "Did I Get Proper Sleep And Nutrition Today And What Is Stopping Me From Getting Proper Sleep And Rest And Eating Healthy?" "How Does That Make Me Feel Eating Right And Sleeping Well?"

10. "Does Fear And Worry Change Or Resolve Anything?" "How Does That Make Me Feel Not Resolving Anything?" "Can I Instantly Change Fear And Worry Into Direct Positive Action?" "Can I Do It Now?"

11. "What Good Or Even Great Things Did I Accomplish Today?" How Does That Feel Right Now To Have Achieved Good Or Great Things?"

12. "What Did I Do Today That I Initially Resisted To Do, But Overcame The Resistance?" "How Does That Make Me Feel To Challenge Myself And Win?"

13. "What Specific Actions Did I Take Toward Completion Of Goals Already Decided And Written?"

14. "What Did I Do Today Or I Am Going To Do Today To Build Stronger Healthier Self Confidence?"

15. "What Did I Do Today Or Can Do Today To Strengthen My Faith?"

The use of well formulated questions when effectively utilized create immediate shifts in focus, emotions and physiology. The use of these fifteen questions enables a person to take strong control of their focus and through that process control the way they feel. It is strongly suggested that these empowering questions be used daily and frequently until a strong and specifically desired feeling, becomes associated with the answer to each of these questions. Once again it is through this process that you will be able to control the way your false feelings led you to believe that your highly successful recovery actions had failed; or have failed to provide the emotional expectation that was desired and motivated the actions that were taken.

In order to be able to exercise your personal power and take control over mistaken beliefs in the context of whether you experience pain or pleasure; it is necessary to condition yourself and finally and at last be able to control your self.

> "An effective method for conditioning new beliefs is to state them OUT LOUD frequently and with passion. Despite your doubt in these new stated positive beliefs the repetition of stating them OUT LOUD frequently and with passion will impact your mind to believe them."

It doesn't matter whether you believe that the new thinking is possible, it only matters that you practice stating these with DEEP DESIRE and PASSION. Here are a few examples, but you are encouraged to create your own.

Some or all the following mindsets should be used each morning:

1. "I will and I am having a great day!"
2. "I will and I am learning great things today!"
3. "I am changing and I will continue to change in great ways today!"
4. "I am helping and continuing to help others to recover today!"
5. "I am patient and tolerant today!"
6. "I am kind, caring and loving!"
7. "My mind and my body will continue to improve today!"
8. "I am motivated and passionate about recovery today!"
9. "I will do great things today!"
10. "I will do good things for others today!"
11. "I know there is much good to do today!"
12. "My life will be greatly improved today!"
13. "I will have abundant energy today!"
14. "I know there is so much to have gratitude for today!"
15. "I am a winner and I will work hard today!"

The following mindsets should be used at night and they directly correspond with the mindsets used each morning.

1. "My day was great today!"
2. "I have learned great things today!"
3. "I have made great changes today and I will continue to change!"
4. "I have had a positive impact on others today!"
5. "I have demonstrated patience and tolerance with others today!"
6. "I have shown care and consideration for others today!"
7. "My mind and body continues to improve and heal!"
8. "I have shown much enthusiasm and excitement about my recovery today!"
9. "I have accomplished much today!"
10. "Others have found me today reliable, caring and supportive!"
11. "I have contributed to the general good today!"
12. "I can see the positive changes I've made in my life today!"
13. "I have been very energetic and motivated today!"
14. "I now remember all the things I'm grateful for today!"
15. "I have worked hard and I am a winner today!"

Before you can begin this change it is necessary to gain strong leverage over yourself by recognizing that you must get yourself to the point that "something must change, you must change it, and you can change it right now." It is through the development of this belief that immediate and effective changes will occur in your life.

Now you must find the negative associations that disempower you and replace them with more powerful ones that will bring you to your goals. You need to identify the beliefs and behaviors you have about people, about yourself, about relationships, about money that are limiting your life, and that are stopping you from achieving the level of success that you deserve in your life.

If you link enough pain to something that you are presently doing it will lead to stopping and changing that behavior. Identify those limiting beliefs and link agonizing pain to them and this will create empowering new beliefs to replace the old ones.

> "You need to do more than just think, but feel deep pain regarding all the areas of your life that's being affected and how much it is costing you and how much you're

losing because you have allowed your feelings to lie, rob, cheat and deceive you."

Through the process of rehearsing these mindsets passionately "OUT LOUD" you'll condition that new strong empowering positive belief, and each time that you think of the new empowering belief as well as verbalize it "OUT LOUD" so you hear it in your own ears; you will feel it that much stronger and positive and as you do it again and again it will become permanently wired into your brain.

We need to understand the importance and the impact on our ability to change our lives and understand the driving forces that we need to know, and to control in order to change our lives.

> "In order for any change to occur in our lives we must have goals in which we develop a new vision that enables us to clearly see the great positive changes we are achieving, and to no longer fall victim to the mistaken belief that in order to succeed we must feel successful."

Once again success is not based on a feeling but a fact, and we must teach ourselves to celebrate each and every successful action regardless of any feeling or emotions that we experience.

> "Placing achievement ahead of emotional expectations enables us to have clear direction and to concentrate not only our mental energy but our physical and emotional energy as well, and gear it towards the acquisition and accomplishment of what we desire and envision in our recovering journey."

CHAPTER FOUR

Relapse Realities

For over thirty years both as a counselor and a recovering human being I have asked numerous others this simple question. "Why do people relapse? Why do they return to the use of a substance that has hurt them and everyone they know?" Many people give many different answers; from "I don't really know why I started using again." or "I got bored." or "I stopped going to support meetings." or "I started to feel my feelings." or "Using is all I have ever done." or "I went back to my old friends or things that I use to do." or "I missed the excitement." and the number one most frequently used justification is "I just wanted to or thought I could control it." The alibis, justifications, the excuses and the rationalizations are endless.

Why does the madness continue? Why do they relapse is the most frequently asked question when it comes to families and friends of an addict or alcoholic. There are many assumptions, as well as many facts regarding why a person may relapse. There are also many fantasies why a person will fail to stay sober.

> "It may be helpful to always remember that we are dealing with a condition that has been referred to as being a disease. Not just any kind of a disease, but a chronic one that is punctuated by denial and progression."

Of all the answers I have heard the most perplexing one is as follows: "They just wanted to use and get high and there is nothing anyone could have done." Believing that people want to get high when it is an obvious fact that it will be very costly financially and emotionally is really to be ignorant of the facts. These facts are as follows:

The first fact is:

> "The addict or alcoholic suffers an obsession they cannot control that wears their resistance down, and one of the main purposes of this book is to instruct people to learn how to build up their resistance. For in the end it is only their resistance that will enable them to avoid repeating their past tragic mistakes."

The second fact is:

> "Most alcoholics and addicts cannot remember their own suffering, nonetheless that of their loved ones-so worry about hurting the ones they love is not an effective deterrent."

The third fact is:

> "The condition that they suffer from is literally mental illness; actually chronic mental illness and in fact incurable mental illness. While most people are cheering an addict for being clean and sober; if that person is not addressing the real problem, which is their thinking, then they are probably doomed to failure."

Since they are in fact seriously mentally ill, means that they are not capable, and in fact it is not possible for them to make healthy decisions, so to say that "They just wanted to get high" is being very ignorant of the facts. Believing that "There is nothing anyone could have done" is probably the cruelest belief a friend or a loved one of an addict could have. It is necessary for a friend or a family member to remember to confront and remind the addict that they need to manage their condition, and to do so in a loving and caring manner and avoid any sarcasm, nagging or ridicule. Avoid any power struggles just express concern, and gently remind them to maintain their recovery commitments.

> "For it is only though strong daily commitments that an alcoholic will be able to stay sober."

The mental illness of the addict or alcoholic can be observed through the use of the following metaphor. When a person is driving a car, they cannot get complacent and take their hands off the steering wheel, especially when moving at high speed, none the less get out of the drivers seat, when moving at very low speed. Does it make sense to step on the gas and let go of the steering wheel? —Yet this is what happens when things begin to improve and speed up in the person's life, and they get careless and lose direction and lose control. By being committed to making and overcoming challenges on a daily basis is the best way to stay alert and vigilant, so they do not crash.

> "In the AA book it indicates on page 89 "Nothing will insure immunity from drinking than intensive work with another alcoholic *or addict*." The AA book outlines a foolproof formula for protecting against relapse."

It should be noted that this concept does not need to be limited to just doing intensive work with another alcoholic. For many addicts and alcoholics this may not be the only way to assure immunity.

> "If the person is a very selfish and self centered type of alcoholic or addict that really cannot not, or will not, engage in this particular activity; then they can utilize the concept that "any intensive work that challenges their resistant attitudes, and feelings will produce the same result."

This will occur every time when a person experiences a feeling of great achievement and self-satisfaction, that comes as a direct result of knowing, and proving that their own immediate needs do not have to come first, and by challenging himself or herself brings great satisfaction, when they are able to help others. Anthony Robbins developed the concept in his books that there are Six and only Six Human Needs. It is helpful to discuss two of these six needs, which are "Growth" and "Contribution." According to Anthony Robbins these last two provide the greatest sense of purpose, fulfillment and accomplishment.

> "Now in the AA world working with others is the epitome of spirituality, and it falls in the realm of "Contribution" but whenever a person overcomes their own negative inclinations, attitudes or behaviors, they

are absolutely demonstrating "Growth" which is just as equally empowering."

It is through these two human needs that all addiction and dependency behaviors can be addressed and contained.

"When a person is so selfish, self centered, self consumed, self obsessed and self directed, they will be prevented from experiencing any kind of spirituality, due to the fact that it is necessary to be sacrificing, and place others ahead of themselves, before they can ever be or feel spirituality."

The AA book speaks about having the need to have a spiritual awakening, but due to the hard wiring of the addict to be inclined to be selfish, this experience is almost impossible to achieve. It is suggested that since many addicts and alcoholics cannot be taught to be spiritual, then instead of the goal being totally altruistic and spiritual as the AA book implies; it may by more expedient and more feasible to teach or guide them towards being less selfish instead of selfless.

"The ability to be self-sacrificing is possible through the concept of making and keeping COMMITMENTS. Regardless of any feeling or emotions to do so or not. COMMITMENTS manage the mental illness by reducing or eliminating the most damaging impact of the illness, which is the tendency to be impulsive."

While people struggle with understanding why a person will relapse, they may be missing the most simple and obvious truth. "They relapse because sobriety sucks!" Now as absurd and offensive as this comment may sound. This thought stopping phrase should initially produce shock and disbelief that a counselor would say such a thing. In my years of counseling, whenever I would express this statement to a group of addicts and alcoholics, most of the group members would begin to nod their heads in reluctant agreement.

"As it may be observed, that when they can actually believe even for a moment that "sobriety sucks," then it

is crystal clear that they are indeed suffering a form of
mental illness."

When they catch themselves expressing this absurd belief, it is at that
moment they begin to grasp some profound truths about themselves, their
denial and their addictive condition. It is at this time it is possible to help them
become painfully aware of the fact that they do indeed have very TWISTED
and PECULIAR perceptions.

"The naked truth is that they are mentally ill, and in
fact "chronically mentally ill," and this is the way denial
manifests itself through PECULIAR and TWISTED
perceptions."

To attack their denial I would confront the addict or alcoholic with
the need to clearly define "sobriety" in as much detail as possible. It would
naturally follow that once they reluctantly agree that, "Relapse must be due
to the fact that sobriety sucks." They now have to discuss and define the
concept of "sobriety," so they can clearly see why they would believe, that "it
must suck," but of course through this process of defining "sobriety," no such
conclusion can be substantiated or drawn that "sobriety sucks."

Addicts and alcoholics due to their denial-due to their PECULIAR and
TWISTED perceptions, have a tendency to have the inability to describe
"sobriety." To assist in overcoming this tendency it is helpful to identify, and
just list the actions and feelings that they have experienced or believe they
would experience, that would, accompany sobriety.

The following is a simple, but not all-inclusive list of the positive things
that the addict or alcoholic will experience as a direct result of staying clean
and sober.

"Physical health begins to return; self esteem begins to
increase; self and other forgiveness also begins especially
if the person is involved with a 12 Step self help program.
In addition to this, the person's family relationships
are improving and the person maybe building healthy
friendships with others in and out of recovery. There's
a new or renewed interests in sports and hobbies long
neglected. There may be financial and personal rewards
in current or new employment opportunities or they

have returned or for the first time entered school or training programs. Relationships with family and others are improving or developing. They may be returning to a more committed practice of religion or may be just beginning new spiritual involvements. If there have been legal problems, those issues may also be getting resolved, just simply because of ongoing abstinence. Continued sobriety leads to resolving guilt and shame. Integrity also builds though the process of making necessary amends to people, that have been hurt. It is through this process people build a stronger connection and trust with a God, of their understanding or Higher Power, as God, is referred to in 12 Step terminologies."

This very short list will demonstrate to the reader an incredible irony that can be observed in the fact that, since sobriety means all the above great and wonderful things, how could a person work so hard to achieve these and then carelessly throw them all away.

"How can they fail to recognize all the GOOD that is occurring in their lives as a direct result of staying clean and sober? An addict or alcoholic will verbalize their gratitude and happiness regarding all the positive things happening in their lives, and then an hour after expressing all this gratitude they will return to substance abuse. How does this happen? What is wrong with this person? What can be done to stop this insanity, this madness, and this life threatening foolishness?"

How can anyone answer these questions accurately? Is it even possible for these questions to be answered accurately? There is a high probability that most people believe that addiction is a matter of choices. Even a large percentage of the addicts and alcoholics I have worked with have argued the point, that "It is my choice." or "I decided to get high and no one made me." In addition to the self condemnation by the addict to themselves; their loved ones and family members also generally will blame the person with the problem; who in reality is as much as a victim as the family who suffers the "fallout," from the destructive behaviors of the addict or alcoholic. In the interest of enlightening the reader to this dilemma of "Choice vs. Disease" it is helpful to examine the benefits and the liabilities of each opposing view. Addiction is it a disease or a choice? — In the chapter "Understanding Addiction" this controversy will be further explained.

When a person is judged or even condemned for "bad behaviors," what purpose does that serve the person who is doing the judging? All values and beliefs serve a purpose. So what is the purpose of "blame?" If blame enables someone to feel better, then that would make the attitude of "blaming" self-explanatory. What is the potential problem with maintaining an attitude of blame towards a loved one, who is dependent on substances? This can be answered with the idea that blaming leads to shaming and a sense of victimization.

> "Shame is a belief that "I am no good" and that means the person who is poisoned by shame believes they have no value." Things that have no value are discarded and usually thrown away. Therefore once a person enters into the state of SHAME they have NO value. As a direct result of this they have NO interest in improving their lives, and if they are trying to get sober; then it follows that their sobriety would have NO value to them, and since they have NO sense of personal value; they have NOTHING to lose by returning to substance abuse. It is in this way they truly suffer victimization as does their loved ones."

Sometimes people take a blaming stance, simply due to being afraid to have any hope that recovery is possible, and by discounting the person with the addiction by shaming them, then it is less painful if the person should relapse.

> "The way this works is that if I blame you and don't believe in you, then I have NO hope for you, and that means I will NOT suffer disappointment and despair should you fail. By blaming you I have successfully protected myself from potential emotional pain, that is associated with the LOSS of hope."

In order to have a more supportive attitude toward their loved one, the significant other or family member would need to have understanding of addiction and or alcoholism from the perspective of a disease.

> "Once someone accepts it as a condition that is involuntary, they will have a tendency towards compassion rather than condemnation."

I will outline briefly how accepting that addiction is a disease is both empowering to the family as well as the addict. To understand the addicts or alcoholics dilemma, it is necessary to understand the following ideas.

> "Addicts are plagued with a condition I call "PECULIAR perceptions," which in reality is mental illness or just plain insanity, but the term PECULIAR perceptions sounds so much less threatening. Telling someone they are insane or mentally ill usually produces a strong sense to argue or rebel against this fact or possibility."

Addicts and alcoholics need to recognize that returning to drinking or drug use measures the severity of the addicts or alcoholics condition. These TWISTED perceptions cause a sensory failure resulting in a problem with "perspective." Depending on the depth of a person's faulty perceptions determines the degree of impairment. The degree of impairment is a measure of how distorted their "thoughts, beliefs and feelings" are.

> "When any person suffers a significant distortion in their perceptions or what can be described as what they "Think, Believe and Feel," then that is referred to as "mental illness."

Many family members and recovering people themselves do not realize, that they are not suffering from a condition called "addiction" but they are in fact afflicted with "mental illness." This condition is chronic and progressive and in fact the addict and alcoholic suffer from chronic incurable mental illness. The proof of this is evidenced by the fact that they continue to drink and or use drugs despite the serious aversive consequences they have or are suffering.

The continued use of a destructive substance is the proof that they have a mental disorder.

"Therefore "addiction" is not a disease but a symptom of a disease, and clear evidence of the presence of "mental illness." With this understanding comes much confusion, when we take a condition such as alcoholism or addiction, and try to answer the question of whether "Is it a disease or is it a choice? "It should be clear now the facts speak for themselves. "The addict or alcoholic does not have the power of choice."

The truth of this statement cannot be denied when every addict and alcoholic, as well as their family members have asked and stated numerous times: "What is wrong with you (me)?" "You (I) must be CRAZY that I did it again." "How can you (I) care more about drugs than my (your) own children (family)." Within these questions the answer has been presented.

"They are in fact CRAZY," for only a CRAZY person could continue to hurt himself or herself, as well as the people they love, and do this over and over. NO sane person who loves his family and his own life would engage repeatedly in self defeating and self destructive behaviors."

They would be willing to do anything to stop the pain and suffering to their family and themselves; but I did say "no sane person" so therefore to engage in this behavior over and over again measures the degree of insanity.

"If and when addiction and alcoholism are accepted as forms of insanity, then it becomes very clear that their using is not "a matter of choice" but more so the manifestation and evidence of a "Disease of the Mind."

"When a person has a demonstrated history of extreme poor judgment, TWISTED perceptions, impulsivity and warped behaviors and attitudes; then it cannot be denied that they are in fact "mentally ill, and therefore cannot exercise healthy choices."

The dilemma that creates all this confusion regarding the issue of "choice," is found in the fact that decision making or "choice making" can be described by the following words—"No matter what decision or direction a person takes or makes, many times they will experience PAIN. In other words they are "Damned if they do and Damned if they don't!! To describe this dilemma the following concept needs to be recognized.

Many times it is a "PAIN or PAIN" experience, and no matter what decision is made, there is acute suffering. This may cause the addict to abandon making that decision; due to it does not seem right, since pain is attached to the decision. An example of this would be to choose to stay in a very abusive and unhealthy relationship, due to the need to avoid the PAIN of ending it. By ending it the person may fear to be alone and feel lonely, which would also create great PAIN. So there must be an understanding that the "PAIN or PAIN" is not the same, and this can be explained by the example of a person with a serious toothache and has fear of going to the dentist. If they do nothing, it will only get worse, but if they go to the dentist, then they may not only experience severe emotional suffering but physical pain as well. Their refusal to take action leads to PAIN that is relentless, ongoing, destructive and permanent –whereas going to the dentist produces PAIN that is temporary, positive and constructive as well as productive.

To explain this in the context of addiction is to recognize that an addict can choose not to resolve a problem, if they can escape the pain as long as they have substances. So therefore even though the pain is destructive and permanent, they can and do have CONTROL over it; but if the addict is sober and clean, and has to make a very painful decision, then they suffer, and even though it is positive, constructive and temporary, they cannot CONTROL that pain.

In other words it is the dilemma of having to face the "PAIN of Active Addiction" vs. the" PAIN of Active Recovery," when in fact substance use provides a guaranteed escape from this dilemma.

> "It is the memory of how substances block or mask pain, that causes a return to using alcohol or chemicals as a means of coping. The addict or alcoholic does not intentionally or willfully nor deliberately intend to do harm to their families nor to themselves; but they are seduced by the power of substances to guarantee the resolution of emotional discomfort that is caused by the above dilemma."

Now a sane person would have a passionate willingness to change their behavior, their friends, their circumstances, to end their family's suffering and their own suffering. However an insane person may not know how to change the situation or organize an effective corrective action. The reason that most addicts and alcoholics never develop enough willingness to change their behaviors is because they are incapable of willingness.

Since they are not sane and do not have any rational understanding that their use of substances is the direct cause of the suffering. Therefore they do not have the capacity to be willing because they are in fact insane. Where is the guilt and shame when they hurt the family and why is guilt not a strong deterrent prior to the relapse?

"The answer to this question may be found in the fact that their feelings dictate their actions. This is why treatment and self help programs fail; due to the addict or alcoholic has never been instructed to develop the ability, to understand how to effectively resist the feelings and emotions that trigger the use of substances."

If he cannot resist what is inside then he or she must learn to resist acting out. This is where the concept of learning to "resist the resistance" comes into play.

"Through the "Power of Resisting Resistance" and practicing the "Art of Self Defiance" enables the person to take effective control of their emotions, and take the right actions regardless of the way they feel. In this way they learn to manage any difficult situation rationally rather than emotionally."

Now regarding this concept of "willingness to change"-can a person afflicted with mental illness really exercise any kind of effective willingness, when they are so delusional that they don't accept the fact that what they are doing is very wrong and they must change this? Since they are so blind, how can they possibly know what it is that they are so "willingly suppose to change?"

The use of substances has effectively enabled them to avoid the dilemma regarding the fact that whatever decision they make, many times will result in feeling pain or at least discomfort. Especially when they are confronted with the fact that whatever choices they make result in intense pain and suffering.

This perception is one of the driving forces behind their TWISTED Thoughts and Feelings.

> "It is through these TWISTED perceptions that they can evade the strong feelings of guilt and shame that should motivate them to change their behavior. The addict has a strong tendency to resist pain, and yet it is pain that leads to motivation to change behaviors, and the strongest pain, which is guilt, is resisted and masked."

Any strong negative emotions that are caused by substance use are masked By What Has Been Referred To As Euphoric Recall. It Is In The Context Of "Euphoric Recall" That "Only The Good Times Are Remembered." This process of repressing the most powerful and painful memories, that have resulted as a direct use of drinking or drugging, are so strong that they literally block any attempt to recognize the severe damage, and deterioration to themselves and their relationships.*

> "Accepting and understanding that addicts and alcoholics destructive behaviors are due to mental illness rather than evil intentions, allows for compassion instead of condemnation."

> "In the same sense that someone who is suffering from untreated Schizophrenia is absolutely and totally innocent in regards to anything they say, and or do while in a psychotic state; the recovering person is equally guiltless when they relapse."

*For a detailed understanding of this concept of how Negative Events and Emotions are Masked by Euphoric Recall. Refer to Chapter Sixteen "Essays and Excerpts" under the subheading of "Relapse Victims and Manipulation," which graphically illustrates this phenomena through the use of "The Highline."

The idea of holding a person guiltless may offend many and may seem absolutely absurd to many others. Most people would not hold a person accountable for being psychotic, and yet the person who has relapsed is judged and blamed and condemned. This view is not just limited to significant others and society at large, but it is also believed by the victim themselves, meaning the person who has just relapsed. The reason they relapsed is that sobriety did NOT make enough sense, or was NOT valuable enough to protect, and this lack of proper perspective, is NOT the addicts or alcoholics fault.

To help correct this perception of victim blaming—Let us return to the guiltless schizophrenic, who is experiencing psychosis, which is manifested in the belief that he thinks that he is "Napoleon." This is referred to as being delusional in that he believes something that is absolutely not true. Does it make any sense to ask the question—Is the schizophrenic choosing to believe that he is Napoleon? Does he have the power to choose the delusional belief that he is a doctor or lawyer or even the President of the United States? Are these within the power of conscious choice? The obvious fact is that the schizophrenic does NOT choose the delusion, but rather the delusion CHOOSES the Schizophrenic. Does the schizophrenic have the power of CHOICE, or is the delusion the proof that mental illness IS present?

In the same sense isn't the alcoholic or addict ALSO in a delusional state. They believe and are obsessed that "somehow some day and in some way" they will be able to drink, or do a drug that they can control, and in fact suffer no harm? Is this NOT identical to the Schizophrenics delusional belief in something that is absolutely NOT true? Do they have the power to CHOOSE the truth, which is to know and understand that their abuse of mood altering substances ARE destroying their lives, as well as the lives of ALL they love.

> "For the addict and alcoholic due to their PECULIAR perceptions; they just fail to register that it will never be possible to safely use any mood altering substances, and that ANY return to USE will definitely be harmful to NOT only themselves, BUT their loved ones also."

Is it their fault they cannot see what is so obvious? What in fact is a simple and absolute naked truth, that, "Using mood altering substances will continue to cause harm and tragedy? There is nothing crueler than a victim to blame himself or herself, for something they have no control over. Does the addict or alcoholic have the capacity for becoming "willing?" Does a schizophrenic have the capacity to become "willing" not to be delusional? It needs to be recognized that neither the alcoholic nor the schizophrenic have a CHOICE to "become willing" because the mind is so severely affected. The concept of "willingness" never presents itself neither for the schizophrenic nor for the addict.

"Once this is understood and accepted we will be able

to develop Compassion instead of Condemnation, Awareness instead of Judgment, Concern instead of Criticism. Failure can then be met with Forgiveness instead of Blame. We can give support, and have empathy for why they failed to stay sober. Rather than blame, we need to accept as well as understand they are victimized by their PECULIAR perceptions!"

This issue of TWISTED and PECULIAR perceptions was addressed twenty-three hundred years ago when a great Greek philosopher named Epicurus expressed.

That there are three standards of truth and that truth or what is perceived as truth is based on our sensations, preconceptions and our feelings. Therefore knowledge— all our knowledge ultimately develops through the interaction of these senses. Epicurus further proposed that since our sensations give us all the information that we can know about the exterior world; the combined information from those three senses are the only way we know the world we live in.

It is through this process we make judgments and take actions. He emphasized that sensation itself is never wrong, since non-conscious processes drive the three sensations. It is a purely passive, mechanical reception of images, and the senses themselves do not make judgments.

All ideas are formed ultimately on the basis of what we perceive through our sense experience. Once again since the world can only be known through the information we obtain through our senses, it is through the right or wrong judgments we make based on the senses that error and mistakes occur.

These judgments are ultimately based upon one thing and that is what we believe will cause feelings of pain

and pleasure and therefore what eventually will be
sought after and what ultimately will be avoided.

Hopefully we can now recognize that in many ways perceptions control
our emotional states. What Epicurus presented over 2,300 years ago implies
that "Nothing in this world can directly affect you unless it enters your skin-
an arrow, rock or spear." He went on to state that, "It is the view you take of
the events in the world and it is not the events in the world that affect you."

"This means that how a person views something or the
way it is perceived determines what "constitutes their
reality. "Reality is not an objective thing but created out
of the words we think and speak."

If we believe that there is no answers to a particular problem and that we
are a failure; then that perception of the problem and ourselves will produce
that result—"The problem has no answer and we are indeed a total failure."
In regards to this concept of CHOICE, and how many people believe that the
addict or alcoholic CHOOSES to relapse; they need to consider that there is a
strong belief or perception that they are powerless to change something, due
to how they perceive what they may or may NOT be able to do.

When a person suffers a loss or when someone or something disappoints
them; then they can feel grief, frustration, depression and or anger. In the
same sense if the person can see the loss or disappointment as just part of the
natural order of things such as the death of an older grandparent; then they
can better cope due to they do not feel like a victim.

"To feel like a victim a person has to use disparaging
language "Why does this always happen to me." or "I
am not going to be able to live without this person." or
"I will never get over this." or "It is just too much to
deal with now." It is this disempowering language that
many times triggers a relapse."

If a person asked themselves the following questions, they would gain a
deeper insight that would help them cope as well as deal with many of life's
disappointments and disillusionments. Those questions are: "Who or what is
making me feel like a victim?" "What is it I am doing right now that is causing
me to feel victimized?" "What action can I take immediately that would stop
me from experiencing victimization?"

By asking these questions removes the tendency of falling into the self-pity trap. These questions forces the person to view their sense of Hopelessness and Helplessness in the context that it is being self inflicted, and once they can recognize this; they ARE immediately empowered to change the feeling of victimization and reduce the risk of using substances to cope.

"Victimization increases stress and when a person can empower himself or herself, this results in a reduction in stress. When a person is building a sense of Hope and Faith, they immediately experience a reduction in stress simply through the act of having Faith."

The following questions will empower the addict or alcoholic and improve their perceptions, which will reduce their possibility of using substances to cope or deal with Disappointments or Disillusionments: "How does anyone deal with something they cannot control or change?" "What do they have to do?" "What are they immediately feeling?"

"When attempting to answer these questions it is helpful to understand how the concept of Faith provides direction as well as the energy to push forward in every manner possible, and NOT get bogged down or paralyzed with Fear and Worry."

"Fear only leads to even deeper fear and overwhelming worry, whereas Faith provides forward direction moving toward some solution or resolution even when the outcome seems improbable."

According to Epicurus our reactions to things in the world are based on how we perceive an event and that perception results in a belief and that belief results in an action. If we have faulty perceptions then we have faulty beliefs and we act in error. In other words what he described as the "Three criteria of truth as sensations, preconceptions and feelings" I am interpreting as "Beliefs, Thoughts and Feelings. Using this understanding of perceptions we can now describe how the TWIST develops that victimizes and causes the recovering person to THROW away their chance and ALL their hard work to achieve sobriety.

It is our judgment of events that determine the desire or undesirability, not the event itself, for it is an obvious fact that being clean and sober should have great and lasting value, but to a relapsing addict or alcoholic it obviously does not.

> "If the addict fails to feel Value in their recovery actions, then they will cease taking those actions. They will "Believe" it is not worth the effort and begin to "Think," in error, of how nice it would be to someday, somehow and in some way control, and enjoy their drinking or drug use, thus creating the "Feelings" and desire to get high one more time."

In attempting to understand that relapse is due primarily to the seemingly poor choices that the addict or alcoholic makes, enables us to remember the cause is due to their delusional thought processes, which embody all that they "Think, Believe and Feel." No one, and I repeat no one deliberately destroys what he or she have worked so hard to build or create, unless they are in fact, very SERIOUSLY mentally ill.

> "It is a contradiction of healthy functioning to throw away what a person greatly loves and desires. How can anyone in their right mind inflict the irreparable harm and damage to their families and themselves?"

> "The answer is of course quite obvious; they are NOT in their right mind due to their affliction of having the tendency to frequently have PECULIAR perceptions about their use of substances, their families and themselves."

I do not believe that the addict or alcoholic woke up on the day they relapsed and asked themselves this question. "Now that everything I have worked so hard to achieve in recovery has now manifested itself in my life; should I now destroy it all by getting high?" I do not believe that the person said to himself or herself "I can't wait to take this drink (drug) and to lose everything I have achieved." Or "Boy if I drink (drug) today I might even get lucky enough to go to jail." Or "Boy I really can't wait to completely ruin my life."

"No indeed the addict or alcoholic has never said to themselves that they are ready to Throw it all Away, but the fact is whatever motivates them to "try it one more time" the result is ABSOLUTELY predictable and certain that the decision to drink or drug IS going to be very costly, if NOT emotionally to them, then CERTAINLY to their significant others."

Here again I want to scream out—Given the fact that so much damage has been done, and will continue to be done, due to getting high, any person in their right mind would immediately cease and desist from that destructive activity or behavior, but the addict and alcoholic never stops no matter how great the suffering of their loved ones or themselves. Therein lies the mystery.

"Why is there NO demonstrated willingness to change behavior? Earlier I stated that when a person IS less than sane, they cannot exercise willingness due to they are Incapable of recognizing the need to make a change, or the need to be willing to change, none the less of what to change."

In the following chapter I will demonstrate NOT only the nature of the insanity, but also the way it manifests itself into what has been generally labeled as denial. How do the best intentions to do well in recovery fail?

"The process or mechanism for this may be found in what I refer to as "Value Exchange." The Value of doing well or staying in recovery is fully exchanged for the Value of doing badly by drinking or drugging and relapse. Due to this observable fact most addicts and alcoholics are incapable of developing the emotion of "Willingness.""

As you will see next in the chapter on Value Exchange the shift is NOT between being "good" vs. "bad" but actually a failure in the evaluation of what is perceived as GOOD vs. BAD.

Therefore, do not Worry about Tomorow,
for Tomorrow will Worry about itself.
Each day has Enough trouble of its Own.

Matthew 6:34

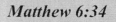

Chapter Five

Vision And Values

What causes a person to FAIL after demonstrating a seemingly strong DESIRE to change? Were they just conning others or themselves or did they sincerely want to stay abstinent? Both of these questions will have very different answers depending on the particular person we may be speaking about. In the latter case there WILL always be people who are insincere and NOT ready to stop.

They are just giving a brief performance of being sober or clean. This particular person has only one desire and that is to be able to use without consequences, and so they stop, or stall their using for a time; but they ABSOLUTELY know that their abstinence is strictly temporary. Despite their unwillingness they can change by challenging their own desires and behaviors that will enable them to create a new destiny that frees them from the insanity of addictions.

Everyone who has had a drink or used drugs has experienced something so powerful, that even if something distressful occurred at the time a substance was used, the unpleasantness that was experienced did not become a deterrent to future use and experimentation. The fact that most people drink and the fact that most people know other people that drink or may do drugs; means that the ingestion of chemicals, that alter the mood of a person, must be felt to be a very EMPOWERING experience. Considering the fact that the great majority of people drink and or use drugs is clear evidence this activity has HIGH value.

"The power to alter emotions and feelings in an almost guaranteed manner, must be seen as a coping device or tool. It provides an experience that is perceived as comforting and soothing. No matter what issues, stressors or concerns a person is experiencing, the USE of a chemical ingested into the body REDUCES the negative sensations that those problems or troubles create."

The concept of value in describing a substance allows a deeper understanding for the reasons so many people struggle to give up their right to use a substance. Despite the high cost they pay to continue their right to use a substance, they either cannot or will not give up this method of Coping or Celebration!

The things that a person may consider to have Value are the things that a person will naturally protect and guard against their loss or theft. The mystery is why, when a person losses control of the use of a substance, they fail to recognize that their use of substances has now become a total liability. When problems or suffering occur, the idea of continuing to use a substance that is the DIRECT cause the suffering, should result in a reduction or elimination of ALL its appeal or measured sense of value. A person who has not developed the perception of reliance on chemicals, as a means to cope or enhance their joy, excitement and pleasure, have no ability to understand this mystery.

"Since the use of the substances results in pain and suffering for not only the user, but the people who are involved with the user, such as their family, friends and the community at large; this pain creates the need for relief, and the simple fact IS that continuing the USE of the very substance that causes this suffering, WILL paradoxically relieve the pain it creates."

Since no matter what consequences have occurred the person perceives the use of substances as Pleasurable and at least ALWAYS Comforting. Expanding on this phenomenon an OVERDOSE may be viewed paradoxically as JUST an extreme attempt to get COMFORTABLE.

"Many addicts and alcoholics are so obsessed with Comfort they pursue it to the point of DEATH. In other words they are Comfort junkies, and will DO anything to escape any discomfort or undesirable feeling or emotions."

In this manner the pain has been removed, and there has been a "value exchange" between what has caused the pain, and what relieves the pain. This is very seductive to the person who has come to rely on a chemical filter to deal with life's Pleasures and Pains.

> "Even when they WANT to abstain, the process of stopping is SO painful, and stopping substance use has such little appeal or low Value, that they will place more Value on how to escape rather than deal with the discomfort. Their discomfort IS intensified by the fact that many buried issues and problems will boil to the emotional surface, overwhelming any determination to abstain, control or stop."

Since the person has developed the factual knowledge through their using experience that EVERY time they initiate a return to chemical use, after a brief period of abstinence, the result is ALWAYS sensed as powerful, pleasant, exciting and appealing, because it ALWAYS reduces or completely removes any negative sensations, feelings or emotions. These feelings cause the person to Value active use of a substance rather than maintaining abstinence. In other words they engage in the process of exchanging "worth for worthlessness!"

Until a person has had a corrective emotional experience they will ALWAYS be at a very high risk, due to the fact that the use of a substance is ALWAYS emotionally experienced as Needed and Necessary. To create the necessary emotional experience that AA refers to as having a "Spiritual Awakening" or "Spiritual Experience," can only be brought about by a determined effort by the addicted person. They will NEED to engage in many physical activities that will FEEL emotionally uncomfortable, and they would prefer to resist, since those recovery activities would have very Minimal appeal.

By using the simple concept of "Value Exchange" we can begin to gain some needed insights to how seemingly highly motivated and not so motivated people fail. It should be noted that any period of sobriety has great Value to not only the addict or alcoholic, but to their family and friends. Anytime we speak of Value we speak of things having great worth. The strange paradox is why anyone would take something of great worth [recovery and abstinence] and willingly trade it for something that is NOT only worthless [drugs and alcohol] but exacts a higher price each and every time they make that trade. How is it possible that they continue to repeatedly fail when it is CLEARLY a losing proposition, and each return to use becomes an accumulative added cost and liability?

"To answer this question it is necessary to understand

that active use of substances, also have great VALUE
and worth [escape, celebration and or can be used as an
effective coping device] at least that is the way the user
experiences it. Therefore to them they are NOT trading
something of worth for something that is worthless, but
they are simply involved in a "values exchange."

A simple metaphor to use to describe this paradox and to give this concept
Crystal Clarity is as follows:

A pile of dirt suddenly has value as soon as someone else shows interest
in it. My neighbor was building a house and I needed a few wheelbarrows
of the extra-excavated dirt that was left over from digging the foundation,
and suddenly one of my other neighbors came over, almost in a panic, and
demanded, "I want some of that too..."

Addiction is a "pile of dirt" that seems to get great VALUE when others
show interest. This is when the desire and interest in drugs and alcohol by
others or their USE of these substances distracts us from recognizing ALL
the opportunity and achievements that were accomplished. Despite our hard
earned success in recovery we begin to see that "pile of dirt" as being worth
making that "values exchange."

You must have a clear understanding of your VALUES and how dangerous
and destructive Values Exchange may be in your life. Whether you are trading
the VALUE of recovery for the VALUE of getting high; or mistakenly placing
more importance on recovery, to the point of devaluing your family and
career, may ALL equally result in suffering great unnecessary losses, due to
exchanging good VALUES for worthless VALUES, Ideas and Beliefs.

The only way that a person can relapse is that they first have to convince
themselves that they will NOT lose anything substantial. They believe that
by drinking or using drugs they WILL experience something that is of even
greater VALUE, and has more worth than their period of sobriety, that they
are now willing to trade.

"They have minimized in their minds what the potential
losses WILL be and therefore have come to believe that
they have NOTHING to really lose by returning to
substance use. Somehow the experience of drinking
or drug use has dominated their sense of what is right
and wrong and what is worth protecting [their right to
use drugs and alcohol] and what is worth risking [their
earned rewards from being abstinent.]"

The process that allows this to occur is driven by pure emotion. Rational reasoning does not exist, and that is why willingness never develops, due to the fact that willingness requires a rational understanding of facts and the ability to compare facts. It is through this awareness a person can begin to clearly recognize, what actions need to be taken, and what actions need to be avoided. Rational reasoning processes in the mind that are not influenced by TWISTED perceptions or extreme emotions are what determine the healthy action.

It is through emotions that a person is able to assess the VALUE of something. The perceived VALUE of something is totally dependent upon the intensity of the feelings or emotions being experienced; therefore the emotional sensation regarding a particular thing determines the level of desire to acquire the object or experience. If there is no or very little emotional sensation or appeal; then there is very little sense of VALUE.

> "It is the addicts and alcoholics failure to develop a strong desire or passion towards the things they worked so hard for in recovery, that makes it so easy to give them up and throw them away. When a person lacks desire and passion they have a tendency to just merely think and talk without much enthusiasm, nor do they have any appreciation for their recovery achievements."

The reason they have this tendency to "merely just think about recovery," is due to the fact that their minds and bodies are completely emotionally detached from this abstract concept, referred by everyone as "recovery." Yet on the other hand from their very first ingestion of a drug or alcohol, they had a deep emotional learning experience, in which they have "emotionalized" addiction, and everything that is attached to the use of substances.

It is not a mystery why addiction has strong positive emotions attached to it, and recovery is devoid of any strong driving emotional attachments. The very essence of the drug or alcohol using experience is defined through emotions; whereas recovery is ONLY known through the prompting and education of others, and NOT experienced as an intense pleasurable sensation as was drugs and alcohol when initially used.

Being pushed and taught for most substance abusers has very minimal appeal. Therefore due to the lack of any emotional intensity and pleasure, recovery or abstinence are NOT valued very much. Recovery most of the time is an abstract concept that is presented to the addicted individual, and since it has NO emotional attachments associated with it; this renders the concept useless in attempting to motivate a person to change their beliefs and behaviors.

If the initial use of mood altering substances were not originally felt to be an intensely pleasurable activity; there would be NO further interest in engaging in drinking or drugging behaviors. Therefore although it is a fact that when anyone ingests a strong mood altering substance they WILL experience some change in moods and perceptions; NOT all people experience the same emotional or perceptual shift.

> "It is helpful to understand; "When a person ingests a mood altering substance they have a mood altering experience" but it is NOT felt by all people in the same way."

When something learned becomes connected to strong emotions, that in turn causes what is learned or experienced to have more permanence.

> "It then follows, that there is a 100% probability that whenever a person ingests a mood altering substance, it WILL ALWAYS be perceived as a powerful and positive experience that creates a strong desire or even an obsession to repeat the experience. It should be noted that NOT only is it experienced as a positive experience, but ONE that is "guaranteed" each and EVERY time."

We can now begin to recognize some of the processes that create the TWISTED thinking that addicts have due to their "PECULIAR perceptional problems." It is the fact that one of the most dangerous things about the use of substances, is the fact that "It Works." Substances DO exactly what a person wants, and that IS to experience something different than what they are currently experiencing. The next paradox is, "Why is sobriety and recovery not experiences that the person will defend, and protect through strong recovery commitments?" "Why does the recovering person at times find sobriety so unsatisfactory and disappointing to the degree that returning to substance use creates such strong desire and appeal?" The answer becomes clear when it is understood that the Powerful, Pleasant experience that is associated with substance use, is guaranteed each and every time a mood altering substance is ingested. Once this is recognized and accepted the next question is what else in this world provides the same guarantee?

"What else in this entire world WILL do for you, what you want every single time without fail? The answer to this question IS drugs and alcohol and there are NO otherworldly guarantees other than death. That is the paradox that will occur once a person has to give up drugs and alcohol. They have to give up the ONLY guarantee that exists on earth!"

Once this is understood we can recognize how something so destructive, useless and stupid, could be so treasured, that they are willing to risk every other thing in their lives. Those other things are perceived to be less valuable, because they all have less of a guarantee in producing that very special desired emotional effect, every time without fail.

"To the addict or alcoholic they are not throwing away anything; their perception is that they are availing themselves of the most powerful guarantee in the world; the ability to have TOTAL absolute control over their moods and emotions."

This ability as well as the right to change feelings at will is a phenomenon that has great VALUE, great worth and therefore great appeal! This becomes especially important when it is realized that for so many recovering addicts and alcoholics, the experience of being totally abstinent comes with great pain and disillusionment.

"It is this pain and disillusionment that makes the concept of recovery and abstinence almost an intolerable state of despair, instead of an exciting time of change and growth. Whereas the ingestion of mood altering chemicals create an instant sense of joy, freedom or relief; abstinence produces confusion and dissatisfaction."

"This is why an addict or alcoholic is willing to give up everything, for that ONE thing, instead of giving up that ONE thing, so they can have everything!"

To further expand upon this understanding, I will outline the entire process of how something that is so desired as "recovery," has very little "perceived value." To generate value it will be necessary to give a "face to recovery," that will create a sense of excitement and appreciation. Unfortunately the "face of addiction" comes automatically loaded with desired emotions and excitement. It is perceived as having greater value than "recovery" due to recovery has no automatic desired emotions or excitement, but instead recovery is experienced as something that has to be grudgingly worked for. This is clearly expressed in Chapter 11 titled, "A Vision For You" in the Alcoholics Anonymous book on page 164 where in states:

> "We shall be with you in the Fellowship of the Spirit, and you will surely meet some of us as you trudge the Road of Happy Destiny. May God bless you and keep you-until then."

The words selected in this statement indicate that sobriety and recovery WILL be challenging as well as VERY difficult. The evidence for this is found in the word "trudge" which means; to walk wearily; to hike; to take a long walk; to march. Many recovering people cannot accept the fact that staying clean or sober does not come with any guarantee that they will feel good about being sober. They become easily disillusioned due to the fact that just because they do the right things in recovery, it does not guarantee that they will have satisfying or good feelings; but using drugs and alcohol ALWAYS provides a pleasurable if NOT exciting emotional experience!

This paradox is due to the fact that emotions are the legal tender used as an exchange between a person and an event or object, and it is a person's senses that establish what is perceived as valuable. It is due to the emotional economy inside the addict or alcoholic, that substances are desired more than their spouse, parents, children, freedom or even their own life. Despite the fact that no person or family member wants to believe that the addiction has more value than they do, it is apparently true, and the truth of this is absolutely indisputable.

> "Addicts and alcoholics who return to substance abuse have obviously placed drugs and alcohol ahead of any good intentions or desires and promises they may have made with others. Anyone who lives with or loves an addict or alcoholic, and has suffered the abuse, confusion bewilderment betrayal and neglect that commonly occur WILL undoubtedly agree."

Returning to the need to give recovery a "face" that is at least equal to, if not surpasses the "face of addiction," it will be necessary to understand that whether a person is an addict, alcoholic or not; all people use some level of emotion to determine value. For instance if you gave a great gift to someone who was deeply depressed, they may not recognize nor appreciate that gift. In another case someone who is very joyful and happy the smallest gift or consideration would be incredibly recognized and appreciated, whereas the depressed person may not even be capable of showing any positive emotions.

Despite how well a recovering person appears to be doing on the outside, many times they do NOT feel any strong positive passionate feelings on the inside, and therefore ALL their good works are perceived as valueless, due to there is NO accompanying positive sense of joy or even accomplishment.

How many times have we seen or witnessed through the news media that some very rich or prominent or successful person took their own life or were engaging in very dangerous high-risk activities or sports, and as a result died or were killed. We have asked ourselves, "With all they had going for them what drove them to this."

The answer can be found in the above concept of "Value Exchange " which can range from "Emotional Euphoria" to deep "Emotional Emptiness." The prominence or success or wealth did NOT create enough of a level of emotional satisfaction causing them to feel deep "Emotional Emptiness" and so they searched for something that would give them the extreme joy, pleasure or reward they SO desperately desired, and they were willing to risk their lives to achieve or trade their "Emotional Emptiness" for "Emotional Euphoria."

> "It is this paradox that NO matter how much someone has achieved or acquired; if there is NOT an accompanying emotional intensity, then there is NO recognition or appreciation. Therefore it has minimal significance to that particular person. Without emotional content NOTHING has value; children have NO value, husbands and wives and friends have NO value, health has NO value, financial stability and security have NO value and recovery has NO value."

When considering the addict or alcoholic and exploring this paradox further, the following becomes very apparent:

"Alcohol has MORE value, drugs have more value,

negative and toxic friends and toxic family members have MORE value and physical and financial ruin have MORE value and of course relapse has MORE value. Now immediately you may want to argue that NONE of this is true and can NEVER be true; but the actions of any addict and alcoholic have made this entirely and UNDENIABLY true."

So how does the most Dire and Dark behaviors become appealing enough to sabotage a recovering persons desire to stay Clean and Sober? To answer this question lets return to the need to give value or a face to recovery.

"The following should hopefully describe the "face of recovery." An individual wearing this face will exhibit enthusiasm, joy, satisfaction, emotional strength, integrity, maturity, compassion, patience, tolerance and most of all acceptance, and the ability to deal with the world on the world's terms, as AA has so succinctly stated it so many years ago."

To establish concepts, and to give them the level of value that will surpass the value that returning to substance use offers; it is necessary for the recovering person to witness how others have established these concepts to be more valuable than substance use. The cofounder of AA Bill Wilson stated that AA has to be a program of "attraction rather than promotion." This statement reflects that only something of value ever has any attraction. He knew that promoting AA or forcing it on others, would NOT be as effective as just demonstrating how valuable the program can BE to the suffering addict and alcoholic.

Unless addicts or alcoholics are able to develop the perception that recovery has great VALUE; they will NEVER be able to put on the "face of recovery" and WILL continue to suffer "Emotional Emptiness." It is then inevitable that this TWISTED and PECULIAR perception of emptiness, which in fact can and is experienced as a very low level of loneliness, WILL lead to an easy decision to trade recovery for relapse to escape this deep despair. To trade their deep "Emotional Emptiness" for "Emotional Euphoria!"

The concept of "value exchange" may seem complicated but it explains how the addict can perceive things that are bad as good or desirable. The addict's view does not wrestle with the recognition of what is right or wrong but more so of what has more perceived emotional value."

One of the most difficult things that the addict or alcoholic has to face, is that there is a tendency for them to inadvertently experience strong emotions and intense passion, when they think about the use of substances. Due to this tendency they have difficulty with building enough desire for this thing that is referred to as recovery. It should be noted that the passion for their use, abuse and even dependency on mood altering substances was learned through the physiological experience of ingesting the substances.

"There is no stronger behavioral reinforcement, than that of an intense pleasurable physiological experience that is guaranteed every single time a mood altering substance is taken into the body."

"On the other hand recovery can seem like a very empty promise in comparison."

"The reason I would indicate that the addict or alcoholic would believe recovery to be unfulfilling, is due to the fact that at least initially doing the right things, and living the right way does NOT produce the same intense desire or passion as that of the ingestion of substances."

This is another one of those dilemmas in which the addict or alcoholic may work very hard with the high expectations that getting clean and sober should lead to Comfort and Satisfaction but instead they experience Disillusionment and Frustration, if not just empty boredom. To better comprehend these concepts there are several key questions that need to be asked and answered.

Some of those questions are: "If you do right will right things happen?" and "If right things happen does that mean you'll feel right?" and "Just because you do right and right things happen does that necessarily mean you will feel right?" and "If you do wrong does that necessarily mean you'll feel wrong." A few additional questions are "If it feels right does that mean it is right." And "If it feels wrong does that mean it is wrong."

When an addict or an alcoholic attempts to answer the first question "If you do right will right things happen?" They have a tendency to believe that doing right WILL mean that right things WILL happen and they WILL have good positive feelings.

> "But the reality is that if a person does right, the fact that they are doing right means that right things are absolutely happening. But due to their TWISTED perceptions they may NOT experience positive feelings, and therefore they WILL have a tendency to discount any positive or correct actions that they are taking and need to continue to take."

To clarify this, all one needs to do is to recognize the fact that, "If you do wrong-then wrong things will absolutely happen."

> "Where the addict or alcoholic gets confused may be found in the fact that even though they put much effort into doing right or forcing themselves to stay right, they still DON'T feel right."

Since they are putting so much effort into this thing called recovery, and then NOT getting any positive reinforcing emotional reward, that should be manifested in experiencing positive strong passionate feelings; then the addict or alcoholic are Disappointed, Disillusioned, Disenchanted and Discouraged, due to this lack of positive emotional reinforcement.

> "Due to the lack of being rewarded for doing the right thing, they begin to think about the tremendous seemingly positive emotional and psychological, as well as physiological experience that they are GUARANTEED to have by ingesting mood-altering substances."

This can be clearly seen in the history of an addict or alcoholics relapse when they appeared to be doing well for an extended period of time, and then "for apparently no clear reason they threw away their recovery and relapsed." After working with addicts and alcoholics for over 30 years there does NOT seem to be any mystery or riddle to why that person returns to substance use. It is just simply a matter of emotional mathematics, they work very hard and they get NO emotional satisfying reward, and therefore their effort seems Futile and Worthless.

> "Addicts and alcoholics are driven by a strong motivation to experience powerful emotional psychological and physiological experiences. Substance use and abuse satisfies this need and many times recovery fails to meet this need."

The evidence for this failure, may be found many times in the persons statements about why they believe they had relapsed, was due to they stopped doing the things that were keeping them sober and clean. The only reason anybody would give up the winning formula or success formula, would be due to the belief that their efforts did NOT feel right, and therefore they did NOT feel like they were winning nor succeeding. As a result of this they would be driven to seek the intense passionate feelings and experiences in some other manner. Once again we can clearly see that the addict is NOT driven by what is right or wrong, but what has the greatest emotional value. It is this perception that causes them to fail even when, and even while they are succeeding.

The next question, "If right things happen does that mean you'll feel right?" Now this question has been partially answered in the previous paragraph; but does need further Expansion and Exploration. The addict or alcoholic is taught and learns that there are certain behaviors that they WILL get recognition and praise for. It is this expectation that motivates them to engage in what can be termed new recovery behaviors. Some examples of these can be found in AA or NA behavioral protocols. A new member or "a newcomer" when they ask for help and select a sponsor, that person will ask them to follow certain disciplines, such as daily phone calls, attending meetings daily, reading specific AA or NA recovery literature, and if the person fails to follow through with this, then they are considered not being ready for recovery. Now many "newcomers" will take these suggestions, and follow through with doing things such as committing to attending 90 meetings in 90 days, in other words, they agree to go to AA or NA on a daily basis for three months. They may even begin calling their sponsor on a daily basis.

What happens to many people is that before they finish their three months of commitments, they abandon these behaviors. If going to meetings on a daily basis, and calling another member of AA or NA on a daily basis were strong enough and powerful enough reinforcement, that would provide a sufficient emotionally pleasurable experience; then that person would NOT abandon these activities, but strongly EMBRACE them and continue them.

The reason that the person fails to follow through with maintaining "right actions" is that...

> "The right actions do not result in the right feelings. Since an addict is obsessed with "feeling right" they have no desire or motivation to continue with behaviors that are so painfully disappointing. Once again they place value on the Feeling rather than on the Action, and therefore they can and do get it completely in reverse."

> "The necessary action that they have to begin to engage in is to do the right things regardless of how they feel, and to learn to <u>NEVER</u> let their actions be driven by their emotions. The addict must learn that their emotions should <u>NEVER</u> dictate their behavior."

The third question, "Just because you do right, and right things happen, does that necessarily mean you'll feel right?" This question has been partially answered in the above paragraph and needs further elaboration. Whether the person suffers from addiction or they have no problems of this nature, that person would expect that it should be logical that if you "do right," then you absolutely should "feel right," especially when right things are occurring. Now there's a high probability that a person who's <u>NOT</u> an addict or alcoholic, when they are motivated enough to engage in behaviors that are positive, uplifting and beneficial, NOT only to them, but the general good as well, that these behaviors would result in experiencing positive sensations as well as emotions that would be very reinforcing, and create a strong desire to repeat these behaviors.

> "Now in the instance of the alcoholic or addict they physiologically and psychologically may NOT have the capacity to recognize or experience positive reinforcing emotions or feelings when they engage in correct actions, and therefore it becomes much easier to abandon right actions because they do not feel right. Here again the driving force behind the loss is that they measure their

actions based upon a Feeling rather than the Actual Result."

"It is this values dilemma that has to be recognized and addressed in the addict or alcoholic, who needs to learn to begin to measure success based upon the positive changes they are demonstrating, rather than the emotional experience that they may or may not be having."

The best way to clarify the addicts dilemma is to use the following metaphor: If the addict or alcoholic was given a job to help place and finish concrete; they would have to work very hard and diligently to assure that the wet concrete is not only placed right but would have to be properly finished. Since concrete has a fixed time in which it sets; there is no debating and no arguing with concrete. If you take a break or think you will come back tomorrow; the job will be absolutely ruined and you will need to rent some Jackhammers!

"You can never do what needed to be done today-"tomorrow" concrete does not wait for you, nor does life!"

I used the concrete metaphor to demonstrate that certain recovery actions must be taken in a timely manner or there is no going back. Placing and finishing concrete is one of the most physically demanding jobs that a person can do, and if the addict or alcoholic completed the job and they worked over ten hours due to there was no time to take a break, then they would be more than physically exhausted.

If the contractor paid the alcoholic or addict a penny an hour or just gave them ten cents after ten hours of demanding, exhausting work, do you think that they would have an issue with the contractor? After all the contractor did pay them for the work they did. Without a doubt the first thing that anyone would say in regards to the question of "Would they have an issue with the contractor?" would be to scream out, "They may have got paid but it surely was not enough!" If someone works that hard they should be paid adequately and fairly.

Now the reason the addict or alcoholic will throw away their Achievements and Accomplishments that they earned while they were sober, is due to, "They believe that they did NOT receive adequate pay for ALL the efforts they put forth in recovery." In other words the compensation did NOT cover their efforts and they felt used, exploited and underpaid. Now in recovery, compensation is measured by an anticipated emotional experience or reward, and when they do not experience that expected emotional reward; they begin to believe that ALL the efforts they put forth in their recovery have NO real value.

> "Therefore it is absolutely necessary for the addict or alcoholic to measure abstinence by celebrating each achievement or accomplishment during recovery, even when it does NOT seem important. In this way they WILL be able to stack positive feelings and emotions, and NOT expect an automatic anticipated emotional reward; but develop Appreciation for their hard earned Achievements."

The last questions, "If it feels right, does that mean it's right?" and "If it feels wrong, does that mean it's wrong?" This becomes even more perplexing for the addict and alcoholic, for it embodies a major confusing paradox. To clarify this all one needs to do is recognize that any major change in a habit or behavior is absolutely going to feel awkward, if not outright "wrong." This means that if a person is driven by the need to absolutely count on a certain feeling or emotion in order to engage and to repeat a new behavior; if that expected feeling is NOT experienced, then in ALL probability that behavior or action WOULD be abandoned and negated. The addict and alcoholic needs to recognize that there is a high probability that as they embrace new behaviors which are referred to as "right actions" they will only do them for as long as they feel "right."

> "The sad fact is that recovery actions and behaviors that would lead to a more fulfilling productive and positive lifestyle, are cast away due to the way the addict or alcoholic measures their actions by their emotional reward, and if there is NO reward, then the behaviors are considered Worthless, Useless and Purposeless."

Now paradoxically the second question "If it feels wrong, does that mean it's wrong?" further causes confusion in that the person who is engaging in right behaviors may NOT experience them as feeling right, and therefore since they feel wrong they would NOT continue to engage in those actions. The best and simplest way to describe how these paradoxical questions operate is to understand that…

> "Drinking and drugging absolutely gives them a "right" feeling. Even though it's absolutely the "wrong" thing to do."

The other question leads to the understanding that just because something feels wrong such as going to meetings every day for three months, is NOT going to be a walk in the park for most people, and therefore it WILL begin to feel very wrong, and there IS a danger of giving up the behavior simply due to the Feeling that it Feels wrong.

> "In the 12 step programs they have a cliché "don't quit till the miracle happens." This can be interpreted, as there is a need to stay fully committed to living in the right manner despite the fact it doesn't feel right. By forcing yourself to engage in correct behavior for a long enough period of time WILL result in finally Feeling good about Doing good."

Before we proceed further I need to present another extremely interesting paradox in regards to taking positive recovery actions. The paradox occurs due to the fact that when a person is motivated and enthusiastic about doing something; it does nothing to strengthen their recovery. It is much like going to the gym and working out with weights and never lifting more than a three-pound weight.

It is virtually impossible to build added strength or fitness when the challenge is so slight and minimal. If the challenge is not worthy, then nothing is gained. In other words when a person takes an action, and they are interested and excited as well as highly motivated to engage in that activity, their actions have very minimal power in helping them change their lives. As absurd as this statement sounds, let's examine this concept in more detail.

Doing the things that you have an aversion towards or resistance against actually works much better to improve recovery chances; than doing the things that are easy and pleasing to do. In other words…

The more someone learns to do the right things when they don't want to; the stronger they become able to resist the moment of temptation; but if they only do the things that they feel like doing or feels right to do, then they will have no defense against cravings or desires. When they feel like getting high or drinking; then it will easily flow in that direction, because they have not learned how to resist a strong desire or feeling.

> "It is this habit of "feeling based decision making" that has been the cause for most failures in recovery." In fact when they are doing all the things they want, they are just merely allowing the feeling or desire to control and direct their actions and decisions. The "Power of Resisting the Resistance" through the practice of the "Art of Self Defiance" provides the ability for resisting the power of feelings to control and direct. Developing this power will sufficiently prepare the person to stand strong against the feeling to drink or drug, if and when that desire arises."

> "This means that if someone loves taking ALL the actions and engaging in ALL the recovery behaviors that they like to do, then everything that they are doing IS almost a total waste of time."

As contrary as this may sound, all we need to do is examine the facts. The only thing between a person and picking up a drink or a drug is the power of their resistance to do so. It follows that if a person just does what they want to do, or have the desire to do in recovery; then they are just merely acting on the feelings of desire and they are not learning to resist or fight desire; therefore when the desire to drink or drug does arise they will honor and act on that desire due to the fact they have not learned the "Art of Self Defiance."

> The "Art of Self Defiance" is to practice the concept that the more things that a person challenges themselves to do, that they ABSOLUTELY do NOT want to do, that is good for them or good for somebody else; then the STRONGER they are becoming. The strength arises from the constant practice of overcoming their negative or resistant feelings and DOING the right things regardless of the Emotional Resistance."

> "Therefore each time they overcome the resistance to

doing the right things they immediately build higher and higher levels of self-esteem. Practicing the "Art of Self Defiance" will ABSOLUTELY result in the building of self-esteem, which in turn AUTOMATICALLY creates an increase in a person's sense of self worth. It is this higher self worth that builds the strength to RESIST temptation, invitation or opportunities to get high or drunk."

If the addict or alcoholic is very enthusiastically engaging in these productive actions and are experiencing associated positive feelings; then where is the challenge to change? Recovery requires a shift in not only behaviors but also attitudes. When a person is doing what they want to do where is the challenge to change?

"It is ONLY when a person suffers from and overcomes adversity that they build self esteem and healthy confidence."

A Proverb in the Bible states "Sorrow is better than laughter for through a sad countenance the heart is made stronger." It is an interesting concept that when we do what is fun and enjoyable it does nothing to build our character, but as the saying goes, "What doesn't kill us makes us stronger."

The irony is that when the addict or alcoholic was actively drinking or drugging they were doing what they want and there was no awareness to change behavior nonetheless their attitudes. In the same sense...

"When a person is very motivated and enthusiastic about a recovery activity such as calling a sponsor, attending meetings or engaging in numerous other recovery activities, such as bringing meetings to a hospital or jail; there is NO adversity and therefore there is NO challenge."

"Without challenge there is NO real benefit derived from the action and that translates to there is NO growth, for without growth the person remains unchanged and remains in a weakened condition as WELL as very vulnerable TO impulsivity and relapse."

This means that the most powerful and positive actions that an addict or alcoholic engage in for their recovery is almost useless in that it fails to provide an opportunity to challenge negative feelings, and change attitudes that WILL result in changed behaviors and actions. The more the person is forced to change their behaviors when they do NOT feel like it; the STRONGER is the change in their attitudes that WILL result in developing strong positive recovery Behaviors and Actions.

> "In other words if a person does what they really want whether it is drinking or drugging or enthusiastically being involved in recovery activities; the fact is they are JUST doing what they WANT to do. So where is the growth, and where has there been any change in their attitudes? Is it NOT just a simple fact that it takes NO effort to do what you WANT to do?"

The foundation for an effective attitude shift will occur when the person doing all the positive actions ALL of sudden NO longer, "Feels like making their bed, cleaning the dishes or going to the meeting or feels like talking to their sponsor or feels like they need to do the step work." It is precisely at this point that the person is challenged with whether they are GOING to allow a dumb stupid sensation- a feeling, dictate their next actions or are they GOING to successfully challenge the negative emotion whichever one it may be and "Resist the Resistance to Resist" and make that bed, clean that dish, call that sponsor go to that meeting in SPITE of the way they feel.

We have a tendency to do what feels right and to avoid doing things that feel wrong. This decision is usually driven with confidence, but just because it feels right does NOT necessarily mean we Should do it. In contrast if something feels wrong, does NOT necessarily mean it is wrong—i.e. taking medications may feel wrong but it is very beneficial to the body and for our health.

To sum of this paradox it can be simply stated:

> "If you are doing what you want to do, whether it is recovery or active drug use or drinking; the fact is you are JUST doing what you WANT to do, and there is NO opportunity for growth or change. In fact everything that you do that you WANT to do in recovery, does NOT count! It is when you do what you DON'T want

to do that is good for your recovery, and COUNTS
the most."

"Your recovery depends completely upon your ability
to FORCE yourself to continue to DO the right things
especially when you DON'T want to."

It is at this point that a significant attitude change has occurred, and until
the attitude that feelings <u>CANNOT</u> be allowed to dictate actions has been
fully embedded within the person, they WILL remain at high risk. Until
this is fully learned and understood the chances for a long lasting recovery
IS very uncertain.

It is helpful to recognize and understand that the addict or alcoholic must
learn as well as be taught <u>NOT</u> to be emotionally reactive, and to develop
the ability to make decisions based on facts and NOT on their Feelings.
When they learn to exercise this perspective, then they can clearly discipline
themselves to follow the actions that lead to the right results and NOT base
the outcome on their Feelings or how they Feel.

"Until the addict or alcoholic is able to step up and
recognize that they do NOT necessarily have to have a
positive feeling to take positive actions and to maintain
a positive direction; their chances for a long lasting
recovery WILL be very doubtful."

By stepping up, they would within an extended period of time realize a
sense of Accomplishment and Achievement that would boost their self-esteem,
and give them a high level of healthy self-confidence.

One last thought on the process of utilizing "Value Exchange" to build
"Resistance Muscle" regards the need to discuss the mistaken belief that many
people in recovery have expressed. Which is the unfounded fear that when a
person forces themselves to get too involved with the AA or NA programs they
may become disillusioned, and this could cause them to burn out quickly, due
to the perceived burden of obligation of having to help others in recovery. Can
others in recovery place such a heavy burden to cause this?

The answer could be somewhat complicated.

"If the person places VALUE, and builds VALUE
with others in the recovery programs, then certain
consequences may occur; but keep in mind most addicts

and alcoholics are naturally too selfish as well as to self centered to get that overly involved with sacrifice, and the 12 step programs."

The issue of becoming addicted to AA or NA has also been a concern to many people, and the only real conclusion is that although you cannot become addicted to the program, as evidenced by the fact that anyone who has walked away from a 12 step program, has never experienced any significant degree of withdrawal or great discomfort, as one would if they suddenly stopped using an addictive substance or stopped engaging in an addictive activity. However it should be noted that…

"You definitely might suffer severe consequences when you prioritize your time around AA or NA. This means that through the process of "Values Exchange" in which AA or NA begins to be sensed or perceived to be more valuable than the job or the family; then the family or job or other things may be lost, due to having poorly balanced boundaries and priorities, and NOT because the person became addicted to AA or NA or any other self help program."

When drugs and alcohol are overly valued there were serious consequences; if recovery actions and behaviors are more valued than anything else, then serious consequences of a different nature may, and probably will occur, if a man or woman becomes too preoccupied with self-help involvement.

"It should be noted that while they may feel and actually be protected from the use of deadly substances or destructive behaviors, they might neglect or inadvertently devalue their family or job and suffer losses in those areas."

"The fact is that each person in recovery, Will have to learn to NOT only establish a strong sense of value in a recovery lifestyle; but they will also HAVE to assure it is balanced with other things in their lives, that have equal value. Failure to do this WILL result in further suffering and losses for NOT only the addict; but also their family, friends and even coworkers."

"Another danger of over valuing the 12 Step Programs can be found in the obligation of helping other addicts or alcoholics, and the possible danger for a person in early recovery, to become overwhelmed with a sense of obligation, to try to save a friend or an associate."

Since the new person to recovery is very fragile and NOT well equipped to deal with the intense emotional burden of watching a friend or family member hurt or destroy their lives; they feel they MUST step in and do something. Unfortunately, due to being so fragile themselves they usually fail, and instead of saving that friend or family member, they get lost back to addiction themselves.

"It should be emphasized that unfortunately there is a higher probability that the friend or associate will persuade the person in recovery to join them in relapse behaviors; than for the person in recovery to convince the person to come back to recovery."

"The best way to deal with a friend who relapses is to find someone else to help, or just avoid any contact."

To clearly visualize this, simply think about yourself in a situation in which you are holding on to a five hundred pound person by the wrist, who is dangling four hundred feet off the edge of a cliff. Will it be possible for you to pull up the five hundred pound person, or for that endangered person to pull you, the rescuer, attempting to save that person over the cliff?

The answer is obvious and indeed a painful truth, it is ABSOLUTELY impossible to save the person, but it is highly probable that if you don't let go you WILL be pulled over, and DIE with the person you tried to save. There is only one answer and that is to know that, "You have to let them go, for you to live, or hang on, and be dragged over to your own death." The decision will be based on a "Values Exchange" predicament.

"As may be observed in the above metaphor, the concept of value in describing not only substance use and abuse, but how "Value Exchange" plays a part any time a person struggles with trying to determine the right or best course of action; allows for a deeper understanding for the reasons why so many people struggle and so many fail. Throughout a person's recovery they will be challenged with weighing critical decisions on a "Values Exchange" process."

The following chapter will provide an effective course of action to enable an Addict or Alcoholic to take control of this "Values Exchange" dilemma. They WILL learn how to develop the ability to change the "Resistance" or the confusion that leads to bad decisions, and turn it into an effective "Resolution."

Chapter Six

Resistance Into Resolution

Taking control of the "Value Exchange" process changes the despair that occurs every time a bad decision is made that undermines a person's recovery, and will enable that person to transform it into a strong and powerful force that strengthens their recovery. This is the process that will enable you to "Turn Resistance Into Resolution."

The simple solution is to understand that it is necessary to teach an addict or alcoholic to challenge their own emotional states and to force himself or herself to take actions they prefer not to take. This is the very essence of a technique that anyone can utilize and it has nothing to do with willingness. The process of "Learning To Resist The Resistance" is the way to build "Resistance Muscle."

One of the most effective methods to build strong Resistance Muscle is using the "Power to Resist the Resistance" by turning "Resistance into Resolution" through the "Art of Self Defiance" The addict, alcoholic and their families as well as loved ones, need to fully understand they are in a desperate life and death struggle. It is only through developing the ability to "Resist the Resistance" that can and will save them.

> "Everything they love and care about is threatened by their tendency to act out on destructive emotional decisions and impulses. In other words with so much at stake, your health, your, family, your job, your sanity, your freedom, your peace of mind, as well as your very life, you better learn the following undeniable truth, and that is you must be strong enough and brave enough to speak loudly and proudly this universal truth for any addict or alcoholic, and that is to "Fuck Your Feelings before They Fuck You!!"

Now for the squeamish who may be offended by the wording of this concept I will now inform you that this highly descriptive sentence and concept will only be used a little over a dozen times in this entire book. Most of which will appear within the following few pages. For the faint in heart that are embarrassed or shocked at this language; I have great news for you! Although I have to keep the Force and integrity of the Power of this language; I will modify it to suit any potential critics. I actually prayed and meditated regarding changing what some people may judge as "offensive" language." It should be clearly noted that I did an additional edit that I had to pay for in regards to changing these words. This was done to clear up any possible future controversy that may or may not arise!

If indeed you are or have been offended then it is clear that the choice of words absolutely do and instantly change a persons state. It really does grab your attention; hopefully in the same manner that an Air Horn on a large truck warns you that you are about to be RUN OVER-if you don't wake up and change what you are doing!

By going the extra mile I have come up with the following strategy to eliminate any controversy. By spelling this questionable word without the offending "K" and through the magical use of the Power of an acronym, I have been able to completely reframe this potential controversy into a mere curiosity! In other words the letters F U C (And remember it is not my fault that this acronym and the questionable word with that controversial "K" at the end sound the same!)

For those of you who are not offended then feel free to proclaim the "K" with all your passion; but if you are somewhat squeamish then only pronounce the "K" as a "C" as in F U C C your feelings. The acronym F U C stands for F EELINGS U NDERMINE C OMMITMENTS. There is nothing more clear than this fact; which is that Feelings absolutely Undermine recovery Commitments! Therefore you have to learn to F U C those self defeating feelings that block taking the necessary recovery actions!

Now enough of this Nonsense at attempting to stay Politically Correct— And lets get back to the Real Deal! Words ARE Power and certain words have GREAT power to instantly change or radically shift a person's focus and break the ADDICTIVE "Hypnotic Lock!" At times to make the reader even more comfortable I will replace the language with the words of "Resist the Resistance" or "Building Resistance Muscle" concepts. As strange and even confusing as it sounds the phrase "Resist the Resistance" has a strong tendency to interrupt an impulsive Thought, Feeling or Belief. This phrase has the Force and the Power to shatter the deadly "Hypnotic Lock" that drives, directs and destroys the addict or alcoholic!

Now despite my strenuous effort to disarm any critics, I have to mention that the word F U C_ at times in this book has been reunited with the offending "K" due to the fact that the Force and Power of this word would be diluted and that would destroy the Maximum IMPACT of certain significant concepts being presented; therefore for those who are offended I will beg for your forgiveness in advance!

> "The addicts or alcoholics feelings seduce them back to active use, by sabotaging any interest in staying sober through the phenomenon of Values Exchange. It is now time to present and identify the real problem, and that problem, is simply and tragically."

> "The addict or alcoholic allow their—Emotions To Dictate Their Actions. One of the most powerful and effective methods to prevent this tendency is to utilize the "Power to Resist the Resistance" as the most potent and immediate method to stop destructive emotions, or impulses at their very core. This concept will produce enough personal power to effect huge changes in one's life even when there is no willingness, or desire to do so."

Willingness is nothing but a simple feeling, and it has nothing to do with taking actions. An action can be taken regardless of how a person feels or whether they are willing or not. In combat a soldier is not willing to die or be wounded, and they die and are wounded not as a result of being willing, but as a result of the actions they took, regardless of any feelings or emotions. In another words they said "Fuck the Feelings" and they engaged in actions despite the way they Thought, Felt or Believed; they carried out their mission! "THEIR COMMITMENT!"

For most addicts and alcoholics, at least for the long term, they will find recovery is more of a mission, rather than a willing choice that is made. In fact, in my personal and professional experiences, it seems common for the addict or alcoholic after even a short time, to find committing or complying with recovery suggestions or recommendations very difficult, frustrating at times, as well as annoying and very dissatisfying. Due to these unpleasant feelings they tend to be resistant and even resentful about having to take certain if not all of the recovery suggestions.

To emphasize this point even more strongly...

"I believe that the addict or alcoholic will virtually not want to do any recovery actions or suggestions. Just because some people will be fully compliant does not necessary mean that they are willing or have any willingness at all. This lack of willingness can easily be resolved by the utilization of "Resisting the Resistance" which strongly confronts the conflict that exists any time a person has a lack of willingness, and it is through the concept of "Building Resistance Muscle," damaging feelings and destructive impulses can be pushed aside enabling the person to take right recovery actions."

As bold and as brazen as these vulgar words are "FUC Your Feelings Before They FUC You" they do have an innate magical and powerful tendency to empower anyone; who chooses to utilize them in the context I will now describe.

"The words themselves by their very forcefulness should be verbalized in a very loud and distinct manner, and preferably with aggressiveness any time the addict or alcoholic realizes they are about to make a very poor decision or take a very destructive action!"

It should be clearly noted that saying these words "loud and proud" absolutely has nothing to do with whether a person is willing or has any willingness. Whereas willingness implies and allows a person to change their behaviors; so does "Building Resistance Muscle" through the process of learning to take on the challenge of "Resisting the Resistance" or "FUC Your Feelings Before They FUC You." The power is found in understanding that desire is only a feeling and feelings have nothing to do with changing or making changes.

Willingness is only a feeling and it is not the only key as has been expressed in most A.A. and N.A. meetings and literature. In fact all feelings can be used as keys; for all feelings have power, but some have the power to create and some have the power to destroy. Therefore regardless of how offensive and crude this language may sound or even be; I have found no other words that produce an abundance of great creative power, than when a person recognizes the truth that the reason they cannot change, or will not change, is not because of the family, not because they are stupid, not because they are afraid, but because they have allowed and continue to allow their "Feelings To Fuck Them."

> "They have continued to allow a dumb stupid sensation, a very destructive sensation destroy their lives, and everyone who touches their lives; just to appease an asinine feeling such as "I don't feel like going to a meeting" or "I don't feel like praying" or " I don't feel like apologizing" or "I felt bored" or "I felt hopeless" or "I felt I didn't need any help" or "I felt like I needed a joint-drink-drug" or "I felt left out" or "I felt I could not resist" or "I felt too good" or "I felt too bad" or "I couldn't feel anything" or "I felt I could control it this time" or "I felt I needed it." And so on and so on. "FUC YOUR FEELINGS BEFORE THEY ROYALLY FUC YOU!"

When a person is oppositional, rebellious and defiant these feelings are usually directed at some person or a person's idea. There is a need to learn to put these feelings in proper perspective and understand as well as accept how self-defeating they are. The addict or alcoholic must make a reversal, from blaming others or things for their drug or alcohol use. By changing the focus gives them the power and opportunity to change their behaviors, and allows them to immediately see the need to target themselves generally and more specifically their emotions-their feelings.

Those stupid things that they have allowed to destroy them and everything they love. After all when everything is said and done, the only thing between recovery and relapse is the moment of truth when a person has to have enough resistance to say no. Through the "Power to Resist The Resistance" when it is used daily, the addict or alcoholic will have "Built the Resistance Muscle" to withstand any threat or temptation.

The needed daily exercises utilising this concept can be as simple as making your bed, washing the dishes, taking a shower, going to bed early, reading a book, apologizing to someone or virtually any behavior or action that either strengthens a persons own recovery or just is a nice thing to do for somebody else. It is very important to note, that any of these or any other activities that a person can force themselves to do, when they do not have the willingness nor the desire, are the very activities that "Build Resistance Muscle."

> "The tougher the resistance that is overcome, the stronger the "Resistance Muscle" and strong resistance muscle gives the person the power to resist any temptations or cravings, and through the "Art of Self Defiance" gives the person the capability of "Turning Resistance into Resolution" which creates the strength to be able to turn down drugs, when the offer or opportunity to get high arises."

Once again I will emphasize that the reluctance or resistance a person may have regarding taking a good or positive action can be easily overcome; when that person has learned to challenge themselves and are able to tell the resistant feeling to go "F" itself, and do the right actions anyway. Even with people who have never stopped or relapsed, learning to practice using the bold and brazen words of "FUC Your Feelings Before They FUC You" will enable them to smash their hypnotic trance, that overpowering "Hypnotic Lock" in their minds driving the deadly obsession to use drugs or alcohol!

It immediately hits a person in between the eyes that they are being controlled by feelings, impulses and desires, and no addict ever wants to admit this. Once the addict sees this, they can then begin the process of challenging themselves to change, and as stated earlier this does not require any willingness.

> "The motivation to take on this challenge is driven by the truth that they now know what is exactly wrong, and they can take immediate action regardless of the way they feel, and in spite of the way they feel. Those actions can be the most simplistic things to do that will radically alter their lives with very minimal effort or change."

I personally believe that one of the main reasons for relapse is that the substance user perceives using substances and controlling that use as a worthy challenge. Since being oppositional and rebellious are common traits found in most addicts and alcoholics, they need to effectively combat this tendency. The person needs to constantly be able to challenge himself or herself in the manner clearly described, and learn to begin to "Build Resistance Muscle" and to use the "Power to Resist the Resistance." It needs to become a daily obligation or discipline to assure that any successful attempts in engaging in positive recovery actions, are clearly connected to, and associated with, great intense emotional reward and pleasure.

It will be through the ongoing process of constantly challenging their own resistance that a strong connection or association will result in the creation of a higher value for their recovery efforts. Each time they successfully use the concept of "Resisting the Resistance" they build stronger and stronger resistance muscle. This will significantly improve their chances for a lasting recovery; since they have learned to manage the greatest recovery threat; which is their tendency to be impulsive, or in other words, to allow feelings to dictate their actions.

> "Once a person has learned to overcome their own rebellious, oppositional, defiant feelings and take actions regardless of how they feel. They will absolutely begin to experience the great reward of building higher levels of self-esteem and self worth.

> "It is almost an iron clad guarantee that each and every time they succeed with this challenge their self-esteem as well as self worth will increase proportionately."

> "In the Bible there is a Proverb that states, "Greater is he who conquers himself than he who conquers a city!"

> "The meaning of this Proverb should be clear. "That even thousands of years ago it was fully known that self control is the greatest of all accomplishments and achievements!"

Before proceeding further there is an extremely important caveat I must add to these concepts, and that is to reinforce the understanding that every human being needs to respect their emotional self!

> "It is very important to clearly understand that we "Do Not Want To Throw The Baby Out With The Bath Water." We always want to stay in touch with our emotions. The focus of this chapter is not to imply that emotions are bad and should be cursed and ignored."

> "In fact it is only through the use of emotions that a
> person can effectively begin positive life changes. Again
> I want to make it clear that the emotions that will
> "SCREW YOU OVER" are the ones that need to be
> fully identified and managed. All the other feelings and
> emotions need to be celebrated and fully experienced."

To differentiate the negative destructive feelings from the healing constructive feelings, we will review some simple examples. When a person procrastinates they are allowing a very negative and potentially destructive feeling to take total control of their lives. What they have done is to allow the feeling of "I Don't Want To Do This." or more accurately it is experienced as an emotional state —"I Don't Feel Like Doing It Now." to create stress, and a loss of that sense of accomplishment that is always felt when a task is completed.

When people allow themselves to procrastinate frequently and for too long. Others will label them as "Being Irresponsible Or Just Lazy." When this reaches a certain point in the view of the people around them, those people will stop relying or depending on that person because they are not "trustworthy." It is very sad, when a stupid and dumb thing like an emotion is allowed to cause the destruction of a person's dreams or relationships.

> "There is no emotion that should dominate and control
> any person's life. If they allow their emotions to do so,
> then they are living a very impulsive life. No addict, and
> in fact no person can live a happy, joyful and productive
> life, if they let emotions control and direct them."

A very common destructive negative emotion or feeling is that of lust. When this feeling is allowed to be unharnessed the person becomes completely victimized by his or her own Dark and Destructive emotions. Lust and uncontrolled desire for anything, can only lead to deep regret and suffering, for not only the person who refuses to take responsibility for managing these Destructive Desires. But great agony for the significant other and family in the event the uncontrolled desires lead to an affair and infidelity, or financial problems. In the event that the person cannot control their desire to purchase expensive products or services, or cannot stop from accumulating an abundance of anything regardless of value the results are the same, it lowers their self-esteem and increases stress on family and significant others!

"Here in lies the paradox that anytime we succumb to our Dark Desires, it creates a tremendous and seemingly rewarding moment; but it will automatically lead to some permanent loss in self-esteem. As our inability to take control of these harmful emotional states continues, we continue to lose more and more self-esteem."

"Since self-esteem is the life's blood of recovery, the loss of self worth begins to cause a severe hemorrhage in the desire to stay clean and sober." Lust and selfish interest in things begin to lead the person down a very destructive path!"

I heard once or read somewhere that when a person's self esteem is reduced they have a tendency to become very extravagant to compensate for the loss. "As Self Esteem Goes Down Extravagance Goes Up." An example of this may be found in the proverbial story of "Good Time Charlie." He is the person who is in financial ruin, and he will go to the bar and buy "DRINKS FOR EVERYBODY." In the event Charlie is an addict he does the same when he or she begins to act grandiose in some manner. This is demonstrated when a low functioning addict makes up stories about the excitement of selling or using drugs, and the "Wild Or Crazy Times" they have had, or are having.

"Since positive feelings and emotions build self-esteem, and are productive and constructive there is no need or concern regarding these states. "Feelings such as love, compassion, appreciation, gratitude, sacrifice, faith, consideration, commitment, charity and cooperation do not need any monitoring and can and should be freely experienced."

"It needs to be abundantly clear that the ONLY emotional states that NEED to be monitored are the ones that are harmful to others and us. A review of these would be uncontrolled anger, resentments, spite, jealousy, lust, envy, pride or ego, and they have been traditionally known as, and described in the Holy Bible, as the "Seven Deadly Sins."

For clarification here is the pairing of the Dictionary Definition of each one of these, with the Biblical verse expressed in "quotes," that describes these seven behaviors or attitudes. The definitions used were found in Merriam-Webster on line Dictionary. [1] Lust – unbridled sexual desire or an intense longing for something: "But I tell you that anyone who looks at a woman lustfully has already committed adultery with her in his heart." (Matthew 5.28) [2] Gluttony – excess in eating and drinking; greedy or excessive indulgence: "For drunkards and gluttons become poor, and drowsiness clothes them in rags" (Proverbs 23:21). [3] Greed- a selfish and excessive desire for more of something than what is needed: "Having lost all sensitivity, they have given themselves over to sensuality so as to indulge in every kind of impurity, with a continual lust for more" (Ephesians 4:19). [4] Laziness – disinclined to activity or exertion: not energetic or vigorous; encouraging inactivity or indolence "The way of the sluggard is blocked with thorns, but the path of the upright is a highway" (Proverbs 15:19). [5] Wrath – strong vengeful anger or indignation: "A gentle answer turns away wrath, but a harsh word stirs up anger" (Proverbs 15:1) [6] Envy – painful or resentful awareness of an advantage enjoyed by another or joined with a desire to possess the same advantage: "Therefore, rid yourselves of all malice and all deceit, hypocrisy, envy, and slander of every kind. Like newborn babies, crave pure spiritual milk, so that by it you may grow up in your salvation" (1 Peter 2:1-2). [7] Pride — quality or state of being proud – inordinate self-esteem: "Pride goes before destruction, a haughty spirit before a fall" (Proverbs 16:18).

In viewing these sins, potential actions or tendencies, it is clear why they are destructive. There is a definite need for them to be monitored and changed the instant they are recognized. For instance with "Lust" a person can immediately change this though the use of the concept of utilizing the "Power to Resist the Resistance" by reversing the emotion by challenging himself or herself to find someone or something that they can freely give their resources to, such as their Time Or Money, and to do so regardless of whether they Want To Or Not. It states in the book Alcoholics Anonymous on page 89 that "Nothing will insure immunity from drinking than intense work with another alcoholic."

With "Gluttony" a person needs to learn to refuse to eat the last two or three bites of a meal, or learn to select healthier meals and foods, rather than the ones they WANT, which may be full of fat, as well as lacking any real nutrition. They need to eat fruit instead of several cookies or drink water instead of an Energy Drink.

With "Greed" a person needs to learn to give freely of their resources and of themselves, especially in amounts that they rather not do. With "Laziness" people need to challenge themselves to take actions every single time they recognize that they are delaying or procrastinating; especially when the action will provide an immediate benefit to anyone other than himself or herself.

In regards to "Wrath" which usually translates to the concept of resentment, rage or anger; the most effective method to manage this negative emotion is through the practice of stress management techniques discussed in this book in the chapter titled "Breathe Right Feel Right." With "Envy" it is helpful to just simply move your eyes or your focus off the desired item or concept, and shift your attention to helping someone with anything or just start or complete some positive need or action.

When it comes to "Pride" one of the clearest ways to identify this negative emotion is whenever false self-confidence is recognized; for it is in this state that there is the greatest sense of Pride. The paragraphs above clearly demonstrates techniques in which the concept of "Building Resistance Muscle" may be fully utilized.

> "It is through the "Art of Self Defiance" or understanding how to fully use the "Power to Resist the Resistance" that will enable the person to effectively manage Dangerous and Destructive feelings. They learn that their negative attitudes, beliefs as well as behaviors can successfully be Challenged or Changed without the need for willingness."

Through this process of "RESISTING THE RESISTANCE" potentially deadly emotions will be instantly dismissed and can be completely ignored. It is in this manner that the person is free to Completely Change at their own pace and in their own way. For the addict or alcoholic that is unwilling— this concept of using "Resistance Muscle" completely frees them from their stubbornness or fears. It is through the harsh strong vulgar language of "Fuck Your Feelings" that the person is empowered.

This is accomplished in two ways. First, as soon as an addict or alcoholic is aware that they have both very destructive emotional states as well as very Creative and Constructive emotional states; they now have Clear Choices. It is though the empowerment of being able to make decisions that resistance is converted into resolution.

> "Up until this time the person had no power to make decisions since they were driven by impulses. Once again a person does not need willingness to make and carryout decisions, all they need is desperation

or determinedness. On the other hand impulsivity is always driven by willingness, in that they willingly follow their feelings."

The second way that this concept empowers the addict or alcoholic is through the shock value of these words.

"When an addict or alcoholic start to focus on and begin to obsess upon getting high or drinking; they become tangled and seized by a hypnotic lock. These words have the absolute power to smash that hypnotic lock and free them from that Moment of Madness!"

When the addict or alcoholic is aware of their Dark Desires and impulsive destructive tendencies or emotions, they can immediately stop them through the use of this concept, because these words are absolutely thought stopping and will shatter any hypnotic locks that grabs them—"FUC Your Feelings Before They FUC You!"

A very effective technique to use that will SMASH and SHATTER that Hypnotic Lock as well as dissolve drug interests or cravings for a drink is to always carry a photograph of someone extremely special who you love, and who really loves you; a person that you may be WILLING TO DIE FOR!

This could be your husband or wife; or son or daughter; or mother or father; or brother or sister; or best friend. The technique that I am telling you to do is as follows: Keep that physical photograph with you at all times. An actual paper photograph is best due to it bends, folds, cracks and tears, which is impossible with a digital photo on a phone or other device. A paper photograph provides more power to this technique. They are just more personal, private and intimate.

Now every time you find yourself Drifting into thoughts about using Drugs or Drinking, which can be memories of past episodes or plans for future use; then take out that photograph and stare into the eyes and face of that person. Do not take your eyes off their eyes and face. Continue to deeply gaze into their eyes, while you are still having Drinking and Drug use Desires.

To clarify this method, do the following: Hold the photograph in you right or left hand and place your thoughts about Drinking or Drugging in the other hand. Make your focus on substance use strong and actually imagine THAT substance in the other hand, but while doing this do NOT take your eyes off the photograph.

It is important to try to intensify your desire to get high while staring in your loved ones eyes and bring the photograph close to your own eyes, until it gets a little blurry and then move it back into clear focus and keep IT as close as possible to your own face. Now do the same thing with the imaginary substance in your other hand. Bring your hand up and try to imagine the substance of your choice in that hand, as if you are ready to immediately Drink And Get High!

Now both your hands are in front and close to your face, but you are only looking at the photograph. As you stare at the loved ones face do it with Crystal Clear Clarity and you will just have some awareness of your other hand, which is a out of focus, due to the fact that you cannot clearly see the photograph and the other hand in the same manner. It is a virtual impossibility to see the other hand with any real clarity when you are keeping your undivided attention and gaze on the photograph in the RIGHT hand.

You may have some awareness of the other hand and what you are imagining is in that hand—but it is absolutely impossible to clearly see it—if your undivided attention in focused on staring the person in the eyes in the photograph held in your Right hand! This is how you want to train yourself to ALWAYS SEE WHAT IS MOST IMPORTANT—the person in the photograph—so it remains impossible to focus on Drugs or Drinking!

As you engage in this exercise you will notice the Desire to Drink or use Drugs will begin to slowly or quickly fade.

> "The reason for this is that when you directly try to want something that you may want and strongly like, such as drugs or alcohol and place them in direct contact with someone you love, it is not possible for the mind to grasp both concepts equally due to the "Values Exchange" process discussed in a previous chapter."

> "In other words, it is VIRTUALLY impossible for your mind to remain focused on drugs or alcohol due to the fact that "you cannot WANT something that WILL destroy The One You Love."

This process builds very strong "Resistance Muscle" in that it effectively replaces the desire for drugs or alcohol with immediate disgust. Whenever you have a thought about using alcohol or drugs that Desire Must Be Destroyed by turning "Desire Into Disgust."

In the event that the hypnotic lock is so strong that this technique fails to weaken it, then there is an additional process that can be added to the above concepts. If you have the unfortunate experience to be able to still "deeply WANT something that will ABSOLUTELY hurt and destroy someone you love and loves you, then you MUST do the following:

Get real! Stare at that loved ones photo and while staring into their eyes —say—NO don't just say this—SCREAM IT! Stare at that face and look deep into those eyes and SCREAM, "I don't give a damn about you—YOU don't mean a rats ass to me—I don't care if this Rips the guts out of you— BABY because this is what I love," and while screaming BABY stare at the hand that the imaginary drugs are in.

If this does not cause a slight change in desire, then add the following step! Stare now at the hand the imaginary drugs are in and SCREAM " this is what I love BABY—this is what I am Willing To Die For—this is my everything and YOU are my nothing! I have NO love for you BABY because you mean nothing, zero,-- zilch!

If you are NOT able to turn that "Desire into Disgust" after doing this process; then you are either a full blown sociopath and only GOD can help you or you do not have the right persons photograph! This process demonstrates the "Power to Resist the Resistance" through the "Art of Self Defiance" Turning Resistance Into Resolution." By forcing yourself, overcoming your Resistance to do this will save you from the horrors of inflicting severe harm on Yourself and Your loved ones! Yours and theirs needless suffering and agony will be avoided through "Building Resistance Muscle" by effectively using the "Power to Resist the Resistance."

To help the reader gain more understanding of this power in an earlier chapter I used the metaphor of the airfoil. Now returning to that example I will discuss and use it to describe how the dynamics of the airfoil can be applied to the process of converting Resistance Into Resolution.

As mentioned in that previous chapter the reason that tons of aluminum can leave the ground in the form of an airplane is due to the airfoil design. The airfoil is a special design that changes pressures so that it results in a lifting effect or conversely it can do the direct opposite creating great downward pressures.

When the addict or alcoholic realizes that they can manage their negative Dark Desires and feelings, then those feelings will NO longer be able to manage them. It is just a simple fact that if they do not learn to manage destructive and self-defeating feelings, then those feelings WILL take control, and the addict or alcoholic will feel powerless to stop or change them. That Hypnotic Lock Will Seize Them!

"It is important to fully recognize that there are certain

feelings or moods that will absolutely pull a person up and away from their recovery. Through the use of the concept "Building Resistance Muscle" the person is able to gain the power to change their feelings, by challenging those feelings or by flipping them upside down. This will result in PUSHING the same person into recovery behaviors and attitudes rather than AWAY from them."

This provides for the power to change your life, your destiny or basically anything that needs changing within you. In the same way that an airfoil can be positioned to lift up or push down this principal can be applied to any and all emotions; both those conceived as good and those considered as bad. The airfoil when it is positioned one way provides for airplanes to fly, and when it is positioned the opposite way it provides the downward pressure that holds race cars on the track when moving at incredible speeds. "Resisting the Resistance" conversely accomplishes the same thing in that Resistance Is Turned Into Resolution WITHOUT The Need For Willingness.

At this time there is some need to reflect on this constant reoccurring theme through out this book, regarding the concept of "willingness."

"I have emphatically stated numerous times that "willingness is NOT the only key or willingness is ABSOLUTELY unnecessary and has NOTHING to do with a person's ability or Determination or Desperation to do an activity, take an action or just CHANGE something."

The reader at this time may want to turn to the Chapter titled "Definitions Determine Direction" and find the definition of "Willingness." They will notice that it is defined:

"As to be happy to do something if it is needed; approving; describes someone who does their work Energetically and Enthusiastically"

It should be blatantly clear that since most addicts and alcoholics have a tendency to be Oppositional, Defiant and Rebellious; that would mean that they are not "happily Engaged or Energetically and Enthusiastically Engaged."

> "No person needs to be "Happy or Enthusiastic nor Energetic" in order to do Something or CHANGE Something!"

> "It should be abundantly clear that "willingness" ABSOLUTELY is unnecessary and in fact completely a non issue when it comes to Taking Control Of Your Life!"

So many addicts and alcoholics have expressed to me that "I just don't think I am ready to stop" or "I am not ready for this change" or "I wish I wanted to stay clean but I just don't want to" or "I don't believe I can do this" or "I don't feel I am ready." All of these comments or excuses have one thing in common; they all reflect that they believe they have to have "willingness" to change and that is absolute nonsense!

One of the most destructive comments or beliefs heard in an AA or NA meeting is "They just don't have enough willingness to stop." Most people that attend AA and NA are indoctrinated into this belief. In fact when a person gets bored or tired of attending meetings or following recovery commitments, they don't even try to challenge themselves, they just stop working a recovery program.

The reason for this is that they have no "Resistance Muscle" and have never had the chance to develop the "Power to Resist the Resistance." They are allowing Stupid, Asinine Sensations To Dictate Their Behavior.

> "It is when a person is challenged with a loss of interest or have lost their "willingness" that they need to step up against the feeling and become directly determined to take the right actions or continue to take the right actions, REGARDLESS of any emotion or feelings."

Once the person takes control away from their feelings and uses the "Power to Resist the Resistance" forcefully and with determination they will have demonstrated they possess the power NOT to allow their feelings to RULE them! At this point they will have broken free of their impulsive tendencies and Will Be Able To Engage In Decision-Making That Is Not Guided Or Ruled By Their Emotions.

"SMASH AND OBLITERATE THE THOUGHT OR BELIEF YOU MAY HAVE"—

"THAT YOU MUST HAVE "WILLINGNESS" BEFORE YOU CAN MAKE ANY CHANGES."

"It Is A Lie And It Is Absolutely Not And Never Will Be True!"

Without making a decision you cannot and will not take any action at all!! Hopefully you can recognize that many of the decisions that we make have nothing to do with the concept of willingness. It is not a matter of learning more; it is a matter of doing things differently despite the way one feels. Willingness and desire are nothing but an emotional sensation and have nothing to do with the ability to force oneself to make decisions that will lead to changing their lives.

"It is through learning to challenge their own emotions and fully recognizing that there are certain feelings and moods that will absolutely pull a person up and away from their recovery and by challenging those same feelings will flip them upside down, thus pushing the person into recovery. The utilization of the "Power to Resist the Resistance" through the "Art of Self Defiance" provides the force behind "Turning Resistance into Resolution" that becomes the driving force that produces those powerful changes."

A demonstration of this principle may be clearly observed when a person who for instance does NOT like to make their bed. Even though they have NO willingness to make the bed, they can easily take on the challenge and FORCE themselves to make that bed, through the ability to build and utilize "Resistance Muscle" Their power to act is found through the ability to overcome the feelings of not wanting to make the bed, through using the challenge of "Resisting the Resistance" they can practice the "Art of Turning Resistance into Resolution." Every time they choose to do something that is Good For Their Recovery Or Is Good For Someone Else they are practicing the "Art"

This is a situation in which the person realizes. "If I follow the feelings of laziness my feelings will be Fucking Me."

"Through the process of doing the right thing, REGARDLESS of whether they want to or feel like doing that particular activity, WILL immediately increase the persons self esteem which Builds a healthy confidence."

Therefore if they fail to take on that challenge, it WILL result in feelings of self doubt, guilt and even the possibility of shame, and in this manner they truly have been SCREWED by allowing their Emotions To Dictate Their Actions.

Taking on the feelings by fully recognizing that all feelings have the power to create or the power to destroy and by a simple cognitive switch any person can change their emotional selection. This allows the person to easily build self-esteem and healthy self-confidence.

"As they continue to challenge and overcome their resistance to engaging in healthy activities, the more value each of those activities will be imbued with, and the greater the increase in self esteem."

"With an abundance of Self-confidence and Self-esteem there is a Significant reduction in desire to change emotional states due to the fact that strong Self-esteem and Self worth are peak experiences."

"Through Self-empowerment there is less desire to seek a change in emotional states, and this automatically lowers the probability or interest in using substances."

We need to take a moment to describe healthy self-confidence from the kind that is a total liability. For our purposes it is necessary to distinguish between "healthy self confidence and unhealthy self confidence." In Step One on page 21 in the book "Twelve Steps and Twelve Traditions" self-confidence is referred to as being a total liability.

To clarify how such a powerful emotional state as "confidence" could be considered as something bad or harmful; it is first necessary to clearly understand that the reason it is a total liability is due to the fact that confidence is not a fact, but simply a feeling and that's all it is, "just a feeling." Too many times it is that feeling that really screws up an addicts or alcoholics serenity and sobriety. A feeling is NOT a fact, and just because someone may have an abundance of confidence does NOT necessary mean that they have the necessary power, skill or ability to succeed with the task or challenge.

"The ability to demonstrate or perform is referred to as competency. Competency is the measure of ability, whereas confidence measures nothing and means nothing other than the positive and pleasing state of mind that it produces. The hidden danger is found in the fact that when an individual is full of confidence they have become unteachable and unreachable."

"The tragedy is that the feeling of confidence causes a person to Believe That They Have Power And Capability That In Fact They Do Not Possess."

"This false belief or false confidence leads to poor judgment and poor decisions, resulting in risk taking behaviors that usually end in relapsing."

In contrast to false confidence is the concept of healthy confidence, which is when a person has a realistic understanding that by taking certain actions will result in predictable outcomes. The major difference is that the person with healthy self-confidence trusts a process or a method rather than an unproven blind belief. One of the fastest ways to build healthy self-confidence is through the daily practice to find ways to build "Resistance Muscle."

"Resistance Muscle" develops when a person resists acting on their emotions, and through that process they build a sense of power that creates healthy self-confidence. When they act counter to their negative emotions they are able to empower themselves. They are literally able to accomplish and do anything when they put their Mind Against Their Emotions.

"Acting against their own feelings and emotions leads to the creation of greater and higher levels personal power. It is this new power that gives the new forced behavior or activity a higher level of perceived value. It is this perceived value that creates and promotes desire to continue to challenge oneself by acting contrary to, or by ignoring self- defeating emotions and feelings. Once this is accomplished the person has learned an effective method to manage and control their impulsive tendencies."

Once again we can return to the concept of willingness and recognize that willingness implies following a suggestion or direction, whereas when a person practices Resisting Resistance they are controlling and are in CONTROL of themselves; whereas to be willing implies being controlled by someone else or at least influenced by someone or something else. In another words, the person develops a sense of accomplishment and satisfaction in overcoming their own resistance, rather than feeling forced to succumb or submit to someone else's ideas or suggestions.

"Since the addict is basically almost my nature Resistant, Rebellious, Oppositional, as well as Defiant it is just much easier for them to "Act Naturally Rather Than Change Their Personality."

"Through the action of using the "Power to Resist the Resistance" they have inadvertently built up their self-esteem which creates a powerful and positive emotional association or reward to the accomplished activity."

"It Is This Emotional Reward That Produces An Associated Powerful Positive Emotional Sensation That Increases The Value Of The Action Taken; And Increases The Probability That The Action Will Be Repeated."

Any action that becomes associated with a positive emotional experience is likely to reinforce the probability that the action taken will in all likelihood be repeated more than once. It is through this reinforcement that a positive value exchange will occur which will naturally strengthen the desire to remain clean and sober.

"This is more powerful to most addicts than the concept of willingness due to Willingness Equates To Admission

Of Powerlessness And Surrender—but—Challenging and Overcoming ones Self Builds Healthy Confidence and Self Esteem."

"Too many addicts and alcoholics are <u>INCAPABLE</u> of surrender due to the belief or more specifically the <u>FEELING</u> that surrender has NO perceived value, and in fact it is perceived to be to threatening."

Due to denial the addict or alcoholic is very emotionally volatile and oversensitive and many times emotionally fragile and the concept of surrender is fully blocked off as a viable option. The addict has spent years in denial and believing that they have control and influence. If They Were Capable Of Surrender They Would Have Done This A Long Time Ago.

"A small handful of addicts and alcoholics are able to recognize the futility of Drinking and Drugging; when they are finally Crushed and Pushed into SURRENDER. But it is a statistical fact the greater majority of addicts Will Die Or Be Killed Before They Surrender."

While the act of surrender may provide for a feeling of relief after countless years of internal and external conflict; surrender will never compete with the feeling of satisfaction and the sense of power of accomplishment that a person will fully experience when they forcibly overcome their own strong negative feelings or beliefs.

"It is indeed very heroic to believe that all anyone needs to do to recover is to become willing; but it is arrogant to believe that willingness can be imposed upon anyone. It is equally tragic to blame the unwilling for being unteachable and or unreachable. "After all is said and done" as the old cliché goes; when dealing with addicts and alcoholics what is easier and most probable for them to do "Change Their Personality Or Let Them Act Naturally?"

The challenge of clearly identifying their destructive feelings and "Fucking

Those Feelings Before They Fuck Them" creates the power that enables an addict or alcoholic to overcome themselves and their own destructive tendencies. It provides for an entire new destiny that is built on a healthy level Self-confidence rather than upon false Self-confidence. It provides for an increasing level of self-esteem rather than being forced into humility and surrender.

> "Since most addicts and alcoholics are <u>NOT</u> capable of gaining enough humility to surrender, empowering them through the process of successfully challenging themselves, provides for a new path and opportunity to change their lives, before they have to crash and burn, and lose everything including too many times, even their own lives."

> "Everything that needs to be done for recovery are actions that the addict or alcoholic are NOT going to want to do. Conversely everything, they Do Want To Do, doesn't really count, due to the fact they ALWAYS have a strong tendency to just Do What They Want To Do."

> "Now they have to Learn To Resist The Feeling and do things that are right and that they Don't Want To Do. The "Power to Resist the Resistance" provides the power to change this self-defeating life long pattern."

By the end of the next paragraph it will be safe to proceed through the rest of the book without any further threat of vulgarity. But in the meantime I will challenge you to find language that you believe is not as offensive but absolutely to the point. I do not believe that there are any other combinations of words that can intervene or interrupt in a powerfully and passionately effective manner and stop the core cause of relapse, Death and Destruction to the addicts as well as their families.

> "The core cause is their impulsivity IS fueled by allowing self-defeating emotions to dictate their actions, and this insanity and madness must be stopped. Since an addict or alcoholic may always be plagued by the obsession

that "some how, some way or someday I can use and get away" and may focus on the fantasy that they can use a drug or alcohol and control the effects as well as avoid any serious consequences; they must be ready to take on the challenge of "Resisting the Resistance."

"This more succinctly may be stated in the following seemingly vulgar manner, "FUC Your Feelings Before They FUC You!" In my experience these specific words seem to have a universal appeal to the substance abuser and addict. It is in fact the very language of addiction. Because at some very deep level there is that TWISTED and PECULIAR perception that makes an addict or alcoholic reach the point of "Fuck It" and they use it as justification to get "Loaded, Drunk or High."

Why do addicts or alcoholics fail to do what they need to do? After they've been in treatment or a 12-step program, and they have learned that there are many things that they can do that will improve the chances for long-lasting recovery; yet they still fail to follow through with these needed suggestions or recommendations. To gain some understanding of why they fail or resist taking responsibility to fully utilize methods, techniques and recommendations that would definitely enable them to stay clean and sober; the following phenomena needs to be understood.

Any alcoholic or addict that has been actively using and their use has been interrupted will experience the initial stages of withdrawal; they become very panicky and begin to experience almost a life and death sense of urgency to find more drugs or alcohol. This phenomenon is due to the fact.

"Addiction has somehow hijacked their survival instincts and turned them inside out. This means that they become obsessed with an intense fear that they will die if they do not find more alcohol or drugs and paradoxically The Very Thing That They Believe They Need For Their Survival, Is The Very Thing That Can Kill Them."

"It is amazing that the mind or brain of the alcoholic or addict has become so TWISTED that it has taken their very basic survival needs and turned them against their Survival."

To emphasize the severity of these TWISTED and PECULIAR perceptions I will now reflect upon the book of Alcoholics Anonymous in which there is a statement on page 44 in the chapter titled "We Agnostics" in which it states "To be doomed to an alcoholic death or to live on a spiritual basis are not always easy alternatives to face" When one examines the significance of this one statement it becomes very apparent that the mind of the alcoholic or addict is severely warped and out of touch with reality.

To clarify how significant their PECULIAR perceptions are is to do a simple analysis of this statement. "To live on a spiritual basis" means that the person is virtually happy, joyfully engaged in life and fully free and living in peace and serenity. They have a clear understanding of what life is about and can live life successfully on life's terms. "Or to die an alcoholic death are not easy choices for us to make" means the person will die in a lonely, agonizing, deteriorated and in a regretful manner.

"It should be clear that there must be something horribly wrong with the way a person feels, thinks and believes when they struggle with what is and should be an obvious decision. As stated earlier the reason for these TWISTED perceptions is that the person has a tendency to Allow Their Decisions Or Actions To Be Dictated By Their Emotions."

"IN OTHER WORDS THEY ARE FROZEN OR PARALYZED FROM MAKING OR FOLLOWING THROUGH WITH A DECISION UNLESS THEY GET PERMISSION FROM THEIR EMOTIONS TO FOLLOW THROUGH."

One of the easiest ways to understand this is to recognize that the alcoholic or addict will NOT do anything outside their comfort zone. For recovery to occur the addict or alcoholic must learn how to step outside their comfort zone and in this way they can begin the process of progress.

The following will enable the person to understand the difference between admitting powerlessness that leaves them in a very vulnerable position due to not having the ability to resist temptation, and the concept of "Practicing

Powerlessness." This enables them to overcome the demands of negative emotions that overwhelm the ability to resist their power.

> "When an addict or alcoholic gets angry over a feeling they don't want to experience, the reason for their frustration is due to the fact that as an active addict they could always change the feeling or any feelings instantaneously by ingesting a drug, and now in recovery they have to learn to accept and tolerate unpleasant feelings and emotions."

> "It is the feelings that take control and the addict or alcoholic follow that negative emotional power and then act within that power. We must understand that we must render those strong negative feelings that have power over us, and harm us, powerless to continue to do so! In other words we use the "Power of Practicing Powerlessness" and this takes away the power negative emotions have over us!"

> "It Is Not Good Enough To Admit That One Is Powerless, They Also Have To Practice It!! You May Have To Give Up Your Rights To Do Just What You Feel Like Doing—Because This Is The Driving Force Behind A Relapse" –

> "You Did What You Felt Like!!"

NOW--Don't Do What You Feel Like With The Challenge I Am Now Going To Confront You With!

The following demonstrates the use of the "Power of Practicing Powerlessness" through the development of learning to effectively use the "Art of Turning Resistance into Resolution," which is one of the most bizarre things you will ever hear. I guarantee this will be the Strangest thing you have ever read; but in the end you will be Scratching your head, because it makes Sense in a very bizarre and unexplainable manner. It may be a matter of Life and Death or Sanity or Insanity to grasp its meaning and to FULLY implement it into your daily life.

It will be essential as well as necessary to read it out loud, and follow all punctuation, this means stop at the commas and periods! This will enable you to hopefully grasp the truth of this bizarre concept. If you do not "READ IT OUTLOUD" you know so that you--Hear It In Your Own Two Ears! YOU will never understand this mystery, nor gain the ability to implement it into your life! Don't cheat yourself- "Set a New Standard, Step Up to this challenge, speak LOUD AND PROUD!" We will begin by using a very simple example that may be found in the situation of whether a person wants to get out of bed or stay in bed.

"Now whether you feel like reading this LOUD AND PROUD does not matter – JUST DO IT! Don't rob yourself of gaining one of the most powerful and easy techniques to take control back from your feelings and Direct Your Life For a Much Better and Greater Purpose, for NOT only yourself but FOR every loved one in your life!!"

"The mystery of getting out of bed when you don't want to, and the forces that either keep you in the bed, or the forces that get you out of the bed may be explained in the following manner.

It is just a simple matter of "Powerlessness vs. the need to Practice Powerlessness."

"Don't make me tell you again—you should be hearing every word at this time in your own two ears and not just be reading entertaining your mind—NOW it is time to stimulate your Ear Drums—Now READ OUT LOUD—you are in your own home or car and even if you are not the REST of the WORLD could benefit from what you are about to LEARN—so don't be shy and share it—at least share it so you Do hear it in YOUR OWN Two Ears!!

For those who may not be familiar with the First Step in the 12 Step Programs of AA or NA it reads "We admitted that we were Powerless over alcohol, (in NA it reads "our addiction") that our lives had become unmanageable." A person must recognize that they have no control over the use of a substance, or this can be expanded to, having no control over an activity. This admission is not AS important or significant, AS the need to NOT just admit, but to "Practice Powerlessness," which I have taken the liberty to phrase as practicing "The Art of Turning Resistance into Resolution" The following ideas will further clarify this statement.

"Verbalizing, "I am Powerless" is a very empty concept and cannot be used in any practical manner, other than as a simple recognition of past or current weakness or deficiency in capabilities. "Practicing Powerlessness" paradoxically addresses weaknesses and increases capability as will now be demonstrated, through some simple questions."

"By the way YOU are verbalizing at this time—Aren't

you—and if you are that Resistant, Rebellious, Defiant and that Oppositional—then I strongly suggest that you "Fuck those Feelings" before they Rob you of one of the most powerful things that you can ever learn—"Practice the Power to Resist your Resistance" to this suggestion and fully implement the "Art of Self Defiance" and unleash your ability to turn YOUR Resistance into Resolution!!!"

When a person refuses to get out of bed! ARE they practicing powerlessness? or ARE they practicing power? By refusing to get out of the bed. ARE they not engaging the force of exercising their POWER!?

Now, if they were to force themselves to get out of bed, and they ABSOLUTELY did not want to get out of the bed; then are they NOT "practicing powerlessness?" You see, you can't have it both ways; it must be one or the other, despite how contradictory it seems. Staying in bed, when you know you should get up, IS using your personal power to overrule your needs (You need to get up and go to work BUT you are refusing and just stay in bed which is absolutely Exercising your POWER to refuse to get up and go to work! So to get up when you don't want to get up is ABSOLUTELY Practicing Powerlessness!)

To clear up any confusion the following idea needs to be fully understood.

"By the way—again are you doing what I ASKED and is absolutely NECESSARY to fully comprehend and fully understand what you are reading—hopefully OUT LOUD and Proud!!"

"Go ahead don't CHEAT yourself Defy those awkward and embarrassing feelings—So Do it anyway and READ LOUDLY!" Get busy and start practicing the "Art of Self Defiance!" Resist Your RESISTANCE" Get Mad—Get Angry BUT GET it DONE!"

"When we speak of "Powerlessness", this indicates a condition of helplessness to change something; but when we expand on the concept by adding to this phrase the "Need to Practice Powerlessness" we now gain power over what seemed to have power over us. It is the feeling or feelings that overwhelm us; and cause us to feel The Great Resistance To Get Out Of

Bed; therefore it follows that When We Force Ourselves To Leave The Bed In Spite Of These Feelings, We Are Truly "practicing powerlessness."

As odd as this may sound if you observe the fact that if we follow the feeling or feelings and stay in bed; then that is ABSOLUTELY Practicing Our Power. "I am NOT ! getting out of bed!" That is when we are Practicing Power of the dominant feeling. Forcing oneself to get out of the bed is NOT Practicing POWER, but actually POWERLESSNESS in context of Practicing Powerlessness over the intense emotions that are demanding that you follow their power to stay in bed."

Another example of this may be found in the following situation. If a person ABSOLUTELY does not want to do something; such as attend a meeting and they say "I am NOT going to that meeting " and say it, with force and authority; then which one are they practicing, Power Or Powerlessness?

The answer is very obvious "They Are Absolutely Practicing Power." Now conversely if they ABSOLUTELY do not want to go to the meeting and despite intense strong negative feelings they force themselves to attend; then...

"It logically follows, that if not going, is practicing their Power then forcing themselves to go must be demonstrating the "Power of Practicing Powerlessness" or the "Art of Turning Resistance into Resolution"

By this time you are probably almost as confused as you could possible get; so I am going to set you free by explaining the justification or juxtaposition of these two concepts.

"DO I HAVE TO REALLY REMIND YOU FOR THE FOURTH TIME—You know what you should be doing—don't you—YES! ARE you still reading so there is still sound in your EARS coming from your mouth!!

"If you truly want to understand this you better still be reading "LOUD AND PROUD!!"

"If a person lets a strong feeling control them, then they are acting with that feeling and they are following or practicing it's power; but when they challenge acting on the feeling they are Practicing Powerlessness. They are refusing to allow the feeling to control them and therefore the Feeling is powerless to control them.

So through this confusing paradoxical practicing of powerlessness you stop the feeling from controlling you and by Practicing Powerlessness the feeling is powerless to control you!

When you Practice POWER you are honoring the negative feeling or emotion, and when you Practice Powerlessness you are honoring the right idea, belief or concept, and the Result Will Be Constructive and Productive; whereas when you honor the negative feeling you are engaging in Destructive and Self Defeating Actions and Behaviors."

If you did <u>NOT</u> get this—then keep reading it till you do; because when it comes to the moment of truth when temptation, obsession or cravings are overwhelming you, then you better know how to engage the "Power of Practicing Powerlessness" through the "Art of Turning Resistance into Resolution" and not just admit that "I am powerless," because that means you Will Have No Defense and will NOT be able to stop yourself or Resist The Temptations Or Cravings.

As illogical as all this appears to be, here are multiple examples to really clear up, what seems or appears illogical is actually "illogically logical." The following statements are presented as quotes that will demonstrate how Admitting Powerlessness Is Destructive and Enables Your Emotions To Take Control, forcing you to do the wrong things against what you KNOW is right.

"Don't cheat yourself I did not tell you to stop reading "LOUD AND PROUD!!"

If a person verbalizes with force and authority and states "I am not going to do that." Are they practicing power or powerlessness? Or if they state, "I will not apologize" are they practicing power or powerlessness? Or they state "I am not going to call" or "I just don't feel like doing it" or "I don't feel it is necessary for me to go there." Or "I don't believe I need to pray."

How would you label those attitudes and decisions? When they follow the feeling or belief are they not absolutely practicing and using its power, and therefore it must follow resisting the feeling or negative belief is engaging in the Power of Practicing Powerlessness!"

"Therefore the concept of Powerlessness vs. the Practice of Powerlessness is the essence of "Turning Resistance into Resolution." Through the use of exercising the "Art of Turning Resistance into Resolution" gives you the ability to ABSOLUTELY overcome negative impulses and tendencies Without ANY Need at all for Willingness!"

"I personally believe that one of the main reasons for relapse is that the substance user perceives using substances and controlling that use as a worthy challenge, and they "willingly" take on that challenge or follow the POWER of that feeling. Rather than fight that feeling or resist that feeling they allow that feeling to control them! They practice its power rather than "Practicing Powerlessness" against it!

Since being oppositional and rebellious are common traits found in most addicts and alcoholics to combat this tendency, the person needs to constantly be able to challenge himself or herself in the manner clearly described, and learn to begin to "Build Resistance Muscle" and to use "Resistance in Action." It needs to become a daily obligation or discipline to assure that any successful attempts in engaging in positive recovery actions, are clearly connected to, and associated with, Great Intense Emotional Reward And Pleasure!"

To become OUT LOUD passionate, excited and celebrate as many right actions as possible, if not all the right actions and behaviors that are achieved and accomplished daily, it is essential to build high value into those activities. Failure to acknowledge "PROUDLY AND LOUDLY" those achievements reduces their value and therefore the probability that the person will continue to take those necessary recovery actions. The failure to Emotionalize And Build Excitement Into Those Activities will lead to losing interest or desire and they will relapse!

"The tougher the resistance that is overcome, the stronger the "Resistance Muscle" and strong resistance muscle gives the person the power to resist any temptations or cravings, and to "Turn Resistance Into Resolution" It is also through learning to effectively develop and use the "Power of Practicing Powerlessness" which creates enough strength to be able to turn down drugs, when the offer or opportunity to get high arises."

To sum up—you do not need to wait for your Feelings to give you permission to make decisions or changes in or to your life—Seize hold of yourself and demand that you Direct yourself and not let Emotions and Feelings Dictate the directions you take in your life!

"YOU ARE IN Control—Seize your power Run your life the Right way—Do Not let Impulses Impact and Immobilize your ability as well as capability to DO the Right Thing!"

"FUC Your Feelings Before they do Royally FUC You"—Out of every one of your Dreams, Desires and DESTINITY!

I have Learned, in Whatsoever state I am,
Therewith to be Content.

Philippians 4:11

CHAPTER SEVEN

Recovery Despair into Recovery Desire

In this chapter you will learn about the "Power of Positive Pressure" and how it will enable you to turn "Recovery Despair into Recovery Desire." You will learn a method to develop the ability to overcome negative emotions and impulses that I refer to as the concept of "Comprehending, Catching and Controlling Click."

The following process is an effective method to utilize the "Law of Attraction" and create strong positive recovery desires when there is none present. The "Law of Attraction," simply means that what we desire with strong emotion we will manifest in our lives. Since the "Law of Attraction" does not differentiate between good desires or bad desires and just works mechanically to manifest what is desired or dreamed; the addict or alcoholic needs to be aware how this law is a driving force behind their repeated failures to recover and therefore they must take control of this powerful force.

"The "Law of Attraction" works on any belief driven by strong and intense desire, since passionate desire creates what is attractive. It is a fact that "What We Feed Our Mind Our Mind Will Attract To Us!"

"This should be of significant importance to the addict or alcoholic who must come to the realization that they have a tendency to frequently, if not constantly obsess on the need or hope that they can safely use alcohol or drugs, despite all the previous facts that would indicate the contrary."

"This strong fantasy, which is really an intense desire, brings devastation to the person due to they attract addiction back into their life; much like a magnet will attract steel, the dream of safely using again, then attracts drugs and destruction!"

Through a very simple step-by-step process you will be able to create strong right desires, rather than allowing wrong desires to dominate as well as destroy everything that has been worked for.

"This process will enable a person to gain the desire, which will fuel the passion that will attract success and recovery, and will enable the person to make a change in behavior, regardless of whether there is any willingness."

I have referred to this process, as using the "Power of Positive Pressure" through the development of the "Art of Controlling Click" The following narrative should help clarify this concept regarding what is "Click."

Many people including myself sometimes have a tendency to just mindlessly watch TV and surf the channels. While doing this I have discovered that there are certain things that "click," and instantly grab your attention but most of the time nothing does. It is just an endless ride through all the channels again and again.

Using this example, it becomes possible to understand why it is so difficult for recovering people to stay focused on the things that will produce and prolong their recovery. The mind of a person whether an addict or not is just a constant stream of thoughts and certain thoughts have "Click Power" and others do not. Most of the thoughts regarding drinking and drugging all have substantial "Click Power", in that the person will stop and pay more attention to these thoughts than the thoughts associated with recovery.

To achieve the ability to develop "Click Control" that will reinforce recovery rather than relapse, it is necessary to understand and engage "The Power Of Positive Pressure" which is achieved through the development of the "Art of Controlling Click." The following method will teach someone how to "Control Click" with recovery thoughts instead of addictive thoughts; so there is a stronger probability for recovery thoughts to grab their attention.

Creating and Controlling "Click"

1. Must Write It Down
2. Thinking About It Will Not Work
3. Know What You Focus On

4. What You Focus On Manifests In Your Life
5. You Select What You Focus On
6. Control The Focus By Writing It Down Daily
7. Select Worthy Challenges
8. A Worthy Challenge Is One That Creates Pressure
9. Pressure Turns Black Coal Into Diamonds
10. A Worthy Challenge Is Worth The Effort
11. Effort Produces Results
12. Review For Results-Repeat Till Resolved
13. Repetition Results In Recovery
14. Read And Reread This Formula And Write Daily
15. Pressure Produces Personal Power

A detailed understanding of each of these actions will help the reader to engage in doing this, whether they want to or not.

"Once again the message I am announcing over and over again in this book is that you and in fact anyone can recover from any addiction or dependence whether they want to or not."

"If the person is highly motivated for recovery from their addiction or dependence; then that person will find that these actions will create an explosion of positive feelings and sensations that will immediately reinforce the desire to change their lives."

"I always must add with great caution that any person who is very motivated to change and "willingly" engages in recovery actions and activities, unfortunately may never build enough strength to resist the opportunity when offered their drug of choice. It will be at that moment of truth when they must face the decision to resist or to relapse. Comprehending, Catching and Controlling Click may be their only defense!"

The first of the 15 guidelines that it "Must Be Written Down" just follows the tried and true method that all people of success know. There is a very powerful and almost magical force that is unleashed with written goals. In case the word "goals" has caught you off guard, please recognize that any action(s) that you engage in whether you want to or not are actually "goals." It should not be a mystery that Anytime Anyone Completes Their Goal It Leaves Them Stronger And More Confident Than Prior To That Achievement. Even if the person did not want to do the activity or play the game The End Result Of Goal Completion Is A Powerful Boost To That Persons Self Esteem.

> "As mentioned in previous chapters; any time a person's self esteem increases it reduces the risk of relapse due to the simple fact that the person has positive and powerful feelings that are more pleasing and pleasurable than that of using drugs or engaging in some other obsessive and destructive behavior."

Most people have found that just a simple "to do list" has the incredible power to lead to the fulfillment or completion of the items written on it. For those who have never tried writing goals then this is just another one of those "Worthy Challenges" we will discuss in the following paragraphs. Through the "Power of Positive Pressure" you can force yourself to achieve anything by creating and succeeding with "Worthy Challenges."

The second rule "Thinking About It Will Not Work" is a continuation and justification of the first rule that it "Must Be Written Down." The reason for this may be found in the following metaphor: Anyone who has had the pleasure and honor of having to do their laundry outside their home, has probably had to visit their local commercial Laundromat. When you walk in all the dryers are spinning and all you can discern is color and shapes when you glance through the circular glass dryer windows, and it is not until you shut it off and take out each item that you discover that there are very expensive items or there are throw away paint rags.

> "The mind is like a constant spinning dryer and All You Glimpse Is The Barest Superficial Understanding Of What You Are Experiencing Or Thinking."

> "Therefore if you want to control what you put back into your mind you must follow this formula."

> "It is through the selection of writing it down rather

that just thinking about it that makes it much more probable to occur."

Thoughts, any thoughts just stream through the mind, and when a decision is made to choose or select certain ideas; then multiple areas of the brain have to be engaged. The More Areas That Become Involved In The Action, The Deeper The Learning is and the more cues to retrieve those needs or desires are created. For instance when you just think about something it passes through your awareness very quickly if not instantly; but when you write things down it is a much more complicated process in which there is review and editing and selection of vocabulary words, and review of the sentence structure, as well as additional review as more words or sentences are added. Therefore the following method needs to be followed for optimum impact and benefit, when using this rule.

"Write things down very concretely and NOT abstractly. The impact of writing a specific task or action associated with a specific time and place that also preferably includes another person, has the highest probability of being accomplished as written. But an abstract approach that does NOT list a specific time place and action; nonetheless being absent of accountability to another person, is probably going to be a complete waste of time and effort."

A few examples of these are "Telling yourself that you will do something." is vague and will not propel someone to accomplish or achieve the "thing." Or "I have to exercise more" or "I have to stop eating so much" or "I need to spend more time with my family" or our battle flag motto "I have to get clean and sober" all of these have no impact in moving a person towards their goals.

"The more effective powerful way to do his is to change these "good intentions" to achievable and measurable goals by first: writing them down and second writing them in a specific and concrete format. Instead of just "telling yourself that you have to do something" Write The Specific Action and Attach Time and Details Necessary for Accomplishing the Thing."

It must be described as if it was already on video. For instance "Tonight when I get home from work at 6:30 I will ask my {significant other} to walk around our neighborhood for 30 minutes or go to a local park and walk for 30 minutes." It should be obvious that this written goal encompasses all three good intentions and does not mention any of them. The person is spending more time with the family {significant other} they are exercising and burning calories and they are not drinking and "they're not just trying to stay sober-they are staying sober."

The third guideline for creating "click" is to "Know What You Focus On" this too is directly correlated to the first two; for to know what you are focused on, requires you to stop the spinning thoughts and write them down.

The fourth rule is the simple fact; "That What You Focus On Is What Is Manifested In Your Life." In the "Law of Attraction" it states that we create our own realities whether good or bad. They are manifested from the energy we create that is directed by our focus. It is this "Law" that this author believes strongly contributes to relapse. Most people that lose their recovery or their sobriety do so because They Refuse To Take Control Of Their Focus On Drugs Or Alcohol. Not only do they not try to control or try to change their focus, they in Fact Energize That Deadly Focus With Intense Passion Bringing It To Life, as did Dr. Frankenstein when he brought forth his monstrous creation.

"Failing to take responsibility for controlling their focus and in fact intensifying that negative focus with passionate desires, is what summons forth drugs and alcohol in the same way that a demon may be conjured up. I have deliberately used the metaphor of Frankenstein and Demons because in reality; when we think or obsess on substance use or abuse we actually become possessed by a "Demon" and do "Monstrous" things."

"We cannot stop ourselves due to the massive obsession and accompanying cravings. Therefore it is Imperative And Essential That You Know Where Your Strongest Thoughts Are Centered, And You Change That Focus Whether You Want To Or Not."

"If you do not control what you focus on; then what you
focus on will ABSOLUTELY control you!"

The Fifth rule which is "You Select What You Focus On" reinforces what
was just mentioned in the preceding paragraph; which is the fact that you
have the...

"Full Power To Select What You Focus On, and The Quality Of Your
Life Is Directly Contingent Upon Your Ability To Direct and Control That
Focus."

In his book "Think and Grow Rich" Napoleon Hill indicated the following
concepts which he obtained from interviews with the most powerful and
influential leaders of his time. After interviewing these prominent people for
years he drew the following conclusions to how they became so successful.

It should be noted that just a few of those people where: Henry Ford
founder of Ford Motors; Alexander Graham Bell creator of the telephone;
Thomas Edison inventor and visionist; King Gillette of razor technology
and dozens of others such as Theodore Roosevelt president of the United
States, Wilbur Wright with his brother who are famous for the first successful
airplane flight that took place at Kitty Hawk, Woodrow Wilson, Howard
Taft, F. W. Woolworth, Clarence Darrow, Charles M Schwab and the founder
of The Standard Oil Company—the first American Billionaire—John D
Rockefeller.

From the meetings with these giants of history and industry, he recorded
the following factors responsible for their achievements: From an in depth study
of these rich and powerful people Napoleon Hill concluded the following:

"First comes thought, then organization of that thought into ideas and
plans; then transformation of those plans into reality. Action is the real measure
of intelligence. All achievements, all earned riches, have their beginning in
an idea. Cherish your visions and your dreams, as they are the children of
your soul, the blueprints of your ultimate achievements. Man, alone, has the
power to transform his thoughts into physical reality; man, alone, can dream
and make his dreams come true. Our minds become magnetized with the
dominating thoughts we hold in our minds and these magnets attract us the
forces, the people, the circumstances of life which harmonize with the nature
of our dominating thoughts."
Napoleon Hill

"As you may observe from these quotes, what is manifested
in our lives is a Direct Result Of What We Imagine and

Focus On, and Energize with Passion Through Our Concentration on that Particular Vision."

"Therefore it is imperative that you take control of your focus before your focus takes control of you. If You Focus on Drugs or Alcohol then They Will Be Summoned and Manifested Back into Your Life."

If this sounds strange and mysterious and metaphysical, then please reread Napoleon Hill's quote that were drawn from the true-life successes of some of the greatest individuals of all time.

"It should also be noted that if you obsess on not wanting to drink or do drugs it is actually no different than obsessing on wanting to do those substances. This is due to the fact that whatever idea, thought or focus you emotionalize with a deep passion has a strong probability of being manifested into your life."

"In the next chapter I will detail exactly the process of how the "mind does not work" and why obsessing on "NOT wanting to do something" will never work due to the brain has no capacity for comprehending a "NOT" concept or desire."

The sixth guideline is "Control The Focus By Writing It Down Daily" this is the only way that you can absolutely control the focus by writing what you want or need to focus on. Once again this reinforces the first guideline of it "Must Be Written Down." For it is only through writing it down that you can actually control the focus. A person that has a good idea that fails to control or focus on it is someone that may be referred to as having "Good Intentions," and as my mother use to say "Good Intentions Pave the Way Straight To Hell!"

Don't be foolish take every good idea you have and write it down. "Good Intentions" are the same thing that in AA or NA refer to as a Half Measures" and they emphasize that "Half Measures will avail us nothing!" Good intentions many times lead to destruction! "Don't Just Say It But Write About "What You Wish To Become!"

The seventh recommendation "Select A Worthy Challenge" This means that you take full control of not only what you focus on, but now you become empowered. It should be noted that once selected then the eighth guideline would enable you to use your personal power and to choose. A "Worthy Challenge Is One That Creates Pressure" to change something, and it is through the utilization of this pressure that enables you to gain the power to change your entire life, future and destiny.

Regarding the ninth concept "Pressure Turns Black Coal Into Diamonds" This is just a simple metaphor to emphasize That Pressure Can Create Great And Valuable Things. Therefore we should not hesitate to pressure ourselves in the right way, by selecting the right challenges that creates healthy pressure, which leads to improving our lives and the people that we care for.

The last six guidelines do not need as much detailed understanding or explanation, as has the preceding nine. Number ten "A Worthy Challenge Is Worth The Effort" is just a continuation of taking responsibility and being sure that Whatever Effort Is Used Was Worth That Effort. Number eleven "Effort Produces Results" is simply a reminder that Nothing New Can Be Created Without Work And Determination. Number twelve "Review For Results-Repeat Till Resolved" is also a simple guideline that encourages Continued Committed Effort That Will Not Be Stopped No Matter What.

Any time there is a goal there is always a strategy to reach that goal, and if a particular strategy should fail to produce the results intended, then a person Must Continue To Look For Additional Strategies Until They Achieve That Result. Number thirteen "Repetition Results In Recovery" is just a commonsense reminder that PUTTING FORTH REPEATED EFFORTS WILL ABSOLUTELY LEAD TO CHANGE AND SUCCESS. We can only fail if we become doubtful and cease the commitment to maintain a strong desire to take on the challenge, and choose to fail to find the strategies and positive focus that we want in our lives.

We need to remember those immortal words "Failure is not an option" as dramatized in the movie Apollo 13 when the ship and all aboard appeared to be doomed; but the staff and engineers at NASA brought the ship and all aboard home safely, against absolutely impossible odds!

In other words we need to believe and give the new focus the equal power to "Click" as did the power of those words "Failure is not an option" led to one of the greatest true miracles of our time!

The fourteenth recommendation:

> "Read And Reread This Formula Daily" comes directly
> out of Napoleon Hill's understanding that all success

is based upon a disciplined and strong daily focus on a written plan or directive that is verbally repeated OUT LOUD and frequently. It is through this discipline, that passionate emotional energy is NOT just created through the words we think but much more importantly the words we CHOOSE and select to speak OUT LOUD. These words we speak as well as think will be brought forth and manifested into reality. The final concept; "Pressure Produces Personal Power," is the last reminder in this process of creating "Click" that this is how to succeed in turning "Recovery Despair into Recovery Desire."

One last concept we need to understand if we are going to learn to manage or control the emotional impulses, that have been directing bad decisions and dictating wrong actions.

"We need to be very aware that what we focus on, verbally and non-verbally, since it controls what we emotionally experience."

The following is an excerpt from a future Chapter titled "Essays and Excerpts Random Facts and Factors." I am presenting it here due to it will greatly clarify the concept of how all emotional experiences are determined by the words we use and think. The Words We Choose Determine What We Believe To Be Our Reality.

"If we pick disempowering words we will feel weak and fragile. If we stay fully aware of the need for careful selection of the words we choose, and use empowering words We Will Feel Confident And Powerful!"

The process to accomplish this is through utilizing the "Power of Transformational Communication" through the "Art of Word Selection."

When working with depressed, anxious or even chronic pain sufferers, I would immediately challenge them to change the words that they were using to describe their condition or symptoms. I would instruct them to choose different words than the ones that they were currently using to describe what they were experiencing.

When a client would state, "I don't know what to do I have always suffered from deep depression?" Or they would state, "I have an intense anxiety condition and I frequently have severe panic attacks and I need medication or I feel like I may kill myself!" Or another client may state, "Two years ago I suffered a devastating car accident and my back and neck are permanently severely damaged and there's no way I can function even one day without drugs-without my pain medication!" And in still another case the client may state, "I have tried getting help numerous times and there is nothing anybody can do for me I will just never understand and I will never change, being here is just a waste of time!"

Upon hearing a client state these discouraging and disempowering comments and beliefs about themselves, I would challenge them to state in depth and detail exactly what they had just previously expressed, but to do so without using the disempowering and discouraging words that they were choosing to use. Many times the client would become frustrated and express their complaint in exactly the same words, and it would take much prompting or even provoking to force them to search for other words to describe a condition.

Take for example the client who stated, "I have always suffered from deep depression." I would instruct that person to repeat that statement, but to do so without using the words "always suffered" and to not use the term or words "deep depression."

> "Upon hearing this the client would be come somewhat confused, disoriented and even extremely frustrated because it would be the first time that they would be forced to THINK about what they were saying rather than just saying what they were feeling without any THOUGHT whatsoever."

What I have witnessed every time a client has taken on this challenge is their surprise in regards to how their reality reorients itself just because they chose different words to describe what they thought they could only feel, which was the degree, depth and discouragement regarding their situation or symptoms. Now returning to the example of the person who stated, "I have always suffered from deep depression." They changed the words to "I have experienced much sadness" or they change the words to "I have felt lost" or another variation of words chosen "I just don't really know what I'm feeling." Although it may be difficult for you the reader to fully understand how this process works.

"It is through the use and choice of words that all of life that we experience is measured and brought to our attention. In other words when people are experiencing "something" until they describe that "something" that "something" does not exist."

It is only when we bring it into our reality by choosing words to describe the event the situation or even symptoms, is when we become aware that any of this even exists.

"Everybody has experienced times when they may have had a severe headache, felt overwhelmed by some situation, or was actually very physically sick; but when they became distracted or preoccupied regarding some other totally different experience, the headache, the overwhelming situation, and the physical sickness mysteriously vanished, until they remembered those symptoms and pains once again."

In the example where the person stated, "I have an intense anxiety condition and I frequently have severe panic attacks and I need medication or I feel like I may kill myself!" that person was confronted with the need to restate their feelings in depth and detail, but to repeat it without using the following words, "intense anxiety" or "frequent panic attacks" or "kill myself." When the person attempted to share the feelings that they clearly stated in the above statement without having access to the words I prohibited them to use, they then experienced a very bizarre and strange change in their previously believed perception of their reality.

They expressed the following, "I am just real nervous and get real shaky and I just don't know how to stop it." As you can see when you compare these two statements there is a massive change in the way these words will create or impact in a very positive way their feelings and emotions. In fact not only is there a significant reduction in the sense of helplessness and hopelessness but there is an immediate shift in how they are thinking about their situation or condition.

"This new choice of words unleash a large degree of new self empowerment and awareness of a larger number of options available as a direct result of using the "Power of Transformational Communication" through the "Art of Word Selection."

To strengthen these new resources I instructed this person to repeat once again the statement they last made to describe in depth and detail exactly what they were feeling, but this time I prohibited them from using the words "real nervous" and "real shaky" and "don't know." When they reconstructed that statement it was presented as "There is something wrong and I have to stop it." This third statement was the most bizarre reversal of a previously stated belief that the person believed that they were absolutely helpless and hopeless in regards to this situation or condition.

> "As can be seen in these two examples when a person chooses to change discouraging, discounting, depreciating, debilitating or disturbing words they can and will completely alter what they perceive to be their reality."

In the next example in which the person stated "Two years ago I suffered at a devastating car accident and my back and neck are permanently severely damaged and there's no way I can function even one day without drugs-without my pain medication!" I challenge this person to repeat exactly what they are feeling in as much depth and detail as was humanly possible, but prohibited them from using the following words and terms, "suffered" or "devastating" or "permanently severely damaged" or "there's no way."

The rapid extraordinary change in their affect or facial expression was absolutely astounding when they rephrased their feelings in the following manner. "Two years ago there was an accident and I hurt my back and neck and I function with pain medication." Although this statement may seem similar to the first statement the change in this person's face showed that an extraordinary shift that occurred or that their reality was indeed reoriented. The reason for this will be clearly seen and how the choice of words created a new sense of hope and a different belief than the one in which they were suffering a hopeless condition in which they were helpless to change or manage.

> "By removing the absolute words "suffering, devastating, permanently, severely, damaged and no way," enables a person to develop a completely different perspective, which enables them to redefine the experience

and therefore to change that previous held belief or reality."

In the last example in which the person states "I have tried getting help numerous times and there is nothing anybody can do for me- I will just never understand and I will never change, being here is just a waste of time!" Upon hearing this statement I challenged that client to restate how they felt, but I prohibited them from using the following words and terms, "tried" or "numerous" or "nothing" or "just never" or "we'll never" and "waste of time."

The client after much arguing and prompting and feeble attempts to change this statement finally was able to construct the following statement, "I have gotten help several times and they couldn't help me." As you can see from this second statement it is significantly different than the first statement, and by choosing to change the words this person now has a new sense of possibilities.

By removing the words that measured absolute conditions, enables the person to begin to recognize other possible options. Although the second statement sounds almost as fatalistic as the first, it absolutely does not have the same impact or negative intensity on the person and therefore changes some of the disempowering beliefs they had about themselves.

"As I did in the previous example I also challenged this client to polish up the statement by prohibiting them from using the additional terms, "several" and "couldn't." They formulated the following statement, "I have gotten help and sometimes it helped." As you can clearly see in this third and last reconstructed sentence or statement, that this person has experienced a complete reversal in their initial sense of helplessness and hopelessness!"

All this power to completely alter your negative realities are at your disposal within a heartbeat moment. Therefore it is unnecessary and needless to suffer, when you have the ability, and so much power to shift things in an instant.

"Learn to be aware and very sensitive to what your thoughts are but even more particularly to what you speak out loud. The words you choose to speak out loud creates the reality of what you will experience; as can be clearly seen in the four previous examples, that they absolutely demonstrate the "Power of Transformational Communication" when you CHOOSE to engage in the "Art of Word Selection."

"Taking control of your own mind and directing it to what ever means or ends you desire is instantly possible and will work faster than any drug you have ever done!"

I feel that these concepts regarding the utilization of the process of the "Power of Transformational Communication" through the "Art of Word Selection" is so essential for the rapid strengthening of recovery and the immediate healing for your life; that I repeat this in exactitude in the Chapter titled "Essays and Excerpts Random Facts and Factors" under the subtitle of "Utilizing Transformational Communication Through Transformational Vocabulary"

"All emotional experiences are determined by the words we use and think. The words we choose determine what we believe to be our reality. If we pick disempowering words we will feel weak and fragile. If we stay fully aware of the need for careful selection of the words we choose, and use empowering words we will feel confident and powerful!"

What we emotionally experience is perceived to be our reality. Since we can change our emotions though the guaranteed technique described earlier, then we can absolutely set ourselves free from whatever limiting beliefs we have ever had regarding our ability to stay clean and sober. Through this process we can achieve a lifestyle only previously dreamed about.

Whenever anything happens to us we are always trying to make sense of it, and this is the simple process of "assigning a meaning" to the event, and anytime we assign a meaning to an event we automatically create an accompanying emotion. The meaning assigned is through a process in which words are said either to us to or to ourselves. This assigned and attached emotion latter on can become unwanted "emotional baggage." We carry this burden and believe we are powerless to change it. Some people will bear this load their entire lives. They will blame others for their current state of affairs, their lack of abundance, their loneliness, and their physical health problems, and never realize that their past trauma was never the cause or the problem; but the meaning they assigned to it and the emotional attachments they unwittingly allowed to occur.

"Since the past does not exist, other than as a past perceived memory or impression, then it only has impact from the words we choose to use to remember it. No matter what has happened, or you want to happen, it all can be successfully challenged or changed as well as overcome by the effective use of the "Power of Positive Pressure" through the "Art of Controlling Click."

It is the "Power of Positive Pressure" that will enable you to turn "Recovery Despair into Recovery Desire" through your disciplined efforts that will enable you to acquire the Power of "Comprehending, Catching and Controlling Click."

"Even though a past event can never be changed the meaning can always be easily changed and that will automatically change the "emotional attachment." It is through utilizing this process of creating "Click" that a person is able to control focus and create desired emotional feelings and experiences that will be selected over the old undesirable and miserable emotions."

"Even though a past event can never be changed, the meaning can always be easily changed, and that will automatically change the "emotional attachment."

All things are Possible to him that Believeth.

Mark 9:23

Chapter Eight

Desire How To Find The Fire

"Are Relapse and Recovery Choices?" Your brain is the most powerful thing in the entire universe, there are more cells in your brain then there are stars in the sky. Just look around you and know that everything you see, first had to originate in someone's brain. Once the person had a clear vision of what they desired to create they then had the ability to make it happen.

For it is absolutely true what Napoleon Hill, stated in regards to whatever a man or women can "Conceive and Believe they can Achieve!" If you are reading this on your computer while sending E-Mail; speaking on your cell phone; or surfing the Internet; watching TV or the latest movie or possibly doing all four on your iPhone, it must be recognized that all these miraculous and incredible creations that we take for granted on a daily basis, all originated in one or more persons minds. "It was Conceived and Believed and therefore was Achieved."

"Therefore you must recognize that you are no different since you have the same creative ability and capacity to use your mind, and therefore you must know that Your Recovery Can Be Created From Your Brain When Properly Guided And You Learn How To Use It."

"There are Many Simple Tools that will absolutely allow you to take complete control of all that gray matter between your ears and it will be through this process and these techniques that Will Absolutely Set You Free From The Madness Of Addiction."

What you have been doing has not worked, because you don't know how to work what will work and that is utilizing the enormous potential power of your own mind and brain. Until this point the brain has been controlling

133

you and in spite of your dreams, your hopes and despite the promises you have made to yourself and others you continue to fail, because you don't understand why you have repeatedly failed. Until you are able to understand more clearly how your mind works your chances to make a change for life will remain slim.

I would like to take a moment here to briefly discuss how the mind does "not" work. Once you understand this concept you'll have much more ability to direct your own mind in a more controlled and effective manner. In order for you to gain awareness and insight of how the mind does "not" work you will need to do the following. Since this is an exercise in which you are going to experience the impact of words that are said to you, despite the fact that you will be given clear direction to "not" listen to any of these words, you will find it virtually impossible to resist or avoid hearing those words.

To do this exercise you will need to find a partner that will be willing to read to you Out Loud the following statement.

> "Do "not" hear anything of what I am going to say. I repeat do "not" think about any of the words or ideas that you are going to hear. Now I absolutely do "not" want you to think about or hear about: A bright green leaf glistening in the early morning sun with a silvery drop of dew running down the center vein of the leaf and dropping slowly to the leaf covered forest floor in the early morning twilight mist."

By doing this exercise you should have discovered that when something is being read or spoken out loud and you hear it in your own ears, it is virtually impossible "not" to think about or "not" hear those words that were read or said out loud. This means that when you try to block an idea or thought by using a negative concept, such as "I am "not" going to drink today" or "I am "not" going to get high today" or "I "don't" want to do it anymore" or "I am "done" with drinking" or "I "don't" want it anymore," thinking this or saying this will "not" stop you from doing what you said you would "not" do!

The reason you will generally fail to persuade yourself to "not" to do something is due to the following. When you take a concept and you try to negate it by adding a word such as "not" or "won't" Or "will not" or "cannot" or "don't" or any other words that are an attempt to convey the opposite of what is being said, will absolutely fail to accomplish what is intended.

The reason an addict or an alcoholic will fail when they are sincerely trying to talk themselves out of taking a drink or doing drugs, is due to the fact that The Mind Cannot Understand A "Not" Concept. In other words when a person states, "I am "not" going to drink anymore" or "I am "done" doing drugs," what they are attempting to do, is to resist taking that action.

The problem or paradox is the fact that since the brain does not understand any "not" concepts, then when the person verbalizes or even just thinks "I am NOT going to drink today" the brain does not recognize the word "not." What this means is that the brain or the mind will not comprehend the word "not" which means this statement is experienced in the mind as "I AM going to drink today."

To clarify this it is necessary to just simply understand that when a visual image forms in the mind, the mind begins to organize itself immediately to acquire the object of that image. In other words a picture that forms in the mind becomes an object of desire and the mind will always move in the direction to "acquire the object of desire."

"Any word that forms a visual image in the brain becomes an object of desire therefore when the addict or alcoholic states "they are "not" going to drink" or "they are "not" going to do it anymore" the words "drink" and "it" create powerful visual images."

"Therefore since the word "not" is not recognized or understood in the brain and the words "it" as in "I am not going to do it." Causes the brain to want "it.""

In the event that there may still be some confusion about the above concepts of how the brain or mind does "not" work I will expand on the explanation by inviting you to consider the following. Most people are aware of how international signs work. In other words when you see the word ENTER and it has a complete circle around it with a single diagonal line striking across the word, then that sign would mean "Do Not Enter." Another example of international sign language would be the words RIGHT TURN and if it had a complete circle around it with a single line on an angle across the word that would really indicate "No Right Turn."

By understanding international sign language you can begin to understand how the human brain does "not" work. The failure to be able to negate the concept by stating that you are going to "not" going to do "it" is due to the fact that the human brain cannot form a circle with a diagonal slash through it regarding the word "drinking" or "drugs."

> "As soon as the mind hears these words or substitute
> words for "drinking" or "drugging" then those words
> create powerful visual imagery that creates a strong
> Desire To Acquire The Objects Of Desire."

It should be especially noted that any word that is associated to "alcohol" or "drinking" or "drugs" or "drug use" would form powerful images. Such as when those words are replaced with: "it" or "stuff" or "garbage" or "crap" or "shit" or "that" as in "I hate "that" or "I am done with "that" or "I am through with "that" or "Take "that" away" or "I am through with doing this "crap" or "shit." As you can see from these examples, any effort to talk yourself out of drinking or using drugs is doomed to failure, if any words or combination of words are used in a sentence that triggers a visual image of what you don't want to do, will actually communicate a strong and powerful compelling message to the brain to "do it."

> "The reason for this phenomenon is that certain words
> create powerful visual imagery, and words associated
> to the use of alcohol or drugs have this power and
> potential, to create "Click Power" as stated in the
> previous chapter."

> "It is this unintended as well as uncontrolled "Click
> Power" that creates the "Hypnotic Lock" that acts like
> a heat seeking missile that causes the intense impulsive
> need to return to drinking or drugging" despite all the
> sincere effort to resist!"

> "Once this is understood then the most effective strategy
> to challenge a thought or an obsession to get high, is
> to use an opposing or competitive term or word that
> can create a completely different vision or image in the
> brain."

An example of this would be instead of attempting to convince yourself "I don't want to do "this" anymore" it is more effective to say to yourself "I need to call my sponsor" or "I need to write in my journal" or "I need to play with the dog or cat" or "I need to clean the dishes" or "I need to pray or read the Bible" or "I need to go to the gym" or basically any word or concept that would be an effective diversion from the thought of drinking or using drugs. As you can observe from the above examples, words like "sponsor", "journal" "play" "dog or cat" "clean" "dishes" "pray" "read" "gym" all provide powerful mental imagery that directly competes with the image of drinking or using drugs.

Now you can clearly see that there are effective ways to use words that will cause your mind to work in more predictable ways. You also are now aware of why the most sincere and strongest efforts to attempt to talk yourself out of drinking and drugging have failed in the past. Once again…

> "If you use any word that creates in your mind a visual image, then your mind will organize itself to acquire the object of that image."

Therefore the most effective way to protect yourself when you are thinking about drinking or drugging or getting high is not to try to "not to think about it" but to distract yourself by choosing words that form completely different or opposing visual images as shown in the above example.

> "The mind cannot <u>not</u> think about something that is being thought" therefore "You cannot <u>not</u> think about drugs when you are trying <u>not</u> to think about drugs." The word drug, conjures an image and that image cannot <u>not</u> be imaged and the image creates interest and desire to acquire the object of desire." You cannot <u>not</u> think of something that you are thinking. You cannot unthought a thought."

You must stay alert and be aware of how your brain cannot understand any statement that contains the word "not" or any other equivalent that is an attempt to negate the concept that the word is used with. By being fully aware of all of these concepts the addict or alcoholic is much more empowered to better manage to take control of their own thought processes and intentions.

> "One final comment regarding the above concepts and paradoxes is to understand the following statement. "Once a thought has been thought, a thought that has been thought can never be unthought."or "You cannot,

not have a thought, that you have, thought" or "you cannot not think about something that you have thought about." When you use any word that automatically fires a strong image in the brain, you cannot, "not" think or undo that image, therefore you must stay very alert to the images you allow to be triggered in your brain."

There is technology available that you can utilize that will enable you to control your own mind and change your life forever, change the way you think, change the way you feel, change what you believe and even change how you physically act. Just as there is technology in computers, technology in transportation, there is a massive technology available that will enable you to take control and change your life; but first you have to make the decision to want to change.

"If you know that you must change; then you must also know that no one can change you, but you!"

As repeated frequently throughout this book "you can make a decision to change something even when you don't want to and have absolutely no willingness to do so."

"The concept of the need for willingness to be necessary is a complete sham; in that since "willingness" is nothing more than just an emotional feeling and has nothing to do with whether a person can take an action or not!"

The technologies of neural conditioning or success conditioning enable a person to change their life through very simple repetitive actions. Once Again A Person Does Not Have to be Willing, just Disgusted and Determined. These technologies will provide you with opportunities and exercises, that when done with enthusiasm and extreme passion; will absolutely recondition your mind to work in a very fantastic and extraordinarily different manner, than it has ever worked before.

So please don't cheat yourself! Do the exercises with strong passion and deep belief. These exercises embody the very essence of the "Law of Attraction" previously mentioned. If you do these things for 30 to 90 days, you will make lifelong changes in the way you think, the way you feel, the way you believe, the way you act, the way you dream and the way you succeed.

It is important to fully understand that in order to succeed many times you must fail. To gain deeper insight into how failure is the building block of any success we will use the following example. In baseball a player who fails to hit the ball 7 out 10 times is considered to be one of the best in the world. This means that a failure rate of 70% is not just only acceptable, but absolutely considered extraordinarily excellent. The player who hits the ball 30% of the time is categorized as one of the world's best hitters.

> "It is extremely helpful to understand that the concept of success is always built on numerous efforts and failures. It is Not Measured by Achieving What We Desire, But Through Determined and Repeated Efforts."

> "We will always achieve what we desire through the process of constantly changing strategies and shifting directions until we do succeed."

In order for any success in any area of anyone's life they must know what they want. Two extreme examples that prove the principal that failure(s) are the strong foundation of any success were demonstrated in the development of a working light bulb and the other was the V-8 engine. We will now look at those two incredible innovations and technologies that we depend on, almost for our very lives.

It has been almost a hundred years since the advent of the electric light bulb and there have been numerous other technologies designed to create the same effect; which is providing light that is safe and reliable. Prior to the invention of the light bulb, the only source to light the darkness, was through the use of an open flame or fire.

In the interests of recognizing how this applies to a person's journey to recovery and making a successful and permanent life change, it is helpful to observe how the human brain and mind was able to achieve this miracle.

First it is necessary to understand that more than one person was attempting to find a cheap safe and reliable alternative to having to use fire and an open flame as the only source of lighting the darkness. It was Thomas Edison who was credited finally with achieving this miracle. Although he has been given full credit for this invention it should be clearly noted that he had a large group of researchers that were simultaneously working on the development of this invention.

The result of all this creative human energy and potential was that in a very short time they were able to fail over 10,000 times before they successfully had the prototype of a working electric light bulb. As you can see from this

139

example, if early on they had given up because it seemed hopeless as evidenced by thousands of failed tries, then they would not have been credited with this success. Success Would Have Been Attributed To The Person Or Team That Was Able To Overcome All Failure.

Every addict or alcoholic needs to understand and accept that their previous attempts or wreckage has absolutely nothing to do with their ability to absolutely succeed in making that necessary and needed life change. In Fact The Person Who Has Failed The Most Is In All Probability The Person Who Will Be The Next To Succeed with changing their life; as can be observed in the process that led to a working light bulb.

The second example is the direct result of the determination and vision of a single person. That person had a vision that existing technology could be completely improved and presented his vision and this challenge to his engineering team. The man having minimal education regarding what he was requesting his engineers to develop was considered by the engineering team to be ignorant of the facts, and the belief that what he was proposing was impossible to achieve.

As a result of their beliefs they proved that they were right and every effort that they tried failed. They brought all the evidence of their failure to the man with the dream and he ignored all the proof that it was impossible, and simply stated that if they could not produce what he envisioned, he would find a new engineering team that had the same vision and determination to create what had not existed before.

Since this engineering team enjoyed their position in that company They Had To Change Their Beliefs and Focus On The Possibility That All Things Have a Probability. Within a few months they had successfully developed a fully working prototype of what the man had envisioned and demanded. They Had Proven The Impossible Was Possible Once Their Beliefs Were Challenged and They Changed Them. As you can see from this example that despite beliefs that were strongly supported by evidence, those beliefs were in fact, not universal truths. The people who had these beliefs acted accordingly and produced the exact result that they believed would occur.

> "Whatever your beliefs about past treatment or efforts
> to control or stop, you must now know that none of
> those past failures have any control over you, other than
> the way you allow it to limit your beliefs regarding the
> possibility of future long term sobriety."

> "This means that if you believe that something is not

possible then you will not be able to achieve or change what you believe cannot be changed. However Once A Compelling Reason Is Seen Or Developed Then Impossible Beliefs Become Observable Facts."

It is through the technologies of neural success conditioning that the impossible is made possible. The human mind is capable of absolutely anything, and It Is Only The Limiting Beliefs That We Place Upon Our Minds That Hold Us Back From Achieving The Things We Deeply Need And Desire. In the case of the addict or the alcoholic that means they can absolutely achieve not only permanent sobriety, but create a fantastic and new future and destiny.

The man in the above story who had the belief and vision that what was believed by the great majority to be an impossibility, proved that Vision And Determination Is Stronger Than Belief, and any evidence that supports this false belief, is also wrong. It should be noted that the gentleman's name was Henry Ford and he was credited with the development of the first V-8 engine that enabled much more power at a much cheaper cost and revolutionized engine technology of the day.

These two examples demonstrate:

"That despite what seems to be facts many times are really only fiction; that developed upon the basis of having deceptive beliefs that ultimately proved to be false."

"It should also be noted that when a person has a strong belief they can, and will actually produce the evidence supporting that belief."

"Despite the reality that the belief and all the evidence may in fact is incorrect."

It is necessary to recognize that it is not recovery that is your goal; It Is Really The Rewards That You Perceive That You Will Receive From Recovery. In other words recovery is not what you want but what you want, are the rewards of recovery, so therefore you must sketch out how your life will be when drugs and alcohol are no longer in your life. The previous chapter on "Creating and Controlling Click" mapped out the exact procedure to accomplish this.

"If you do not sketch out a clear vision of what your life will be like after you stop using drugs or alcohol, then you absolutely cannot move towards that goal, you will not be able to make directional changes. Recovery efforts will have no "Click Power.""

"In fact just not using drugs or alcohol is not what your life is about. Your life is about everything that starts after you stop using, and you need to define, as well as to know what you want in your life, once you stop abusing substances."

To make a change in your life, you must first get clear on what your outcome is, and to know what you desire before you will have the ability to make a decision. The power to move towards that desire is created when you take action to get yourself to follow through immediately, regardless of any feelings to make a decision. It does not take time and you can change anything you desire right now.

"It is important to notice that while you are working on achieving your goals and desires that you must also be alert and determined, that if one thing does not fulfill what you desire, then move onto something else; but continue to move and continue to adjust until you reach your ultimate goal and that new vision of the new you."

One of the most powerful ways you can change yourself is to use a role model by finding someone who's getting the results that you want. Many times you may not know or be able to decide what action to take and that's why a role model is so important. A role model shows you the way, and in fact shows the accurate new direction to take. The senior members in AA or NA who are dedicated and enthusiastic about recovery are highly recommended. Although many people may have difficulty relating to these senior players in the 12 Step worlds, their experience and knowledge needs to be considered invaluable.

"It is important to remember that knowledge is not power it is only potential power. Even the AA book indicates in the chapter titled "More About Alcoholism" on page 39 states that:

"The actual or potential alcoholic (*or addict*) will be absolutely unable to stop drinking on the basis of self knowledge. This is a point we wish to emphasize and reemphasize, to smash home upon our alcoholic readers as it has been revealed to us out of bitter experience." (End of quote.)

"Therefore it is necessary to apply knowledge, but only action is what ultimately will lead to making changes, not just more information. Knowledge Is Not Enough, We Must Condition Ourselves And To Train Ourselves To Follow Through. As a direct result of taking action and following through, rapid changes begin to occur. The major obstacles of fear and indecision that are getting in the way can be pushed aside when you're ready to drive forward."

By working enthusiastically and passionately, whether you have the willingness or not, you will be able to develop the ability that will enabled you to breakthrough those fears, in much the same manner as when you go to the gym and workout with weights. You initially start with light small weights and then eventually you work up to the ability to lift very heavy weights.

It is just a matter of conditioning and determination. It is a matter of discipline and deciding that every failure we've ever experienced needs to be seen as well as appreciated for the opportunities that those experiences have given us. Not only have we received a tremendous amount of knowledge and understanding; but also it has given us even more wisdom.

"Wisdom is what life is made out of, and knowledge is what you have been taught. Wisdom is what you know and you know what you know because you live what you have lived. It's not someone else's theory and it is not someone else's opinion. It is your life experience and your life experiences give the invaluable wisdom to direct your own life. You must keep changing your approach until you succeed and with determination and persistence you absolutely will succeed."

It is essential that when you do the following exercises, that you do so with a very open mind and with strong determination. Regardless of whether you believe it will not work, it will absolutely work, if you work for it. By committing and doing these exercise every single day you will build the momentum to break through whatever obstacles have been in the way. You will succeed if you consistently take the recommended actions. You must use the principal of momentum; once you've made that decision, once you have decided you know what direction you will take, you must then take immediate action towards that path.

"What changes us is accessing the power to act through on the decision; that is how we change our lives. When a person fails over and over again despite all the effort, and they do not get the result they desire despite all the determination, All This Means is That the Plans Failed, Not the Person, and By Changing the Approaches Will Lead to Success."

This process of decision-making is the driving force that we need to understand in order for us to be able to push through obstacles till we do succeed. There are no problems, but there are challenges, and Each Challenge Requires The Right And Effective Decisions To Find The Best Strategies. To develop effective strategies it is necessary to gain understanding of the invisible forces that are driving the process of decision-making and to understand how Emotional States and Mental States are Definitely the Driving Forces in Our Decision-Making Processes.

If you're in a depressed state then you will make very different decisions then if you were in a joyously excited state. If somebody was to invite you out to dinner and you were very depressed, your decision would probably be, not to go, but if you were in a great mood, then without hesitation you would probably accept the invitation. In regards to emotional states it is our physiology the way we move our body and our gestures that actually defines and gives meaning to a particular emotional state.

A person who is depressed has a very specific and identifiable pattern of behavior that would be associated with depression and conversely someone who is very happy and excited will have a very different type of physiology. They Would Be Moving Differently, Talking Differently And Breathing

Differently; so it is the way we move our body that determines the way we feel.

Now many people believe that feelings just occur and they are without control; but it is very important to understand that in fact, it is the way you move your physiology, which will have much to do with the way you feel.

The next thing that has a very strong impact on the way you feel is what you focus on; If You Focus On Sad Things, then You Will Feel Sad and Or Depressed; But if You Focus On Positive and Good Things and Things that You're Grateful for; Then You Will Have Very Strong, Healthy Optimistic Positive Emotions as Well as Feelings.

The third thing that affects the way you feel has to do With the Meaning That You Assign to Events that Occur in Your Life. An example of this may be observed when searching for employment. There is much stress and pressure to find a job. It may take much effort and much investigation to succeed. Therefore when the person is looking for a job and they do not find work; they may go home and feel very discouraged, depressed and possibly even experience a sense of impending hopelessness.

If the same person who has been out there looking all day long has not found a job, and they go home with the positive attitude that they had achieved their job search for that day; then they would experience a sense of accomplishment in that they went to seven interviews today. They would believe that even though nobody hired or even showed any interest in them today, their effort was still fruitful.

This healthier attitude or belief enables them to Change the Meaning From Failure to Success by just Relabeling their Effort. By simply viewing it from the perspective or belief that they are getting much closer to being hired, because they know as well as believe that it is Just a Matter Of Getting Past the "No's" Before they Can Get an Acceptance.

If you expect to get immediately hired as soon as you walk into a place you may be setting yourself up for some real agonizing disappointment as well as deep discouragement; but if in reality you know it may take being rejected 20 times before you finally get accepted, then you will feel hopeful and satisfied with the efforts being made in your job search. Therefore It Depends On How You Define Your Actions That Will Cause You To Feel Deeply Depressed Or Even More Excited And Hopeful; Due To Your Belief That It's Going To Be A Short Period Of Time Because Each Rejection Means You Are Coming That Much Closer To Your Success.

"It should be clearly noted at this time that life is about
an endless stream of experience and it does not have
any significance to us until we assign a meaning to

any specific event. Different events will have different meanings and that meaning will be determined by the words that we choose to describe the event."

In the previous description of the people looking for a job, they could either assign their behavior with the meaning of "I will never get a job it's hopeless" or they can assign the same behavior with the idea of "I am getting very close now because I know that there is a certain amount of times that I'll be turned down but I will soon be accepted."

Since words drive and direct much of our emotional states, we need to be very much aware that in the event of a relapse the meaning that we assign will determine very different ways in which we would address it. If we choose to use words like "I have failed again, I am hopeless, I am helpless, I will never be able to stay sober" or we view it like "This is a valuable experience and gives me further information that will help me find the path to lasting sobriety."

Whatever belief we pick will create our reality through our ability and power to take responsibility for the words that we choose to think. It is even more important to understand that the words be choose to speak OUT LOUD have the greatest impact and influence on how we feel.

"It is the way we define our experiences and the meaning that we assign that controls the way we feel. As soon as words are expressed OUT LOUD describing the experience they trigger the sensation that we refer to as an emotional state, and it is our emotional state that creates what we perceive to be reality."

As you can see from these two very diverse and different responses to a life experience such as a relapse. There will be very different mental as well as emotional states that will occur as a direct result of the language chosen. In the first situation the person feels helpless, hopeless, depressed and this may create a lack of desire or motivation to improve or make any further changes.

In the second case the person may feel more positive and motivated to understand why they had failed, and then to make specific and certain changes based on what they had learned from the experience. So instead of feeling as a failure they would feel that the experience was a valuable lesson to be learned.

Therefore we can begin to see that our emotional states are a direct result of the meaning that we assign to events in our lives. The Meanings Of

Those Events Are Filtered Through The Way We Define The Words We Use. Emotions will also occur based upon the way we physically act when we are in or experiencing a specific situation. In addition to these is the fact that both are significantly influenced by what we choose to focus on.

These powerful forces (language-words we assign to an experience; physiology-the way we move our body or gestures or facial expressions; and our focus-what we see or more so how we choose to see an event) all influences the meaning we assign that in turn drives our emotional states, and ultimately our decision making processes

> "Many people drink, drug or use medications as a means of controlling their emotional states, as well as their mental states. They blindly do this without ever understanding that they could use their own ability and capability to make a decision to control what they focus on, how they use their body and the words they choose to use to describe their human experiences."

The most important factor to consider is that we have developed many habitual ways, in which our focus as well as the way we use our bodies, and the words we select to use all combine to give meaning to the experiences we have. Once certain habitual patterns have been well established they continue to occur almost invisibly, and we are not aware of how much influence and impact they are having on our lives.

> "Many times just becoming aware of the fact that there are basically millions of other things to focus on and there are many ways to view life experiences, gives you the absolute ability to make a decision to use your body and mind in new ways, that will significantly enable you to create new healthier habits."

We Need To Use Our Ability As Well As Our Capabilities If We Are Going To Learn To Manage Or Control Our Emotional Impulses And Effectively Break Those Old Patterns. It has been these patterns that unfortunately have been directing bad decisions and dictating wrong actions.

To Improve Our Lives We Need To Be Ready To Change What We Focus On. In Addition We Need To Be Alert To What We Speak OUT LOUD, As Well As Our Unspoken Non-Verbal Thoughts. We Need To Also Always

Remember That The Way We Move Our Body, All Contribute And Control, What We Emotionally Experience.

"We can change our emotions though the guaranteed techniques described earlier. Regarding utilizing the "Power of Positive Pressure" as well as developing the "Art of Controlling Click" and the "Power of Practicing Powerlessness" through the use of the "Art of Resistance in Action" as well as the "Power of Resisting Resistance" and practicing the "Art of Self Defiance" all enables the person to "Build Resistance Muscle" and take effective control of their emotions, and take the right actions regardless of the way they feel. It is through the use of these Powers and the Art of applying them that we can absolutely set ourselves free from whatever limiting beliefs we have ever had regarding our ability to achieve a lifestyle only previously dreamed about."

Emotions can be managed and even controlled, once a person understands that there are Three Components Of Emotion; Which are "Physiology, Focus and The Use of Language." Therefore we have the power and ability to change any emotion in a split second by taking control of all or any one of these three functions (Physiology, Focus And Use Of Language.)

A simple, effective and powerful demonstration of this may be experienced by doing the following: Hopefully you are sitting down and if you are not sitting down then do so at this time. Sit with your legs together but slightly apart and just bend your head down, placing your hands on your thighs or knees and look at your left foot only and stare at the left foot only for a few minutes and think sad or depressing thoughts and notice the feelings you are experiencing. If you are actually doing this exercise then you are probably not having a joyful nor pleasant experience, and in fact some people will not just begin to remember dark and unpleasant memories, but deeply feel sorrowful emotions as they look down and to the left!

"Now quickly shift your glance to your right foot and notice a distinct change in the intensity of the feeling that immediately results from CHOOSING to making a deliberate abrupt direct CHANGE in the direction of your focus."

148

> "You will feel a distinct change to a better sensation
> or at least some reduction in the sorrowful feelings.
> Now change your glance to straight out in front of you
> and notice an even greater improvement and change in
> feelings."

When you now look straight up at the sky or ceiling the feelings change even more noticeably in a very positive manner. In fact I challenge you to think those same sad thoughts that triggered sorrow and try to maintain them at the same intense level while looking up. In fact as soon as you glance straight up the corners of your mouth also turn up causing an involuntarily almost unnoticeable smile, but none the less a smile and that immediately changes and reduces the intensity.

To maximally experience rapid and radical changes in feelings and physiology by manipulating your focus do the following: Once again look at your left or right foot and try to smile and notice it is an absolute struggle to do so! Now looking down try to laugh, really laugh and see what results you get. If you are the rare person who can do this, even if you are able to smile or even laugh it will be empty and superficial. In other words you will not have a physiological change that mirrors the efforts.

Now quickly look straight up at the ceiling or the sky and smile and laugh. Do You Notice The Radical Changes In Your Feelings By Just Making This Change In Focus?

> "By CHOOSING to lift your head and changing the
> direction of your eyes NOT only made it very easy to
> Smile, but to genuinely Laugh and to experience it at
> a deep physiological level, NOT superficial, hollow or
> empty, but TO the physical core."

By doing this exercise you now know BEYOND A SHADOW OF DOUBT THAT YOU HAVE FULL CONTROL OF YOUR OWN EMOTIONS FROM DEEP SADNESS OR DESPAIR TO INSTANT LAUGHTER AND JOY. Notice that this exercise did not require the feeling of willingness, it only required following suggestions REGARDLESS of any feelings to do it or NOT do it.

> "In the end it boils down to just one thing, we want
> to be able to manage our emotions and to be able to
> absolutely create the mental and emotional states that

we desire, and to get the expected result for all the effort that we have made."

"It Should Be Clearly Seen By Now That Our Ability To Change Is Not Based On Our Ability Or Willingness To Change, but IT'S BASED ON THE STATE THAT WE ARE IN AT THAT MOMENT."

"If We Are In An Empowered State We Can Accomplish Almost Anything; but IF WE ARE IN A DISEMPOWERED STATE, WE MAY FAIL AT ALL WE ATTEMPT TO DO."

In the above exercise when you are looking down to the left you are physically positioned in one of the most disempowering ways possible and it is the poorest place to put your Focus, which results in minimum or even NO access to resources within yourself.

"When you look up, you automatically open up vast access to huge resources that just will NEVER materialize while looking down. This is the reason why depressed people feel depressed and stay depressed."

"All They Have To Do Is Look Up, Straight Up and Smile and Laugh, Laugh Loud, Laugh Deeply and Proudly—Get Ridiculous, Get Hysterical, it does NOT take Willingness To Look Up And Smile!"

"It is Automatic and Involuntary when a person does this the corners of their mouth will automatically turn up-it is just a matter of gravity!"

Depressed people do NOT look up and if they DO it is only for a brief moment. If you are depressed I challenge you to do this, NOT just try this! But DO this and DO it with Anger or Passion, but Lift Your Head High and laugh like an Ass!

By the way the reason I sad laugh like an ass is because it definitely changes your existing Focus and your inner dialogue or language to: "What Did He Say?" "What Is Wrong With This Man?" or "He Is Fucken Crazy." or

"I Won't Do It" or "It Won't Work For Me" or "What Do I Have To Lose?" or "I Will Do This Just To Prove This Asshole Wrong." Go Ahead, "What Do You Have To Lose??" Prove Me Wrong-PROVE GRAVITY WRONG!"

> "Management and control of our states is the key to basic freedom and it's not about our ability or capability. If you're in a state of fear then that is what you will experience, but if you're in a state of confidence then you improve your chance to be successful. So the key is the state and the Control Of the State Is Essential to Being Able to Change any State Into an Empowering Force. It is this power to change our states that is the driving force behind change and success."

It is this ability to shift and change states that enables you to access greater and greater resources. When you are feeling depressed you will access different resources then when you're happy and joyful. When in a disempowered state such as depression or anxiety; then there will be limited access to needed resources.

YOU HAVE TO KNOW WHY YOU WANT TO DO SOMETHING BEFORE YOU WILL BE ABLE TO DO IT. It is NOT as important to figure out how to stay sober, as it is to Have Strong and Compelling Reasons Why You Should Stay Sober. Therefore if you know why you should stay sober you WILL have stronger reasons to do so.

STRONG OR EVEN STRONGER REASONS WILL DRIVE YOU TO FIND MORE AND MORE WAYS TO MAINTAIN SOBRIETY. The stronger the reason the more deeply it is experienced as a Feeling or an Emotion. Weaker and less important reasons remain in the form of just a passing thought and "A Passing Thought Does Just That—It Just Passes!"

Another term for a passing thought is when the person may have had what I earlier referred to as "good intentions." By the way, remember, my mother always yelled and preached "Jerry, Good Intentions Pave the Way Straight to Hell!!"

It is very important to recognize that the reason most addicts and alcoholics have so much difficulty with staying clean and sober, is due to the fact that the Experience of Using Substances is Felt Deeply in their EMOTIONAL CORE. Conversely most of the experience of recovery or sobriety occurs only in the mind and there is very minimal impact at the emotional core.

"In other words using creates a deeply Powerful and

> Profoundly felt emotional experience, and the feelings and experience of recovery can NOT compete or reach the same depth of feeling."

> "As a Result of This Fact, Recovery has Much Less Attraction due to there being MUCH less emotional intensity or reinforcement." "Although many recovering people would argue with this, it is still nonetheless a fact for most addicts and alcoholics, at least in their initial beginning stages of sobriety."

It needs to be also noted that if the person has become involved with a 12 Step program, the only time they will really experience a powerful and strong reinforcement in regards to staying clean and sober is when they achieve specific periods of clean time. Depending on the program they are involved with, the number of times they will experience strong reinforcement is limited to only six or seven times in the first year.

The ritual that provides this reinforcement to celebrate successful continuous sobriety is the "Chip or Key Tag" ceremony. This means that only after the 24 hour "Chip or Tag," or after the 30 day; 60 day; 90 day; six month; nine month or one year time periods, that they are provided a Potentially Profoundly felt and deep Emotional Experience. It is at those times and ONLY at those times that the person is given applause and public recognition for doing the right things.

> "It is obvious that ONLY six or seven opportunities in an entire year provides a very minimal emotional reward in return for the immense work IT takes to stay abstinent."

> "Once again it must be strongly emphasized as well as recognized that any time the person thinks about their past drinking or drugging experience or about alcohol or drugs, the very thought has a Stronger emotional impact than their previously Appreciated or their upcoming Anticipation of Participation in the ritual of the "Chip or Tag" ceremony."

The only effective method to provide a strong competitive emotional experience is to understand the IMPORTANCE THAT "RIGHT ACTIONS" NEED TO BE REINFORCED WITH THE "RIGHT EMOTIONS." Any and every identified as well as unidentified emotion in your life must be filtered through your nervous system. It Is Impossible To Experience Any Feeling Unless It Is Experienced At Some Physiological Level.

Any change in your physiology is a change in your nervous system and by changing the nervous system you change the way you feel. The most effective way to change the way you feel is to change your motion. When you change the way you move your body, such as the rate or depth of breath, it immediately changes the emotions you are experiencing. Additionally the way you move your body whether you move fast or slow will completely change the way you feel. Changing Your Physiology Is Actually Faster Than Doing Drugs. DRUGS REQUIRE MINUTES OR SECONDS TO WORK AND CHANGING YOUR PHYSIOLOGY WILL CREATE CHANGE IN FEELINGS INSTANTANEOUSLY.

"Every time you take "right actions" you must connect that effort to creating the "right feelings." Failure to do this means that taking "right actions" will quickly lose its appeal. The only method on earth to accomplish this is by engaging your ability to FORCE yourself to celebrate passionately and loudly EACH and EVERY "right action." To celebrate you must fully engage your body through STRONG changes in your PHYSIOLOGY, and unless this is done, there is Absolutely No Way To Build Strong Interest in Recovery."

"FAILURE TO BUILD STRONG INTEREST ALLOWS THE PASSION ATTACHED TO DRUGS AND ALCOHOL TO CONTINUE TO DOMINATE THE EMOTIONAL CORE OF THE PERSON."

"This results in the addiction becoming more emotionalized than recovery. This will lead to probable failure to maintain interest in staying abstinent."

When a person speaks with much animation, Emotion, Excitement and even Enthusiasm when telling war stories they are Emotionalizing the addiction. It is vital that they abandon any Out Loud verbalizations about substance use, abuse, drinking, or drugging lifestyle, and LEARN that it is equally; but even MORE essentially important to speak Out Loud with strong passion, as well as positive ENERGY when describing actions they are taking or will be taking in recovery.

To demonstrate this principal or Power of Right Actions—Right Feelings," it is strongly recommended you engage in the following exercises. For the next ten days it is essential that you learn to force yourself to take "Right Actions" to recognize the "Power of Right Actions—Right Feelings" achieved through the effective practice of the "Art of Service and Sacrifice." (See the chapter on "Definitions Determine Directions" for more detail regarding the use of the "Power of Spin" through the use of the "Art of the Second Thought".)

After completing any "Right Action" you MUST force yourself whether you Want to or NOT and especially if you do not WANT to! You MUST do this whether YOU are Willing to or NOT! You have to CELEBRATE the fact that you took the Challenge and did the "Right Action(s)" that YOU in fact accomplished this achievement. The only way YOU can MAKE this matter and FEEL this SUCCESS is by doing the following:

> "Bring your arm up and make a tight fist, now snap it down aggressively as you state OUT LOUD and with passion "I DID IT!!!" this may seem too simple but it will guarantee that you WILL begin to embed it into your nervous system."

"To strengthen the experience add words or phrases such as "YEA I DID IT.!!" or "YES YES!" such as "I did it!! YES-YES!"or whatever you say when you experience a great achievement. It will also be necessary to say the phrase OUT LOUD every time and to do so with high verbal energy and stretch out the words "YEAA I DIDD IT!!" While verbalizing and celebrating your completed "Right Action" it will also be necessary to repeat this several times rapidly in a row and each time saying with more intensity until it is Really—REALLY felt!!

If this seems awkward or strange to do just remember the last time your team won during the last minutes in the game. If you verbally expressed your happiness and satisfaction with the spectacular achievements of the team you were applauding for, how did you show it? Most people "yell" at least and most people repeat OUT LOUD "DID YOU SEE THAT, DID YOU SEE THAT." Then they repeat what they saw "HE CAME IN AND

SLAMMED THAT BALL LIKE HE WAS PLAYING TENNIS!!" or "That Toss Was In The Air And There No Way Could Have Done It- But WOW!!" This excitement that is easily expressed during a sporting event can easily be done when you recognize that by taking "Right Actions" You Have Won And Won In A Huge Way!

> "The mere fact that this is a true challenge and the only thing getting in the way is your "asinine idiotic sensations in your body, and you overcame the sense of awkwardness or discomfort, when you yelled out "YEA I MADE MY BED-YEA Yea!!," means you WON-you overcame your emotions and took control of the play and directed your emotions."

> "REMEMBER IF YOU DO NOT TAKE AGGRESSIVE "RIGHT ACTIONS" TO MANAGE YOUR EMOTIONS, THEN YOUR EMOTIONS WILL MANAGE YOU!"

> "As you challenge yourself, and overcome yourself and direct yourself in the manner described, you will experience "Right Feelings" through the use of the "Power of Right Actions—Service and Sacrifice."

It should be emphasized that anything and everything that you engage in on a daily or hourly basis can offer opportunities to practice this suggestion. Every time you stop yourself and become consciously aware to make the bed, put the glass or dish away, to apologize, to hold the door open for the old lady or anybody else, to turn the TV off or glance away from the computer when someone is trying to talk to you, stop at the stop sign, pray on your knees in the morning, eat breakfast or choose to eat healthier, to do the laundry, put away the clothes, clean the bathroom or virtually anything else that upon "First Thought" you would fail to do. When you act on "Second Thought" then you are forcing yourself to become more consciously aware.

> "It is though this process that you will "Build Strong Resistance Muscle" that will give you the strength to resist the offer or opportunity to use drugs or alcohol when that temptation presents itself. Through aggressive

effort with this process you will be well prepared to manage any threat to your recovery. ALL THREATS GET THEIR POWER FROM UNCONTROLLED EMOTIONAL STATES. By practicing the "Art of Second Thought" frequently the action of acting on "Second Thought" which is always focused on doing the "Very Next Right Thing" and forcing yourself to celebrate it LOUDLY and PROUDLY will enable you to more easily manage uninvited and destructive emotional impulses that could undermine recovery work and efforts."

At this time it needs to be reemphasized that whatever we are Focused on at the moment is what determines whether we are moving towards something or away from something. It is NOT a mystery of why addicts and alcoholics QUIT doing the things and behaviors that were keeping them sober. Since it is emotional states that drive direction and motivation, then whatever you Focus on is what's most real to you at that precise moment and what determines whether there is an association to pain or pleasure in regards to what you are doing in that moment. If you want to control your Focus, then you must condition yourself to know, that NOT taking a positive action, is going to be more painful than taking a negative action.

"There is NO choice you must take on this ten day challenge to stop and make yourself consciously aware of each and every action you take, and to take a significant moment to CELEBRATE—Really Celebrate each and every "Right Action.""

"Each time you see yourself making the winning play celebrate OUT LOUD you are indeed a champion! Act like a champion, sound like one and most of all FEEL LIKE ONE!! Feel the "Power of Right Actions—Right Feelings.""

Another example of this is when someone tries to diet instead of Focusing on trying to lose weight; it is much more powerful to FOCUS on how wonderful it will be to be thin and healthy. To Focus on that vision is a more effective method than resisting eating too much and when you eat better, yell, "I DID IT!!" "YEA YEA! YES YES!!"

"IF YOU CHOOSE TO IGNORE THIS SUGGESTION THEN ALL YOUR EFFORTS TO MAKE A CHANGE WILL BE FUTILE AS WELL AS A TOTAL WASTE OF YOUR TIME!

"In Order To Be Properly Compensated For All The Hard Work That You Do To Stay Clean and Sober, You Must CELEBRATE Each and Every Success with LOUD Very OUT LOUD Passion and Enthusiasm.

If you fail to add this to each and every achievement and accomplishment in your recovery, then you will be short changing yourself and feeling short changed!

"IT IS ONLY THOUGH THE FORCED AND DELIBERATE ENGAGEMENT OF YOUR NERVOUS SYSTEM THAT ANY RECOVERY EFFORTS HAVE ANY CHANCE OF BEING REINFORCED."

You do NOT need to wait for a specific period of time to celebrate success such as the way the "Chip and Tag" ceremony does. You can create your own recognition and develop healthy pride and healthy confidence through this ten-day challenge. ONCE YOU HAVE DONE IT FOR TEN DAYS IT IS STRONGLY RECOMMENDED THAT YOU DO IT FOREVER!! Why wait for a few passing moments to feel and celebrate success, when you have the constant opportunity to do so from hour to hour and day to day.

"All your recovery actions must be forcefully connected to positive and pleasurable feelings and emotions. Remember that whatever you FOCUS on becomes your immediate reality and by changing your FOCUS you can immediately change how or what you associate to or evaluate in terms of pain or pleasure. The controlling force in your life is what you link up to pain and pleasure. If going to meetings daily is exciting, challenging and fun then you WILL feel strong motivation to attend; but if they become boring, repetitive and tiresome that WILL lead to quitting meetings."

"This shift in emotional states will cause you to stop

doing something you really need and should want to be doing. It is NOT a mystery of why we fail to do what we know we need to do." "The reason for the lack of motivation is that we attribute more pain to doing it than not doing it and until this changes you CANNOT control your behavior and you will still fail to have any real CONTROL over your life."

There's nothing stopping you from having the quality of sobriety that you crave; you have the ability; you may even have the desire and you certainly have made the promises to stay clean; but if you are not clean, then there is something inside you; somewhere deep inside you; there is the belief that sobriety means greater pain than active addiction.

"We need to use this pain and pleasure force within us to produce lifelong success by learning how to USE pain as your greatest motivator to give you the ability to Change Your Focus and therefore the ability to Change a Behavior Instantly by learning how to control the driving forces of pain and pleasure."

The mere fact that most of the actions that you take to recover will NOT come with an automatic "Right Feeling" means it is absolutely essential that you force a connection of a "Right Feeling" by consciously taking the time and making the effort to truly CELEBRATE each and every "Right Action," LOUDLY and PROUDLY! Then use the "Art of Second Thought" to alert you to Fully Celebrate Moment to Moment Each Daily Achievement and Accomplishment.

If you are still struggling with comprehending or understanding this concept of the "Art of Second Thought" then I will politely remind you that I strongly suggested way back in the beginning in this book's Introduction that the reader first read the chapter titled "Definitions Determine Direction" which fully explains the "Art of Second Thought."

The next exercise is drawn from one of Anthony Robbins most powerful techniques that he refers to as the "Dickens Method or Model" To gain the greatest benefit from this you need to write down and do this exercise with deep passion and commitment, or you will never learn how to manage, the creative and destructive forces within you. By doing this exercise you are going to build your muscle to achieve control over these powerful influences.

First you need to write down the things or attitudes or feelings that have been blocking you from taking right effective actions in the past, then you need to write the pain in depth and detail that you have experienced through failing to change. Next you will write all the positive things that you associate to using drugs and alcohol in depth and detail and then recognize and REALLY feel the pain and loss you will experience once drugs and alcohol are NO longer options for you to use.

Include how relationships will be changed or lost, the way you will never be able to celebrate in that certain manner ever again, how New Years will be different and therefore virtually every other special occasion as well as every holiday will also be very different, in fact Every Day Will Be Different Once You Recover!

For this moment forget about being an addict or an alcoholic and with all its attendant suffering; just remember the glorious rush when the chemicals of your choice were ingested and savor the memory of the moment they Slammed Into Your Brain! This will lead clearly to seeing all the benefits you experience as a direct result of using mind and mood altering substances.

Now write in depth and detail all the bad and terrible things that you have done to yourself and any loved ones. Write down at the very least ten or more things that you will lose or cause you or your loved ones to suffer if you fail to recover. It will be even more effective to write twenty or thirty things that will happen if you continue to fail to stay clean and sober. Express strongly and write next to those ten to thirty or more consequences, all the pain you will suffer if you are irresponsible about following through with more positive, productive and healthier self directed recovery actions.

Take a moment and simplify this challenge and write easy actions that you're going to take. Such as making the bed every day or attending AA or NA daily or doing a physical work out, going to the gym, saying prayers or practicing meditation and doing Yoga, eating healthier foods, putting the dishes away, cleaning the bathroom or putting your clothes away. Once again the choice of actions are limitless and entirely in your personal control. There are pages of suggestions in the chapter 17 titled "The Power of Right Actions." Select ten or twenty things to challenge yourself with and then write next to each action why you should take it, and the pain that you will experience if you don't follow through.

"The Next Part Of This Exercise Is Vital For Your Success, And Failure To Fully Follow Directions Will Greatly Reduce Your Chances For Staying Sober And Clean Or Changing Your Life."

You will now need to write down in depth and detail all the pleasure and all the good things that will happen or occur by following through with your self directed Right actions and activities. It is important that you capture with words all the excitement and joy not only you will experience, but your loved ones too.

> "It is through this process that you will be able to create clear direction and a vision that will pull you forward and create the driving force that will lead ultimately to your success not just with the ability to stay clean and sober; but to change your entire life and destiny."

This process is so important and effective I will repeat the instruction and warn you that failure to take on this work and challenge will be to not only cheat yourself, but to rob the ones that love you. If You Do Not Want To Do This For You, Then Do It For The Ones You Think You Love, And By Doing It Prove That You Indeed Do Love Them.

> "It does not matter how awkward, annoying, strange or especially uncomfortable this challenge seems to you. Do not let those asinine, stupid and silly sensations that block you from trying new actions, STOP YOU."

Step up against those dumb feelings and take possession of your own mind, use your birthright that enables you to take possession and control your own mind. Learn to direct your own mind to whatever ends you desire. Take control of your feelings so they stop dragging you around like a ring in a bull's nose that enables a powerful beast to be controlled and dragged about. Take charge of your life, and tell those disempowering, sabotaging and destructive feelings to go "F" themselves. Force yourself to do this work!

> "Remember my passion is to prove to you, and have you prove to yourself that recovery does NOT require any willingness at all!! All that is required is that you passionately and deliberately and forcefully take control of your behavior, IGNORE WHAT YOU THINK AND FEEL! Just change your actions and NOT only will you be set free from addiction but An Entire Universe Of Opportunities Will Open Up To You!"

"Now without further hesitation, if you have not done
the above exercise do it NOW whether you want to or
not, and ESPECIALLY if you <u>do not</u> want to do it!!"

Once again step one is write down the things you should have been doing and write down the pain you experienced through failing to do what was Right, needed and necessary. Step two—write down all the pleasure you got by NOT being responsible and having failed by NOT taking that action.

Keep in mind that even though you may have failed, you may still have experienced a sense of relief by not having to take responsibility. Now step three is to write the opposite, meaning to write all the PAIN that you will SUFFER if you fail to take these self directed actions, and what you will LOSE if you don't take these actions.

Carefully detail how much it will COST you personally, emotionally, financially, the damage and destruction that WILL be done to relationships in your life, your self-esteem, if you don't make a change. NOW write the loss and suffering that results from NOT changing. List the extensive loss, misery and deep suffering and project this insanity, this madness out for ONE year, TWO years, FIVE years, TEN and even TWENTY years.

"Do not minimize, diminish or decrease the discomfort,
but feel the ache and feel the deep DEEP torment as
year after year passes and you refuse to use the tools to
enable you to succeed and CHANGE your life."

See and feel the loss of all your dreams and potential. Feel the depth of hate others will have towards you instead of pride and admiration. Feel the intensity of your own shame and self hate! Now do step four and write a list of all the things that you will immediately gain by taking these self-directed actions, all the good things that will happen by taking these actions. Recognize that as a direct result of taking these actions that IMMEDIATELY you will gain strength as well as a sense of spirituality.

If you have done this exercise thoroughly and honestly as well as passionately, then you will teach yourself how to instantaneously… Change The Desire To Use Drugs Or Alcohol Into Pure Disgust!

"You need to be in charge of your own desires and to set
your own destiny and to control the two driving forces
of pain and pleasure."

"You need to develop the skill in controlling what you associate to pain or pleasure and to redefine them and make them work for you instead of against you."

"ASSOCIATING ANY PLEASURE TO THE USE AND EXPERIENCE OF USING DRUGS OR DRINKING MUST BE SYSTEMATICALLY DESTROYED WITH EXTREME PREJUDICE."

"Only you can force this connection that will discourage the use of mood altering substances."

"Once again failure to FORCE yourself to do these exercises and the TEN DAY CHALLENGE, means that you are allowing the intensely pleasurable, exciting, appealing natural occurring feelings that are associated with drug as well as alcohol use to Control And Dominate Your Decision Making Process!"

The issue of why so many recovering people allow their emotions to direct their decisions needs to be understood in more depth. Regarding this tendency, it is helpful to first explore whether feelings have the power to control our actions. Many times after a person returns to active substance abuse, they will relate that the Urge Was Too Strong To Resist, and in fact, they may have had the telephone number of a sponsor or some other supportive person; but they Felt Totally Paralyzed From Being Able To Call For Help. This paralysis is due to the fact that addictive desires are like a "Hypnotic Lock" not only on a persons mind but their emotions as well!

"The perception that they were powerless to take control of the moment has been reinforced too many times in the 12 step meetings."

The person hears almost at every meeting that one or more people attending the meeting "were powerless to stop themselves," from picking up a drink or a drug. "I could have called someone, but I guess I just wanted to get high." When a person says this they are acknowledging that it is indeed a matter of choice to relapse or return to substance abuse.

"Although it sounds like it is a choice, it is helpful to understand that when a person becomes intensely overwhelmed, by some kind of feeling or emotion that they cannot manage or control, this feeling or belief often leads to acting out behaviors."

The acting out many times is in the form of returning to active substance abuse. Through the "Power of Resisting Resistance" and practicing the "Art of Self Defiance" the impact of this acting out behavior can be reduced and even possibly eliminated depending on the strength of the commitment to utilize the "Eleven Arts and the Essential Eleven Powers"

Acting out behaviors can also manifest themselves in many other ways; such as resisting or refusing to maintain certain needed recovery actions and attitudes. When a person acts against their own good judgment they are referred to as being "impulsive." If you believe that impulsivity is the cause for many relapses; then you might conclude that the person "Could Not Help Themselves Due To Being Just Too Impulsive." In my opinion a person who is truly "too impulsive" usually spends most of their life in jail and prison. The mere fact that someone has no control over their own actions means that they are going to break the law and suffer the associated consequences.

Many addicts and alcoholics have been wrongfully convinced that they are "powerless" and basically a victim of their "chronic progressive illness." Once they have accepted that they are "powerless" many of them use this as an excuse and justification for their ongoing failure to maintain any long-term sobriety.

"The failure to stay clean and sober is NOT due to "powerlessness" and or "being too impulsive" it is the direct result of being to lazy to utilize effective management options and techniques that have been previously described in great detail."

"Sometimes this is due to ignorance rather than lack of motivation. Whatever the reason the result is the same the person is incapable of maintaining any lasting recovery.

"The Ignorance Lies In The Belief That They Cannot

Change Their Behavior Unless There Is Willingness To
Do So."

As mentioned numerous times this belief is a tragic lie and no one needs
to wait for his or her feelings to give him or her permission to change.

"Change is neither determined nor dependent upon any feeling."

"Change has nothing to do with neither the way a person feels nor what
they are feeling."

"Change has nothing to do with intentions or impulses."

"Change only requires one simple action—

"Change It, Whatever it is!"—Regardless of any feelings whatsoever."

Let's return for a moment to the proposition that one of the reasons for
a person to relapse is due to "impulsivity." I believe that almost all people at
one time or another have thought about killing themselves or someone else;
but that person and the other people are all alive at this time, so therefore the
thought of killing did NOT manifest itself in their own or anyone else's death.
It was just a passing thought and no matter how frightening it may have been;
the Thought Alone Could Not And Did Not Cause Any Deaths.

To expand on this for a moment, I also believe that there are people
that when they go to a bank to withdraw cash or cash their paycheck, have
experiences in which they sometimes think "It would be nice if I could just
reach over and take more of that stuff than what they are giving me." Or some
people when they are in a store may have the thought "I could put that in my
pocket" or "No body is looking."

What stops these people is the awareness that indeed if they "follow the
feeling" they will become criminals and in the case of taking the money from
the tellers draw, that is referred to as "Bank Robbery" and comes with some
nasty consequences.

Therefore most people do not act on impulse and most addicts do not act
on impulse despite their belief otherwise. Any one that is too "impulsive" to
control themselves has usually been apprehended and identified as a criminal
or they spend much of their time in the criminal justice system.

"What is it that makes us believe that we cannot use the
same restraint when it comes to returning to the use of
substances? The truth of the matter is that addicts and
alcoholics drink and drug because somehow it makes
sense for them to do so."

"For a person to be consciously aware that they are

about to risk everything that they have worked so hard for, to get back into their lives, for just a brief moment of chemical bliss; certainly does not make any sense at all."

"The deep dilemma for the person who relapses; is the sad fact that they usually have not carefully thought out or weighed the pros and cons of giving up their sobriety."

Afterwards they try to reason out what happened, but they absolutely are unable to find any identifiable causes.

"The reason they have relapsed is that they allowed their emotions to dictate their actions. In other words they failed to develop or use the "Art of Self Defiance" as well as the "Art of Second Thought!"

Some people may reflect that it is because they became "impulsive," but the real matter is to know why they allowed themselves to fail. Is it really a matter of choice or is it actually due to being totally powerless?

"If It Is A Matter Of Choice, Then It Absolutely Can Never Be A Matter Of Powerlessness, Because You Have To Be Able To Exercise Some Kind Of Power Whenever You Have To Choose Between Alternatives."

"If it is a matter of being totally powerless; then it can never be a matter of choice, because to exercise choices a person must have the ability and the power to select."

Since most people do not understand the true nature of addiction, they tend to get very caught up in these two perceptions of the cause of relapse.

Is there possibly another more obvious reason for recovery failure, such as being too lazy to care about the need for management? A good parallel disease to compare this to, is Diabetes, and just simply stated, does the Diabetic have control, or are they powerless over their personal health. It is quite obvious that the Diabetic is completely in control of the management of the disease, even though they may be powerless to cure their Diabetes.

"In the same sense the alcoholic or addict are powerless to be cured from their addiction; but they have 100%

control over the management of their disease, as does the Diabetic."

Earlier it was stated that the addict is just lazy and that is why they fail. Is the Diabetic also at risk for being lazy, and if they fail to manage their disease would that lead to severe medical consequences? Does the alcoholic risk medical and other consequences if they are just too lazy to take the necessary precautions to maintain a lasting recovery? In both these situations the answer is of course" yes." Is it also possible that both allowed their idiotic sensations and feelings to dictate irresponsible decisions resulting in failing to take effective actions to manage these conditions?

In returning to the original question of whether an addict or alcoholic have choice or power over their feelings; it needs to be accepted that first, any human being has absolute and total control over number one, their actions; but to a lesser extent, number two, their emotions. Despite what they may say or how they may act they have the absolute ability to speak and act differently!

"If a person acts in an irresponsible manner that is potentially harmful to them or the people around them, are they then choosing to put themselves and others at risk for injury? Would a loving caring person deliberately endanger the welfare of their spouse or child? Of course they would not and yet their actions definitely do."

Since it is not rational to believe that a loving caring person would deliberately hurt someone they care about, but do. This needs to be understood in the context of the paradox of how "love and caring" fail to change a person's behavior.

Therefore "Is it a Disease or is it a Choice?" This is presented in great depth and detail in the Chapter on "Understanding Addiction." It should be emphasized however "If you believe something to be so—then it is so!" The next thing that must be asked is "So is that the way you want it to be?" The debate of whether a relapse is a choice needs to be settled.

"If we examine this from a common sense point of view, then it is more than obvious that no addict or alcoholic who has gained some clean time or sobriety would intentionally and deliberately hurt the people whom they love and who loves them. To believe that

they have a choice is to also believe that they do not care
about the ones they love."

If they say and believe they love someone they could never deliberately harm them; so therefore there must be another reason than that of choice. If it follows that it was not a choice, then it has to be accepted as a disease or a symptom of a disease. Any time someone drinks or drugs it can only be attributed to one of two things. Was it a choice? Or the failure to remain clean and sober was due to a disease.

"Many times a person may state "I was clean for a few years and relapsed and then I just did not want to stop." It should be noted that when a person states that "I just did not want to stop" they falsely accuse themselves of having made or currently making bad decisions; whereas their inability to stop or control their own behaviors simply demonstrates the degree and severity of their condition."

"Also the belief that they somehow are responsible creates a strong sense of toxic shame. Shame is a very deadly emotion and feeling and needs to be carefully defused. Shame creates a sense of worthlessness and this significantly and severely undermines their chance to remain clean and or sober."

It is also helpful to notice the contradiction that is expressed through the words of "I didn't want" or "I was not ready" or "I just did not have the willingness." The contradiction occurs in the sense that the first step of the program indicates that "We are powerless" and the addict's or alcoholic's words "I didn't" and "I wasn't" and "I just" all indicate that the person has power over choices, and in fact they are expressing that they intentionally and willfully chose to engage in a destructive action that is harmful to them and destructive to the relationships they have with other people.

It was emphasized that no healthy minded person would intentionally and deliberately engage in behaviors that are harmful to themselves and others. In fact anyone who would observe a person's self defeating behaviors would conclude that "the person must be crazy or just stupid." Little does anyone realize how accurate an assessment this is by that person.

> "The truth is that an addict or alcoholic suffers from severe chronic mental illness and their use of a substance is just the symptom of the problem and not the cause of it."

The proof that they are mentally ill is found in the continued use of a destructive substance despite the severe consequences it causes.

> "It can also be found in the fact that the addict or alcoholic become overwhelmed with the feeling or belief that if "I don't get a drink or that drug I WILL die."

This obsessive driving force that leads to total self-destruction is a huge paradox.

> "To avoid the devastation and obliteration of your life you will need to develop or create a counter force to this obsessive driving force."

What can be done to control this force when it is almost equal to a violent and powerfully intense forest fire that is burning out of control—threatening everything in its path?

> "This obsessive force just like the raging forest fire if left unchecked will absolutely totally annihilate everything you have or are working for!"

What do you do when an entire mountain is engulfed in fire so intense that there is no amount of water, firemen or resources to put it out? Do you let it burn itself out and just accept the destruction of homes, loss of property as well as people's lives? Do you just stand by and let the forest fire of your addiction destroy you and your family's lives?

> "When you have to fight an unstoppable force greater than anything you can stop it with. You need to fight that force by using that very same force against itself—in other words you have to "Fight Fire with Fire!"

When there is a driving force almost as strong as natural instincts, that dictates that a person has to put a poisonous substance into their body, or they will die, and it is the very act of putting that substance into the body that can cause death; then this is a very TWISTED perception. Like the forest fire you need to "Fight Fire with Fire!"

Since everything involving the use of substances and addiction is highly emotionally charged; then the addict or alcoholic will need to find and engage an equally intense emotional force or power.

This force is created by developing the ability to resist the temptation or seduction of the deep desire to drink or drug, through a conscious effort.

> "The person MUST scream out passionately, LOUDLY and PROUDLY verbalizing OUTLOUD statements such as: "Get the FUCK out of my life!" Scream it so you hear it LOUDLY in your own ears! Yell and Shout for this is—the only way to "Fight Fire with Fire!" Scream and cry LOUDLY "I don't want to hurt my family anymore!" "I want to be a Good father or a Good mother—I want this out of my life!" Feel the rage against the drug or alcohol and don't be a WIMP! Attack Aggressively this Obsessive Destructive Driving Force with an equal level of Power, Personal Power, the Power to effectively find and use "Fire to Fight Fire!"

If you have not already read about the concept and absolute NEED to emotionalize your statements and experiences regarding recovery; then the above is a reminder. Addiction is a raging force in your life and it is fueled by intense passion. It is this overwhelming intense passion that undermines most addicts efforts to stay clean and sober.

> "There is NO choice you must engage equally deep passion for recovery efforts and achievements or they are futile useless efforts. The only way that you can create the level of force that can overpower your addiction is to literally SCREAM back at it!"

By strongly engaging your vocal cords and involving your nervous system is the only way that you can empower yourself against the "Unstoppable Force" of addiction!

"The addiction is deeply woven into your nervous system and that is where the constant obsession to drink or use drugs originates. Due to it being so deep in your nervous system it maintains a strong "hypnotic lock" on your thoughts as well as your feelings."

To smash this lock you need a Force that is equal to it, and that force is your ability to choose to intensely engage your nervous system in the manner just described.

"The addicts or alcoholics natural instincts for survival have been supplanted with an obsession, that taking a deadly substance somehow is necessary to stay alive."

"To fight this you must use the power of emotions, you must engage your nervous system in a strong "LOUD and PROUD" positive manner to counter act the TWISTED "Thoughts, Feelings and Beliefs" that drive addiction and alcoholism!"

"It should be further noted that the mental illness that blinds the person from recognizing the truth and the paradox that hides the truth, occurs due to the sad fact that at times—

"Since The Mind Is Sick, So Are The Components Of The Mind Which Are "Thought, Feelings And Beliefs."

An example of this that most people can relate to is: After making serious mistakes the person asks themselves the question. "What was I thinking?" Then it should be noted that anytime a person reflects back to some awareness, that they just did something stupid or wrong, they also become painfully aware that this can only occur; when it matches the "belief" part of that wrongful thought.

The person would only take the action when they "believe "they know what the outcome will be." Therefore the next question they would ask is "What made me believe I could do that?" Since the mental illness manifests itself in these ways it is also important to recognize that even more important than "thoughts and beliefs;" is the fact that most addicts and alcoholics take actions based on "feelings."

> "Multiple examples of this would be "I did not feel like calling my sponsor, doing the steps; attending a meeting, washing the dishes, taking a shower, apologizing, putting away the laundry, getting out of bed"...etc, etc—

> "They allow their feelings to dictate their actions and this is the formula for absolute and complete recovery failure,"

> "It is only when a person learns and practices resisting acting on their feelings; that they become stronger and more capable of saying no when temptations arise. If the person has been more focused on doing what they feel like doing or not doing; then they are that much more prone to acting carelessly and impulsively and relapsing due to having had no practice, resisting actions based on emotions."

We will explore how throughout your entire life there is only one principle that will lead you to lifelong sobriety. "Resistance is the Key" and by learning to effectively utilize and manage your "Power of Resisting Resistance" you will not only be totally free from any risk of returning to substance abuse; but you will be completely liberated to pursue any dream you have, and will actually be able to achieve them all.

Failure to learn and utilize this key will throw tremendous counter forces of destruction back into your life and instead of practicing the "Art of Self Defiance" and the discipline to use the "Power of Resisting Resistance" you will by default absolutely be subconsciously, and possibly, and even foolishly consciously "Reaching" for drugs and alcohol.

> "In the final analysis as they say "You are either moving away from a drug or you are moving towards a drink or a drug" and it really is "just that simple." To put it clearly

> "If you are not Resisting then you are Reaching."

> "Resistance in the very end is the only thing between you and picking up trouble and the stronger your Resistance the healthier you are."

It really is no different than when your body builds resistance to bacteria or a virus. This chapter has absolutely taught you the "Art of Second Thought" which is the "Power of Spin."

"The Art of Resistance into Resolution" which is the "Power of Practicing Powerlessness" The "Art of Self Defiance" which is the "Power of Resisting Resistance." The "Art of Word Selection" which is the "Power of Transformational Communication."

You now, if you choose have the ability to build daily strength in yourself with these techniques. In the same way a person uses determination and frequently forces themselves to go to the gym and follow the ridged discipline of lifting weights, will absolutely result in building muscle, stamina and transformation of their physical body; you will in the same manner become strong against temptation and foolish seductive thoughts of drinking or using drugs!

The next chapter will arm you effectively with many concepts, ideas and suggestions that will enable you to begin to practice and gain understanding of the "Power of Paradox" through the "Art of Resistance in Action."

> "Remember the "Art of Resistance in Action" is the "Power of Paradox" that occurs every time when you will follow suggestions of doing things and reading things that you may have absolutely no desire or "willingness" to do so!"

> "It is always a matter of CHOICE, which has nothing to do with, and never will have anything to do with Whether You Want To Or Not. Certainly "willingness" to do something or not do something is totally irrelevant!"

The challenge you will face in the next chapter will be the fact that you will experience much doubt, suspicion and cynicism and want to avoid or ignore many of the "Eganisms." You will find yourself judging and even condemning me for my arrogance to create a language, and title it with my last name. However it will be great practice to finally stop the madness and take full control over your mind and especially your feelings and fully go out and practice the "Art of Resistance in Action!" –Whether you want to or not, but even more importantly if you absolutely do not!!

> "So go ahead and "Practice some Powerlessness" and feel really FEEL the "Power of Paradox" by developing the "Art of Resistance in Action"— following suggestions of doing things and reading things that you may have absolutely NO desire or "willingness" to do so!" But may in fact really greatly benefit you!"

Chapter Nine

Eganisms—Snippets and Shortcuts to Sanity

Some of the following snippets I have developed to communicate RADICAL views and suggestions. Clients have referred to them as "Eganisms" after my very own last name. Yes I know you must be asking yourself is the author an egotistical maniac? The answer is a huge no. By using my last name as a way to label a group of ideas and concepts, some of which are not my own, creates some novelty and humor. You will also observe that some of these are just simple universal truths that have existed since the beginning of time.

Since there is no rhyme or reason to what will follow I have just listed all the "Eganisms" in no particular order; but every one will clearly stand on its own! It should be noted that if you have not puked or vomited regarding the audacity as well as the egotism to call a bunch of unrelated ideas and concepts by my last name; most of which are my own, and a few belonging to others. You should be aware; it was my clients that coined the name; NOT me—I am completely innocent from any charges of any arrogance or self-importance!

Hopefully you have enough tolerance to continue through this chapter and be willing to accept and fully implement the following truths: As I mentioned in this book's Introduction "The chapter on "Eganisms" will absolutely have your head "Spinning" in the right directions!"

"The time to start spinning is NOW!! SO here goes—and hang on!!"

My first suggestion for the reader is for you to accept the following challenge if you are smoking cigarettes. Since I personally witnessed the agonizing deaths of many great men and women "Who had recovered from a hopeless state of mind and body" and yet failed to recover from tobacco; as well as many of my family members die such terrible deaths due to this nasty habit—

"I decided to attack tobacco, and as you are well aware
of by now, it doesn't amount to a "sack of potatoes"
what you "Think" "Believe" or "Feel" regarding this

challenge—do it regardless of how you feel—use the "Power to Resist the Resistance" and start building that "Resistance Muscle" through "Practicing Powerlessness" using the "Art of Resistance in Action" and experience the awesome "Power of Paradox!"

"After all it is just your life! Fight for it! Don't cheat yourself, you have nothing to loose but a few cigarettes and a chance to accomplish one of the greatest achievements of your life!"

Before I state what the challenge is please be aware that the Tobacco problem "IS" the number one Drug Problem in America—nothing even comes close.

It should be noted that tobacco kills over 166 people every hour of every day, which translates to over 450,000 deaths annually, which is approximately 4000 people a day die from smoking cigarettes. That is the equivalent of eight fully loaded Boeing Jumbo jets crashing Every single day of Every single week of Every single month of Every single year! You may think there is some pressure and protest against smoking—but is there Really—when you consider if EIGHT fully loaded jets crashed daily—I believe there would be more of a STINK—

Speaking of "more of a STINK—An interesting "Eganism" I have used to help people deal with their tobacco and nicotine dependency is to suggest that when they get to the last cigarette in each pack, to take a very close look at that empty pack with that one lonely cigarette, and then make a fist and "Crush It" and "Smash It" with that one remaining cigarette nestled safe inside!

"It is important to feel anger, frustration and rage at the fact that because there is only one cigarette left, it is triggering a feeling of anxiety and even panic. This intense negative emotion will occur even if you already have lit the first cigarette from the next pack. Get disgusted that your mind and emotions have been taken completely hostage!"

Respond to that intense negative emotion as if it was a bully that was threatening and harassing you. "Get Mad" "Get Real" and "Get Even" and feel the Power, Strength and the Determination and absolutely teach yourself through this very entertaining challenge that you are Stronger and more Powerful than that feeling—as you Crush and Smash that empty pack with that one cigarette in your Fist!

Do you see where this is going?—When you can dispatch that last cigarette in the pack and do it more than once with a sense of Deep Pride and Strength—Then it is time to destroy the two last cigarettes in the next pack, until you reach the point of no return—and smoking has become a thing of the past!!

"Try this suggestion—After all what do you have to loose!! Just ONE LOUSY CIGARETTE and hopefully you Know that your life and health has got to be worth more than one wretched miserable coffin nail!"

"Did I say TRY well that is just another word for "Choosing to Fail" trying is Lying and Dying!

"When you say you will Try—that shatters focus and direction –anytime you use the word Trying you are "Lying and you are Dying!"

"Do Try this!! Say to yourself "I am going to "Try" to meet you tomorrow at some time." Now "Try" this, and state "I will meet you tomorrow at 2:30 in the afternoon in front of Starbucks." You "DO" notice that the first statement feels and seems very indecisive and therefore has a much lower probability of you actually meeting that person—but the second statement is forceful and very concrete and "Will" cause your brain to organize itself around achieving the decision and intention of meeting that person. Where as the first statement is vague and non direct and will actually disorganize the brain due to the brain or mind only works on very direct and concrete concepts and ignores anything else!

The rest of the following twenty-five or so pages will demonstrate this clearly!!

Do read these with an open mind and do take the time to fully understand each one. To help the reader I have added an explanation below each "snippet."

"Never ask for a sponsor but always ask for a telephone number."—

You will always get a person to give a phone number but not all people will agree to sponsor!

"Always call any telephone number within six to eight hours after receiving it." –

Within a few hours most people will lose the desire to make that call!

"Practice obtaining at least one to three telephone numbers at each AA or NA meeting." –

Call at least one to three of those numbers daily.

"Always ask for a specific time the person can be reached" –

[Early morning or late evening is best] -- The person will be more likely available to talk to you at the beginning of the day or at the end of the day rather than during the day.

"Despite what is said or believed –we are absolutely not powerless"—

We can engage in any activity that we choose to- that will result in keeping us clean and sober.
"We are not powerless over our actions; but it may feel at times we are powerless over our feelings and thoughts."

"A feeling should never dictate an action." –

Actions taken should be directed by clear rational thought but never dictated by an emotion.

"All relapses are a direct result of allowing a feeling to dictate an action." –

Any time and every time you allow your recovery program to slip or be neglected it is due to allowing your feelings to dictate your behaviors.

"There are more things occurring in this world than our limited view allows us to see" –

Therefore when we believe there are limitations we are blind to the fact there are actually a boundless number of possibilities.

"The GREAT news is that our limited perceptions can never limit what we can do and achieve."

Since perceptions are dictated by our feelings and emotions, it is only the feelings and emotions that are perceived as limiting us. Regardless of these we have unlimited potential and therefore unlimited opportunities!

No addict or alcoholic should ever identify himself or herself as an addict or alcoholic; as in when we state, "Hi I am Jerry and I am an alcoholic." The reason for the need to change this is three fold.

"First the admission of identifying myself as the problem makes me begin to believe it is an attribute instead of a condition and it also does nothing to build self-esteem or self worth."

"Second, by identifying myself as the problem significantly reduces my ability to view myself in a more empowering manner."

"Third, every human being on earth should never identify himself or herself as the condition that they have."

In other words you are more than the condition that you have; you are a million other possibilities and you have a billion other potentialities and probabilities.

"I really want to emphasize this universal truth, and that no one should ever express or have beliefs that limit them. No one is an introvert, no one is a loner, no one is an addict and no one is an alcoholic. They are just behaviors or conditions acquired or learned and they absolutely are not attributes."

"The person is not the disease. They have the condition but they are not the condition that they have"

They are so much more and should not limit themselves to this designation.

179

"An emotion has no real power to dictate the choices we
ultimately make."—

It is the feelings and emotions that betray us; in that they blind us from
seeing or knowing the real truth regarding almost anything.

"In addiction there are no benefits or rewards there are
only suffering and confusion."—

The addict is obsessed with the Feeling they experience from the use of a
substance and then allow that feeling to dictate their choices.

"It is essential for an addict to develop a sense of joy or
even achievement with every passing day they are clean
and or sober." –

We need to learn to recognize and remember on a daily basis the small
and yet vitally important things that will insure that we maintain joy and
deep satisfaction and gratitude for recovery.

"The task at hand, is to identify frequently throughout
the day, the special gifts that are present with each
moment of recovery." –

They may be found outside ourselves or inside ourselves. It may be a
feeling or an event or a simple word or even just gazing at the sky, clouds,
sun, moon or stars!

"Since addiction is a very intense and a deeply
emotionally charged experience that appears to have
had some significant rewards, it is difficult to overcome
the fascination and pleasure of getting high."—

Any memory of the pleasure and joy that getting high produced or the
tendency to verbalize past using experiences, which is known as a "War Story",
is detrimental to the chance for a successful sobriety.

"The addict must be very aware and vigilant to notice,
when they are having fond pass memories, they need

to confront the memory with the reality that substance
use has inflicted severe harm on them and their
families."—

It is only through this process that the pain of substance abuse can be
retained in the memory and when coupled with enough disgust, repulsion
and revulsion these powerful negative emotions may trigger a strong enough
deterrence to push out the pleasing drug use memory.

"Never discount yourself or depreciate, degrade doubt
or curse yourself."

Because, who do you listen to the most?— YOU!!

"Do it all! Don't cheat yourself."—

It is absolutely true- half measures will avail you nothing!

"Tears are a spiritual experience."—

Tears are to the soul as soap is to the body.

Don't say "I am having a good day or even a pretty
good day"—

Say, I am having a GREAT day!!

"Trying is lying and trying is dying."—

TRY- is the dirtiest three let word in the entire recovery vocabulary-it
dilutes and weakens possibilities!

"There are no problems only opportunities."—

Problems paralyze but opportunities open- endless possibilities!
"In far eastern philosophy the word "crisis" is defined as

"Danger plus Opportunity"—

Every crisis sows the seeds of advantage as well as opportunities- Move cautiously- but reap rewards!

> "Anger is about now. Fear is about having negative fantasies about the future. Resentment is about the past."—

Manage them now—FEAR Forget Fear; find FAITH;- Resist Resentment; Resolve Anger. NOW!

> "To thine own self be true" –but on page 62 In chapter five of the AA book it states "the alcoholic is an extreme example of self-will run riot-though they usually don't think so"—

In what ways are you self will run riot and have you finally come to recognize this.

> "Half measures availed us nothing—Some sponsors only teach half measures"—

So they cause us to "avail nothing" no matter how sincere or how much effort we are putting forth.

> "AA is a program of perfection despite its claim that "we strive for progress not perfection."—

It views the person who used one time in an entire year in the same capacity as someone who has been drinking every day for the past year—it seems unfair that if a person can put together months and months of clean time- THEN they should be recognized and even be able to celebrate at some level.

> "We need to change and switch to asking better questions such as "Will I be able to control this drug or my drinking" to the question "Will this hurt my family?" or "Do I want to give up this current change and improvement in my life?" or "Will drinking or

using drugs improve anything in my life?" RIGHT NOW!

Learn to ask questions of "Concern"- instead of questions of whether "I can Control!"

"Nothing can stop an action—but a feeling can"—

When you let them dictate your actions –you must learn to take right actions regardless of any emotional states you are experiencing.

"AA is a program of action –meeting action—sponsor action—sharing action—helping others action—and what can stop an action?"—

A "dumb stupid feeling."
"Actions LEAD to and CREATE Advancement and Achievements."

"Messy Bed means a Messy Head!!!!!!! And if you are in your HEAD you are DEAD!!!"—

"Protect yourself through the 3-B's of recovery— BED—Bath—Breakfast!" Making your "Bed" is pure DISCIPLINE- Showering or taking a "Bath" is guaranteed jump-start to FEEL GOOD (after all, have you ever heard of ANYONE coming out of a shower screaming "oooo water and soap how horrible—I can't believe I took a shower, I have to stop this shower crap" no contrary WATER hitting the body-always FEELS GOOD—it is GUARRANTEED! So why cheat yourself from a guaranteed jump-start FEEL GOOD every morning when you wake up! Now for "Breakfast" It Is absolutely necessary and STABILIZES the blood sugar in the brain! Unstable blood sugar causes hunger, and hunger is experienced in the mind as "craving" and the brain does not know whether it craves "Cheerios" or "Cocaine"-DO NOT CREATE UNNECESSARY CRAVINGS—

EAT BREAKFAST!

Take control of the main problem, which is your HEAD. —Start the day out and consciously practice some DISCIPLINE; make yourself feel GOOD; and for Gods sake STABILIZE your brain! Make a "BED" you don't want to, take a shower-"BATH" you don't want to; eat "BREAKFAST" you don't want to.!! Discipline!-Discipline!-Discipline!

" In your Head you are Dead but—In your FEET no DEFEAT"—

The feet do not lie. When you go to bed at night- look at and ask your FEET, What did we do today to stay SAFE SANE and SOBER? Did we spill coffee on them at a meeting? Did we crunch them in prayer? Were they present when we did something loving or caring for another?

"Write 20 things to do daily that support recovery and you absolutely do not want to do. Things done that are good for you is practicing DISCIPLINE and things done for others is practicing SACRIFICE."—

What ever you do that YOU want to do- does not count-you must constantly challenge yourself and MOVE past your comfort ZONE! Addiction lives in YOUR comfort zone!

"All things that are done without resistance results in reluctance."—

Reluctance forms when desire deteriorates. When desire deteriorates, determination disintegrates and recovery detonates!

"Recovery Actions taken and completed despite resistance- strengthen the ability to remain persistent to stay abstinent when threat or desire to get "Higher" becomes insistent." –

The actions that you force yourself to do that are right for you or right for someone else provides the power to resist any threat or temptation to recovery.

"When Resisting the Resistance to Resist – You-Stop

the unstoppable- even when you can't or don't want to stop!

Since only a feeling can stop an action-then fight the feeling-your life depends on decisions made with mental Discipline and Determination- not left to the control of emotional impulsivity or desires.

"Its about the "have to's" and "got a do's"- Not the "want a do's!"

Addiction is about doing what you want-it is about impulsivity. Recovery is about "having to do" and "got a do"-it is about discipline.

"RESISTANCE INTO RESOLUTION"

Use of resistance produces self-esteem and true self-confidence through the demonstration of competency. It is the ability to control, manage, direct and resist acting on your own feelings. The Bible has many good references that I will now state in regards to the concept of turning "resistance into resolution."

"What good does it profit a man if he gains the whole world and loses his own soul" Mark 8:36

Greatness is measured by self-control and discipline-not just by achieving success.

"Greater is he who conquers himself than an entire city." Proverb

Managing emotions and directing your own emotions and mind are the true attainment of greatness.

Here are the rest of these universal truths and they need no further explanations from me!

"I have learned, in whatsoever state I am, therewith to be content." Philippians 4:11

"Yet man is born to trouble as surely as sparks fly upwards." Job 5:7

"In your anger do not sin": Do not let the sun go down while you are still angry... Ephesians 4:26

"Everything is permissible"-But not everything is beneficial. "Everything is permissible"-But not everything is constructive. Nobody should seek his own good but the good of others. 1 Corinthians 10:23-24

"Therefore, do not worry about tomorrow for tomorrow will worry about itself. Each day has enough trouble of its own." Matthew 6:34

"Set your mind on things above, not on things on the earth. Colossians 3:2

"For where two or three are gathered together in my name, I am they are in the midst of them." Matthew 18:20

"There is a way that seems right to a man, but in the end it only leads to death. Proverbs 14:12

"Sorrow is better than laughter, for by a sad countenance the heart is made stronger." Ecclesiastes 7:3

"Do all things without complaint or dispute." Philippians 2:14

"For where envy and self-seeking exist, confusion and every evil thing are there". James 3:16

"Now faith is the substance of things hoped for, the evidence of things not seen. Hebrews 11:1

Whether you are a Christian or not —find books or spiritual teachers and memorize more universal truths—for me I found that these words pushed out of my head the thoughts and ideas of drinking and drugging once I used the Discipline of writing them down, and reading them, and rereading them, and reading them even more—till I no longer had to read them—Because I had memorized them!

We will NOW return to more "Eganisms" and "Snippets."

"Set up competing thoughts—Defiance means Determination!"

Defy unhealthy feelings and impulsive actions-use your Discipline and Determination to force yourself to stay on task! When you think about or obsess on a drink or a drug then with strong Determination pull a picture of your son—daughter—mother—father—husband—wife—boyfriend—girlfriend—fiancée OR your dead Parrot or Cat and just stare and focus on their eyes and their face and know the Damage and Destruction they will suffer if you give in to that stupid desire or impulse to USE! The competing thought will obliterate the DESIRE to USE!!

"All conflict creates value-conflict creates new direction!"

All struggles require energy to make a choice and anything that makes you choose- forces you to choose a new direction.

> "Challenges produce creativity-creativity produces corrective actions-corrective actions produce confidence, confidence produces self-esteem which produces increase in value."

Value creates desire to acquire the object of desire. Desire to acquire the ability to overcome unwanted and unhealthy objects of desire.

> "Once the person is feeling strong and confident they become virtually unreachable and unteachable."

In the book "Twelve Steps and Twelve Traditions" fondly known as the "12 & 12" on page 22 it states "Self-confidence is no good whatever; in fact it is a total liability."

> "There is a limited period of time in which a person will be willing to ask for a sponsor."

Due to the rapid development of false self-confidence the desire or need to ask for help-fades quickly. In matter of fact, asking anyone for assistance will be blocked due to feeling confident.

> "Learn to resist yourself, to insist upon yourself, better mental health"

Take healthy control of your feelings and emotions and eliminate regret, remorse and relapse.

> "The way to begin to build "resistance muscle" is to learn through out each day to challenge the feelings of desire, for instance "while you may like a greasy cheeseburger it may be better for your body to eat dry Tuna and despite the fact that you "feel" like having the burger, you can resist the feeling, and have Tuna instead. As soon as this is done you have just strengthened yourself against a relapse."

"Another simple exercise is to delay smoking a cigarette when you feel like one and instead look at a clock or a watch and delay lighting the cigarette for one to five minutes. Even though you are not resisting this dangerous deadly habit at least this teaches you to better control your feelings and impulses!"

"Learning to delay leads to—Control and control leads to— Decision and decision leads to—new Directions and new directions lead to—new Destinies!"

"Giving in, is caving in, and caving in, is the END"

Never give in or cave in to negative feelings, thoughts, beliefs or actions-it will spell the end of all your dreams and all you have worked for!

"To excel, just rebel, against what you know so well"

Resist telling or listening to any War stories, romancing the stone, drug interests and desires. Anything that excites, attracts or distracts from recovery efforts.

"Whether you want to or not, you must know that you can."

Feeling a certain way does not control or direct going a certain way.

"What they choose to do should have nothing to do with the way they feel, but what they choose will definitely create very different realities, which will directly determine the feelings that they will experience! Our realities are really our choices!"

"…that in all things God works for the good of all those who love Him, who have been called according to his purpose. Romans 8:28

The meaning of this is that for those who Serve and Love God—all things that happen to that person will be for their Good or for the Good of others!

188

By the way my belief about atheism is that:

"An atheist is someone who has the deep belief that there is no God, but since it is only a belief and no one really knows, then an atheist is a person with deep faith in the concept that God does not exist. But since it requires deep deep faith to believe in Nothing; then believing that deeply in Nothing, is really deeply believing in Something and therefore they have a devout faith and that makes them very rigidly religious! If you really, and that strongly believe in Nothing; is it not possible that really believing in Nothing is really truly believing in Something that some people and I prefer to call "God;" but you prefer to call "Nothing" and by believing that strongly in "Nothing" is really strongly believing in "Something;" therefore it follows you cannot be a true atheist for if you truly believed in Nothing then this entire paragraph should mean absolutely nothing to you!" Either way it is not necessary to know or accept if God exists for the "Power of Spirituality" is never denied to any one. Any one has full access to this Power regardless of what they Believe, can't Believe or don't Believe!"

It is good when things go bad. It helps us search for solutions to find GOD or
<u>G</u>ood <u>O</u>rderly <u>D</u>irection

"Just because it feels good does not mean that it is good"

Getting high or drunk felt good-getting and staying clean and sober may not feel so good.

"Just because it feels bad does not necessary mean that it is bad"

Doing the right things many times does not feel right and we should never stop doing the right thing just because it feels bad!

> "If addiction crushed you, and drove you to your knees,
> let your knees drive you to Freedom and Faith."

Whether you pray on your knees or not. —To be truthful didn't drugs and alcohol drive you to your knees? Did you crawl on your knees searching your pockets frantically or have laid on the ground or Prayed before the "porcelain alter"(The Toilet) screaming or mumbling—OH GOD! And were singing gut busting Praises in the form of (the sounds) of wet and dry vomiting into (the toilet)—get on your knees voluntarily—get on your knees in Gratitude-rather than in Regret! BUT get on your knees to remember—you never want to be on your knees in THAT way ever again!!

> "Wisdom always trumps an opinion"

Knowledge is not power, knowledge is only an opinion — what others tell me is not mine. But what I have done is mine- Wisdom is power!

> "Have to do's and want to do's don't count-Got a do's
> get it done"

A "have to do" is about- Discipline and Structure. Activities of daily living.

A "want a do" is about – Desire and Pleasure. Activities willingly and joyfully engaged in.

A "got a do" is about –Decision and Determination. Actions taken not because you "have to" nor because you "want to" but because you "got to." Activities that produce a strong and mature person is what "Get it Done" Things that are done not necessarily with joy nor willingness, but things that build character through sacrifice and makes you kind, Caring, Compassionate, Considerate, Concerned, Conscientious and most of all driven by Commitment that may include, but not necessarily requires neither Discipline nor Desire, just a clear Decision and then sheer Determination!

'False Self Confidence"

Is at the core of most relapses. It is the false certainty; conviction and coolness that makes a person not only believe, but also FEEL they can do anything they want, but they have no proven capacity or competency to accomplish it.

"I have no friends, if all my friends drink and do drugs-they are my ...."FRIENEMIES."......................................

Because they, "once were my good friends, but we got high together, and now that I am in recovery they are an enemy to my chances for recovery." Therefore they are enemies to my recovery, so I called them "friend-enemies" whether they are friends or family.

"Resistance is Insistence"

When desire or temptations occur we must be Insistent on being Resistant.

"In recovery if we get things back Fast, we go Fast, and
then Crash."

When going fast in the right direction if we let go of the steering wheel-we will crash.

To prevent this from occurring we need to know "when you are driving a car you must be intensely involved in what you are doing from second to second, and it is equally necessary for us to figure out ways to stay intensely involved with our recovery, or we "WILL" absolutely crash!

"Insistence is persistence and persistence is to rebel, or
is it to propel, the choice is yours"

"Resistance is to rebel or repel against something"

Challenge yourself daily and build persistence. By failing to challenge yourself is to stay resistant and to rebel. Transform this Resistance into Persistence and have both the power to repel and propel. Repel "push the thought away" or propel " push the thought that has been thought and to Embrace or Resist that thought," the choice is always yours!!

"Desire always drives the Power to Acquire"

What we strongly want we will always achieve to acquire. This starts the fire for the Good as well as Bad and the Power has no preferences or favorites for either. Desire is the power you use to Create as well as to Destroy!

"The implementation of Self Defiance results in strong Self-Reliance"

Self defiance is self sacrifice and leads to delayed gratification and mature adult function.

"A thought that has been thought- has been thought and cannot be unthought."

The mind cannot <u>not</u> think about something that is being thought" therefore "You cannot <u>not</u> think about drugs when you are trying <u>not</u> to think about drugs." The word drug, conjures an image and that image cannot <u>not</u> be imaged and the image creates interest and desire to acquire the object of desire." You cannot <u>not</u> think of something that you are thinking. You cannot unthought the thought.

"You cannot choose your first thought but you can, and always, do choose your second thought"

Choose wisely for the thought creates the image to desire and acquire what ever you set on fire with your imagination. Whether it is to get high, drunk or pray to God your imagination will feed the passion that drives the determination but you always set the direction!

"Then it follows that "Since desire is a feeling and the feeling sets direction you must learn to FUC_ your feelings before they FUC_ you!"

We must do what we have to do, and not just do, what we want to do." We are hard wired, to do what we want to do and not what we have to do. "Doing what we <u>Got</u> to do is how we get recovery done!"

"Must counter desire with disgust"

The choice is always yours- you can and always do choose the second thought-remember the good times or remember the bad times.

"Remember how good it felt or instead remember the Horror and Hell!"

The dreadful and sickening suffering done to your family and yourself!

"Give expectations instead of limitations."

All things are possible-know no limits! But know your LIMIT!

"Following feelings leads to failure"

It is the habit of "feeling based decision making" that has been the cause for most failures in recovery.

"Challenges create changes; Changes creates connections."

Connections to others, yourself, recovery and ultimately to God! For those who may still be squeamish when the word GOD is seen or heard-please refer to the earlier "Eganism" or "Snippet" regarding the Bible Verse "... that in all things God works for the good of all those who love Him, who have been called according to his purpose. Romans 8:28

"To try to stay clean and sober completely on your own. To refuse to ask for help from God, or his designee which is your fellow man, is actually the most inhumane thing you could do to yourself!"

"Addicts and alcoholics whether by nature or simply due to the habitual use of a substance have become very self-centered, self focused, self obsessed as well as self directed and when they are so consumed with only thoughts about themselves it is not possible to recover."

"If a person can place one other persons needs genuinely before their own needs then that person will not relapse."

"Relapse always occurs because the person is self obsessed and only cares about his or her own feelings. By learning to sacrifice for others they engage and have access to the "Power of Right Action" through the "Art of Service and Sacrifice" which changes this negative tendency, and strengthens their ability to resist an opportunity or offer to drink or do drugs."

"Addiction is about surviving and lying"

"Never forget that "Trying is Dying and Trying is Lying! And it directly causes us to fail due to it allows us to believe our own "Bullshit."

"The implementation of Self-Defiance results in strong Self-Reliance."

"Recovery—it is about sacrifice and service. Turning Resistance into Resolution."

"Must counter desire to relapse with equal passion to resist."

"Do not bring a deck of cards to a gun fight-it is no time to gamble!"

"We are playing Russian Roulette every time we have an unchallenged thought or memory about alcohol or drugs"

The bullets we load into the gun are made of DEEP DESIRE and IF they are fired into our brain then our recovery is seriously injured or dies! If we load all Six Chambers of a gun with DEEP DESIRES then we might as well be playing Russian Roulette with an Automatic!

"We must counter the desire to use, with the passion to fight-"Fuck you I'm not giving in!"

Just as if someone was trying to abduct or kidnap your child, or talk you into a dangerous activity and they will not take no for an answer-you explode with the intense passion "Leave me alone-Go FUCK yourself get the FUCK away from me."

"Passion is the Power that fuels Resistance"

We cannot quietly and cognitively resist temptation! For this to work it has to be LOUDLY and PROUDLY stated with all the desperation and passion that can be generated to break the "hypnotic lock" that is created when we desire or crave drugs or alcohol.

"It is only when you fully Emotionalize a word or statement that it is given value, and only what we Value will we do—and Pursue!"

"Fear can always be used as a motivator to find Faith."

But fear can never be used as a deterrent. Only the force of Faith can deter desire!

"Recovery is like a gold mine in which someone else has thrown large nuggets of gold all over the floor."

All you have to do is pick it up; all the work has been done for you!

"Relapse is being in the same mine with the same opportunity to pick up a kings ransom in gold without any work"

But you feel it is too much trouble to reach down and start picking it up!

"Despite what they say "AA is a program of perfection"

Try to pick up a medallion or coin, if you even have had only one joint or one beer for an entire year-there is no wiggle room, and it is better to celebrate any time clean and sobriety, than to compare and regret that you are not perfect.

> "To recover, "something has to shift." Here is the simple ultimate test to determine your ability to "Resist the Resistance to Resist." Try moving your watch or jewelry to the other hand and see what a challenge this becomes- DO IT NOW! Don't question ME! DO IT! Now that you have done it – Did you do it because you wanted to do it or desired to do it or were even willing to do it. NO!—You did it because "Want a Do's" and "Have to Do's" don't count, what counts is the "Got a Do's" and they get it done! NOW try committing to leaving it on the new location forever, or at least until you RELAPSE then wear it where you want!" Not so easy to do is it! Guess what! When facing recovery challenges will you or will you not be able to force yourself to "Get it Done!"

Your rituals; possibly the way you dress; the side of your face you start your shave or begin to apply make-up; where you wear your jewelry; the side of bed you sleep on; how you wear your hat or where you wear your watch may all need to change. This action scrambles your brain and scrambles the rituals surrounding drinking and drug use.

> "Willpower is doing what I want"

Willingness is listening to others.

> "With addicts, wrong comes easy and doing right is hard to do"

Wrong feels right and right feels wrong.

> "If it feels good, does that mean it is good, and if it feels bad does that mean it is bad"-

> "We love what drugs do for us—we can't stand what drugs do to us."

Meaning drugs give us great feelings or power and that is what they do "For" us. But they hurt others and us and that is what they do "To" us.

"When feelings rule our actions and behaviors."

We are reacting from emotional logic that manifests itself in the following manner:

"If it feels good it is good and more is even better" and
"if it feels bad then it is bad and should be avoided."

Where this becomes very obviously problematic is that attending meetings or working a Fourth Step may be stressful or feel bad; so does that mean it should be avoided at all cost, and conversely thinking about drugs or giving into the resistance to not attend a meeting feels good, so does that mean skipping meetings is a good thing, just because it feels easier to avoid than to engage.

"Any one at any time has the absolute ability to change
anything they want. But if they believe that they have to
have willingness or a "feeling of willingness" then that
belief could literally kill them!"

The word "willing" is a feeling saturated word, but has nothing to do with ability.

"When you get better they get bitter."

Make no mistake about it when you change your life some people will resent and reject you. So always remember that those who judge—Don't matter and those that Don't judge Matter!

"Selflessness vs. Selfishness"

That is the definition of Spirituality!

"It is more through the words we speak than think- that
the seeds of all emotions germinate."

We have little control over the First Thought of what we think but we always and do have much control over the Second Thought and absolute total control over what we speak OUT LOUD!

> "On the material plane, all material rewards, will always pale in comparison to drugs and alcohol."

Which are the pinnacle rewards on the material plane and therefore will out weigh family, friends and any and every other material acquisition or achievement.

> "Therefore the "high" from alcohol or drugs will always be selected as the final reward."

> "It is essential that the addict or alcoholic learn to be less selfish at the very least; if they cannot achieve the state of being selfless and altruistic."

Then the person must develop a more selfless attitude instead of maintaining a selfish attitude.

> "There is one thing all people have in common, and that is when anyone any where helps another human being it gives them a guaranteed feel good sensation."

> "The degree of selfishness can be observed by doing the following exercise: List ten situations in which the addict or alcoholic "deceived, disappointed, disillusioned, disturbed, discouraged or discounted someone whom they really love or loves them."

For none of these things would have been possible without the elements of pure selfishness!

> "If it's a Disease, then the person experiences Symptoms, and if it is a Choice, then that person would experience Consequences."

> "If it is a Disease it is about Powerlessness, Concern and

Compassion and if it is about Choice it is about Shame,
Failure and Condemnation!"

The very nature of having a disease means that the person is powerless
and the very nature of being able to exercise choice means that the person
is not powerless. In other words if it is a disease it is about powerlessness
and compassion and if it is about choice it is about experiencing shame and
condemnation since the person had the power to change but did nothing.

> "When a person identifies himself or herself as the
> "problem" rather than having the "problem" they
> immediately limit their power and resources to make
> an immediate change or adjustment. They fall victim
> to the myth that their condition is an attribute and due
> to that they believe "It will take a long time to make
> changes."

In reality any change can be done instantly, unless it is an attribute.

> "Tension is that force in all of us, that is the driving core
> of all creativity."

TV and drugs reduce potential due to they reduce Tension. TV, substance
abuse or any other non-productive form of distracting ourselves, prevents
this FORCE from producing the motivation and direction that comes from
properly and appropriately RESPONDING to that TENSION!

> "Willingness is not a natural state or drive in addicts or
> alcoholics, but defiance and rebelliousness is."

It just makes more sense to use "what comes natural" than to try to create
an unnatural desire or attitude.

> "It is great fun to challenge yourself and to defy the
> odds-what do you have to lose? After all what is easier
> to do "change a personality or act naturally?"

By utilizing the addict's natural tendency for rebelliousness and defiance
we can flip it around and direct the negative energy in a very positive manner

back towards the addict or alcoholic. "Challenge them to challenge their own impulsive tendencies.

> "In recovery once you give up one Thing then it is easy to give up another Thing until you have given up Everything."

Do not be careless, complacent or confident about changing a winning recovery formula. It is important to always place commitments to recovery actions ahead of everything for failing to do so means the probable loss of everything. ANY changes in the formula need to be reviewed with a sponsor, coach, trusted friend or family member before any change is made! Just because it feels right to change it- does not necessarily make it so!

> "Teach yourself that any time you have a thought about a drug or alcohol to then immediately bring to your mind a memory and a feeling of a terrible thing that happened as a direct use of substances. By conditioning yourself in this manner you will be able to stack up Disgust against the Desire."

The addict or alcoholic needs to passionately use this technique and it will enable them to create not only a satisfying, but also a sober and clean spectacular life.

> "Recovery is Discovery."

> "Clean and Serene"

> "Stick and Stay in AA or NA.

> "Sobriety Is Variety."

> "To Be Cool Was to Be a Fool."

> "There Are No "Not" Concepts in the Brain."

> "We Can and We Will If We Follow through."

"Since Addiction Is a Mind and Body Disease-The Solution Must Be a Mind and Body Solution."

"While the 12 Step Programs Help so Many, There Are so Many More They Fail to Help-The Statistics Speak This Truth."

"Where Do You Run for Cover and Comfort When the Most Important Person in your life Is No Longer Available to You Because Addiction Has Destroyed the Relationship."

"To Recover Is to Re—Discover-My Wife, My Life, My Husband, My Children, My Mother, My Father, My Sister, My Brother, My God, My Peace, My Purpose!"

"Motion Creates Emotion!"

"Single Events That Occur in Less Than a Microsecond of Time Can Change Our Lives Forever-Your First Drink Or Use of a Drug Was One of Those Events!"

"It is most important to understand that the "subjectivity of reality" allows us to manipulate what we believe to be reality."

If you have read up to this point and have not judged me for my arrogance in referring to this chapter as "Snippets and Eganisms", then the following concepts that were presented by Anthony Robbins in his live presentations, seminars and tapes are well worth a closer investigation!

"The past does not equal the future!!"

"It Is not a matter of learning more!—it is a matter of making a decision and taking an action!!"

"The smallest action taken daily equals huge changes in your destiny!!"

"In order to take an action you must have desire and if you have strong desire you will take strong actions!!"

"If there is no strong desire then there is no power to make a decision—and without making a decision you cannot and will not take any action at all!!"

"A desirable future must be envisioned that will give power to make a decision to move towards it!!"

"Always see it as it is—But not worse than it is—But see it better than it is—and make it that way!"

And my favorites from Nepoleon Hill-

"For it is true, for what ever a man feeds his mind—his mind will attract to it!"

"What Ever A Man Can Conceive And Believe He Can Achieve!"

Well we have now had our commercial break or advertisements; now it is time to return to "Snippets" and "Eganisms"

"Make sure you are growing and cultivating the right kinds of seeds. Use and plant the seeds of a recovery lifestyle and you will reap great riches in every area of your life. Cultivate the wrong seeds of an addictive lifestyle, then watch every dream, hope, desire, promise, vision and aspiration be slowly choked and shattered!"

"The future is completely unwritten so anybody can "Write or Right" their present life to create whatever future they Choose. It is only in the now that we Can Control the future."

"You can't mow the lawn today with yesterdays gasoline and you cannot cut the lawn again today for next week- you do not have any power to address anything that has already occurred or has not yet occurred."

"Be aware of the ILLUSION of SELF SUFFICIENCY"

We are all dependent on highways, gas stations, Wal-Mart, Home Depot-refrigerators and stoves and Publix etc –etc. There for we all are interdependent on each other and need each other especially in recovery.

"The Essence of Time The great paradox of time is that "nobody has enough of it, yet everybody has all that there is". Nobody knows exactly how much we have but we should appreciate that time is precious. During the next 24 hours another 86,400 seconds will have passed by. Will you have had a good return from it?"

"It is a huge responsibility to know you have to manage your thoughts-do I have what it takes—Do I know what it takes—will I do what it takes- Am I truly willing to go to any length or will I accept half measures which have always availed me absolutely nothing- Will I force myself whether I am willing or not, to experience an entire psychic change and if I am not determined to force myself will I accept the fact that for me there is very little hope for recovery"

"It seems that the more costly continued use is, the more value is created to continue use is."

Since no matter what consequences have occurred the person perceives the use of substances as pleasurable and at least always comforting. Expanding on this phenomenon:

"An overdose may be viewed paradoxically as just an extreme attempt to get comfortable."

"What else in this entire world will do for you, what you want every single time without fail? The answer to this question is drugs and alcohol and there are no otherworldly guarantees other than death."

That is the paradox that will occur once a person has to give up drugs and alcohol. They have to give up the only guarantee that exists on earth!

> "An addict or alcoholic is willing to give up everything, for that one THING, instead of giving up that one THING, so they can have EVERYTHING!"

Addicts and alcoholics are driven by a strong motivation to experience powerful emotional psychological and physiological experiences. That one "THING" Substance use and abuse satisfies this need and many times recovery, that other "THING" fails to meet this need!

> "It is this values dilemma that has to be recognized and addressed in that the addict or alcoholic, who needs to learn to begin to measure success based upon the positive changes they are demonstrating, rather than the emotional experience that they are having."

It is absolutely necessary for the addict or alcoholic to measure abstinence by celebrating each achievement or accomplishment during recovery, even when it does not seem important. In this way they will be able to stack positive feelings and emotions, and not expect an automatic anticipated emotional reward; but develop appreciation for their hard earned achievements.

> "Addicts and alcoholics have mastered the principles of success and use those very same concepts to assure their own failure and destruction!"

Since thoughts are things, then the intense passion of thinking and talking about drug and alcohol use, assure that opportunities to drink and use drugs will actually in fact materialize.

> "The sad fact is that recovery actions and behaviors that would lead to a more fulfilling productive and positive lifestyle, are cast away due to the way the addict or alcoholic measures their actions by their emotional reward, and if there is no reward, then the behaviors are considered worthless, useless and purposeless."

"Drinking and drugging absolutely gives them a "right" feeling. Even though it's absolutely the wrong thing to do."

When a person is very motivated and enthusiastic about a recovery activity such as calling a sponsor, attending meetings or engaging in numerous other recovery activities, such as bringing meetings to a hospital or jail; there is no adversity and therefore there is no challenge.

"Without challenge there is no real benefit derived from the action and that translates to there is no growth, for without growth the person remains unchanged and remains in a weakened condition as well as very vulnerable to impulsivity and relapse."

"If you are doing what you want to do, whether it is recovery or active drug use or drinking; the fact is you are just doing what you want to do, and there is no opportunity for growth or change. In fact everything that you do that you want to do in recovery, does not count! It is when you do what you don't want to do that is good for your recovery, and counts the most."

Your recovery depends completely upon your ability to force yourself to continue to do the right things especially when you don't want to.

"The more we learn to manage any feelings that cause us to do the wrong things or to procrastinate regarding taking or completing necessary recovery actions, the more we will be prepared, when a stupid "feeling" can undermine and even destroy all the effort and hard work that a person has invested in their recovery."

"Until the addict or alcoholic is able to step up and recognize that they do not necessarily have to have a positive feeling to take positive actions and to maintain a positive direction; their chances for a long lasting recovery will be very doubtful."

Once time frames are stated the mind begins to organize itself around accomplishing the task. Without clear stated time frames the mind does not know when or where to make this a priority. Therefore the task will not be done and it is only a "Good Intention" but has no chance of being carried out."

> "It should be emphasized that unfortunately there is a higher probability that the friend or associate will persuade the person in recovery to join them in relapse behaviors; then for the person in recovery to convince the person to come back to recovery."

The best way to deal with a friend who relapses is to find someone else to help, or just avoid any contact.

> "Here in lies the paradox that anytime we succumb to our dark desires, it creates a tremendous and seemingly rewarding moment; but it will automatically lead to some permanent loss in self-esteem. As our Inability to take control of these harmful emotional states continues, we continue to lose more and more self-esteem."

Since self-esteem is the life's blood of recovery, the loss of self worth begins to cause a severe hemorrhage in the desire to stay clean and sober.

> "Lust and selfish interest in things begin to lead the person down a very destructive path!"

> "To recover—A person does not have to be Willing, just Disgusted and Determined."

Success is always built on numerous efforts and failures. It is not measured by achieving the feeling of what we desire, but through determined and repeated efforts. We will always achieve what we desire through the process of constantly changing strategies and shifting directions—until we do succeed— BUT we may not FEEL successful even though we absolutely did accomplish what we Desired! Therefore "NOT" "FEELING successful does "NOT" mean THAT we are not SUCCESSFUL! Always learn to measure your success by what is ACHIEVED rather than what "IS" or was EXPECTED to be FELT!

> "If you believe that something is "not" possible then you will "not" be able to achieve or change what you believe cannot be changed."

However once a compelling reason is seen or developed then impossible beliefs become observable facts.

> "It is only the limiting beliefs that we place upon our minds that hold us back from achieving the things we deeply need and desire."

In the case of the addict or the alcoholic that means they can absolutely achieve not only permanent sobriety, but create a fantastic and new future and destiny.

> "What changes us is accessing the power to act through on the decision; that is how we change our lives. When a person fails over and over again despite all the effort, and they do not get the result they desire despite all the determination"

All this means is that the plans failed, not the person, and by changing the approaches will lead to success.

> "If you are not Resisting—THEN—you are Reaching."

Resistance in the very end is the only thing between you and picking up trouble and the stronger your Resistance the healthier you are.

> "Once a thought has been thought, a thought that has been thought can never be unthought."or "You cannot, not have a thought, that you have, thought" or "you cannot not think about something that you have thought about." When you use any word that automatically fires a strong image in the brain, you cannot, "not" think or

undo that image, therefore you must stay very alert to the images you allow to be triggered in your brain."

Or in another words…

"The mind cannot <u>not</u> think about something that is being thought" therefore "You cannot <u>not</u> think about drugs when you are trying <u>not</u> to think about drugs." The word drug, conjures an image and that image cannot <u>not</u> be imaged and the image creates interest and desire to acquire the object of desire." You cannot <u>not</u> think of something that you are thinking. You cannot unthought a thought."

What more needs to be "THOUGHT" or said!
Understand REALLY UNDERSTAND the following ULTIMATE TRUTH and POWER!

"Change is neither determined nor dependent upon any feeling."

"Change has nothing to do with neither the way a person feels nor what they are feeling."

"Change has nothing to do with intentions or impulses."

"Change only requires one simple action—

"Change It, Whatever it is!"—Regardless of any feelings whatsoever."

The CHOICE is truly yours…Choose CHANGE and…

"Free Yourself from this Madness!"

Sorrow is Better, than Laughter.
For by a sad Countenance the
Heart is made Better

Ecclesiastes 7:3

Chapter Ten

Desperation To Determination

Since addiction is a form of mental illness that has to be managed for life; this means that we have trouble seeing things clearly and everything is distorted and out of focus. Due to this we have to resist the tendency to let our feelings dictate our actions. It is only through gaining sufficient resistance to acting out on our feelings, or what I refer to as developing the "Power to Resist the Resistance" through the "Art of Self Defiance" which will enable us to change our behavior. The mental illness is clearly seen in the way we surrender to acting on our feelings, instead of our knowledge and intelligence. To manage you must deal with the illness, which is expressed through your "resistance" tendencies, which blocks off the ability to change! Just because you want to change, and even if you know you must change, learning more will not fix you or change you!

Learning More Will Not Fix It- Or Change It!

Knowledge Will Not Fix It

The Best Intentions Will Not Fix It

It Will Not Magically Fix Itself

The Only Thing That Can Fix It Is To!

First: On A Daily Basis Write Five Reasons Why Change Is Desired And Needed!

Second: On A Daily Basis Write Five Changes You Will Do Daily.

Third: Do The Five Things You Said You Would Do Before You Go To Bed Each Day

Fourth: Do Those Things When You Want To But-

Fifth: It Is More Important To Do Them When You Don't Want To!

There is a simple principle behind the above five suggestions—In an earlier chapter I described that principle as the "Art of Resistance in Action" through the "Power of Paradox" and it is through the further application of the "Art of Self-Defiance" that these practices unleashes the "Power of Paradox."

In all the years that I have had the opportunity to be a counselor and assist others in helping them change their lives; I have noticed the deciding factor has always been a persons "willingness to change." Now the big question is, "does someone have to have willingness" to succeed in recovery, or for that matter in making any adjustments to their lives.

"If "willingness" is supposedly the key as Bill Wilson, wrote in his book "Twelve Steps and Twelve Traditions on page 35 in the quote "Once we have placed the key of willingness in the lock and have the door ever so slightly open, we find that we can always open it some more." (End of his quote.)

> "Then does that mean an alcoholic or addict that lacks "willingness" is doomed? Is that the reason it appears that AA has been so unsuccessful due to the belief that "willingness" is necessary for recovery? Why would I state that AA is "so unsuccessful?" Is it possible that there is another key besides "willingness" and that key is actually a "skeleton key" or a "master key" that will open any door, which is blocking an addict or alcoholic from their chance for recovery?

A generally accepted sediment in AA is that it is absolutely necessary to have the "willingness", or to develop

"The willingness to give up your pride and self-will to a Power greater than yourself. This has proved to be the only ingredient absolutely necessary to solve all of your daily problems. Even the smallest amount of "willingness" if sincere is sufficient to allow God to enter, and take control over any problem, pain, or obsession."

Let us all begin to radically shift our views and beliefs and challenge the notion that "willingness" is the only key, and the only state of mind, that can lead to changing lives and behaviors. In the book Alcoholics Anonymous, in the chapter titled "The Doctor's Opinion" on page XXIX it reads, "Unless this person can experience an entire psychic change, there is very little hope for recovery." This is significantly reinforced in the chapter titled "There Is A Solution" on page 27 where it states, "Here and there once in a while alcoholics have had what are called a vital spiritual experiences."

What these statements are meant to communicate is that "an entire psychic change" or " a vital spiritual experience" has to occur in order for any addict or alcoholic to have any chance for a long lasting recovery. A description of that change can be seen in that same chapter, where it states on that same page 27. "To me these occurrences are phenomena. They appear to be in the nature of the huge emotional displacements and rearrangements. Ideas, emotions, and attitudes which were once the guiding forces of the lives of these men are suddenly cast to one side, and a completely new set of conceptions and motives begin to dominate them."

It indicates that "suddenly there is a vast change in outlook and the guiding forces of these men, are cast aside and a completely new set of conceptions, begin to dominate them." Where in any of the above descriptions does it imply "willingness?" The simple answer is that "willingness " had nothing to do with it. If willingness is not the answer; then what word or concept can be selected to describe the redemption from addiction?

"I believe the more effective method to succeed with establishing the necessary attitude and behavioral changes, that will result in enabling an addict or alcoholic to recover, is not that they have to have "willingness," but they have to develop the "Art Of Resistance in Action." Resistance is the last defense that a recovering person has. It is only through the ability to employ resistance that the person will be able to keep safe and keep their sobriety."

"Whereas, "willingness" requires a major shift in attitudes as well as behavior; "resistance" is a method that aligns itself, with the addicts or alcoholics natural tendency towards defiance and selfishness."

"Since challenging the addict to be willing to change,

has not achieved wide spread success; we need to open our minds, to more creative and innovative approaches; rather than just fall back on the same old lame excuse, "they just are not willing, or they just don't have the willingness to change."

What I propose is that we accept and recognize that while AA is a very effective program that provides a ready to accept lifestyle; it fails to provide the necessary methods that would attract more active alcoholics to join that lifestyle. Since the entire AA premise of recovery is based on the "need for willingness" how do we help those that are just not "willing?" Can they be helped? Should we wait till they are more willing? Do we sit back and let the natural consequences of being an active addict or alcoholic, finally catch up, and make them willing to accept the need for recovery?

"Almost sixty years after Bill Wilson, wrote in the book "Twelve Steps And Twelve Traditions on page 35 that "willingness is the key" that "key," unfortunately has failed to open the door for literally millions of addicts and alcoholics."

Therefore we need to reexamine its validity. (AA's own statistics indicate that current estimates of members is approximately 2,000,106. The National Survey on Drug Use and Health (NSDUH), in an annual survey sponsored by the Substance Abuse and Mental Health Services Administration (SAMHSA) statistics estimate that there are 18,000,000 Alcoholics and 5,000,000 Addicts.*

*See these facts located in the beginning of this book in the chapters titled "Introduction" and "Awakening Awareness".

I strongly believe that besides "willingness being a key," there are other "keys." The concept that an addict or alcoholic has to be willing to change, before they can change, needs to carefully reviewed; since a very small minority of addicts and alcoholics ever make it through the door and stick and stay in AA or NA.

We need to find ways that will enable the "unwilling" to change their lives. Just because a person may be experiencing an emotional state that may be labeled, as being "unwilling" does not mean they are "unable" to make some subtle changes. In not only what they think, but more so in what they do.

"There is a bizarre paradox in the fact that while in the
process of demonstrating being "unwilling," they have
to be thinking about, what they are "unwilling" to do.
When anyone thinks about what they are unwilling
or believe that they are unable to do, they are actually
contemplating its opposite."

"They are by default considering the alternative to what
they are resisting, and therefore in their mind, they are
actually considering taking the very action, that they
seem to be unwilling to engage in."

Their decision to do or not do something, or their willingness, or lack of
willingness, hinges on one simple concept. That concept is that addicts and
alcoholics are plagued with the tendency to allow their feelings to dictate
their actions.

"Therefore what I like to call "a stupid and dumb thing
like a feeling" is allowed to destroy, not only their lives;
but also anyone and everyone directly and indirectly
involved with the addict or alcoholic."

Through all the years I have been a counselor working with addicts and
alcoholics, the most common response to why they relapse is, "I just don't feel
like stopping," or "I have just always been this way, kind of stubborn." Over
and over I have heard each and everyone that failed to get sober or lost his or
her sobriety state that, "I just was not ready" or "I just thought I could control
it this time" or "I thought it would be different this time." In addition to these
explanations or excuses or justifications, I have heard them state "I just wanted
to be around my old friends." Other responses were "I didn't know what to do
when (some traumatic event) it happened; I just did not know where to turn."
Still others have said, "I really thought that it was behind me" or conversely
they would state "everything was going so good" or "I just always ruin things,
that is the way I am."

The common thread running through all these expressions is that there
is a specific "belief" behind each one of them. It should be noted that behind
every one of these beliefs there is what I call "a dumb stupid feeling." As
everyone should know by now a "feeling" is not a "fact." Yet the alcoholic or
addict act on their feelings, their (emotions) their "dumb stupid feelings as if

they are "facts." As if they are massive concrete and steel levers that have the torqueing power to pry them out of recovery or prevent them from moving towards recovery.

Just as a "dumb stupid feeling" can pry a person apart from their recovery or their chance for recovery, there is a counter force that can and will hold a person tight to their recovery or enable freedom from the madness of addictions. If feelings are such powerful levers that they can lift a person off their road to recovery causing them to crash; then hopefully there is an equally powerful force that can hold them down on that road to recovery.

A simple well know concept used in professional racing is the use of a "spoiler." It creates the dynamic force that the faster the racecar is traveling the more it holds it to the road. Through the complex science of Aerodynamics the same principle that enables tons of massive tubes of aluminum to become airborne, through the use of a very specialized shape called the "airfoil;" when turned upside creates a paradoxical effect, the opposite effect, and pushes things like racecars down, instead of lifting them up like it does an airplane.

I am using this analogy to demonstrate that one design can be used in two totally different diametrically opposing directions, and yet there is no significant structural change to accomplish these tasks. I believe in the same way that an "airfoil" can be utilized to "lift up" or "hold down" a fast moving object; "defiance" can be flipped over and effectively produce it's very opposite effect.

What I am proposing here is a unique perspective that may seem confusing initially; but if you the reader can simply open your mind to these concepts, that will not be found anywhere but in this book; then you may discover the other "key(s)" that Bill Wilson, never believed existed. Where I would like to begin, is to discuss how unlike Bill Wilson, referred to "defiance" as a serious character flaw as was expressed in his book "Twelve Steps And Twelve Traditions" in his comments written regarding Step Two on page 31 that expressed that "Belief meant reliance, not defiance" and on that same page he wrote "As psychiatrists have often observed, defiance is the outstanding characteristic of many an alcoholic" and the last reference, "When we encountered A.A., the fallacy of our defiance was revealed."

In addition to these references to "Defiance as being a serious character flaw" he wrote on page 28 that, "The roadblocks of indifference, fancied self-sufficiency, prejudice, and DEFIANCE (all capital letters are my emphasis) often prove more solid and formidable for these people than any erected by the unconvinced agnostic or even the militant atheist."

I believe that "Defiance" may be the greatest asset of and for the addicted. Instead of attempting to get rid of it or destroy it or force someone to accept or comply; I propose to just simply flip it over. I am convinced and I hope to convince you, that once you learn to "flip" defiance, the result is its opposite. Now you may be saying to yourself –you must be lying because to "flip" defiance means the person has to be "willing" and therefore this whole proposal is a giant contradiction. If you view it in terms of "willingness" your argument may have some plausibility; but remember I am asking you to briefly open your mind and your "willingness" to hear the rest of the proposal.

To begin to understand how this may work is to recognize the following: Even when a person is very resistant, they are strongly considering the thing that they do not want to do, and then with "defiance" as their guiding force they choose not to do it. One of the key concepts here is that any and every action a person takes, is simply a matter of choices they choose to make. The choice is not made without their knowledge or awareness; although they may not be aware of the serious consequences that may result from the choice they made.

> "Since the addict and alcoholic always has the power of choice, and in fact unless they are in a total decompensated psychotic state, they will always know, they are making choices. Making choices has nothing to do with "willingness," it is just a matter of making choices."

> "The tendency for the addict or alcoholic to be defiant merely means; they make choices others do not agree with, and then they are labeled as being "defiant." If they made a different choice, they would get the label of being "willing." It should be apparent now that "willingness " has nothing to do with decision-making; it is only a label that is given to a decision made by one person from another person, who judges that decision."

> "This should debunk the myth that "willingness" is necessary for a person to recover. I am so passionate to alert the world to the falsehood of this myth, that I am willing to create an alternative reality, that in the end you may consider to be the "real" reality, and not the false constructs of an idealistic fool."

I have witnessed the death and destruction of hundreds if not thousands of addicts, alcoholics and their families. It is this agonizing suffering I am obsessed with ending. I believe that what I propose is solid and sound, and anyone can adopt and accomplish changing their lives for the absolute good for them, for their families and for society as a whole.

> "At the risk of sounding too grandiose, maybe the entire world can learn that "willingness" is a lie, and that everyone who has ever told another person that "you have to be willing" has done them a great disservice at the least, and at the most may have cost them their lives."

At this time I would like to remind the reader that in the book Alcoholics Anonymous in the forward of the first edition it stated the following paragraph, which then became the original preamble of Alcoholics Anonymous. If you are a recovering alcoholic and have attended AA meetings you are very much aware that they read the Preamble before every meeting and for the uninitiated it goes like this:

> "Alcoholics Anonymous is a fellowship of men and women who share their experience, strength and hope with each other that they may solve their common problem and help others to recover from alcoholism. The only requirement for membership is a desire to stop drinking. AA has no dues or fees. It is not allied with any sect, denomination, politics, organization or institution. Does not wish to engage in any controversy. Neither endorses nor opposes any causes. Our primary purpose is to stay sober and help other alcoholics to achieve sobriety."

But it should be noted that the last statement in the Preamble is "the only requirement for membership is a desire to stop drinking." Yet in the Forward to the first edition of the book Alcoholics Anonymous it also states all the above; but they added one simple word that has been deleted from the current and most popular version. That word is "HONEST" in the version in first edition of the A.A. book, the Foreword reads as follows; "the only requirement for membership is an "honest" desire to stop drinking." The quotes on the word "honest" are my own and to establish the radical contrast between what was originally written, and what was finally accepted, as being what we would call, "being politically correct." I challenge you the reader to come up with some kind of plausible reason the word "honest" has been deliberately left out of the verbalized as well as the written version read and heard at the beginning of any AA meeting literally in the entire world.

This decision was made as part of the evolution of AA; the "Honesty" phrase had been dropped from common usage, after the midsummer 1958 meeting of the General Service Board of Trustees ratified the deletion, and since then the Preamble has read simply "a desire to stop drinking."

While AA has always made a big and important point in regards to what is read out loud in the beginning of many meetings, which are pages 58-60 of, "How it Works" in the book Alcoholics Anonymous regarding the first paragraph, where it references three times the conceptual importance of being "honest"; "rigorous honesty" and "capacity to be honest"; then why has addicts and alcoholics deleted this vital word from the ears of any newcomer or visitor, that has ever attended an AA meeting?

While you take your time and struggle to answer this riddle, I will give you my interpretation for this incredible deletion. "It was done to save lives," period. Now you may ask yourself how can leaving the word "honest" out of the AA Preamble save lives? Well then, it is time to remind you of the comment stated in the book Twelve Steps And Twelve Traditions on page 31 "Defiance is the outstanding characteristic of many an alcoholic."

"Since it was so clearly spelt out that "defiance " is an outstanding characteristic, then it would follow that "being honest or having the capacity for honesty would have no bearing or weight in the thought processes of an alcoholic or addict."

"Defiance is driven by an emotion and an emotional state has absolutely nothing to do with the concepts of honesty or being honest. In fact defiance may be the manifestation of an action, which is in opposition to the concept of being honest."

"Since this may be true, and I certainly believe it to be true, it would further follow that since the natural tendency is to be defiant, the alcoholic and addict are

going to be defiant toward being honest, or in other
words, being truthful or believing the truth. If this
was not so, then the alcoholic and addict could not be
defiant nor practice defiance."

The word "honest," that is in the Foreword of the first edition was left out
because in my opinion, it was a deadly word to use, and as I have discussed in
the chapter on "language" that indicated that words can kill, and the sentence
that described that membership in AA was limited to only those who "had
an "<u>honest</u>" desire to stop drinking" (emphasis is mine) may have, and would
have killed thousands of addicts and alcoholics.

Now you are probably becoming confused, perplexed or down right
angry and hostile towards what I am conveying. In fact hopefully you are
still reading this and have not done what Bill Wilson, wrote after the A,B,C's
found currently in any AA book on page 60. In the original manuscript it
stated, "If you are not convinced on these vital issues, you ought to re-read
the book to this point or else throw it away!" Bill was definitely an alcoholic
after my own heart-he did not "mince" words nor was he fearful of the truth
nor of controversy.

Well, for those who have survived so far, I will now offer a clear and
plausible statement regarding why the word "honest," could have and probably
has been responsible for numerous deaths that I believe could number in the
millions.

Now you are asking yourself, is this author insane or crazy; before judging
me, reflect that the Bible states that "the truth will set you free," then how can
a simple word like "honest" be bad for certain people. For it is only though
being "honest" that one can find the "truth" and when you are truthful, you
are being automatically honest.

"It is not the concept nor the word that is the problem, it
is the alcoholic's tendency to be "defiant." If in the past
when an alcoholic or addict had decided to attend AA
or NA, and if they were to hear the original version of
the Preamble, they would be presented with a quandary
and paradox; in that upon hearing the word "honest
desire " they would have to question themselves whether
they do "In Fact" have an "HONEST" desire to stop
drinking. This tendency to second guess or question

their willingness comes from that tendency toward "Defiance."

"By deleting the word "honest," from the sentence describing the criteria for membership has enabled many people to make the decision; without it having to do with a "feeling" or how they "feel" it is just a matter of whether they meet the membership criteria of accepting that: "the only requirement for membership is a desire to stop drinking or using."

Anyone can clearly see, without any confusion over "feelings", that they may be ready to stop drinking or using drugs; but once the person has to filter the desire or decision through the concept of "honest desire" they would then start with second guessing: "But do I really have an HONEST desire-I know I have a DESIRE—but I am not sure I have an HONEST desire; so therefore I may "not" be ready to meet the membership criteria or requirement."

"Therefore by deliberate design or by accidental default leaving the word "honest" out of the popular version of the Preamble has resulted in saving thousands and maybe even millions of lives."

"Leaving out the word "honest" removes the "emotional filter" and by removing the "emotional filter" removes the ambivalence that contrasting emotions create, and this in turn results in reducing or even eliminating the "Defiance" tendencies, that could and have blocked a persons entrance into AA or NA."

The admonition in the AA book indicating that the person has to be "willing" is the same pitfall that befell early alcoholics when the preamble stated "you have to have an "honest desire" blocked them from taking actions, due to it created doubt in their sense of commitment to change. The requirement that "you have to be willing" blocks the addict or alcoholic from making a change in behavior, due to it leads them to believe they have to have a specific and certain type of "feeling" that they just simply may not have, nor may ever be capable of having-"willingness."

"So many addicts and alcoholics over the years would state to me "I just wish, that I just wanted to want to stop, but I just don't feel ready" or they state, "I am not sure I feel I want to stop" or the most sad reason of all "I just don't have the willingness now" or even worse "I lost my willingness."

As can be clearly observed in these statements- they "Do Want To Stop" but they are confused because they do NOT have the "Feeling That They Want To Stop." A simple question to ask, that many times is a matter of life and death is; does a person have to have a "FEELING" in order to change a "BEHAVIOR" do they have to "feel" like they want to stop, in order to stop? The word "willing" is a feeling saturated word, but has nothing to do with ABILITY. Any one at any time has the Absolute Ability To Change Anything They Want At Any Time They Want! But if they believe that they have to have "willingness" or a "feeling of willingness" then that belief could literally KILL them!

"Over and over and over again I want to scream that you do not need "an emotional feeling" to give you permission to change your life! Change Your Behavior, Change Your Life Regardless Of What You Feel Or Don't Feel! No feeling is necessary, since "emotions and feelings" have nothing to do with a person's ability and capability!"

"Everybody is able and capable to make changes without the need for "willingness." So do not allow an asinine stupid feeling rob you of your birthright which gives you the "ability and capability" of virtually doing anything you want regardless of whatever emotion you may or may not presently be experiencing."

In all the years of my experience, I have observed that the addict and alcoholic most of the time seem to be predisposed towards doing the wrong things, especially when it comes to drinking and drugging.

"They drink too much, and use too much, and they get

into to much trouble, and they just don't listen to others
too much- that want them to change."

It seems that there is an unnatural, and automatic negativity and resistance to taking advice, or even really objectively looking at their own behaviors. They have a tendency to blame people, circumstances and situations for the problems they experience as a direct or even indirect result of using drugs or alcohol.

"Many people, and in fact most addicts and alcoholics,
believe that their feelings actually do control what they
say and even what they do; but the truth of the matter
is what they "feel" has absolutely nothing to do with the
"actions" they take."

To prove this point, all you have to do is remember the last time you were driving a car or shopping in a store, and just for a moment you thought about or "felt" like taking something or punching someone or crashing into someone or just pushing someone out of the way, or just drive recklessly through traffic, due to being late or want to run that red light or stop sign. Be honest with yourself, you HAVE experienced these thoughts and "feelings," but you did not act out on them, or at least most of the time you did not act out on them. If you or someone else is indeed a person driven by "impulsivity," then chances are they or you spend most of your time in court, and or, in jail.

Since most addicts and alcoholics are "not" dominantly "impulsive," why do they act as if they are? Why do they drink or use drugs when they feel like it? Why can't they stop themselves; just because they have an overpowering feeling to drink or drug, they do not have to, yet they do, why is this? They do it, "because of a stupid feeling," that they are inclined to follow, or give into, they risk not only their lives but the loss of family, friends, health and freedom, not to mention the actual and potential financial consequences from an arrest or just the cost of the substance use itself, over a dumb ass stupid emotional sensation!

The addict and alcoholic seem to naturally give into temptation, and they seem to "resist" acting on common sense, and fail to register the fact that what they are doing; is just not worth the risk and cost of continuing the addictive behaviors. While they are actively using, and have been doing so for a period of time; it is fully understandable as well as explainable, that the feelings of "withdrawal" would dominate their common sense, and they would ignore any worry, or concern, over actual or potential consequences; due the intense and overwhelming "feeling" that they would die if they did not get more.

> "The fascinating and frightening paradox is that they are chasing after a substance, due to having the "feeling" that if they did not get it; they would DIE, and the very substance that they are so desperate to continue to use to "live," is the very substance that could KILL them."

How is it that a person could have warped their instinct for survival, their common sense, to such a degree, that they believe they need something to live that will actually take their life? Once this paradox is recognized and understood then the principle of utilizing "resistance" instead of "willingness" will make more sense.

I have found after over 30 years of being a counselor that most addicts and alcoholics have demonstrated over and over that they just "don't have the willingness to change or stop." This has deeply concerned me and frustrated me since I have dedicated my life to relieving the suffering that an addict and his or her family suffer. I have asked myself for many years and have taught the concept to many addicts and their families that "willingness is a lie and it is not necessary in order to start and maintain lasting changes."

> "By learning the "Art of Resistance in Action," the addict and alcoholic can more easily access the ability to make shifts, in their behaviors regardless of any "willingness" to do so. Upon reading this you are probably asking yourself how is that possible? How can anyone change unless they are willing to change?"

> "The answer lies in the obvious fact that "it is absolutely unnecessary to want to change, or to have the "willingness" to change; simply due to the fact that "actions" or "behaviors" are not contingent upon any feeling or emotion and "willingness" is nothing more than just an emotion."

Emotions do not and never will "dictate actions." Many people, and in fact most addicts and alcoholics, believe that their feelings actually do control what they say and even what they do; but the truth of the matter is what they feel has absolutely have nothing to do with the actions they take.

> "Through practicing the "Art of Self Defiance" the person gains complete control over their impulsive tendencies. By challenging their resistance to doing the right things, they immediately reap huge rewards consisting of, automatic increases in self-esteem and self worth."

It is very confusing for most people who suffer from addictions, to grasp the real nature of their affliction. Addiction has been defined as a pathological condition that is manifested in behaviors that are conducted in an obsessive and compulsive manner. The definition of an addict, which will be used here, describes people who have lost control, or never had control, over a mood-altering chemical, whether it is alcohol or some legal or illegal substance.

In contrast to this there are many people who engage in very destructive and self-defeating behaviors that have absolutely nothing to do with the use or abuse of drugs and alcohol. These behaviors include; but are not limited to sex, food, gambling, shopping, working, exercising, using the Internet, video games and virtually any other activity that results in harm to self or others. This harm can be classified into the following categories: Financial; relationships (which include significant others), family and friends; emotional as experienced through a sense of bewilderment and confusion, as well as guilt and possible shame. There may be physical harm as in engaging in poor eating habits leading to poor nutrition, or overdoing physical exercise leading to injuries.

All these pathological behaviors have one thing in common; they are suppose to be healthy productive and fun and instead they cause mental and physical harm and illness due to abuse of health and abandonment or destruction of relationships.

> "When any person selects an activity that completely absorbs them for extended periods of time; then the people who are around that person become neglected and frustrated, at the seemingly rude or insensitive behavior of the obsessed person."

Since the obsessed person is not aware that their obsession with an activity, is systematically cutting away their healthy intimate contacts with others, there is total denial that he or she is paying a very high emotional cost, by investing themselves into things, whether it is the Internet, watching T.V. or shopping; instead of developing and maintaining emotional and physical interaction with people.

In other words they have replaced the need and comfort of being around people, with the detached mechanical involvement with their obsession. Since there is no use of a damaging substance, the person can easily minimize the negative impacts of their behaviors.

> "When a person finds interaction with things more important than being with other people, then they have developed a serious mental illness. The nature of this illness causes the person to have a tendency to follow the dictates of their feelings and not the advice or opinions of others. Once they allow feelings to dictate their actions they have cut themselves off from influence of others."

That is why although they can clearly see the need to change their self destructive or inappropriate behaviors they fail to take any actions to change. They become indecisive or confused due to "not feeling ready." Even though they absolutely are actually listening to and may in fact agree with the concerns of other people; they still believe and act on feelings that are contrary and irrational. The irrational feelings block any positive influences that could encourage a change in behaviors.

> "It should be noted that when an addict or alcoholic begin recovery or abstinence; they frequently begin to engage in other pathological behaviors, whether it is working overtime, overeating, sexual promiscuity overspending, or overextending themselves to others including the AA or NA programs."

> "In this way they continue to perpetuate negative and self-defeating behaviors that hurt not only themselves but also their loved ones. They become so preoccupied with trying to make more money or just trying to

escape unpleasant emotions; that they bring more pain
and discomfort into their lives, instead of escape and
relief."

This frustration leads to disillusionment, discouragement and
dissatisfaction, which will potentially trigger a return to substance use and
abuse. As noted through out this book the driving force behind most recovery
failures is due to the inability to control or manage emotional impulses.

"When a person allows their feelings to dictate their
actions and behaviors; whether the person is recovering
from a chemical dependency, food issues, gambling
problems, codependency, sex or relationship dependency,
or is a workaholic or shopaholic; it is this tendency to
follow destructive feelings and emotions that remains
the greatest challenge and threat.

"The most powerful method available to manage any
type of threat to any type of recovery is to be able to
successfully overcome this challenge by fully utilizing
the "Power to Resist the Resistance" through the "Art
of Self Defiance."

Alcoholics and addicts are people who have never grown up due to never
learning how to build healthy self-esteem. Instead of developing behaviors
that would lead to the development of healthy self esteem, the addict and
alcoholic developed behaviors that led to the development of defiance!

"Maturity requires the ability to delay gratifications and
to sacrifice for others. Since the addict and alcoholic
failed to adequately develop these adult characteristics,
they remain childishly selfish and impulsive."

To compensate or cover up for their failure to learn how to function as
a responsible adult, they will attack anybody who reminds or alerts them
of their serious deficiencies. Instead of learning to do things that build self-
esteem and self worth, through sacrifice and giving, they have become self-
centered takers.

The ability to force yourself to do something that you really do not want to do, that is good for you or good for someone else, will result in an increase in self esteem and self worth. Virtually every time a person is able to sacrifice their time, efforts or resources for another person, they automatically feel an increase in their self esteem. Any time you have given a "buck to a bum" on a street corner, how did you feel? Anytime you gave or did something for another person, and absolutely expected nothing in return, did it not feel like a positive experience?

> "It is the ability to give and sacrifice in a healthy way that measures how mature or adult a person is. The addict and alcoholic due to being so self centered, selfish, self obsessed and self-absorbed, protect themselves from this truth by being oppositional, rebellious and defiant."

> "All people need to develop ongoing self-esteem and self worth, and since the very small self focus of the addict or alcoholic prevent this from developing, they have learned to use the passion of Defiance as a substitute to having or knowing how to gain self-esteem."

> "The Power Of Paradox to power addiction extinction is employed when a person forces themselves to do the right things and overcome their selfish oppositional, rebellious and defiant feelings, by using Their Oppositional, Rebellious Defiant Feelings-Those VERY Same Feelings To Overcome Their OWN Resistance. The result of being able to accomplish this on a very regular basis is the development of mature adult functioning that gives the strength to resist doing the wrong things."

When the person has finally gained the ability to do this regularly and frequently they have achieved one of the greatest accomplishments in their lives! The Bible states "He who conquers himself has won a greater victory than he who conquers a city." - King Solomon. This proverb reflects the massive achievement of anyone who takes control of his or her own personality.

> "When a person refuses to challenge their wrong feelings or impulses; then that person is just a slave with an empty and meaningless existence. Don't be that person

for your sake, your family's sake or your loved ones sake and for God's sake please use the powerful forces inside you to be free and to have that "Redemption from Addiction."

Regardless of any feeling or emotion you are experiencing teach yourself you are in control of yourself-

"Be greater than he who conquered a city!"

Once again the technique to accomplish this to fully commit to do the following:

Always remember in order to change you must first deal with the illness, which is expressed through your "resistance" tendencies, which blocks off the ability to change! Just because you want to change, and even if you know you must change.

Learning More Will Not Fix You Or Change You!

Knowledge Will Not Fix You!

The Best Intentions Will Not Fix You!

There Is No Magic To Fix You!

The Only Thing That Can Fix You—Is To Know You Should!

First: On A Daily Basis Write (Not think about but take a pen or pencil in hand and WRITE) Five Reasons Why Change Is Desired And Needed!

Second: You Need On A Daily Basis To Write (On paper NOT a computer.) Five Changes You Will Do Daily.

Third: You Need To "Do" (Not THINK that you "did"—but ACTUALLY "did" do!) The Five Things You Said You Would "Do" Before You Go To Bed Each Day!

Fourth:	You Need To Do Those Things When You Want To- But It Is FAR, FAR—More Important!
Fifth:	For You To DO Them When You DON'T Want To!

There is a simple principle behind the above five suggestions—The Power of Paradox is released when "The Art Of Self Defiance" is practiced!

> "The Power Of Paradox is unleashed when a person forces himself or herself to do the right things and overcome their selfish oppositional, rebellious and defiant feelings, by using their oppositional, rebellious defiant feelings-those very same feelings to overcome their own resistance."

> "The result of being able to effectively practice the "Art of Resistance in Action" and the "Art of Self Defiance" will result in the ability to create consistently strong mature adult functioning that gives the strength which essentially leads to addiction extinction and the improved capability to resist doing the wrong things."

*Ask, and it Shall be given You; and You
Shall find; Knock, and it Shall be
Opened unto You.*

Matthew 7:7

Chapter Eleven

Visualizing Victory

In this chapter, we will explore the "Power of Imagination" through the "Art of Visualization" that is found inside all people. There are awesome and powerful creative forces that can be fully tapped; that will absolutely unleash our dreams and hopes transforming them into a desired reality. Or these same forces will send us into the deepest darkest Hell we have ever known!

Many contemporary philosophers and motivation specialists discuss the nature of this creative force, which can transform anyone's dreams into realities or what I refer to as turning "Possibilities into Probabilities." Many spiritual teachers convey the actual laws and formulas to bring about these desired realities. Rather than paraphrase these great teachers I will now present their own views and I will guide you to properly use this great power—The Power of Imagination!

> "If a person fails to understand that they have a great responsibility to take full possession and control of this power, then that failure to take this responsibility will always lead to these forces taking control of the person in an undesirable, destructive and potentially deadly manner."

> "All addictions are a manifestation caused by the poor or improper use of these forces and powers!"

-Wayne Dwyer's- view of this power is as follows:

He indicates that it is through the attachment of love and especially loving yourself that leads to the manifestation of any reality you choose. He specifically expresses that:

> "The power of creation through imagination" in which

each night he recommends as we go to bed and just before drifting off into sleep that we focus on and deeply envision any desire, goal, dream or future reality; for the "subconscious through some powerful and unknown force converts and transforms our thoughts into a manifested reality."

Any addict or alcoholic who day dreams and night dreams about the substances they used and focuses on memories of the feelings they experienced under the influence, are summoning this power to provide what they long for and desire—which is to get high or drunk again! If the person fails to challenge these feelings and memories, then their "subconscious through some powerful and unknown force converts and transforms their thoughts into a manifested reality." In other words opportunities and temptations to use will present themselves as a direct result of failing to take control of these forces or misusing their power!

These powers and principles were first discovered by Napoleon Hill, and then documented in his book "Think and Grow Rich," in which the concept of "autosuggestion" was first presented in 1937.

-Napoleon Hill-

"Every man is what he is because of the dominating thoughts which he permits to occupy his mind. Thoughts which a man places in his own mind, and encourages with sympathy, and with which he mixes any one or more of the emotions, constitute the motivating forces which direct and control his every movement, act, and deed!"

For the addict or alcoholic this is the driving force for their repeated failures! They have a strong tendency to feed their minds with not just the memory of past drinking and drug using experiences; but also emotionalize them with strong desire and passion!
-Napoleon Hill-

"Those who go down in defeat, and end their lives in poverty, misery, and distress, do so because of the negative application of the principle of autosuggestion. The cause may be found in the fact that all impulses of thought have a tendency to clothe themselves in their physical equivalent. The subconscious mind makes no distinction between constructive and destructive thought impulses. It works with the material we feed it, through our thought impulses. The subconscious mind will translate into reality a thought driven by fear just readily as it will translate into reality a thought driven by courage or faith."

Since "the subconscious mind works with whatever we feed it and it makes no distinction between constructive or destructive thought impulses" then this is the way that the addict or alcoholic does the greatest damage to their chances for recovery, when they engage in exchanging "War Stories" with great enthusiasm, humor and intense passion. Their unwitting destruction is driven by the concept:

-Napoleon Hill-

"All thoughts which have been emotionalized (given feeling) and are mixed with faith begin immediately to translate themselves into their physical equivalent or counterpart."

Since thoughts are things then the intense passion of thinking and talking about drug and alcohol use, assure that the opportunity to drink and use drugs will materialize. In other words addicts and alcoholics have mastered the principles of success and use those very same concepts to assure their own failure and destruction!

Before a person can begin to think and speak with great passion about recovery and sobriety, they will have to abandon verbalizing all references to drinking and drug use. Failure to exercise the discipline or determination to take control of not only their speech but thoughts as well; will continue to lead to failure to achieve long term recovery. This is due mainly to the fact that any positive thoughts or speech about using alcohol or drugs will always be emotionally experienced as being exciting and therefore appealing. The purpose of this book is to alert the addict and alcoholic of the dynamics that undermine their efforts to recover and to provide methods to create the necessary desire and actions that will absolutely enable them to change their life. In regards to this Napoleon Hill stated:

> "The starting point of all achievement is desire... keep this constantly in mind weak desire brings weak results, just as a small amount of fire makes a small amount heat. If you find yourself lacking in persistence, this weakness may be remedied by building a strong fire under your desires."

By forcing yourself to do what you don't want to do enables you to gain hold of and grasp these powerful forces and turn them in the direction of success instead of failure! He emphasized that:

> "Through some strange and powerful principle of "mental chemistry" which she has never divulged, Nature wraps up in the impulse of strong desire, "that something" which recognizes no such word as impossible and accepts no such reality as failure."

> "I have never known anyone to distinguish himself, to accumulate riches of any consequence, without possession of the secret."

> "Whatever a man conceives and believes he can achieve."

But it is absolutely necessary to emphasize that he or she can and will achieve what they conceive whether it is good for their life or harmful and destructive to their existence!

The power is truly in your own hands and you must consciously use it for your good! In regards to this he expressed very strongly the concept:

> "That we were born with the gift to control and direct our own mind to achieve whatever ends we desire...If we accept this gift and responsibility then the following will occur.

> "You will have sound health, freedom from fear and

worry, a labor of love of your own choosing, a positive
mental attitude, peace of mind and material wealth of
your own choice and amount."

But if we failed to take control of this gift; in another words-let our feelings dictate our action then...

"These are the penalties we will absolutely suffer-Poor health, fear and worry, indecision and doubt, frustration and discouragement through out our lives, poverty and want and a flock of evils consisting of: Envy, jealousy, greed, anger, hatred and superstition."

A vision or imagery creates a plan to acquire the object of desire, therefore be very alert and aware and do not allow wrong visions and wrong desires to dominate or rule your mind. For failing to exercise due caution and control over your thoughts will crush and destroy any good intentions or good desires about getting clean and sober! Unmonitored unhealthy and harmful thought will take root in the same way that an unattended garden will grow weeds that if not attended will grow out of control. The Law of Attraction is driven by desire and desire creates what is attractive. The addict or alcoholic has a great responsibility to monitor their thoughts and feelings. They must be able to direct their desires to assure they are positive and will be productive.

Therefore it should be especially noted:

"Thoughts which are mixed with any of the feelings of emotions constitute a "magnetic" force which attracts, from the vibrations of the ether, other similar, or related thoughts. A thought thus "magnetized" with emotion may be compared to a seed which when planted in fertile soil, germinates, grows, and multiplies itself over and over again, until that which was originally one small seed, becomes countless millions of seeds..."

--Napoleon Hill—

Make sure you are growing and cultivating the right kinds of seeds. Attend the seeds of a recovery lifestyle and you will reap great riches in every area of your life. Cultivate the wrong seeds of an addictive lifestyle, then watch every dream, hope, desire, promise, vision and aspiration be slowly choked and shattered!

Since these concepts and principles were based upon the study of the most powerful and successful people at the turn of the last century, it may be very important to not only consider these views but to aggressively apply them to your life and experiences.

-Emmett Fox- related in his book "Sermon on the Mount" that…

> "As soon as you know the Truth and take your thinking in hand, if you are steering correctly, you can find the true place for you, you can be what you want to be, you can do what you want to do, you can have what you want to have. Your thinking is directed. You are no longer drifting in the breeze; you are directing your thinking. You are what you think. That is your identity. And remember that in Mind, there is no extension. Until you learn the Truth, you dwell in the senses: sight, hearing, touch. You are where you think… Until you take your thinking in hand and begin to steer it, you cannot get anywhere. Your direction is in your thought…"

Dr. Fox is reflecting on the fact that if and when we take control of our "thoughts" we can accomplish anything. But if we allow our senses "emotions" (emphasis is mine) we will live an undirected life and remain, "drifting in the breeze." In another words remain at the mercy of impulsive reactionary decision making, rather than taking control of our ability to direct our own minds to achieve whatever ends we desire.

In Emmitt Fox's book "The Sermon On The Mount" he expanded on the above concept. The principal that he relates is the same one that was identified by Napoleon Hill. Since both these books deal with understanding and managing personal power, it is important to fully understand this power. It must be recognized that it is absolutely essential for a person to take control of not only their feelings and emotions, but it is even more vital to manage and control their own thoughts. Since the addict and alcoholic utilize the very principles that are the foundation for success and achievement in a negative and self-destructive manner, it is essential to fully comprehend the following in which Emmett Fox emphasizes that…

"All day long the thoughts that occupy your mind, your Secret Place, as Jesus calls it, are molding your destiny for good or evil; in fact, the truth is that the whole of our life's experience is but the outer expression of inner thought. Now we can choose the sort of thoughts that we entertain. It will be a little difficult to break a bad habit of thought, but it can be done. We can choose how we shall think—in point of fact, we always do choose—and therefore our lives are just the result of the kind thoughts we have chosen to hold; and therefore they are of our own ordering; and therefore there is perfect justice in the universe. No suffering for another man's original sin, but the reaping of a harvest that we ourselves have sown. We have free will, but our free will lies in our choice of thought."

Once we begin to understand this concept we will be able to recognize and accept the absolute fact that if we fail, or continue to fail in our recovery attempts, then it is directly related to our choice in regards to the thoughts we permit to occupy our minds. It is essential that you grasp this truth and immediately apply it to your thinking and then fully understand the following profound view of Dr. Fox!

"If you really do wish to alter your life, if you really do wish to change yourself—to become a different person altogether in the sight of God and man—if you really do want health and peace of mind and spiritual development, then Jesus, in his Sermon on the Mount, has clearly shown you how it is to be done. The task is not an easy one, but we know that it can be accomplished, because there are those who have done it—but the price must be paid, and the price is the actual carrying out of these principles in every corner of your life, and every daily transaction, whether you wish to or not, and more particularly where you would much rather not."

All through this book I have emphasize the importance of not allowing your feelings to dictate your behaviors and actions. I also emphasized that willingness is not necessary for a person to change their life. These universal and ancient truths that are being presented should be fully self-evident. The addict and alcoholic in order to recover must take responsibility for not only the way they emotionally react, but more importantly they need to totally control the thoughts they permit to occupy their minds. As can be seen in the above concept, the person must change and take actions that they have no willingness to take.

It is just a simple fact that in order to change your life a price must be paid. As Dr. Fox indicated that price is the "Carrying Out Of These Principles In Every Corner Of Your Life And In Every Daily Transaction, Whether You Wish To Or Not, And More Particularly Where You Would Much Rather Not."

Elsewhere in this book I had emphasized the important technique of doing five things every single day that you rather not do, and through forcing yourself to take actions that you just don't "feel" like doing, provides the power to change your life in positive rather than destructive ways.

TO RECOVER YOU MUST PRACTICE THE "RESISTANCE TO RESISTING" HEALTHY CHANGES AND Force Yourself To Do The Right Things EVEN WHEN THERE IS NO PERCEIVED EMOTIONAL RETURN OR REWARD, since Dr. Fox explicitly believes and states that....

"The great Law of the Universe, however, is just this— that what you think in your mind you will produce in your experience. As within, so without. You cannot think one thing and produce another. If you want to control your circumstances for harmony and happiness, you must first control your thoughts for harmony and happiness, and then the other things will follow. If you want health, you must first think health; and, remember, thinking health does not mean merely thinking a healthy body, important as that is, but it also includes thinking peace and contentment, and goodwill to all, for, as we shall see later in the Sermon destructive emotion is one of the primary causes of disease."

Please take a close note of the concept that "destructive emotion" is one of the "primary" causes of disease. To be happy, but more importantly to stay clean and sober it is absolutely essential that we must be "Thinking Peace And

Contentment, And Goodwill To All People" for Emmett Fox further clearly stated the following:

> "The principle involved is perfectly simple, but unfortunately the doing of it is anything but easy. Do not dwell upon the mistakes or upon the slowness of your progress, but claim the presence of God within you, all the more, in the teeth of a discouraging suggestion. Claim Wisdom, Claim Power, or prosperity in prayer. Have a mental stocktaking or review of your life, and see if you are not still thinking wrongly in some section or other of your mind. Is there some wrong line of conduct that you are still pursuing? Is there somebody whom you have not forgiven? Are you indulging in any kind of political, or racial, or religious sectarian hatred or contempt? Get rid of this evil thing for it is poison in your life. Waste no more time worrying about the past it is over and done, make the present and the future a splendid realization of your hearts desire."

It is this principle that is the foundation supporting the AA directive stated on page 64 in the AA book regarding "Resentment being the number one offender" and "from it stems all forms of spiritual disease." It is literally the greatest threat to recovery. On page 84 in the AA book it states "…we resolutely turn our thoughts to someone we can help. Love and tolerance of others is our code." The addict or alcoholic has a vital need to "practice, love, patience and tolerance" and make "it their code."

AA emphasizes the need to have a "spiritual awakening" or "spiritual experience" and Dark And Spiteful Feelings Towards Anybody, Whether Warranted Or Not, Will Block And Destroy Any Chance For A Lasting Recovery. In some cases where there has been severe harm done to a person and they have to deal with justified anger or hate, that if permitted to continue would literally destroy them, they will have no other choice but to utilize and engage in the process of prayer!

ALWAYS REMEMBER THAT AN ACTION OR A DECISION DOES NOT NEED YOUR EMOTIONAL APPROVAL!

Dr. Fox relates the following in regards to the benefits of prayer:

> "The great essential for success in prayer—for obtaining

that sense of the Presence of God, which is the secret of healing oneself and others to; of obtaining inspiration, which is the breath of the soul; of acquiring spiritual development—is that we first obtain some degree of true peace of mind. This true, interior soul peace was known to the mystics as serenity, and they are never tired of telling us that serenity is the grand passport to the Presence of God—the sea as smooth as glass that is round about the Great White Throne. This is not to say that one cannot overcome even the most serious difficulties by prayer without having any serenity at all, for of course one can. In fact, the greater the trouble one is in, the less serenity he will be able to have, and serenity itself is only to be had by prayer, and by the forgiving of others, and of oneself. But, serenity you must have, before you can make any such true spiritual progress; and it is serenity, that fundamental tranquility of soul, that Jesus refers to by the word "peace"—the peace that passes all human understanding."*

Since negative feelings as well as thoughts towards others are one of the primary causes of disease, and addiction is a disease; then it follows that the only solution is to seize hold of these destructive impulses and forcefully remove them from your mind. Failure to take control and responsibility, because you just don't "feel" like it, is no different than taking your hands off the steering wheel because you "feel" tired, while driving fast on treacherous twisting, zigzagging, high mountainous roads—you will literally go over the edge and die!

*It is highly recommended that you read Emmett Fox's book "Sermon on the Mount" which can be found easily through the Internet and is available in most bookstores!

"FEELINGS SHOULD NEVER BE ALLOWED TO DIRECT YOUR ACTIONS!" YOUR ACTIONS SHOULD ALWAYS BE FILTERED THROUGH STRONG POSITIVE RECOVERY PRINCIPLES; PRINCIPLES THAT ARE BEING PRESENTED HERE, THAT ARE VERY CLEARLY LAID OUT

AND DESCRIBED IN DEPTH AND DETAIL."
More of these principles have been eloquently presented
by...

-Anthony Robbins-

Who believes in and lives by the concept that "all things are possible" and
he expresses specific ways that this "fact" can be manifested into anyone's life
that chooses to follow his directions. He also emphasizes the absolute need
to not only control what you think and feel, but what you allow yourself to
focus on.

> "Changing our belief system is central to making any
> real and lasting change in our lives. In life lots of people
> know what to do but few people actually do what they
> know. Knowing is not enough! You must take action.
> You literally begin the change in life the moment you
> make a new decision. When you decide that your life
> will ultimately be shaped not by conditions, but by your
> decisions, then in that moment, your life will change
> forever, and you'll be empowered to take control.
> Take control of your own actions because if we don't
> consciously direct our own thoughts, we will fall under
> the influence of those who would have us behave in the
> way they desire."

--Anthony Robbins—

Once again it is clear that for a person to succeed with anything, not just
recovery, they must take control of their decision making power. The power
to make a decision has absolutely nothing to do with whether you "feel" like
doing something or do not "feel" like doing something. If you do not take
responsibility for making a decision then you will fall under the influence of
others. In other words if you choose to be around people who are toxic, you
will be poisoned and become sickened and your recovery will die!

To improve your chances you must learn how to force yourself to do the
right things and to absolutely learn to ignore any person, feeling or emotion
that would counter that effort or right action. When a threat arises within, or
outside of yourself, then you must be able to gain control and apply leverage

to remove that thought, feeling or person from your life. In regards to this Mr. Robbins relates:

> "To get new results in our lives, we can't just know what we want and get leverage on ourselves. We can be highly motivated to change, but if we keep doing the same things, running the same inappropriate patterns, our lives are not going to change, and all we will experience is more and more pain and frustration.

It is our "inappropriate pattern" of allowing our feelings to dictate our actions that leads to failure after failure in not just our recovery efforts, but also if unchecked, will literally undermine any and all our efforts in every area of our lives. By taking control of our feelings and directing our own thoughts we are able to access the power to do or change anything in our lives! Once this principle is completely understood and fully grasped, an addict, alcoholic or in fact anybody will be in complete control of their lives and destiny! Indeed as Anthony Robbins expressed "all things are possible." The only thing that can stop you or get in the way—Is An Asinine Stupid Meaningless Feeling Or Emotion; That Absolutely Has Nothing To Do With Whether A Person Can Make A Decision And Fully Follow Through With A Strong Commitment. Make A Commitment To Change Yourself, Your Beliefs, Your Thinking, Your Feelings, Your Attitudes, But Most Of All Your Actions And Behavior.

Mr. Robbins expresses in order to improve and change your life…

> "We need to expand our view of who we are. We need to make certain that the labels we put upon us are not limits but enhancements, that we add to all that's already good with us—for whatever you and I begin to identify with, we will become. Begin asking yourself, "what more can I be? What more will I be? Who might I becoming now?" "I will consistently act as a person who is already achieving goals. I will breathe this way I will move this way I'll respond to people this way I will treat people with the kind of dignity, respect, compassion, and love that this person would" if we decide to think, feel, and act as a kind of person we want to be, we will become that person. You are now

at a crossroads. This is your opportunity to make the most important decision you'll ever make. Forget your past. Who are you now? Who have you decided you really are now? Don't think about who you have been. Who are you now? Who have you decided to become? Make decision consciously. Make it carefully. Make it powerfully."

In regards to his suggestion that "the labels we put on ourselves are not limitations but enhancements," then the following very controversial practice that I recommend and encourage with any addict or alcoholic I work with, may be better understood appreciated, and hopefully adopted.

This practice consists of having a chemically dependent person "never" introducing themselves as an addict or an alcoholic. No person should limit himself or herself to calling themselves a condition that they have. They may have a condition (addiction) but they are not the condition that they have; they are far, far more than their condition—they are a human being with a million potentialities or a billion possibilities; they are not just an addict or an alcoholic!

They are absolutely capable of so much more, they are so much more-they are mothers and fathers; brothers and sisters; sons and daughters; parents and grandparents. They are miracles—made from God and from Stardust; they are the essence of all creation and the greatest accomplishment in the entire universe! Why should anybody call themselves anything less and after they have conditioned and developed the "inappropriate pattern" of referring to themselves as an "addict or alcoholic" then what are they?

If you are confused, offended or angered by my views then try this simple exercise. Call yourself a name, the name is "addict" or the name is "alcoholic" and that is the one that is absolutely required to gain or be accepted in a self help 12 Step program. "Hi my name is Jerry and I am an alcoholic and addict." Now keep in mind this salutation is stated several million times a day by several million people. Now how about saying something like: "Hi my name is Mary and I am a miracle!" Or "My name is Frank and I am a great father!" or "My name is Jean and I am a Gem!" Now if this was said a few million times a day by a few million people the world may be a much better place to live.

Now before you throw this book away—I mean I hope you are still reading, give me a moment to explain my heresy. While we give lip service and believe that addiction is a disease, most people who are not professionally involved with addiction, don't accept it as a disease. Therefore no matter how much effort is made to convince the general public that it is a disease, just like any other disease, it is not accepted as such. Since the majority of people do not accept or view it as a disease, then they view it as a weakness and instead of having compassion they have judgment and condemnation. This in turn produces stigma and this creates a sense of failure, guilt and shame.

Since most people view it this way including most addicts and alcoholics, the admission of being an "alcoholic" or "addict" is not the same label; such as when someone identifies themselves with a disease that is more accepted, a disease; such as Diabetes. A person who states they are "a Diabetic" everyone immediately views as someone who has a problem with sugar and it goes no further. They are not judged and condemned. But any person who states they are an "alcoholic" or an "addict" people immediately view that person in very different terms. The label of addiction unfortunately is a personality attack. It cuts deep into the heart, soul and spirit of the person. It destroys the very essence of feeling human. I believe it is this tag that has been partially responsible for the fact that although AA has helped millions of people; it has failed to help many millions more! The purpose of this book is to not reinforce limitations but to explode the enhancements and turn "possibilities into probabilities!"

After all, one of the greatest teachers in the world expressed:

"We are what we think. All that we are arises with our thoughts.

With our thoughts, we make our world."

...Original Saying of the Siddhartha Gautama Buddha.
(560 B.C. — 480 B.C.)

The next man was a total failure but then he discovered these principles and not only changed his own life but the lives of hundreds or even thousands of sales men and women around the world by teaching and applying these principles.

-Joe Gerard-

"Want. My want. That was all I knew. And that want was enough to drive me to say and do enough of the right things... And the more you want the more you drive yourself to do what it takes... But you have to want something. And you have to know what it is. And you have to see every move you make is a way of getting

> whatever it is you want. Once I saw that Coca-Cola
> salesman as a bag of groceries I had to bring home to
> my family, he was sold."

By envisioning or imagining the customer as a bag of groceries for his family he developed enough determination to overcome any resistance and by the way he went on to become the greatest car salesman in history. He is in the book of the Guinness Book of World Records having sold 13,000 new cars and trucks in his 15 year career in car sales. It should be especially noted he sold them one at a time—he did not do fleet sales, but sold one car at a time to one customer at a time to achieve this distinction of being the best car salesman in history!

-Louise Hay-

Also discovered these same principles and has successfully transformed her life and those people who have read and studied her wisdom and understanding of the world have gained much personal power as well as the ability to take control and direct their own lives in whatever manner they desire. The following quotes do not need any interpretation or reference to addiction.

They speak universal truths and clearly demonstrate how Applying Their Meaning To Addiction Explains Why We Continue To Use Drugs And Alcohol. BUT IF WE BEGIN TO APPLY THIS WISDOM AND THE POWER OF THESE WORDS, TO RECOVERY we may find an extraordinary source of positive power to change our lives! The following is a quote from her home page:

Recently dubbed "the closest thing to a living saint" by the Australian media, Louise Hay is also known as one of the founders of the self-help movement. Her first book, Heal Your Body, was published in 1976, long before it was fashionable to discuss the connection between the mind and body. Revised and expanded in 1988, this bestselling book introduced Louise's concepts to people in 30 different countries and 23 different languages throughout the world. Through her healing techniques and positive philosophy, millions have learned how to create more of what they want in their lives, including more wellness in their bodies, minds and spirits.

A few of Louise Hay's quotes that will emphasize concepts discussed throughout this book are.*

> "No matter what the problem is, our experiences are just
> outer effects of inner thoughts."

"The past is over and done and cannot be changed. This is the only moment we can experience."

"Your thoughts and beliefs of the past have created this moment, and all the moments up to this moment. What you are now choosing to believe and think and say will create the next moment and the next day and the next month and the next year."

"Look at the problem in your life. Ask yourself, what kind of thoughts am I having that created this?"

*If the reader is not aware of the extraordinary exceptional insightful and healing works and words of Louise Hayes-then it would be extremely beneficial to Google her, or find a plethora of her works in any bookstore in the self-help section!

"You are not a helpless victim of your own thoughts, but rather a master of your own mind."

"We are each responsible for all of our experiences."

"Every thought we think is creating our future."

"The point of power is always in the present moment."

"You are the power in your world."

"You get to have whatever you choose to think!"

"See God in every person, place, and thing, and all will be well in your world."

"What we believe about ourselves and about life becomes true for us."

"All the events you have experienced in your lifetime up to this moment have been created by your thoughts and beliefs you have held in the past."

"Your mind is a tool you can choose to use any way you wish."

"Explain to people that everything they say is an affirmation. Everything they think is an affirmation. Everything! What you want to do is to get control of what you are saying and thinking, so these things bring you good experiences in your life rather than rotten experiences."

"You have the power to heal your life, and you need to know that. We think so often that we are helpless, but were not. We always have the power of our minds... Claim and consciously use your power."

"Remember, you're the only person who thinks in your mind! You are the power and authority in your world."

"The thoughts we choose to think are the tools we use to paint the canvas of our lives."

In addition to these the following classical affirmations should also be strongly expressed and stated loudly!

"All I need is within me now!"

"Every day in every way I'm getting better and better!"

"Everything comes to me easily and effortlessly!"

"I love and appreciate myself just as I am!"

"I love doing my work and I am richly rewarded creatively and financially!"

"I now have enough time, energy, wisdom, and money to accomplish all my desires!"

"Infinite riches are now freely flowing into my life!" "I am relaxed and centered!"

"I feel happy and blissful!"

These quotes should be read out loud every day since it only takes a few minutes to fill your mind full of some of the greatest thoughts and concepts that have ever been written. By reading them out loud will jump-start your mind to give strong positive feelings.

"Incantations are much more powerful than Positive Affirmations due to how an incantation is stated OUT LOUD with passion and as an absolute undeniable truth about oneself; while Positive Affirmations are spoken quietly and softly to oneself, and is only perceived as "wishful thinking that the mind can argue with, and therefore diminish or defeat totally."

"Always be aware that our thoughts are creating a future and by controlling the words that we speak OUT LOUD, strong and proudly will enable us to gain control of our thoughts and therefore our future destiny."

It is also strongly suggested you use the following Anthony Robbins incantations: for maximum effect and benefit these should be said very loudly and strongly at least five to seven times with intense passion!

Now I Am The Voice!

I Will Lead Not Follow!

I Will Believe Not Doubt!

I Will Create Not Destroy!

I Am A Force For Good! I Am A Force For God!

I Am A Leader!

Defy The Odds!

Set A New Standard!

Step Up!

Step Up!

Step Up!

Anthony Robbins also had Seven Power Questions that a person should ask themselves at least once a day and preferably upon waking up. Those questions are presented here for your convenience, but as you may recall they were first presented in an earlier chapter titled "Resisting the Resistance." At this time you now know the vital importance of strongly emotionalizing your answers to each of these questions.

Questions asked at least daily:

1. "What Am I Excited About In My Life Right Now?" "What about that makes me excited?" "How Does That Make Me Feel?"
2. "What Am I Happy About In My Life Right Now?" "What About That Makes Me Happy?" "How Does That Make Me Feel?"
3. "What Am I Proud About In My Life Right Now?" "What Is It That Makes Me Proud?" "How Does That Make Me Feel?"
4. "What Am I Enjoying Most In My Life Right Now?" "What Is It That Is So Enjoyable?" "How Does That Make Me Feel?"
5. "What Am I Committed To Right Now?" "What About That Makes Me Committed?" "How Does Being Committed Make Me Feel Right Now?"
6. "What Am I Grateful For In My Life Right Now?" How Does It Make Me Feel –To Be Grateful Right Now?"
7. "Who Do I Love Right Now And Who Loves Me Right Now?" "How Does That Make Me Feel To Love and be Loved Right Now?"

By asking yourself these questions invoking strongly on identifying and fully experiencing the feeling and emotions associated to each answer, will enable you to achieve control of your thoughts!

These are the feelings that you want to create that build resistance muscle against drinking or drug use desires. By speaking them loudly you will recognize the Power, feel the Power and most of all know the Power that can transform your life.

"The power that I am speaking about is your God-given right your— birthright, "to take possession of and direct your own mind to whatever ends that you desire!"

"Reading and studying these quotes is not enough; you MUST speak them OUTLOUD! Through hearing these incantations and affirmations in your own ears from your own mouth; will ABOLUTELY enable you to gain understanding of the deeper truth that all of your life is but the outer expression of your inner passionate thoughts and therefore you must take responsibility for your own thoughts!"

You must put forth all the effort that is absolutely necessary to change, control and to direct your own thinking for what is great in your life, rather then to continue to allow yourself to destroy not only your own life, but also everyone else who loves and cares about you! On a daily basis force yourself to follow what all these people do unleash the power that is within this Anthony Robbins has expressed.

The greatest gift a person has in life is their own mind and most people do not know how to master it. Through creating a powerful positive mental vision {learning to choose and use words that are strong and potent} then what ever you can conceive, it can be achieved. The "Law of Attraction" brings great responsibility. What you focus on is what will manifest in your life as can now be clearly seen and understood from the teachings described above from Napoleon Hill, Emmett Fox, Joe Gerard, Anthony Robbins, Wayne Dyer and Louise Hay. They all reinforce the fact that you must Take Full Responsibility And Use All The Necessary Effort To Challenge Any Memory Or Thought about using alcohol or drugs.

The easiest way to succeed with this challenge is to teach yourself that any time you have a thought about a drug or alcohol to then immediately bring to your mind a memory and a feeling of a terrible thing that happened as a direct use of substances. By conditioning yourself in this manner you will be able to stack up disgust against the desire. The addict or alcoholic needs to passionately use these principles and it will enable them to create not only a satisfying, but also a sober and clean spectacular life.

The first and simplest thing to do to harness this power is to say affirmations OUT LOUD and you will gain deeper perspective and ability to take control of not only your thoughts but feelings as well.

BY READING AND SPEAKING THESE QUOTES OUTLOUD ENABLES YOU TO VISUALIZE GREAT AND WONDERFUL THINGS IN YOUR LIFE THAT WILL HAPPEN AS A DIRECT RESULT OF STAYING CLEAN AND SOBER!

It is by doing this that the Power of Imagination" is unleashed through the "Art of Visualization" This is what enables a person to begin to implement the Law of Attraction through the use of Autosuggestion —For instance instead of attempting to force yourself to deny wanting to use drugs or alcohol by verbalizing statements such as "I am never going to drink or use again" or "I am done with this stuff" or the classic mistake "Just for today I am not going to drink or get high." It will be more powerful and effective to begin to replace these thoughts or statements with learning to develop powerful mental pictures of family, wife or children or just contemplating the great things occurring or that will occur as a direct result of staying clean and sober.

It would be very helpful and effective to carry actual pictures of the good things in your life and to stare at them, whenever a thought or a flashing memory of drug use or alcohol enters into your mind. Stare at the actual or imagined family picture of a loved one and do not take your eyes off of that vision till all desire for the drink or drug fade as strong feelings of disgust form. The reason this works is due to the fact that your mind will not stay focused on something that you like and maybe want, such as to get high, if fulfilling that desire will destroy someone you love! You cannot want SOMETHING that will destroy SOMEONE you deeply love!

It is the old adage that "out of sight out of mind" is how addiction destroys your loved ones, because you have been training your mind to not think about them when the desire for drugs or alcohol develops. THE MORE YOU ALLOW AN UNCHALLENGED THOUGHT OR MEMORY OF DRINKING OR DRUG USE TO CONTINUE UNCHECKED THE STRONGER BECOMES THE DESIRE AND ATTRACTION. You must destroy this cycle by challenging the thought with a counter image of how and who will suffer if you succumb to the craving or intense desire. You must train yourself to connect a disgusted feeling from a painful past memory every time you think about a drug or alcohol.

The use of Autosuggestion can eliminate and replace any tendency of being constitutionally just too selfish, and through repetition learn to think or envision how others would directly be benefited by sobriety. If a person is insensitive towards caring about others; then they could still use Autosuggestion to strengthen their recovery by using the following example, of a powerful and selfish visualization. They can focus selfishly on visualizing the car they want as a direct result of recovery "that powder blue ES 400 Mercedes with the white leather interior and the California burl nut wood accents on the dashboard with the interactive voice, that personally speaks to you, when you open the door and first get in.

Whether you are a caring and loving person or just a very self-focused and selfish person; LEARNING TO DEVELOP VIVID AND SHARP AND POWERFUL IMAGERY WILL CREATE STRONG MOTIVATION TO STAY IN RECOVERY. If words are difficult to select then "a picture is always worth a thousand words." Find pictures or brochures and take pictures of your family, your car, your dream home, your physical self and through visualization, Autosuggestion and the Law of Attraction, any good and desired goals will become an automatic compelling force to stay clean and sober.

"But remember it has been these very same principles and powers that have kept you and your loved ones in a living dark Hell! You have used the forces of creation to successfully fail."

"Your deep passionate feelings in the past have always been focused on the belief "That some how, some way, some day, I will be able to use and get away.""

"As a direct result of allowing yourself to have this passionate vision is the very reason recovery has either not been desired or has failed repeatedly."

As we end this chapter I want to express an extremely important and vital fact that absolutely proves these concepts, that the above authors have expressed in such an eloquent manner. After speaking to literally hundreds of addicts and alcoholics I have observed a very strange phenomena that involves the power of thought and feelings.

When discussing their experience when they were suffering intense withdrawal the following phenomenon presented itself. The addict would relate that when they were suffering great withdrawal discomfort and pain, they would have the desperation to virtually do anything to relieve themselves of this physical agony.

Upon waking up, "or coming to" they would frantically search for more drugs and begin the difficult process of finding resources (money or some other tangible means of exchange) in order to acquire more drugs to quiet the fire. Depending on the level of focus and concentration, the process of acquiring more drugs many times was almost impossible and overwhelming.

It Should Also Be Emphasized Again That The Addict Not Only Believes But Also Feels They Are In A Life-And-Death Struggle. IT IS THE FEELINGS ONCE AGAIN THAT BETRAY AND LIE, CAUSING THE PERSON TO BELIEVE THAT "IF THEY DON'T ACQUIRE MORE OF WHAT WILL KILL THEM, THEN THEY WILL DIE!"

Once again it can be clearly noted that the survival instincts of the addict has been hijacked by the addiction and completely turned inside out. The person is overwhelmed with an intensity of desperation that drives them into almost suicidal behaviors, with the belief that it is only through acquiring more drugs that they will be able to survive. This is not only quite obviously a complete delusion, "it is absolute madness." But this is not the phenomenon I am speaking about.

The phenomenon that I have observed is that the severe emotional, mental and physiological distress and suffering of the addict, that is directly caused by withdrawal, suddenly becomes completely managed or even vanishes, like magic, once the person has achieved their connection.

> "In other words once the person knows that within 15 to 20 min. they would be able to acquire the product that would relieve their suffering, their suffering is immediately relieved!"

Now the question to ask is how is it possible that a simple thought and a belief could provide such physiological relief? How is it possible that when a person is suffering severe physiological withdrawal and they are shaking, and nauseous, as well as confused mentally, and overwhelmed emotionally; feel instant relief not only from all their emotional anguish, but also from the physiological symptoms of withdrawal? Herein lies the proof of what all the above authors were expressing as universal truths.

The addict is fully aware of this truth, because they know whether consciously or not, that once they know that they are going to be relieved of their withdrawal suffering...

> "...that simple "thought of knowing" immediately reduces their distress or actually magically removes it."

> "This Means That A Simple And Powerful Thought Has Completely Changed Not Only The Way They Mentally Felt, But WHAT THEY WERE ACTUALLY PHYSIOLOGICALLY EXPERIENCING AS WELL."

As Napoleon Hill had indicated "thoughts are things" and therefore a thought ("knowing that I am soon going to get drugs) is as powerful as the thing (drugs) itself! The simplest way to understand why this phenomenon may occur, is to think about the fact that there are receptor sites in your brain that are specifically geared to what ever particular drug you put in your body.

Not only is there a receptor site for a particular drug there is also a memory component involved in that brain process. It is this so-called memory site or memory cell that gets triggered, as soon as the person knows that they will be able to get relief. Once this memory cell fires the person experiences instant relief. This cell that is fired by just a simple thought has the power to completely alter everything instantly that a person is thinking feeling and believing.

In regards to this phenomenon it should become very apparent that there is imminent and great danger for most addicts who engage in "war stories" or permit repetitious thoughts regarding past or future use of substances.

> "Since "thoughts are things" the person by allowing themselves to obsess or repeat verbally out loud with passionate energy, past using experiences or future desires to use, may result in bringing their thought into reality."

This chapter has been titled "Visualizing Victory" which was designed to demonstrate that "whatever a man can conceive and believe he or she can achieve." As clearly presented here the choice is yours, to conceive of the greatest good or to conceive of the greatest evil…

> "…But Be Very Aware That Whatever You Conceive Will Manifest Itself Into Your Life, Whether You Want It Or Whether You Don't Want It."

> "For Whatever You Conceive "Is A Thought" And "A Thought Is A Thing."

Do not be a victim of your own uncontrolled thoughts or impulsive emotions, and seize control of your own mind, and learn to control and direct your thoughts; thoughts which control your emotions that control your feelings, so you can achieve the greatest good for you and everyone that loves you. Now that you know these facts and you have these tools, use them very wisely. Take back your birthright and direct your mind to what ever ends you desire and refuse to be victimized by your tendency to have unhealthy harmful thoughts and useless feelings.

The following will provide you with effective ways to take control of your thinking, and to actually provide a means to direct your mind through learning to maximize the "Power of Imagination."

> "Visualization provides for the ability for a person to actually change their outer world by first changing their

inner thoughts. It is an actual technique used by many people to effect changes in their lives and to promote more rapid progress towards the actual realization of what was first just their imagined dreams and goals."

I believe it is the careless use of the "Art of Visualization" that is one of the primary causes for addiction and especially relapse! As stated earlier in this chapter it is the principle of Autosuggestion driven by the "Law of Attraction" that causes relapse.

"The very laws that govern the ability for anyone to accomplish anything in their lives for their good; are the very same laws that also govern the ability to accomplish anything bad in their lives!"

"The Law of Attraction does not know right from wrong—it works for the greater good of a person or if used improperly will absolutely destroy that same person!"

"It is no different than Nuclear Power—if properly used it provides the greatest Heavenly gifts, such as electricity and nuclear medicine. If improperly used it creates the greatest dread and literally a fiery blazing HELL ON EARTH!"

These guidelines or directions are as follows:

You need to visualize specific behaviors or events occurring in your life. When you do this it is necessary to create a clear mental picture of what one desires and then keep visualizing it over and over again with all of the senses, till you are not just imaging it, but you are feeling it deeply emotionally. The specific details of: What do you see? What do you feel? What do you hear? What does it smell like? All these details are necessary to maximize the potential or probability for successful realization of the dream or goal.

"SINCE THE ADDICT OR ALCOHOLIC HAVE A STRONG TENDENCY TO CONSTANTLY OBSESS ON DRINKING OR DRUG USE, THEY ARE USING THESE VERY SAME SPECIFIC

TECHNIQUES IN A VERY DELETERIOUS, SELF DEFEATING AND SELF DESTRUCTIVE MANNER!"

Visualizing or what I have called the "Art of Visualization" is a very real force that is operating in any person's life and one that should be taken very seriously. It should be used carefully and consciously so it is not destructive. However When Used In A Constructive As Well As A Positive Manner The Results Are Absolutely More Than Astounding.

This power has been dramatically demonstrated in many areas of life, but it has been ABSOLUTELY proven to improve performance of athletes in many types of sports.

In a well-known study Russian scientists compared four groups of Olympic athletes in terms of their training schedules:

- Group 1 = 100% physical training;
- Group 2 — 75% physical training with 25% mental training;
- Group 3 — 50% physical training with 50% mental training;
- Group 4 — 25% physical training with 75% mental training.

The astounding result was that Group 4, with 75% of their time devoted to mental training, performed the best.

This study demonstrated the "Power of Imagination" through the "Art of Visualization" in that it proved that mental images could actually condition physical muscular responses. It should be noted that Visualization is used extensively in many types of sports and the athletes that utilize this principle demonstrate significant improvement as well as success in their particular sport.

> "It is sad and ironic that most addicts and alcoholics spend much energy and time complaining about the results that they are having in their life, and fail to recognize they have absolutely been responsible for producing those results."

It has been scientifically proven that complaining about the results that you create will not change the future.

The path to recovery has to be based upon a careful review of the various aspects of your life and the need to identify what's working and what's not working in your life, in regards to your recovery efforts.

> "If something's not working it is necessary to try
> something new and to keep trying until you find the
> path that gives you the results that you want."

In another study of almost 200 men and women Visualization was used as a primary method to determine whether it would be effective in a weight loss program. In this study the individuals were required to visualize himself or herself having lost a substantial amount of body fat. The results were again astounding due to the fact that those who were practicing daily Visualization of losing body fat actually lost more weight and demonstrated significant progress over those who did not.

THIS STUDY PROVES THAT JUST BY VISUALIZING A RESULT WE ARE SIGNIFICANTLY MORE LIKELY TO ACHIEVE THAT RESULT.

It seems impossible and improbable that a person's mind can work this efficiently, effectively through such a simple process of directing and engaging one's imagination to visualize any result that one desires.

This study once again proves the "Power of Imagination" when the "Art of Visualization is consciously practiced!

> "But these forces will work to the destruction of the
> addict or alcoholic when they are used in the context
> of "war stories" or "romancing the addiction" or any
> thoughts or verbal exchanges that "glorify or celebrate"
> past drug or alcohol use or experiences!"

The following historical people will demonstrate this power.

Kathy Turner who won the Olympic champion speed skater gold-medal related that when she was a seven-year-old girl she would imagine herself in the Olympics standing in the center platform with the gold medal around her neck. She stated that in October 1991, a sports psychologist "Told me that I had to visualize my race, see myself win it in the Olympics and see myself receive the gold medal—all in my head! How hard could that be?!"

She stated there were many challenges along the way but she NEVER stopped visualizing that gold medal around her neck and in 1992 she was crowned as Olympic champion.

"From the top of the awards platform, the view was everything I had imagined when I was the little girl standing on my parents' overstuffed chair. At that moment, I had become my own vision. We can make it happen."

"Whether you are struggling with recovery or you are a person with a great dream, then whatever you do, you should have that goal foremost in your mind."

"To succeed it is always necessary to first visualize yourself having already achieved it."

"No result can always be guaranteed, but practicing active Visualization is definitely guaranteed to massively increase your chances of success."

"By using the amazing "Art of Visualization" through the "Power of Imagination" you can attain what you want in your life!"

As can be clearly seen in the next success story.

Air Force Colonel George Hall was a POW in a North Vietnamese prison for seven grueling years. In his imagination he played a full round of golf every day, and one week after he was released from his POW camp, he entered the "Greater New Orleans Open" and shot a 76.

"How is it possible that NOT picking up a golf club in seven years, NOT to mention the horrible suffering he endured as a prisoner of war; that he could perform so outstandingly? Was it a miracle or was it just the fact that he used the principles of Autosuggestion found in the "Power of Imagination" developed through the "Art of Visualization!"

"In my efforts to free the alcoholic and addict from their madness I must point out that when a person constantly focuses on something it not only becomes a PASSIONATE desire, but It Actually Will Materialize Or Manifest Into Their Real Life!"

"THEREFORE ONCE AGAIN FOR THE THOUSANDTH TIME—THE ADDICT OR ALCOHOLIC MUST BE AWARE THAT "WAR

STORIES" AND INTENSE DISCUSSIONS
REGARDING THEIR DRUG AND ALCOHOL
USE WILL ABSOLUTELY INCREASE THE
PROBABILITY OF RELAPSE!"

In another case involving a teenager hiding from the Gestapo during the Holocaust named Vera Fryling she imagined herself as a doctor and more specifically as a psychiatrist practicing in a free land. She came to America and earned her M.D. and was on the faculty of the San Francisco medical school.

"How is it possible once again for a person to be under such terrible fear and stress to stay focused on her dream and then due to the intense passion of daily imagination lead to the fulfillment of that specific dream? It is the Art of Visualization" manifested through the Power of Imagination!"

The next case concerns a man who was a former Governor of California, not to mention he also had achieved great Hollywood fame due to many successful movie roles! But before all that he was the five-time Mr. Universe and four-time Mr. Olympia and stated the following: "As long as the mind can envision the fact that you can do something, yes you can." He visualized himself being there and having already achieved the goal as Mr. Universe long before he ever started. The Hollywood star and former Governor of California is Arnold Schwarzenegger.

"AGAIN AND AGAIN YOU CAN SEE WHAT
WILL OCCUR WHEN THE "POWER OF
IMAGINATION" IS CONSCIOUSLY APPLIED BY
PRACTICING THE "ART OF VISUALIZATION!"

Returning a moment to the astounding results of the Russian study regarding using Visualization techniques with four different groups of Olympic athletes; in which the study was conducted by having each group receiving progressively lesser degrees of Visualization with their regular training. The astonishing result was the ones who spent the majority of their training time, on Visualization techniques had "Outstanding" results.

"When the scores were tallied after the 1980 Moscow Olympics as well as the Lake Placid Olympics, the group that had 75% of their training time focused on Visualization had won the most medals."

"Imagination is more important than knowledge. Your imagination is your preview of life's coming attractions." "The power of imagination is the ultimate creative power, no doubt about that. While knowledge defines all we currently know and understand, imagination points to what we might yet discover and create."

—Albert Einstein—

Peter Nivio Zarglenga an American author and businessman stated.

"I am imagination. I can see what the eyes cannot see. I can hear what the ears cannot hear. I can feel what my body and heart cannot feel" What he's expressing here is that imagination occurs beyond the senses. A person must have the ability to first make something real in their mind before they can bring it into reality. You must have a vision of being, a dream, a purpose, and a principal. You will become what your vision is.

"Once again it should become very clear that the reason most addicts and alcoholics relapse or fail to recover, is due to the dominating thoughts they permit in their minds or allow others to place in their minds!"

"Guard yourself well from destructive thoughts and Visualizations that can be damaging to your recovery chances and efforts, and most of all protect yourself from the negative impacts others can have on your mind!"

The next historical figure is Nichola Tesla who was born in 1856 in Croatia and moved to America in 1884. Life magazine in a special double issue listed Tesla is one of the (100 of the most important people in the last 1000 years." He had the distinction of being numbered 57 out of those 100 most important people in the past thousand years. He has been credited with inventing AC electricity, electric car, radio, the bladeless turbine, wireless communication, florescent lighting, the induction motor, a telephone repeater, the rotating magnetic field principle, alternating current power transmission, the Tesla Coil transformer and more than 700 other patents.

He possessed an extraordinary ability to visualize, and his thinking powers were beyond that of most people. When an idea came to him he actually built it and tested it in his own mind and he was so effectively able to visualize every aspect of its construction as well as its performance, that when he actually built the prototype it would operate exactly as he had imagined it would.

> "His successful inventions were a direct result of his extraordinary power of Visualization that he trained himself to do, from a very early age. Once again we can see how the "Law of Attraction" and the "Power of Visualization" are the twin driving forces behind all that a man or a woman creates!"

In 1957, Earl Nightingale, speaker, author of "The Strangest Secret." Related that the "Secret is that we become what we think about all day long."

> "Again and again I cannot stop emphasizing that it should manifest itself in the mind of every addict and alcoholic, the significance of these concepts that have been proven to exist even though they cannot be seen; the results of what these forces can do are clearly seen in anyone's life, especially in the person who appears to refuse to abstain!"

Whether they consciously use the "Strangest Secret" they are definitely unconsciously using this force and many times to their own destruction due to their pure ignorance!

> "If it is true " that what we think about all day long is what we become" then the obsession that "some day and in some way I will be able to use a drug or alcohol and get away without consequences" must be destroyed."

> "The constant thoughts of using drugs or drinking or just memories of these actions will absolutely lead to the

263

return to their use, simply because of the misuse of the "Art of Visualization" and "Power of Imagination" that are the driving forces behind the Law of Attraction!"

"It just therefore follows that if you think thoughts of defeat or failure you're bound to feel discouraged. If you maintain constant and continuous thoughts of worry, anxiety and fear, you will experience this in your body as stress, panic attacks and depression."

"YOUR BELIEF SYSTEM NOT ONLY DEFINES YOUR REALITY, BUT IT ALSO SHAPES YOUR CHARACTER AND DETERMINES YOUR POTENTIAL."

This next study should make it more than clear the danger of NOT taking control of your own mind and learning to direct it to the good things you desire in your life as well as your loved ones lives.

"THE FACT IS THAT WHAT YOU VIVIDLY IMAGINE AND HOLD IN YOUR SUBCONSCIOUS MIND BEGINS TO ACTUALLY CREATE YOUR REALITY."

This can be clearly seen in the following study in regards to the placebo effect. A placebo works on your belief and what feeds your imagination. The ability of the mind to cure a disease even when the medicine is known to be worthless is known as the "placebo effect." It's the power of the patient's belief and expectation alone that produces the improvement in his or her health.

There was a group of cancer patients who thought they were being treated with chemotherapy, but were actually given a placebo. Before their treatment began, the patients were informed about the complications associated with undergoing chemotherapy treatment, such as fatigue and loss of hair. Amazingly, based on nothing more than their belief and expectation, nearly one third of the patients who were given the placebo reported feeling fatigued and actually experienced hair loss!

This study demonstrates and proves the "Art of Visualization" and the "Power of Imagination".

Use this powerful tool that will enhance your self- esteem and allow you to reach your full potential. By using Affirmations, but even better make them full Incantations by speaking them LOUDLY and PROUDLY, you may obtain the same results as these well known celebrities.

It has been reported that late at night Jim Carrey would drive into the hills overlooking Hollywood and yell at the top of his lungs "I will earn ten million dollars a year by 1995." When 1995 finally arrived, Jim was the star of the movie "Ace Ventura: When Nature Calls", for which he was paid twenty million dollars.

> "An affirmation is a positive statement that represents your desired condition or outcome. You must understand that your subconscious mind doesn't know the difference between a real experience and a visualized experience."

Therefore any time you catch yourself saying or thinking something negative about yourself, counteract the negative self-talk with a positive affirmation.

> "When you select an affirmation you must understand that your subconscious mind works in the present tense, so avoid words such as can, will, should or could. For instance state, "I love being clean and sober and I am richly rewarded creatively and financially." Rather than "I should stay clean" or " I could stay sober if I try." Nor should you state, "I can stay clean" or "I will stay sober." Or "I really want to stay clean."

In addition you must say it with strong conviction and passionate emotions and repeat them every morning and evening upon waking up and going to sleep. Close your eyes each time and actually visualize the result and feel the emotions that would be associated with the Affirmation and its Accomplishment.

The next man that utilized these principles and achieved extraordinary success who grew up in Louisville, Kentucky. He dreamed of someday becoming the heavy weight-boxing champion of the world. While working out in the local gym he would continuously affirm to all within earshot that he was indeed the greatest boxer of all time!

While many felt he was brash and boastful, few people actually took this 89-pound youngster seriously. Regardless of anyone's opinion he continued to verbalize loudly and proudly his affirmation that he will become the undisputed heavyweight boxing champion of the whole world. That 12-year-old 89 pound light weight was Cassius Marcellus Clay, better known as Mohammad Ali who indeed became NOT only the World Champion as he stated he would year after year with his "affirmations" and "incantations" but he also became one of the most popular and recognized sports figures of all times!

"Was it a coincidence like the rest of these historical figures previously related or was in a direct fact that he maintained the strong belief manifested through the "Power of Visualization " and the "Law of Attraction."

"Watch your thoughts, for they become words. Choose your words, for they become actions. Understand your actions, for they become habits. Study your habits, for they will become your character. Develop your character, for it becomes your destiny."

—Anonymous—

"Any person who has the determination to use this force will have full access to completely changing and transforming their lives, through the same active Visualization and mental imagery processes that the above men and women demonstrate through their life stories."

When the addict or alcoholic utilize these forces they will more easily achieve success due to the fact that through the use of these processes, they will clearly be able to see success. In the same way that the athletes see themselves achieving their goals and obtaining desired performance outcomes; the addict or alcoholic can gain the same results.

"It is through the Visualization process that the result is clearly seen and this automatically triggers strong motivation to work towards its achievement."

This process will vividly remind the person of the desired objective, which will cause an increased intensity in working a program of recovery.

The "Art of Visualization" will be found in the way it can successfully prepare the addict or alcoholic to effectively manage a high risk situation; because they will have rehearsed every aspect of the situation and fully visualized exactly what they would do and how they would do it.

In sports mental imagery is often used to facilitate the learning and refinement of skills. The best athletes "see" and "feel" themselves performing perfect skills, programs, routines, or plays on a very regular basis. The addict must use this same technique to prepare for any high-risk situations that they can perceive ahead of time.

The addict or alcoholic can use it to familiarize themselves as does the athlete use mental imagery to effectively familiarize themselves with all kinds of things, such as a competition site, a race course, a complex play pattern or routine, a pre-competition plan, an event focus plan, a media interview plan, a refocusing plan, or the strategy or plan they need to follow. The addict or alcoholic can effectively prepare in advance to know how they are going to deal with or manage a high-risk situation or event!

Addicts and alcoholics need to be very open to the fact that what I am encouraging them to do has been scientifically proven to effectively work. They must embrace this technology and fully recognize how mental imagery sets the mental stage for a good performance in athletes, who will do a complete mental run through of the key elements of their performance. This helps draw out their desired pre-competition feelings and focus. It also helps keep negative thoughts from interfering with a positive pre-game focus.

> "The addict or alcoholic needs to use these principles to maintain a positive and determined focus, feeling and attitude. They need to train themselves to avoid any talk or conversation about drug or alcohol use, past or present, so they can effectively keep negative thoughts from interfering with their recovery efforts."

By developing a habit of practicing mental imagery the person will be able to more easily refocus when the need arises. For example, if a person starts to feel sluggish towards maintaining their recovery commitments and efforts they can use imagery of a previous completed commitment and the feelings associated to the completion of that work and this will help them get things back on track.

> "It is important to note that when using Visualization the person should not focus on the outcome, but on the

actions to achieve the desired outcome. The person needs to see themselves actively involved with the recovery lifestyle, Seeing Themselves Doing Things There NOT Just Seeing Themselves There. It is better to visualize yourself participating either verbally or behaviorally in some way."

Whether the addict or alcoholic wants to use these techniques—they need to whether they want to or not. The benefits of learning to use this technology are awesome as demonstrated in the next story about a well-known Golf professional who wrote:

"I never hit a shot even in practice without having a sharp in-focus picture of it in my head. It's like a color movie. First, I "see" the ball where I want it to finish, nice and white and sitting up high on the bright green grass. Then the scene quickly changes, and I "see" the ball going there: its path, trajectory, and shape, even its behavior on landing. Then there's a sort of fade-out, and the next scene shows me making the kind of swing that will turn the previous images into reality only at the end of this short private Hollywood spectacular do I select a club and step up to the ball."

—Jack Nicklaus—

It will take strong determination and discipline to become highly proficient at the constructive use of imagery. To accomplish this ability the person will have to use it every day, numerous times through out the day and in the evenings before sleeping.

"To perfect and use mental imagery to the fullest advantage, the person will have to use imagery as perfectly and precisely as possible to see, feel, and experience all your recovery actions in your mind."

"Visualize the exact actions in recovery and as you would like them actually to unfold. The person should see themselves enjoying the activity and feeling satisfied with their involvement. They need to enter fully into the image with all their senses. Sight, hear, feel, touch, smell and interaction, as they would like to engage in a recovery lifestyle."

When you imagine yourself in recovery doing precisely what you want and imagine that it is greatly enjoyable and you are indeed happy, joyous and free, will actually trigger you physiologically which results in creating neural patterns in your brain, just as if you had physically performed the action.

"Visualization is a powerful technique that will train a person's mind and create actual new neural patterns in their brain."

Through this process the future becomes more defined. When the person sees himself or herself having already achieved their goal, causes the brain to believe that attaining that goal is possible. This persistent and consistent effort to practice daily Visualization on any given goal will lead to the ability to achieve that goal far sooner than if you didn't focus on it at all.

It is extremely important to gain the greatest benefit from using this technology, when a person visualizes they need to see themselves achieving their goal through their own eyes, rather than watching themselves from the outside. Also it needs to be noted that the more real the image is, the better this works. The Image Should Not Just Be A Still Picture, But A Spectacular Movie With You In The Starring Role. The more detail the greater the effective power that is unleashed. Therefore it is necessary to see it again and again in your head and to see yourself as the hero, achieving your goal.

To increase the force and power even more add background music that you not only hear but really feel. See your actions clearly, loudly and vividly and take a moment to determine where your mind is locating the picture: top, bottom, right, upper left, etc. One of the most effective and powerful ways to become fully engaged in this process is to take another moment and recall an important action or activity that has been already accomplished, and think about where that goal is located in your mental image frame.

You now have the memory or image of two actions or activities, one in the past and one hoped for in the future. Notice in your mind where are they located? Are they together or very separate? What are the colors how are the colors the same or different regarding these two images? Are they big, bright, and clear, or are they small, blurry, and distant? Notice your feelings regarding the two images. Which ones are associated to feeling happy, nervous, and excited or feel depressed, sad or regretful?

Take the goal you have not yet achieved and give it the same qualities as the goal you have achieved. Make it bigger and brighter; move it to the same location as the image of the already-achieved goal; make it feel the same by inserting every detail. Adjusting your mental image of the current goal to mirror the one you've already achieved. This will make the future desired action or activity seem easier to accomplish, since it has been connected to the already achieved action and therefore there is the feeling that you have already achieved it.

> "Each day find a quiet spot where no one will bother you for at least 10 to 30 minutes every day for engaging in the "Power of Imagination" through the active practice of the "Art of Visualization." The more repetition a person has with this technique and technology the sooner they will realize all its benefits. These actions will absolutely change the direction of a person's life."

> "Success is nothing more than a few simple disciplines, practiced everyday; while failure is simply a few errors in judgment, repeated every day. It is the accumulative weight of our disciplines and our judgments that leads us to either fortune or failure."

—Jim Rohn—

Kaizen is a Japanese belief that many small improvements leads to massive leaps in excellence. Roughly translated Kaizen means continuous improvement.

> "The Japanese philosophy of Kaizen should be a driving force to give the addict or alcoholic person the determination and discipline to aggressively, apply and fully utilize the "Power of Imagination" through the "Art of Visualization" that has been explained in great depth and detail in this chapter."

We too can achieve excellent results by adopting this Kaizen philosophy in our lives. Being aware of the immense power of incremental improvements can inspire confidence and drive.

Gerard "Jerry" Egan

Chapter Twelve

Definitions Determine Direction

In this chapter I will demonstrate and express the "Power of Spin" which is achieved through developing and effectively using the "Art of the Second Thought." The concept that we fully control what we believe or perceive to be our reality will also be explored through learning how to control our perceptions, by using the "Power of Spin" through the effective use of the "Art of the Second Thought."

Many times through out this book I have expressed that it is by developing the "Power of Resisting Resistance" through the "Art of Self Defiance" that an addict or alcoholic can tap the awesome forces and powers that will enable them to change their lives, without the need for any "willingness" at all. Now as bizarre as this may sound it is nonetheless true. To demonstrate this truth it will first be necessary to understand the difference between "resistance" and "willpower." The definitions I will use to support my view all came from dictionaries found on the Internet. So feel free to check my research! Since this chapter is focused on words, then the "Power of Transformational Communication" through the "Art of Word Selection" will also be briefly introduced. A more detailed discussion of the "Power of Transformational Communication" through the "Art of Word Selection" will be presented in Chapter 16.

"Once again I want to repeat my belief that when a person forces himself or herself to take actions that they would rather not take, they are not being "willing," but they are absolutely using willpower to the fullest extent possible. Willpower is the underlying as well as the driving force behind the concept of all "resistance." It is this intense emotional challenge that needs to be fully appreciated, understood and utilized that provides the energy to change, and not "willingness."

The definition of "willingness" in the Cambridge dictionary defines:

> "Will-ing-ness"- as to be happy to do something if it is needed; approving; describes someone who does their work energetically and enthusiastically: a willing helper/worker; inclined or favorably disposed in mind; ready willing and eager to help; prompt to act or respond; lending a willing hand; done, borne, or accepted by choice or without reluctance.

Another dictionary defines: "willing"- as ready and eager to do something." As can be clearly observed the emotional states that these definitions demonstrate are not found in most addicts or alcoholics; they are neither "happy" nor "enthusiastic" nor "ready and eager" to do anything. In fact they are resistant and defiant and not "favorably disposed in mind." Lastly most do not do anything "by choice and without reluctance."

To gain some perspective on how a person can utilize their natural tendency for "resistance" or its manifestation, which is "defiance," it will be necessary to outline the following unique concepts. First it is necessary to redefine these two words, for the purposes of expanding the available tools that a person needs or can use to build a lasting recovery. It may be helpful to take a moment and open a dictionary as the old saying goes; or you may turn to your computer and search for the word "resistance" and among the many definitions there is one that will suit the purposes of these controversial concepts.

> "Re-sis-tance" — an act or instance of resisting; opposition; a means of resisting; the power or capacity to resist: as a: the inherent ability of an organism to resist harmful influences (as disease, toxic agents, or infection); the capacity of a species or strain of microorganism to survive exposure to a toxic agent (as a drug) formerly effective against it; an opposing or retarding force; the opposition offered by a body or substance to the passage through it of a steady electric current; a source of resistance; a psychological defense mechanism wherein a patient rejects, denies, or otherwise opposes the therapeutic efforts of a psychotherapist.

Now we can clearly construct usable concepts from this collection of meanings. The most important one to consider for our purposes is the last one, which states "Resistance" as a psychological defense where the person rejects, denies and opposes therapeutic efforts. In addition to this meaning the first one has significance in that it defines "resistance" as an act or instances of resisting; opposition and the third one "resistance" as an opposing or retarding force. When these definitions are used to describe attitudes and behaviors; they clearly demonstrate the dilemma that the addict and alcoholic experiences, and explains the frustration encountered by any person who tries to help them, and ultimately why they are incapable of developing "willingness or surrender."

Returning once again to the dictionary we can observe what it means to be defiant.

> "De-fi-ance"- proudly refusing to obey authority: a
> defiant attitude/gesture; not willing to accept criticism
> or disapproval.

Anyone who has worked with or lived with an addict or alcoholic is well aware of this behavior. Now the concept of defiance or being defiant has a few more twists; defiance is when you "refuse to obey someone or something" and when you add to this mix the act of resistance, which is defined as "to fight against something or someone that is attacking you; to refuse to accept or be changed by something" then you certainly have the ingredients of being oppositional and rebellious as well as defiant.

An interesting twist and paradox that I am exploiting here, which is the foundation for this book, is found in the definition of resistance – "to stop yourself from doing something that you want to do; - not wanting to accept something; especially changes or new ideas: Why are you so resistant to change?"

Now Bill Wilson in the book Alcoholics Anonymous indicated that no amount of willpower could save an alcoholic or stop or control his or her drinking, and in this understanding he is absolutely right, but what he failed to comprehend is that although the alcoholic could not control or stop his drinking through the use of willpower; he or she could use willpower to change other behaviors. I propose that…

> "Willpower can be fully utilized successfully to force a
> person to change many other behaviors, and it is through

the changing of those other behaviors that drinking and drug use will simply be automatically postponed, until hopefully other healthier emotions create the necessary momentum to permanently abstain."

Willpower is defined as:

"Will-power"- the ability to control your own thoughts and the way in which you behave; determination: It took a lot of willpower to stay calm.

To resist is defined as:

"Re-sist"-to keep or stop yourself from doing something.

Whereas defiance is defined:

"Defiance"- proud and determined opposition against authority or against someone more powerful than you are.

Now after a careful review of some of these actual definitions that are being utilized, to clarify abstract concepts described in this book; you can now begin to ascertain that the views of this author have, if not solid foundations for further discussion; then certainly at least my ideas need to be given some consideration.

If what I am proposing has credibility; then my argument is valid that Bill Wilson committed an error of omission when he wrote that "willingness" is the key to recovery. Since the AA program seems to have helped very few people; when it should have been a solution to the great majority and not the great minority; how could it have failed?

The answer may be found in the fact that most addicts and alcoholics are defiant and resistant. As is clearly observed through the use of the above definitions they do not have the "willingness" and most will probably go to the grave in that defiant state. Therefore I am proposing radical new ideas that allow all addicts and alcoholics to recognize that there are many more keys and they don't need to be doomed; due to their inability to be "willing" or to even comprehend how to even find "willingness."

In their minds this concept is not readily accessible and the prison fortress of their minds; only teaches and reinforces the concepts of resistance and defiance, as the only means of survival. The emotional states of frustration; anger; spite; resistance and defiance or in fact any word that creates an intense emotional state can be used to force shifts and changes in a persons behavior. One final word, "willingness" is just one of many, many emotional states that may be utilized to motivate any person to do anything that is necessary.

The dictionary does not lie and if my observations are correct and I believe that they are absolutely accurate, based upon my 30 years of experience, then most addicts and alcoholics do not have the capacity to develop the feeling of "being willing or willingness." Having worked with addicts and alcoholics and being one myself; I have found that the 12 Step Programs have failed to help the great majority of addicts and alcoholics. The AA and the NA programs adamantly express or at least imply that "willingness is the key"

In fact whenever someone relapses or fails to stay sober the pat answer to "Why did they go out?" is "They just were not willing" or "They just have not surrendered" or "They never worked the steps." All of these admonishments focus on the belief that a person has to "Give up and be willing." The goal and purpose of this book is to provide, "Help to the hopeless and hope to the helpless" by acquiring the ability to take their natural tendency to be resistant, and to learn to resist that resistance, without the need for the feeling of "willingness or being willing." Since being rebellious and oppositional makes it literally impossible to become willing, then we must find other ways to motivate, than to wait for someone to die, who will never become willing.

As I stated in the beginning of this book "What do we do for the addict or alcoholic who does not have willingness?" I implied that the concept of "having to have willingness" in order to begin recovery was absolutely wrong and that there are many more keys that can effectively change lives than "willingness." Yes willingness is absolutely a key for the minority of suffering addicts and alcoholics, but it is not working for the great majority.

I will now demonstrate the power of "Resistance and Defiance" as powerful keys to recovery. Bill Wilson in the 12 Steps and 12 Traditions book reflected on page 31 that, "Defiance is the outstanding characteristic of the alcoholic." It is unfortunate that he failed to recognize that this intense rebellious state, is also a key that can be utilized to set the addict or alcoholic free from the madness of drug or alcohol dependency.

In my decades of experience in working with addicts and alcoholics it is the rare individual that can just grasp the need to be open and willing and embrace all that we teach and recommend. There are very few addicts or alcoholics that are able to utilize therapy and education to stay abstinent, and indeed it is only the rare individual, that simply as a result of committing and cooperating can change their lives.

It is more natural and in fact much easier to mobilize an addicts natural tendency to be "defiant" and "resistant," and to coach them to utilize this attitude in an effective manner to defeat their addiction. In the past the resistance has defeated the addict due to they did not understand the "Power of Resisting the Resistance" through the "Art Of Self Defiance." This principle can be stated in the following manner

> "Since resistance is a more natural occurring state in the substance abuser, it would make more sense to utilize it, than to attempt a complete transformation of their personality, and then hope that they become willing."

Again the question is what is easier to do, force a person to undergo a complete personality change, as was expressed in "Spiritual Experience" found in Appendix Three of the AA book "that the personality change sufficient to bring about recovery from alcoholism *or addiction*" is absolutely necessary? Or the fact that within the same sentence it states "…has manifested itself among us in many different forms." Or is it more practical to encourage and support the concept that, "What is easier to do— change a personality or act naturally?" In the following manner I will describe how the common or natural tendency of being "Oppositional", "Rebellious" and "Defiant" that is found in most addicts and alcoholics can be completely turned around, and demonstrate by utilizing these traits or dynamics that this process may work better than "Waiting for the person to become willing."

To begin this process we need to understand and review the following concepts regarding "words and language," and a technique used by many people especially counselors, coaches and sponsors that I refer to as the "Power of Spin." As thoughts are things as previously demonstrated in the prior chapter; then a thought is composed of words. Without words a thought cannot be experienced.

Prove this to yourself right now! Try really hard to have a thought without words. Although it may be possible to have thoughts without words, such as when you dream, whether it is a daydream or night dream, the only way you can retrieve that experience is by choosing words to describe that dream experience. Anytime you notice that you had a thought or were thinking about something it required choosing words to experience it. Therefore all thoughts that come into our awareness can only do so, through the conscious or more often the unconscious choice of words, which alert us to the fact that we are having a conscious thought. Thoughts without words will remain unnoticed by us and wait in our subconscious mind perhaps waiting to create our future dream material. It is only through words that whatever is in our subconscious can be brought into our conscious awareness.

It is helpful to understand and learn how to effectively use the "Power of Spin." Usually a thought will spontaneously appear in our minds and we only know that we are having that thought because we have chosen words to experience it. Without words it remains unknown and invisible. For instance a thought like "I want a beer" or I want to get high" can only be experienced in that particular manner by choosing those specific words.

Since most if not all thoughts occur without prior planning, invitation or notification, then they are what I call "First Thought(s)." Every human being that has some mental capacity to function can then consciously choose the "Second Thought(s) and the words they choose will create the next moment that they will experience as their reality. In the case of the desire or craving to drink or use drugs, which were the uninvited spontaneous "First Thoughts", the person now has a choice to choose wisely the words that will create their "Second Thought" regarding the "First Thought."

They could choose to select the following words "…and I want that drink right now" or "Where can I score and how soon." They also have the absolute power to choose the words that create the "Second Thought" that could change things by "Spinning" it completely around. They could change the entire direction by changing the meaning of the "First Thought" by choosing words such as "I will not hurt my family anymore" or "I need to pray" or "I need to call my counselor or my sponsor." By consciously choosing these words leads to a completely different set of "Second Thoughts" as well as feelings and emotions that change the behavior or actions that will occur or manifest from them.

"Spin" is when entire meanings and experiences are transformed, by just choosing different words to describe or express a view or a situation. An example of spin is when someone hears something that makes him or her very upset or angry, and just before they are going to confront the source of the slander; someone takes them aside and explains they were not attacked nor slandered. In fact the person had actually complimented them, but did so in a sarcastic manner, that was completely misunderstood. The emotion of anger or even rage was immediately changed to forgiveness and appreciation through "Spin." When a person in AA or NA are fearful or upset or worried, they may hear things in a meeting that enable them to see things completely differently, and this completely changes the emotions that they were experiencing. It is due to the "Power of Spin" through the "Art of the Second Thought" that many addicts and alcoholics have been spared from relapsing.

This may be exemplified in the following situation: A person has been unemployed for an extended period of time and has been diligently looking for work with no positive results. They are becoming so overwhelmed with anger and fear that they begin to obsess on how getting high would provide relief and especially escape from all the desperation they are experiencing. They share in a meeting or with another person how they feel and discuss in detail "the terrible problems" they have to deal with. Then that person or someone informs them "The only real problem you have is the need to stay clean and sober and the rest of what you are experiencing are just temporary inconveniences."

A statement like this absolutely will "spin" the person into recognizing not only their priorities, but even promote a sense of gratitude when they realize being clean and sober, "IS" the most important thing in their life. Another person may create "spin" when they state in that same meeting, "My four year old daughter just had surgery to remove a tumor and the surgeon said don't have a lot of hope." The man or woman who shared being overwhelmed with fear and anger about not finding a job, would instantaneously forget what they described as "the terrible problems" they were experiencing.

If you have ever had a loved one diagnosed with a serious condition, then you know how from the moment prior to being informed; your life, your thinking, your beliefs changed in a heartbeat, and what seemed like an overwhelming problem immediately paled in comparison. This is the "Power of Spin." The words that a person chooses does not need "willingness" and you do not have to be "willing" to be impacted and changed by words and language.

The question to ask is "Do words create emotions or do emotions create words?" For example when I would teach others these concepts and ask the group to express "Words" that have significant impact to change the "First Thought," most of the time a favorite with not just addicts and alcoholics, but even Hollywood is that stand by four letter word "Fuck" and if it offends the reader then it absolutely demonstrates its power. If you recall in the Chapter describing methods to develop "Resistance Muscle I used this word numerous times and if it affected or offended you, and it probably did, then you now know the reason I have struggled to find a replacement word that may be less offensive and more politically correct, but that carries equal impact, influence as well as power.

The question is where and how does a word arrive at having such impact? It should not be a secret at this time to fully understand that the words we choose will either construct a better future reality and or will destroy a promising relationship or reality.

"Words are the building blocks of all realities." Any word
that creates a strong emotion creates an equally strong

vision. A vision can only occur with strong emotion and a strong vision forms the basis of "whatever a man or woman can conceive and believe they can achieve."

"Make no mistake about it, "the awesome force of words," will control and influence what we focus on and therefore what we pursue."

Once again the thoughts that you allow to be unchallenged- the "First Thought" can and most of the time lead to great suffering and heartache. Choose the words that will allow the "Second Thought" to change any and all negative or potentially destructive "First Thoughts."

"You always have the "Power of Spin" to change direction, by changing the meaning through the "Art of the Second Thought." What we choose to say creates the meaning of any event in our lives, and therefore we are absolutely responsible to understand that "Definitions Change Life Directions."

It must be fully accepted and recognized that we are completely responsible for the words we say out loud in our own ears, and to absolutely know that our spoken words create the reality we live in. Although it is the words we say deep down within ourselves that contribute to the development of the space we live in; it is the verbally spoken word that forms the "Definitions" that cements the individual bricks of our thoughts, our "Second Thoughts" into what we perceive to be our reality, which will "Determine" the "Direction" of how we shape our lives.

"In this manner our life and destiny is a matter of choices. The choices we make throughout the day become the bearing walls of our existence; since words are so powerful that they are the substance of all creation, for without words nothing would be possible."

"Words bring forth a previously invisible thought and the words we choose to think and speak out loud creates the vision that produces the strong and intense emotional desires to acquire that object of desire."

As there are words that lead to visions that lead to great creations, such as the electric light bulb or the Internet. Is it possible that the wrong choice of words could actually have the power to kill? If you remember earlier I spoke about a man who lived over two thousand years ago who was one of the lesser-known Greek philosophers. He observed that there is nothing in this world that can affect you unless it enters into your skin, by arrow, rock, sword or spear; otherwise nothing can hurt you.

> "If you suffer it is due to the view you take of the event—not the event itself. Here we see that there is a little known truth that has been around for thousands of years and that is "If I feel bad it is because I choose to and not because I have to" and it is not due to some unfortunate event in my life. "I have the absolute power to choose not to be affected."

The time for blame and being a victim or a martyr must end now. It is through the full utilization of words and language; through the deliberate use and understanding of the awesome force created by words; and the "Power of Spin" that we create the world we choose to live in, and that in turn creates the feelings that we experience that drive the direction of our life.

> "Nothing in this world can harm or hurt you unless it enters through your physical skin barrier, otherwise it is the words you choose or allow others to choose for you that you allow to enter into your mind, that causes your death or destruction."

> "Words are absolute power. Words are absolutely "things." Words can and will kill but only if you allow them by refusing to challenge them. You always have the power and right of the "Second Thought!"

In regards to how the "Power of Spin" and the "Art of Second Thought" are an integral part of appreciating and maintaining a Recovery Lifestyle the following Internet story demonstrates this concept. There was a very positive man who was so positive, helpful, sensitive and caring that you literally could hate him for being so good all the time.

The story unfolds that the man fell 60 feet off a tower he was working on and the paramedics, doctors and nurses believed he was going to die, when they routinely asked the question of whether he was allergic to anything, he took as much breath as he could and voiced "YES," as the medical team waited for an answer he stated "GRAVITY."

Everybody laughed, and when they laughed their reality and his reality radically was changed and altered due to the "Power of Spin" through the "Art of Second Thought." He then informed them "I am choosing to live and I hope you are choosing to operate on me, as if you thought I would live." Throughout the story the main character would say that "I choose to have a good day" or "I choose to live" or "I choose to be positive" or "I choose to not be a victim." In regards to this story you NOW need to choose between two questions in respect to this story. [1] "Are you going to delete this message?" or [2] "Are you going to choose to live your life differently?"

> "Most addicts and alcoholics are plagued with self pity, and they need to know that whatever they perceive their reality to be, those situations or events that they believe are causing such deep despair, could lead to the justification to drink or use a drug."

> "Therefore they Need to Choose to- Just grow up, Buck up, Tough up, Get up, and choose to change that reality. Through the choice to use the "Power of Spin" they can change anything they are feeling or experiencing as clearly seen in the above story of the man who could even choose to joke at a time when he may have been facing his own death, due to his great fall from the tower!"

> "Since words control all that we experience of what we perceive to be our reality, then anything and everything can be changed by using the "Power of Spin" through the "Art of Second Thought."

Remember and never forget all that Reality really is- "Are
the words that you use to describe it—words that you
have absolute control to choose! Therefore by changing
the words describing a situation or incident you Reorient
the Reality you are perceiving at that time."

By using this Internet story are you able to gain some perspective to the
power to change and the power to choose to make a change? All it takes is
changing your language—to choose to use the "Power of Spin" through the
"Art of Second Thought" will immediately change your focus and feelings,
which in turn creates a corresponding shift or a Reorientation to the Reality
you were previously perceiving.

The following will provide four examples to further demonstrate this
concept and will enable you to clearly see the "Power of Spin." Before we
proceed further you need to be informed that in the English language there
are estimated to be between 600,000 to over 1 million words. Now with an
absolute arsenal of word weapons why is it that addicts and alcoholics only
use an extremely narrow and limited number of words. It should be noted
that it is not just addicts and alcoholics but most people in general have only
been using very limited vocabularies.

It should also be noted that of the 1 million or more available words
in the English language there are approximately 4000 that specifically and
accurately describe feelings as well as emotional experiences. It is absolutely
astounding and shocking that the people who study the use of language
indicate that it is not just addicts or alcoholics; but the great majority of people
on a weekly basis only habitually use 10 to 12 words that describe emotional
states and feelings.

This terribly impoverished use of words to describe emotional experience
leaves the addict and alcoholic in a very vulnerable state. The reason for this is
that when they only have a very limited number of words to describe feelings
or emotions, then simple situations or events may be mislabeled with words
that inaccurately described the level of the experience or the degree of intensity
associated to a situation. A simple example of this would be when a person is
offended by or hurt by another person and the associated feeling is described
by the words such as "I am so angry I never want to talk to you again." Or "I
am so mad I want to hurt you!"

When a person is limited to such words as "angry" or "mad" or on the flip
side limited to words such as "happy" or "glad" then there is very limited scope
to what a person is capable of feeling, and this could lead to an inaccurate
sensation of feeling overwhelmed by a very minimal and minor situation or

event. Conversely it could cause a person to fail to recognize a very intense, positive pleasurable experience or to minimize the joy that they could have experienced, simply due to a lack of words that would enable them to feel that level of joy or happiness.

"Since there are almost 1,000,000 or more words that can, and will enable a person to clearly state precisely what they are experiencing, in regards to their perception of reality; then there is a real need to have access to a large vocabulary, so that we can better describe what it is that's happening, has happened or we would like to happen."

There are many variations to the most frequent and commonly used words, and depending on the word chosen to describe a particular feeling, will determine the intensity of the level of that feeling that the word represents. In other words if someone states that they felt "angry" then if they stated instead that they felt "rage" is there not an obvious difference in how these words describe that particular feeling, and how they measure differently the level of negative emotions they are experiencing. If a person states they are "happy" or they state they feel "excited" or "joyful" or even "thrilled" are not these last three words more intense and increase the measure of positive emotions they are experiencing.

> "The following IS a major list of 0ver 2,500 FEELING and EMOTIONAL words." Words that JUST represent the feelings a person may experience. Please take the time to carefully read each of these words and notice how each one will absolutely create a different sensation or feeling!"

Emotional Vocabulary Feelings List

A

abandoned
abashed
abominable
abraded
abrupt
absent-minded
absolute

absorbed
abused
abusive
accepted
accepting
aching
active
acute
adamant

adaptable
adequate
admiration
admiring
adoration
adoring
adrift
adventurous
affected

affection
affectionate
afflicted
afraid
after my own heart
ageless
aggravated
aggravation

aggressive

aggrieved

aghast

agitated

agonized

agony

agreeable

airless

airy

alarm

alarmed

alienated

alienation

alive

alone

amazed

ambitious

ambivalent

ambushed

amenable

amiable

amicable

amused

amusement

analytical

anger

angry

angst

anguish

animated

annoyance

annoyed

antagonized

anxiety

anxious

apathetic

appalled

appealing

appreciated

appreciative

apprehensive

approachable

approving

argumentative

armed

arousal

aroused

ashamed

asleep

assertive

astonished

astounded

at ease

at heart

attached

attacked

attracted

attraction

attractive

authentic

authoritative

autonomous

avoided

awake

aware

awful

awkward

B

bad

balanced

bashful

beaten

beautiful

befuddled

belittled

bellicose

belligerent

beloved

benevolent

bent

bereft

besotted

betrayed

bewildered

biased

big heart

bitten

bitter

bitterness

blah

blame

bland

bleeding heart

blessed

bloated

blocked

bloodcurdling

blooming

blue

boastful

boiling

bold

bored

bothered

bottom my-heart

boyish

brash

brave

brave heart

breathless

bright

brilliant

broken

bubbly

bugged

bullied

bummed

burdened

burned out

bushed

bushwhacked

C

caged

calm

can-do

cantankerous

carefree

careful

caring

cautious

certain

challenged

change of heart

charmed

charming

chatty

cheerful

cheerfulness

chilly

chipper

choked

chronic

clean

clear

clever

close

clumsy

cockles of heart

co-dependent

cold

cold heart

cold-blooded

comfortable

comforted

committed

communicative

companionless

compassion

compassionate

competent

competitive

complete

compliant

composed

compulsive

concern

concerned

condescending

confident

conflicted

confused

connected

considerate

consistent

constipated

consuming

contempt

content

contentment

contrary

contrition

controlled

controlling

converted

cool

cooperative

cornered

courageous

cowardly

creative

critical

criticized

cross

cruelty

crushed

compassion

compassionate

competent

competitive

complete

compliant

composed

compulsive

concern

concerned

condescending

confident

conflicted

confused

connected

considerate

consistent

constipated

consuming

contempt

content

contentment

contrary

contrition

controlled

controlling

converted

cool

cooperative

cornered

courageous

cowardly

creative

critical

criticized

cross

cruelty

crushed

cuddly

culpability

curious

curt cynical

D

daring

daunted

dazed

dead-eyed

debauched

decayed

decisive

dedicated

deep

defeat

defeated

defective

defensive

deferential

defiant

degraded

dejected

dejection

delight

delighted

delightful

demanding

denying

dependent

depressed

depression

deprived

deranged

desire

desolate

despair

desperate

despicable

destructiveness

detached

determined

detestable
devastated
devoted
dictatorial
diffident
dignified
diminished
diplomatic
disabled
disagreeable
disappointed
disappointment
discerning
disgraced
disgust
disgusted
disgusting
disheartened
dishonest
dishonor
disillusioned
disinterested
disliked
dismal
dismay
dismayed
disorganized
displeasure
disruptive
dissatisfied
dissociated
distant
distracted
distraught
distress

distressed
distressing
distrustful
disturbed
dithering
discomposure
disconcerted
disconnected
discouraged
discredited
dizzy
dominant
dominated
domineering
doubtful
doubting
down in the
dumps
down
drained
drawn toward
dread
dreamy
dreary
droll
drowsy
drunk
dry
dull
dumb
dutiful
dynamic

E

eager
earnest
easy
eat my heartout
eccentric
economical
ecstasy
ecstatic
edgy
effective
effervescent
egoless
elated
embarrassed
embarrassment
embryonic
emergent
emotional
empathetic
empathic
empowered
empty
empty heart
enchantment
encouraged
energetic
energized
engrossed
enjoyable
enjoyment
enmeshed
enraged
enraptured
enthusiasm
enthusiastic

envious
envy
esteemed
estranged
euphoria
evasive
exasperation
excited
exhausted
exhilaration
exposed
extravagant
extroverted
exuberant

F

facetious
faint heart
fair
faithful
faithless
false heart
fanciful
fancy
fantastic
fascinated
fast
fateful
fatigued
fault
fear
fearful
fearless
feckless

feeling
feral
fertile
festive
finicky
fixated
fixed
flagrant
flat
flighty
floating
flourishing
fondness
foolish
forced
forceful
forgivable
forgiven
forgiving
fortunate
foul
free
frenetic
fretful
friendless
friendly
friendship
fright
frightened
frigid
frisky
frowning
frustrated
frustration
fulfilled

full heart
full of life
fulsome
fuming
funky
funny
furious
fury
fussy

G

gaga
gallant
game
gasping
gay
generous
generous heart
genial
gentle
giddy
giggly
girlish
giving
glad
gladness
gleeful
glib
gloom
gloomy
glowering
glum
gnawing
goalless

good
grace-filled
gracious
grateful
grave
great
greedy
green-eyed
grief
grief-stricken
grieved
grim
groovy
gruesome
gruff
grumpiness
grumpy
guarded
guilt
guilty
gutless
gut-wrenching

H

half-hearted
happiness
happy
hard
hard heart
hardy
harmonious
hate
hateful
hatred

have a heart
have my heart set
heart and soul
heart attack
heart break
heart burn
heart in my mouth
heart of the matter
heart on my sleeve
heart song
heart stopping
heart stricken
heart throb
heart wounded
heart wrenching
heartache
heartbreaking
heartbroken
heartfelt
heartless
heartrending
heartsick
heart-to-heart
heartwarming
heavenly
heavy
hedonistic
helpful
helpless
hermit-like
heroic
hesitant

high an mighty
high heart
high strung
hilarious
hollow
honest
hope
hopeful
hopeless
hopelessness
horrified
horror
hostile
hostility
hot
humane
humble
humiliated
humiliation
humorous
hung up
hurt
hysteria

I

icky
idle
ill
ill-natured
ill-tempered
imitation
immature
immobilized
immoral

immortal
impassive
impatient
imperious
impersonal
important
impoverished
improvident
impudent
impulsive
in a bind
in a rut
in a stew
inactive
inadequate
incapable
incensed
incontinent
indecisive
independent
indifferent
indignant
indignity
individual
indomitable
inebriated
infantile
infatuated
inferior
inflamed
infuriated
ingenious
injured
innocent
inquisitive

insecure
insecurity
insensitive
inspired
insulted
insulting
intelligent
intense
intent
interested
intimate
intractable
intrepid
intrigued
introverted
intuitive
invalidated
inventive
involved
irate
iron heart
ironic

J

jazzy
jealous
jealousy
jerky
jittery
jolliness
jolly
joy
joyful
joyous

jubilant
jubilation
judged
judging
judgmental
jumpiness
jumpy

K

keen
kind
kindness

L

laid back
languid
lawful
lawless
lazy
left out
lewd
liberated
licentious
licked
lifeless
light
liking
limitless
limp
lion heart
listening
listless
lively
livid

loathing

loneliness

lonely

lonely heart

longing

long-suffering

lose my heart

loss

lost

loud

lousy

love

loved

loveless

lovely

love-struck

loving

low

low-spirited

loyal

lucky

lustful

M

mad

malevolent

manic

manipulative

manly

martyred

matter-of-fact

maudlin

mean

mean-spirited

meditative

menace

menacing

mend my heart

merry

mettlesome

miffed

mindful

miserable

misery

misfortunate

misgiving

mistrustful

misunderstood

mixed-up

monotonous

moody

mooning

moping

moral

morbid

morose

mortal

mortified

motionless

mournful

moved

mutilated

mysterious

mystified

N

narcissistic

narrow

nasty

naughty

nauseated

negative

neglect

neglectful

nervous

nervousness

neutral

nice

nit picking

nonchalant

nostalgic

nosy

numb

nurturing

O

obedient

objective

observant

obsessed

obstinate

offended

offensive

officious

on a limb

on tenterhooks

on the spot

open

optimism

optimistic

ornery

out of touch

outgoing

outspoken

over used

over-bearing

overjoyed

overwhelmed

P

pain

pained

panic

panicked

panicky

paralyzed

parasitic

particular

passionate

passive

pathetic

patient

patronized

peaceful

pedantic

peeved

pensive

peppery

perfectionistic

perky

perplexed

persuasive

perverse

pessimistic

petrified

petty

petulant
pissed off
pitiful
pity
pitying
played-out
playful
pleased
pleasure
plucky
pooped
poor
positive
powerful
powerless
prayerful
precise
preoccupied
pressured
pride
private
privileged
projecting
protective
proud
provocative
provoked
prudent
punished
pure
pure heart
purple heart
purposeful
put on
put out

puzzled

Q

quaking
queer
quick
quiet
quirky
quivery

R

rabid
rage
raped
rapture
rapturous
rash
realistic
reassured
rebellious
receptive
reckless
reclusive
red-blooded
re-enforced
reflective
refreshed
regret
rejected
rejecting
rejection
rejuvenated
relapsed
relaxed

release
reliable
relief
relieved
reluctant
remorse
repressed
repugnant
repulsive
resentful
resentment
resigned
resilient
resolute
respected
responsibility
responsible
responsive
restless
restrained
retarded
retiring
revengeful
revulsion
ribald
rich
righteous
risk taker
romantic
rotten
rough

S

sheepish

shocked
shut-out
shy
sabotaged
sad
sadness
safe
sappy
sarcastic
sassy
satiated
satisfaction
satisfied
savvy
scared
scorn
search my heart
secretive
secure
seductive
seething
self-assured
self-doubting
selfish
self-possessed
self-righteous
self-sufficient
sensitive
sentimental
serene
serious
set heart against
shabby
severe
sexual

sexy

S

shaken
shaken up
shaky
shame
shamed
shameful
sharp
silly
skeptical
sleepy
sloppy
slow
sluggish
smarmy
smart
smiley
smug
sneering
snobbish
snoopy
social
soft
soft heart
solitary
somber
sore
sorrow
sorrowful
sorry
sotted
sour

spaced out
spastic
speculative
spineless
spirited
spiritless
spiteful
spleenful
spontaneous
squeezed
stabbing
stable
stagnated
starry-eyed
sterile
still
stilted
stir-crazy
stirred
stolid
stout heart
strangled
stressed out
stretched
strong
stubborn
stuck
stupefied
stupid
suave
subjective
submissive
suffering
sulky
sunny

sunshiny
superior
supernatural
supportive
sure
surly
surprised
suspicious
sweaty
sweet
sweetheart
sybaritic
sympathetic
sympathy

T

tactless
take heart
take to heart
talkative
tame
tearful
teed off
temperate
tenacious
tender
tenseness
tentative
terrible
terrified
terror
terrorizing
testy
thankful

theatrical
thick-skinned
thin-skinned
thorough
thoughtful
thoughtless
thrashed
threatened
thrifty
thrill
thrilled
thriving
ticked off
tickled
tickled pink
tickled-to-death
timid
tired
to my heart's content
tolerable
tolerant
tongue-tied
tormented
torpid
torrid
tortured
touched
touchy
tough
tragic
tranquil
transcendent
trapped
trepidation
tricky

trustful
trusting
turned off
turn two-faced

U

unbelieving
uncaring
uncertain
unchanging
unclean
unclear
uncomfortable
unconcerned
unconquerable
unconscious
undaunted
understand
understanding
undeserving
uneasiness
uneasy
unfeeling
unflinching
unforgiving
unglued
ugly
unafraid
unassuming
unguarded
unhappiness
unhappy
unimportant
uninterested

unique
unmanned
unmoved
unnatural
unnerved
unpleasant
unreasonable
unresponsive
unsettled
unshrinking
unsure
unsympathetic
unwholesome
unwilling
upset
uptight
urgent
used
useless
unbelieving
uncaring
uncertain
unchanging
unclean
unclear
uncomfortable
unconcerned
unconquerable
unconscious
undaunted
understand
understanding
undeserving
uneasiness
uneasy

unfeeling
unflinching
unforgiving
unglued
ugly
unafraid
unassuming
unguarded
unhappiness
unhappy
unimportant
uninterested
unique
unmanned
unmoved
unnatural
unnerved
unpleasant
unreasonable
unresponsive
unsettled
unshrinking
unsure
unsympathetic
unwholesome
unwilling
upset
uptight
urgent
used
useless

V

vacant

vain
valiant
vengeful
venturesome
vibrant
victimized
vigorous
vile
vindicated
violent
virginal
virile
virtuous
visionary
vivacious
vulnerable

W

wakeful
wanted
wanton
warm
warm heart
warmth
wary
wasteful
watchful
weak
weakening
weary
weepy
weighty
weird
whacked

			Z
whimsical	wishy-washy	worry	
whiny	withdrawn	worshipful	
wholesome	withholding	worthless	zealous
whole-souled	woeful	worthy	zestful
wicked	womanly	wounded	zingy
wild	wonderful	wracked	zippy
wilted	worked up	wrathful	
wimpy	worn	wretched	
wincing	worn out	wronged	
wired	worried	wry	
wise	worrisome		

To really drive home the point and the need for not only every addict or alcoholic to expand their GENERAL vocabulary but far more important to enlarge their EMOTIONAL vocabulary; this brief "Feelings Vocabulary List" was presented.

> "DON'T CHEAT YOURSELF! Remember you use or used substances to change the way you feel or felt, and that is the only reason you use or used substances. If you learn or expand your EMOTIONAL VOCABULARY you will experience a BRAND new world!"

> "A world that can and will be fully experienced through words instead of DRUGS and ALCOHOL!!"

> "Once again it is only through words that the invisible stream of all experience is brought to our consciousness. When we stop to notice, and label a fleeting moment of that eternal stream of invisible experiences that are occurring in us, within us and around us—IS when and only WHEN we gain awareness and potential control of ANY experience!"

The following chapter will go into great depth to help the addict and their families understand each other. After all, the number one reason for relapse is problems with relationships, family relationships, friendships, job relationships, or any other interaction between two people that can lead to confusion, and intense feelings that can trigger an unchallenged "First Thought" that could lead to a destructive impulsive action.

The following chapter on "Relationships" will provide you with much opportunity to recognize the absolute need to begin to practice the need to always choose a right "Second Thought" and learn to choose the "right emotional word" than choose a wrong "Second Thought" and the "wrong emotional word." If you then act on that wrong thought or use that wrong word, this will be the cause of deep emotional regrets afterwards. In other words by understanding and developing the ability to utilize the "Power of Commitment" through the "Art of Accountability" will not only enable the person to heal, strengthen and significantly improve any damaged relationships; but will appreciably increase the quality of all relationships!

PLEASE NOTE IF YOU JUST READ THIS CHAPTER AS A RESULT OF JUST FOLLOWING THE SUGGESTION IN THE INTRODUCTION OF THIS BOOK—IT IS NOW RECOMMENEDED YOU RETURN TO THE BEGINNING OF THIS BOOK BEFORE YOU CONTINUE INTO THE RELATIONSHIP CHAPTER!

But if you are currently experiencing problems or concerns with a relationship—then maybe you should just continue with your reading—"So You Can Immediately Begin The Process Of Healing Your Damaged Relationships!"

Do not be Deceived, God is not Mocked; for Whatever a Man sows, that He Will also Reap.

Galatians 6:7

Chapter Thirteen

Addiction's Impact On Family

The need to explore relationships is fundamental to establishing an understanding of the value as well as the vital importance of a relationship; in regards to an addicts or alcoholics chances for a lasting recovery. As you may remember in Chapter Five on "Value Exchange," the reason that any human being will choose one action or thing over another; is strictly based on the value they assign to it, and the value is determined directly by the intensity of the emotion they attach to it.

In all my years as a counselor, relationships appear to be the number one reason an addict or alcoholic will relapse. Therefore it is essential that the reader be aware of the awesome benefit and need of being in a healthy relationship, as well as to be sensitive to the very fragile nature of relationships.

As we proceed we need to expand on this concept that "relationships are the number one reason for relapse." The reason for this is…

"Where Are You Going To Run For Cover And Comfort?" When the most important people in your life are no longer able or willing to support you—due to your "addiction" and "madness."

"There is only one place to run and that is back to the very "MADNESS" that drove all the people that care—out of your life!"

When describing relationships it is helpful to recognize that any involvement with anyone else basically meets the definition of relationship, for the simple fact that two people when engaged in an activity with each other are relating. It is in this sense that relationship encompasses all the following: families, friendships, romance, business and pleasure. It is the fact that anytime two or more addicts or alcoholics, who are in early recovery are engaged in a joint activity, things can and usually do go wrong. Many times the addict or alcoholic becomes easily disillusioned and disgusted, and this leads to almost an automatic desire to drink and drug to deal with their discontent with the other person or people. In the early and initial stages of recovery this impulse to drink or drug to mange stress may occur. Therefore any interaction with others has the potential to derail an addicts or alcoholics recovery.

The reason for this may be found in the fact that for the addict or alcoholic who has used substances as a primary coping mechanism, unconsciously desires that the people in their lives do whatever is necessary to keep them comfortable and free from stress. Unfortunately the other people are unaware of this expectation and they have their own needs and desires and generally will not compromise just to make an addict comfortable or happy.

The alcoholic is so accustomed to taking a substance into their body to experience or to not experience certain feelings; this tendency causes them to consciously or unconsciously want to manipulate people to do their bidding, and in fact they think about the interaction in the same way they viewed or used drugs and alcohol.

In another words they want people to do for them exactly what the substances did for them. They want and expect the person to make them feel good, and unfortunately many times, and maybe even most times this is not going to be the case. As the process of recovery develops hopefully a person can learn enough sensitivity, sacrifice, compassion, patience and tolerance; that is always necessary to maintain a healthy relationship.

Despite the fact that most addicts and alcoholics are still involved with others in healthy and unhealthy relationships makes relationships seem fairly resilient and even "bullet proof" especially after all the constant suffering and history of emotional abuse, neglect and in many cases physical abuse as well.

This chapter will explain the development of relationships, the destruction of relationships and ways to delay and defuse the risks of probable or potential dissolution.

> "Failure to accept or take responsibility or to deny these risks and threats will undermine and destroy the chances for a lasting relationship and since no relationship is absolutely "bullet proof" –do not take for granted any family or loved one that is currently sympathetic or struggling to be supportive."

What is a relationship? The Miriam Webster dictionary defines it as:

> "Re-la-tion-ship" the state of being related or interrelated; the relation connecting or binding participants in a relationship; a state of affairs existing between those having relations or dealings; had a good relationship with his family; a romantic or passionate attachment "intimacy."

For our purposes we will utilize the meaning, which is "the state of being related or interrelated" and "a state of affairs existing between those having relations or dealings." Why do people get into relationships with each other? Is it not to develop a means or develop strategies in which there are dealings between them? What is the primary reason for close and intimate relationships? Is it not to get emotional needs, human needs met? What are those needs and how do we obtain satisfaction of those needs from another person? How do we know which person will best meet those needs? How do we select a partner to help us acquire satisfaction of our human needs?

Let's begin with the fact that there are strong innate needs inside all people, and they can only be satisfied by developing a healthy connection to another person. This would be the ideal case but unfortunately many people select unhealthy partners and they get some needs met; usually unhealthy ones, while the healthy needs continue to be neglected.

> "It is the neglect of healthy needs or the inability to find a partner to help identify and get these needs met, which leads to pathological relationships not only with people but with objects and things also."

These include but are not limited to objects such as money, food, drugs, sex and rock and roll. Music can be very addictive; as in the case of the person ignoring or neglecting a family member or a friend because "I just got to hear this one more time." When in fact they have listened to it a thousand times. Also things like shopping, gambling, pornography, TV or computers and the Internet, all can significantly meet many healthy needs but more probably unhealthy ones.

The first step in the process "of having relations or dealings" is to pick a partner. How does one select one person out of over six billion to be the ONE? Well nature answered this with the fact that in your brain there are numerous chemical compounds and some of those create an incredible intense pleasurable feeling, and almost anything that has any appeal will set this in motion.

Therefore a person just looks around their environment and something stimulates them or "grabs their attention." It is at that precise moment that the selection process has been engaged, and all things that have less stimulus value will have less "grab" power.

> "The awareness of that person, event or object that now is being fed by pleasurable brain chemicals, causes the loss of awareness of everything similar or even not similar at all."

In the case of "lust" or romantic attraction, which both produce an almost identical chemical pleasurable experience; it is really only some sort of rationalization that separates these two intense forces. Once there is awareness of desire to acquire the object of desire the selection process is now fully engaged. The driving force and focus will be the belief that acquisition will meet certain conscious and subconscious needs.

When two people encounter each other for the first time they begin to explore their attraction and the feelings that drove them to meet. The problem is that since it is really just simply a matter of brain chemistry, there is nothing rational in this process and therefore they will believe anything simply because "what feels so good, cannot be bad."

It is interesting to know that very early on and sometimes deep into the history of a relationship, there is an unrealistic acceptance of unacceptable behaviors. This occurs due to the feeling or stimulation that continues to cause the release of these powerful neurotransmitters; that literally blinds the person to the faults or deficiencies of their selected partner. This unfortunately is recognized way too late in the development of the relationship and when the moment of truth does arise; it can be recognized by statements or thoughts like these: "what did I ever see in her" "what made me believe he was the one?"

> "The REAL reality is that you never saw anything and you never had to believe in anything. It was the sight, sound, smell or even the memories of this person that stimulated your brain to an immense level of pleasure, and it absolutely had NOTHING to do with the quality of the relationship."

"The passage of time will ALWAYS result in questioning the feelings once they become less important, which leads to finally noticing ALL the negative behaviors that a person had been exhibiting since their first meeting; but was virtually invisible due to the excitement and pleasure that they were stimulating in each other's brain."

As with any repetitive exposure to a stimulus a person becomes progressively less stimulated and this spells the death of any relationship, which has never evolved from the neurotransmitter state, to a deep level of intimacy. Nature or God has given humans this gift of selecting, but after that we have a very limited time to begin to build healthy or even unhealthy foundations for deeper intimacy. This has to occur for any interest to be maintained, for the stimulation provided by the neurotransmitters, will fade slowly away; sometimes in just weeks and more rarely in years, but without the development of deeper intimacy the relationship dissolves.

We need to pause here for a moment and search the dictionary again but this time we need to understand the abstract concept of:

"Intimacy" the state of being intimate; familiarity; something of a personal or private nature.

In line with this definition we can include a description of "intimacies." There are many types of knowing "something personal or of a private nature" between two people. Now for most addicts and alcoholics intimacy many times is limited to having a sexual experience with their partner.

"In the world of intimacy there are many things just as intense as sex."

For instance when one partner knows exactly the right gift to buy for their significant other without hints or prompting; they just know, intuitively know just what their partner likes or loves. Another form of intimacy is just sitting quietly watching a sun set or enjoying a movie or studying a painting and knowing the other person is just as much involved in the experience and not one word is shared.

An even deeper level of intimacy is experienced when one person knows precisely how the other feels, in some given situation and as a result of that deeper true empathy they provided encouragement, support and can celebrate with that particular person in a manner they never experienced before. That person uses the precise words that comfort, heal, or appropriately excites their partner. Another type of intimacy occurs when the couple is apart for extended periods of time and they still only think about each other without any visual cues or stimulation despite being separated and not being able to see or hear from each other.

> "Notice when intimacy has reached this depth, it no longer has anything to do with the initial energy that formed their alliance; but is now driven by love. Some authors have written that it may take five to seven years for this depth of intimacy or connection to occur between two people."

Now that we have a vague understanding of the types and levels of intimacy and how this is the true bonding energy that holds a couple together for the long term; we need to now explore the obstacle to its development; which is the failure to enlarge the connection beyond the initial chemical attraction period of the relationship and failure to accomplish this, will cause that relationship to die on the vine. This failure will always lead to disillusionment, dissatisfaction, disharmony and the inevitable dissolution of that relationship whether they still live together or there is separation and divorce, that relationship will be dead.

> "It is at the time that the stimulation fades that the impatience and intolerance for the other person's defects and deficiencies come into full light, and have to be wrestled with, and for the relationship to survive, the couple will need to successfully negotiate solutions."

> "Unfortunately many times it is just easier to allow a stranger to begin to create that same excitement in the brain and leave the less stimulating partner for the more stimulating person. Yes—once again "if it feels good how can it be bad." The inability to negotiate solutions destroys all the "Good" things that were being developed or worked for, in the existing relationship."

Now I want to take a moment to show the selection process by simply comparing picking a partner to that of picking a pair of sneakers. If you enter into a sports store and they sell a variety of sneakers of all makes and styles, how do you choose the pair you are going home with?

Although this is a complicated process it is also a simple one at the same time. You will select the pair by the way they feel and the way they look. Now that is the simple part but how will you know that you know? What tells you that it is so? Where is it happening that you are so sure? The process entails neurotransmitters and that is the complex part. How does this happen and which chemicals are driving the choice. The details of this process are not important and way beyond the purposes of this book.

To further simplify this process lets use another common situation in which decisions are or have to be made. Now instead of struggling with the decision of which pair of sneakers to buy, lets think about this in the same manner of how the mention of certain foods absolutely grabs your full attention. It is this same chemical process that alerts you to know, what type of food you desire, or which pair to pick and ultimately which person to partner with.

> "Once there is interest, then there is desire and once
> there is desire; the plan is developed to acquire that
> object of desire; whether it is a particular pair of sneakers
> or a special or specific type of food, a drink or a drug, or
> a strong attraction toward another person."

How does a relationship develop once there is attraction? How strong is the connection once there is attraction? How much effort will be expended to achieve contact or acquisition? To answer these questions we will explore the process that leads to contact or acquisition.

When a person notices that they are gaining interest in another person and they have a desire to get together with them and to develop the connection further they first have to meet and greet. A common and general manner in which this takes place is when one asks the other for contact information such as a telephone number or even an address where they can find that person. If the person is not willing to give up this personal data about themselves; then the next step is to explore their willingness to meet somewhere to talk or have dinner.

> "Once a time and place has been agreed upon, it appears
> the foundation is being developed for more involvement
> and this further excites the brain chemistry in a very

> pleasurable manner as evidenced by "Wow this may be
> the one; I never felt this way before I hope they like me;
> I can't wait till we meet again."

The strength of desire or the fact that the thoughts about the person are becoming powerful stimulants, may be tested early on by the simple fact that the desired person may not show up at the time and place agreed upon. That means there will be deep disappointment and even possible anger but definitely a sense of frustration and some sense of betrayal.

Now these are very powerful negative emotions that could lead to a quick decision, not to have or try to make another contact with that person, due to the pain they just caused. One simple word or concept that describes this is "mistrust" in that the person whom they have had a great attraction; has just proved they cannot be trusted.

At this point several immediate things will happen. The person stood up will no longer have any interest or desire to try to meet or be with the other person again. Whatever intense and pleasurable sensations they were experiencing while anticipating the meeting will be obliterated and destroyed. The other thing that will immediately happen will be engaging in rationalization to help make sense of the disappointment and prevent disillusionment due to the stimulus memory of the person is stronger than any negative emotions they have caused by their selfish or neglectful behavior, in not showing at the time and place previously agreed upon.

Since they never exchanged any personal data such as telephone numbers or addresses, it is now virtually impossible to immediately find out why there was a "no show." In the event that there should be a chance meeting again, this issue may surface and be explored if the other person is still interested or showing interest.

In the event that at least a cell phone number was exchanged, then the injured party would immediately call and inquire and want to know why the other person did not show. Now at this point that person may be very apologetic and sincerely sympathetic to the disappointment and possible hurt they may have caused and be willing to agree to set up another date or meeting. After an activity and time and place has again been agreed upon, the brain chemistry of the injured person and even possibly the offender will create an exciting and intense sensation and the anticipation would be at least equal to or even greater than before.

> "That intense neurotransmitter stimulation results
> in acceptance of unacceptable behavior, which will

really play itself out, if there is another failed meeting. Depending on a person's ability to trigger an intense and powerful stimulus of excitement, may leave the other person to fall victim to his or her own neurotransmitters, resulting in possibly accepting unacceptable behavior in another person over and over and over again."

This can become so pathological that one person could treat another person as a doormat and they still would not mind or resist. Some authors would refer to this state in a relationship as codependency and that is not what this book is about; there are numerous volumes that have been written and may be found by simply going on the Internet and Google "Codependence."

"Generally it seems, that what should bring two people together, is having some small grain of awareness that they can trust each other. When one person fails to follow through with something agreed upon; whether it was a planned date or the agreement to purchase some item; the failure triggers a sense of mistrust."

"Depending on the force of attraction or the flow of neurotransmitters, will determine if there is forgiveness and tolerance, or disillusionment and dissolution of the brief or even not so brief relationship."

If we may generalize even more, is it not possible that the only thing that is present when two people are attracted to each other is some sense of being able to trust the other person. If very early on that sense of trust is broken, then is it not highly probable that one of those people would walk away from the other. Frustration and disillusionment of not being able to rely upon a person you have just met, but have developed strong feelings towards, could and probably would cause much confusion regarding further efforts to continue trying to develop that relationship. Keep in mind that once again, "strong feelings," are nothing more than just a neurotransmitter release.

I hate to wreck the sense of romanticism and romance but it really is only the force of brain chemistry and nothing mysterious. What is truly mysterious is how a newly formed alliance between two people develops into a lifetime experience together. Some would refer to this as "Being married a long time" or "They have been together for most of their lives."

"Is it possible that a relationship can develop without trust? I personally have been asking this question for decades and most of the people have responded with the answer of absolutely NOT! Although there are exceptions to everything and I will be the first to admit that; it is also necessary to admit that it is just common sense that if you cannot trust a person, there is a high probability that you would cease interacting with that person."

Now what does this have to do with addiction and alcoholism?

If I have lost the reader let me help you come back to the beginning. What we need to know is how addiction and alcoholism impacts a relationship. First let's understand the nature of trust and that means, it is either there or not there, but it is never half or barely there.

"When a person seriously deceives or betrays another person only one thing occurs and that is the trust is broken—not bent, but completely broken. Now it follows that if there is no trust, then there can be no relationship and if this is true, then what holds people together regardless of the development of mistrust."

Since many people continue in relationships in which betrayal and deceit have created mistrust, it is helpful to recognize what the bonding energy is that holds people together, even though trust has been lost or destroyed.

Now let's take a moment to return to the original issue and that is recognizing what addiction does to trust. It absolutely destroys it! Despite the greatest efforts and intentions it is possible that one person will never be able to convince another person that they can ever be fully trusted again. Too many times the relationship has been damaged almost beyond repair and other times it is already a lost cause.

"The purpose of this chapter is to guide the addict or alcoholic into understanding the significant importance of protecting these relationships. In order to protect the relationship, it is necessary to identify the threats to the relationship, and how to avoid further damage to that relationship."

The feeling of trust will have to evolve over a long period of time and can only occur when the distrusted person learns to be very reliable, accountable, consistent, caring, sensitive and considerate. While this process is occurring, it is absolutely necessary to identify the bonding energy that holds people or families together, when trust has been completely lost.

First of all, do not lie to yourself, for if you have lied, deceived, or betrayed someone the trust has been destroyed. Trust is not something that can be stretched or bent and it cannot and does not exist in any manner as partially broken or almost broken; it is destroyed and may never be fully restored; but fortunately trust is not necessary for the survival of long term and established relationships; but it is absolutely necessary in the development of a new relationships.

When working with addicts and alcoholics I would emphasize to them that their significant other or family member has absolutely no trust in them. Although they would find this comment initially disturbing they inevitably would recognize the truth of this. The next question that I would ask is why does the family or significant other still talk or support them, even though there is no trust?

It becomes apparent that there are greater emotional states that bind people and families together than trust and the one that is still holding the family or the significant other together is probably that of "hope." Now hope is much more resilient than trust and it can take more pounding and bending, but once it breaks or is lost then the situation has now become "hopeless" and there is no interest or desire to interact or reconcile with the addict or alcoholic.

> "The addict and alcoholic must see the danger in inflicting any more damage to their family's sense of hope; since it is a well known fact that having family support and involvement in recovery improves the persons prognosis; it is extremely important to protect that relationship."

Too many times the relationship has been damaged almost beyond repair and the addict or alcoholic has to understand the significant importance of protecting these relationships. It is necessary to identify the threats to the relationship and how to avoid further damage to that relationship.

"Why do people get into relationships and what do they get out of them or from them?" Some people would state "for love; for companionship."

> "The concept of love needs to be viewed in the way that 'love' is not what people get into a relationship for and instead see love as the container that all their needs are placed inside."

Love is really like a container or may be seen in the context as a "Bucket of Love." Now what is it that goes into or should fill this bucket? Especially when people will sometimes want to kill or commit suicide due to a relationship; why is it so hard to describe what they need or desire in a relationship- what they want to put in that "Bucket of Love?"

The purpose of a relationship is to enable the meeting of certain human needs. The following will describe some of these needs through the use of words that describe specific emotions. This list is to just illustrate and should by no means be considered all-inclusive; but it is provided here to just provide a hint of the magnitude of the benefits of being in a healthy relationship and sometimes even an unhealthy one. Whether a person is an addict or alcoholic or has no substance use problems, the following list should make it very apparent what is at stake if a relationship is destroyed.

> "People get into relationships for support, understanding, encouragement, affirmation, acceptance, acknowledgement, security, reassurance, friendship, celebration, sex, intimacy, sympathy and empathy or simply stated "A shoulder to cry on." This list should demonstrate why "People need People" as that very old Barbara Streisand song exemplified. Now each time a person interacts with another person it is to meet one or more of these emotional needs."

Some people have also added love and trust to this list but for our purposes it may be helpful to view love and trust, as the necessary container that holds all these human needs. A simple metaphor may demonstrate this concept. If we think about love and trust being a bucket in which all the above mentioned needs are contained within, as well as any and every other human need is also contained within; then we can see how essential love and trust are.

Now to further understand the nature of love and trust let's expand upon this illustration. If you view the bucket as a "Bucket of Love" in which you reach down to pull out these emotional needs, then you can see that love and trust are not in the bucket, but are absolutely essential to carry needs and to have a place to draw them from.

For instance when one person speaks to another person they are actually reaching down inside that persons "Bucket of Love" and drawing out desired human needs and emotions such as "support, acknowledgement, understanding, recognition, affirmation, friendship, security, reassurance or celebration."

Now if we modify this illustration and replace the "Bucket" with a fine crystal bowl and we again place all these human needs in that glass container, then what would happen if someone dropped it? Depending whether it was dropped from a roof and crashed onto the concrete below or just hit a tile floor there is the highest probability that it would shatter and then what would happen to all the contents? Would they remain in place or would they be scattered and lost?

When dealing with addiction and relationships it is necessary to understand the fragile nature of that type of relationship and the necessity to protect it from harm and loss at all cost. In order to better understand how a relationship is damaged by addiction it is necessary to identify the threats. In the same sense of how emotions within relationships meet human needs, other darker or more painful emotions, can destroy the ability to get those needs met.

Just as there are very powerful positive needs such as the ones described in the previous paragraph; there are very equally powerful negative ones. These negative emotions become equally blended when addiction begins to impact the relationship.

> "This means that when a person reaches out to another person in an addictive relationship; then instead of support, acknowledgement, and understanding; they receive rejection, suspicion and doubt. As can be clearly seen there are good and very bad emotions inside that bucket and when the person reaches in they don't know what they are grabbing. Due to addiction there are many poisonous feelings that have been deposited in the bucket and If they grab rejection and hate then they will feel much resentment towards their partner and this could trigger a relapse."

Many times the addict or alcoholic is not aware of the damage they have done to the relationship, due to the progressive nature of their partner accepting higher and higher levels of unacceptable attitudes and behaviors. I would like to take a moment to explain how one person learns to accept greater and greater levels of unacceptable behaviors from their partner. Lets just look at this from a common sense point of view.

If a man came into his house and saw his four year old son watching "Barney the Dinosaur" and the man absolutely hated that purple Dinosaur and took out his Nine Millimeter gun and shot the T.V. what do you think the child's mother should do? Common sense would say to get the child and herself out of the house and or call the police, but absolutely not stay around this madman!

What if the woman's response was "Come Johnny we need to go upstairs to bed, your dad is mad again." Now as she was putting little Johnny to bed she tells him—"Don't worry we will get you another TV and keep it in your room, so daddy doesn't shoot the T.V. anymore and you can finish watching Barney." What would your reaction be if this occurred in your life? How would you handle it?

If you ever stayed out late or even overnight and did not inform your loved ones where you were; what reactions do you think they experienced? Some addicts or alcoholics can binge for days at a time and no one knows if they are still alive, in the hospital, in jail or dead. When they return they do not want to hear any feelings or complaints about the fact they did not come home. In fact most of the time they will not tolerate being informed of the massive suffering their irresponsible addictive behaviors caused the loved ones.

"If you are reading this and you are guilty of this type of behavior and you are good at justifying, rationalizing or minimizing your reprehensible behaviors; then just simply ask your self the following question. Would you accept and tolerate it, if your loved ones did exactly what you did and they stayed out all night or for days at a time and you knew nothing where they were or who they were with?"

The answer to this question is absolutely NOT and you could not because as an addict or alcoholic you do not possess the capacity of tolerance nonetheless patience. You absolutely would not cope or accept such irresponsible, hurtful and inconsiderate behaviors in your partner and you would leave them, possible the first time they did this, and without a doubt if they frequently did this. The next question is why would any person continue to accept greater and greater levels of unacceptable behaviors? Whether it is tolerating their partner shooting the T.V. or staying out for days at a time.

To answer this question we need learn about frogs! If you took a healthy living frog and dropped it into a hot shallow frying pan full of water, what would the frog immediately do? You are probably right-it would jump out! But if you were to put a healthy living frog in a cold frying pan filled with water and turned the heat up slowly; what would the frog do? Now if you said that, "once it got hot it would jump out" you would be wrong! You see when you turn the heat up slowly on a frog; the frog fails to recognize or register that it's environment is progressively becoming more and more life threatening and the changes appears to be so slow and incremental, the frog fails to respond and dies.

> "The mechanism in which people learn to accept and tolerate unacceptable and intolerable behaviors is due to the fact that the behaviors initially were not that dramatic and just like the frog the person fails to recognize how sick and unhealthy the relationship has become."

To drive home this point lets use the example of a couple whom just got married and they are on their Honeymoon, and the first night their new spouse leaves the room and does not come back for a day and a half. Do you think that the other person would tolerate this and what if this is just a sample of behavior that their partner is going to exhibit into the future?

Now suppose a man and woman went on their first date; had dinner and a movie and maybe sex; but the next day the man calls her up and states "I had a great time with you last night" and the partner stated "Wow you are so interesting and you have done so many things, I have never known anyone quite like you before." Then the man shares—"You know when I left you last night I sort of got myself into a situation and I has wondering if you could come down to the town jail and bail me out!"

Now any woman in her right mind may immediately recognize this man is not "Mr. Right" and gracefully or not so gracefully hang up and make sure there is never any further contact. Now a very codependent woman may follow the tradition that Tammy Wynette expressed in that country song "Stand By Your Man." (Google it –you will find the lyrics quite insightful if not very alarming-reminds me of frogs.) Depending on your level of self-esteem and your sense of self-respect as well as your ability to have healthy boundaries will determine your actions.

> "In fact I have found that the healthiest people that addicts and alcoholics meet do not stay in relationships

> with them due to they have a clear sense of boundaries
> and enough self esteem that will not accept or tolerate
> bad behaviors. As frightening as this next observation
> may seem to you; it does appear the addicts current
> relationship is with some of the sickest people they
> know, simple because the healthier people ended and
> left the relationship."

A simple case in point is when domestic violence develops; it usually was preceded by a period of time in which the couple began to berate, be unkind, be inconsiderate and verbally abuse, degrade or call the other person ugly names and use profanity.

> "Even though some couples will banter and call each
> other foul names in a "cutesy" manner, they need to
> realize that once they begin to disrespect each other
> the quality of the relationship is being destroyed and it
> becomes easier and easier for violence to begin to occur.
> Healthier people (since they are not frogs!) will not
> allow this deterioration of the relationship and will not
> tolerate disrespectful, inconsiderate behaviors and they
> would end the relationship if rude and hurtful behaviors
> were to continue or escalate."

What exactly are the impacts that interfere with the ability of one person to meet the needs of another person in the addictive relationship? What are the things that poison the "Bucket of Love?" What can be done to heal or cleanse the hurt and damage? What are the emotions or feelings or beliefs that block one person's access to getting their needs met? To answer all these questions we will need to explore more specifically what those impacts are.

The easiest way to demonstrate how alienation will develop in an addictive relationship is to ask one simple question. What emotions does a person experience as a direct result of living with the addict or alcoholic? When a family member or significant other suffers due to addiction; what exactly is the cause of that suffering?

> "Whether it is done vindictively or simply due to the
> fallout of being with the addict or alcoholic, the family
> or significant other will experience a massive amount of

negative emotions. The following is a list of some of those negative emotions. They will suffer betrayal, confusion, doubt, worry, fear, anger, frustration, disillusionment, disgust, depression, sadness, helplessness, terror, guilt, shame, mistrust, distrust, vindictiveness, depreciated, unappreciated, anxiety, used, abused, neglected, manipulated, despair, desperation, bewilderment, dissatisfaction, rage, homicidal and suicidal thoughts, and this is just a very small and non inclusive list of negative emotional impacts directly due to living and being in a relationship with the addict or alcoholic."

Now it can be clearly seen that addiction has the power to totally destroy any good in a relationship or family. There are far more darker and destructive emotions than there are loving intimate ones. Therefore when the addict reaches out to their partner for support and understanding, they may instead receive anger and rage or despair and depression. The addict experiences these negative emotions as rejection and this sense of rejection will lead to the abandonment of seeking comfort from the family or partner. They then would seek relief through the use of substances.

It is clear that no person will tolerate the pain of not getting needs met and when the most important person in their life is no longer capable of meeting these needs; where will the addict or alcoholic run for cover and comfort? That is absolutely right they will go back to drugs and alcohol. Rejection is the most negative and destructive emotion that an addict or alcoholic may experience; and the equally destructive emotion for the significant other of the addict, is that of being pushed into a state of hopelessness.

"There is no greater damage done to a human being, than to take away their hope and addicts don't just inflict this suffering one time on their loved ones but countless and numerous times. Every time the addict or alcoholic conveys a message that they are going to stop or control their use, the loved one builds hope that this may actually occur. How many times can a person have their hopes built up, only to suffer disappointment and disillusionment over and over again, before they are pushed into a complete state of hopelessness?"

"Is not the act of destroying another human being's hope the cruelest action of all? Is it not probable that the injured person will eventually refuse to believe in the other person after several disappointments? Due to this lack of belief or support for the addict, where will the addict or alcoholic run for cover and comfort. Will not this force the addict to turn back to drugs when they have unmet needs?"

It is helpful for the addict or alcoholic to recognize that when they are being rejected or ignored or they feel minimum or no support from their families or significant other, they should not take this personally.

"An alcoholic or addict has to accept the fact that every human being has a right to protect himself or herself from injury. In fact doesn't human beings have the right to protect themselves from even further injury, and the only way they can do this is though refusing to have hope or believing in the possibility of change. Of course anybody has that right and should exercise that right. Unfortunately for the addict or alcoholic when that person takes a preventive stance to protect themselves; that action is perceived as blatant rejection."

Many times a strange paradox occurs when the addict starts to feel better their significant other will become bitter. The best antidote to this is to accept the fact that due to the overwhelming damage the addict has done to the relationship, the most effective way to bring on the healing is for the alcoholic to accept that they owe one hundred percent and to expect nothing in return from the family or significant other.

Think about the fact that when a person is in need of another person's love and affection, they will do many things to receive it. Now in the event that an addict or an alcoholic relapses after a few weeks, months or even years, then their loved one will immediately lose any trust in that person. Now the addict or alcoholic will be desperate to be back with the loved one they hurt, so they will "woo and coo" them. Think about this in the following manner. When two people need each other, then that means one of them has to give up more than the other one. You can disagree but regardless of what you believe it is never fifty-fifty. Since one is at a slight or even major disadvantage, then it is that person who is at the risk of the greatest harm. To make it crystal clear of the need to accept a loved ones reluctant or even cold attitude towards the addict or alcoholic the following metaphor will be very informative, for it describes how the loved one or significant other allows themselves to be held high in the arms of their partner.

Now visualize the following: The man is holding his partner cradled in his arms at shoulder height. Now if he was to drop this person on the floor or on the street, do you think that person would notice that their so-called loved one just dropped them on their head? Do you think the person would still trust the person that was holding them or would all trust be lost? Now if the addict or alcoholic "wooed and cooed" them to the point that they were willing to get back up in their arms again, would they trust the person not to drop them again or would the only reason be to get back up in their arms, was that they now only had hope, they would not be dropped again, since the trust was absolutely broken.

Now depending on the mental health of the person they may not risk being dropped again, and so they would leave the relationship rather than risk serious injury a second time. Another person without a clear sense of boundaries, and who has low self-esteem may be willing to get into the arms and be dropped several more times, before they refuse to be hurt anymore.

"To make this metaphor even more compelling and dramatic, think about each time the person is dropped it is from a greater height each time. This means that each time they are abused they feel the pain at greater levels of intensity, until they can no longer bear it, and that is when they refuse to get back up into the arms of their partner, when they finally say "enough is enough and I am not going to allow you to hurt me anymore."

"It is at this time the addict or alcoholic becomes desperate and angry due to the overwhelming feeling of being attacked and rejected. As a result of this intense feeling of rejection they may become vulgar and threatening, demanding the attention and affection from the person that they have so severely injured."

Think about it in the following manner: You just dropped your loved one off a ten-story roof and they hit the ground and they are a splattered bleeding road pizza and they tell you. "Take a hike Jack-I never want to see you again-the locks have been changed-don't try to see the children-you will be hearing from my lawyer" Your response is to become progressively more angry due to the fact that you can no longer "woo and coo" them and that means you are not going to get your needs met.

"Now due to your twisted perceptions you are going to feel attacked, misunderstood and abused. Your response will be like this. You will look at the bleeding mess on the sidewalk and start to shake as your adrenalin begins pumping due to the rejection, and you will scream a big-(pardon the language, but you know it is true) —FUCK YOU!! Now lets examine the details, you just threw or dropped this person from a ten story building, and due to the fact that they are finally practicing self preservation and refusing to allow you to hurt them any more; your response is to curse them out! This truly is the meaning of insanity!

> "You must accept the fact that every human being has an absolute right to protect themselves from injury and an even greater absolute right to protect themselves from further injury. If your loved one is treating you coldly or in a detached, unfriendly manner, and they are not very enthusiastic about this, your ninth time you are trying to recover; then do not under any circumstances take it personally."

The alcoholic or addict must clearly understand that stress and uncontrolled emotions slowly destroy a human beings health, by damaging the immune system and therefore the addict or alcoholic must recognize that their bad behavior has physically harmed their loved one(s).

> "The simple fact is that the family or significant other has literally placed their life on the line for the addict. Some research has indicated that the loved ones of the addict or alcoholic are at a greater risk of dying from stress related conditions, then the substance abuser."

There seems to be a high level of cancer, heart disease, bone disorders like arthritis and breathing disorders like asthma and headache conditions that all are disproportionately higher in the family members and loved ones of the addict or alcoholic.

"Therefore the addict or alcoholic owes that person one hundred percent and their loved ones owe nothing in return. The alcoholic must be ready to make the most extreme sacrifices without reservation for their loved ones and the addict must be absolutely patient and tolerant of any hurtful behavior that they may experience from the loved one(s). It is essential that the addict or alcoholic demonstrate this through behavior that reflects care, concern, compassion, and consideration. In this manner they will show the family that they are sensitive, dependable and reliable."

To illustrate this let's take a simple example: Suppose in the morning your spouse or significant other asked you to pick up something from the store such as cigarettes, milk or bread. Of course you would impulsively reply "sure" or "yes I will get that." Now when your walk in the house in the evening and have forgotten your promise-and yes it was a promise and now you broke it-now what you do next will change the destiny of the relationship one-way or the other.

"Like most selfish self-centered, self consumed, and self obsessed addicts the notion of leaving the house to get the items would never enter into the mind. What would enter into the mind was a bunch of useless and worthless justifications or rationalizations of why you did not get, what you had promised in the morning to bring home. Now to forget is human; but since you have committed to always give back a hundred percent, you must be willing to immediately leave the house and pick up the promised items and return immediately. Failure to follow this second option will result in reinforcing the fact that you are selfish and uncaring and worse of all unreliable and untrustworthy and any previous efforts being made to rebuild the relationship will be seriously undermined, if not totally destroyed."

Conversely if you leave and return with the promised items, then you are engaging the "Power of Commitment" through the practice of the "Art of Accountability" and then that person would be greatly delighted and pleasantly surprised at your sacrifice, and this would significantly strengthen the intimacy that is necessary to help build trust back into the relationship. Due to the damage your addiction has inflicted upon the relationship, it may be so fragile that any act of selfishness may be enough to break it and permanently separate you from your loved one.

To further expand on this issue please note the following metaphor: If you hold a large wet bar of soap over your head in one hand and squeeze it hard and quickly it would in all high probability slip out of your hand. Now if you just held that hard large wet bar of soap in that same hand and wait long enough and not put any sudden pressure on it; that soap bar would dry out and then you could handle it with any amount of pressure in any way you might want to. Your relationship is just like that bar of soap and you have to hold it gently, and put no sudden pressure on it or it will in all likelihood slip away from you.

It is through being totally accountable for the first year, that trust will be regenerated and the intimacy will strengthen and all you have to do is be kind, considerate and caring. This would be demonstrated through the following example:

"When you go out at night or anytime you leave the house you must inform your loved one(s) where you will be going and how long you intend to be there and who you will be with and if any of these conditions change you will make an immediate courtesy call to the house and inform them of the change(s). The reason for these actions is to assure that the people who may worry about you, will be spared unnecessary fear, worry or apprehension when they know where you are, whom you are with and when you are expected home. These actions demonstrate care, concern and consideration for others." In other words you are demonstrating the "Power of Commitment" through the "Art of Accountability."

It should be noted that if you tell your loved one(s) that you will be somewhere and you are not there or you come home latter than you had promised, then that person will view that behavior as being irresponsible, deceitful and that you are unreliable and undependable. In addition it must be fully recognized, that even if you were doing great works with your sponsor or church, that person would not know and would be experiencing much fear and worry. Your failure to be courteous and considerate would not be off set, when they find out "you were feeding the poor and homeless."

"In fact during the time that they are anxiously waiting for your return home, they may actually experience all the dread and terror that the reason you have not called or come home is due to having relapsed. Once the person feels this terror and worry, there is nothing that is going to remove this experience. Despite the fact that you may have been doing good or great things with others, does not offset the fact that you did even more harm to the relationship, just because you were so selfish and preoccupied you never thought to be considerate enough to make a simple call to the house."

By not demanding things or pressuring your loved ones to meet your needs, and instead by staying focused on meeting their needs, as well as being always sacrificing and giving with no expectations of getting anything back, will create attraction that reestablishes affection and a strong sense of love. This is the Great reward for using the "Power of Commitment" by exercising the "Art of Accountability!"

"At the risk of not sounding too alarming, I can only emphasize that the recovering person has much work to do in helping to repair their relationship(s) and that failure to be aware of the previous situations stated, and failure to aggressively learn to become a more caring reliable and considerate person, may cause irreparable damage or the total loss of a vitally needed support system, that is absolutely necessary for a lasting recovery."

Do all Things without Complaining and Disputing.

Philippians 2:14

Chapter Fourteen

Understanding Addiction

This chapter will describe in depth and detail the question most addicts and alcoholics have asked themselves, "What is wrong with me?" They struggle with trying to understand why they do the things that they do. Many people as well as the addicts and alcoholics themselves "think" and "believe" that they are "unwilling" to change their addictive behaviors; when in fact they have made some serious sincere attempts to at least control it; if not cease using it!

The concept of using the "Power of Commitment" through the "Art of Accountability will be fully explored as the number one FORCE that can address the addicts and alcoholics deep dilemma; that no matter how much they try and fully understand the need to "change" they still fail to "change!"

The concept that what they do is caused by a disease, the disease of addiction, causes much confusion. This chapter is designed to absolutely clarify any misinformation or misinterpretation of what is meant by the disease of addiction. In regards to labeling their behavior as a disease, it is helpful to understand that any time a person engages in behaviors that are not in their best interest, or are hurtful to the people they love; then their actions can only occur from two sources. They either have a disease or they have made terrible choices.

Most professionals in the field of addictions refer to an addict or an alcoholic as someone who is suffering from the "Disease of Addiction." If a person does not believe that they suffer from the disease of addiction, then they must conclude that they are fully responsible for the bad decisions that they have made, and this could lead to a deep sense of self hate, shame and overwhelming guilt. These intense dark feelings will continue to push the person deeper into active addiction as the only means to deal with the severe psychological and emotional turmoil they are experiencing.

Unfortunately for that person they will continue to believe that it is their fault and condemn and berate themselves. Deep toxic shame occurs when a person believes they can control something they absolutely have no control over. They blame themselves for being weak, or lazy, or crazy; yet little do they know how close to the truth they actually are, when in fact they do start to believe "I must be crazy to keep doing this and hurting myself and all the people I love as well as all those who loves me!"

For the addict or alcoholic to do this to himself or herself is equally as crazy for a person who has a amputated leg to try to run a race without wearing a prosthetic leg, and then blame themselves, because they could not even take the first step without falling on their face! So now it is time for you to ask and answer the question.

"Is it a disease or is it a choice?" By believing it is a disease and even more importantly, accepting and in fact knowing it is a disease, takes the emotional burden of responsibility away and eliminates the deep toxic shame. This does not mean that you do not have to take responsibility to manage the disease, which you must do whether you want to or not; but it does mean that you will choose to manage the condition and absolutely know that the condition in you does not have the power to manage you! You may be powerless over having this condition but you absolutely are not powerless to effectively manage it!"

In an effort to clarify the concept of the disease versus a choice, it will be helpful to discuss in more detail, the disease concept of addiction. To help the reader gain some deeper awareness in regards to how these concepts may be interpreted; it will be necessary to take each concept and explore it in depth and in detail.

When a person accepts that they have the disease of addiction, then that belief enables them to reduce or eliminate the sense of shame or guilt that develops, when a person allows their life to swing out-of-control. When people believe that they do not have the disease, then that leaves them in a very vulnerable position in which they view their poor decisions and bad actions or choices as conscious choices. To sum this up briefly the question that needs to be asked. "Have I done what I've done due to a disease or was it a choice." As confusing as this may seem, anyone can see that their behavior was either driven by a choice or they did the things because they had a disease.

"The people, who believe that addiction is a choice,

also have to accept responsibility for all their negative, irresponsible and reckless actions. At the extreme they may have to wrestle with the idea that what they've done, they did without any regard, concern or care about their family or loved ones."

"Since no person would deliberately harm someone they love, then by accepting that their behaviors were driven by a disease process, frees them from the intense shame that they would experience as a direct result of believing that they had deliberately harmed the ones they love."

A simple metaphor I will use to explain the difference between the concept of a disease process and the ability of making a choice or choices in general may be seen in the following. If a person had a serious head cold and they had an extremely nasty running nose, could they just simply say, "Stop the snot" and due to the fact that they commanded their nose to stop running—would their nose stop running? It is quite obvious that when a person has a disease they cannot exercise choice. Many people confuse the choice to manage it with the ability to control it, but there is no choice to will it out of your body. It is just not possible, due to the fact that when you have a disease, you have no control. You may manage the symptoms; but you cannot just make a decision or a choice not to have the disease or the symptoms the disease causes.

In other words if a person was diagnosed with something say as horrible as cancer, could they just simply say the next day that they are going to choose not to have cancer. When you have a physiological condition that is destructively working on some organ in the body, then that is referred to as having a disease. A person cannot choose to have the disease and equally they cannot choose not to have the disease, if some organ system in the body has become symptomatic. It should always be emphasized that although I cannot chose to have or not have a disease, I always can and have absolute power to choose to manage it in the best possible manner.

"The harmful and disruptive behaviors that the addict or alcoholic have caused to themselves or their loved ones, has either been driven by choice or caused by a disease. There are just simply no other options to describe or explain a person's poor judgment and irresponsible behaviors, when using mood-altering substances. So it is either a disease or it is a choice and it cannot be anything else."

"If it's a disease then the person experiences symptoms and if it is a choice then that person would experience consequences. The very nature of having a disease means that the person is powerless and the very nature of being able to exercise choice means that the person is not powerless. In other words if it is a disease it is about powerlessness and if it is about choice it is about power to change or do anything."

For the people that accept it as a disease, then the next question that needs to be asked is where is this disease located? Since many people suffer physiological symptoms as a direct result of abuse or dependency on drugs, then there definitely is a component that is physically related, and therefore the disease is in the body. At the same time when we recognize that the disease is in the body, where else does the disease have a presence? It should be quite obvious that the disease is also located in the brain, since it also is part of the body. The toxic substances that are ingested into the body affect the brain; and when toxic substances affect the brain its functionality is compromised in some way. If the brain is affected then the mind is also affected.

It is helpful at this time to describe what we mean when we refer to as a person's mind. To simplify things we may want to view the mind as the place where thoughts, beliefs, and feelings all occur. Now if the mind is affected, then it follows that the thoughts, beliefs, and feelings also would be equally affected.

"This means that at times the addict or alcoholic cannot trust what they are thinking, what they believe, or even what they're feeling. Any alcoholic or addict could relate to the following. After doing something that they deeply regret and they're all confused how or why they could've done that regretful action, they will ask themselves the question "What was I THINKING!?" Another question they will ask is "What made me BELIEVE that it was going to work!?" And the final question is "Why did I FEEL I could have done this!?"

As can be seen by these questions the person has acted out in a way that they deeply regret, but at the time they took the regretful actions, their MIND permitted them to do so. It needs to be pointed out here, "What is it that makes a person step out in time and space and take action whether they want to or not." Do people take actions based on a THOUGHT, a BELIEF or a FEELING? Now if you review bad past actions it becomes quite apparent that thoughts, do not automatically create actions. It should also be noted that neither do beliefs automatically create actions. To prove this point, most people that are reading this have probably at one time thought about killing himself or herself or somebody else. Despite the fact about thinking of killing someone or themselves, that person and the person they wished to kill are still alive; therefore thought does not create an event. In regards to beliefs, many people have had strong beliefs about doing something or not doing something but never followed through; therefore beliefs to do not cause a person to act out and take action.

"The driving forces behind most, if not all the actions that an addict and an alcoholic take, are driven by their FEELINGS. In fact many times they know their thinking is wrong and they know their beliefs are also wrong and despite this knowledge and even wisdom, they will still allow their FEELINGS to dictate their actions."

The word impulsive describes people who act out on their feelings without any regard for the risk or consequences. In other words they allow their feelings to dictate their actions. The question to ask "Is it possible to successfully recover and remain abstinent if you still are an impulsive person?" The answer should be quite obvious that an impulsive person will not be successful in their ability to control their wants and desires.

The addict and alcoholic are absolutely plagued with the desire that "Some how, Some way and Some day, they will be able to use substances and get away WITHOUT consequences." Unless they learn how to manage this very destructive thought impulse it will be absolutely impossible to maintain any long-term clean time or sobriety.

When a person is not able to trust what they Think, Believe, or Feel, then that would indicate that there is something wrong with their mind. When a person's mind is working in a dysfunctional manner, we would refer to that as a person who is suffering from Mental Illness.

"When a person's mind does not work correctly then that person is a victim of mental illness. It is at this point I would like to emphasize that what people refer to, as the disease of addiction is really a symptom and not a disease. In other words when we refer to addiction as a disease; addiction is NOT a disease but a symptom of a disease, and THAT disease is mental illness."

Addiction is proof of the severity of the mental illness as can be demonstrated by the person's inability to change their behavior no matter how much they wish or try. In fact most addicts would relate to the following statement. Addicts and alcoholics obsess on the belief "that some how, some way and some day they will be able to use and get away" from suffering consequences from using. They frequently obsess on the belief that they will be able to use substances without causing pain or suffering to themselves or others. The proof of the severity of the mental illness may be found in the fact that despite the severe harm, suffering, injury and disgust that they have cause themselves and their loved ones; this does NOT act as a deterrent to stop further use and abuse of substances. The question to ask is:

"How is it possible that a person will continue to obsess and crave to use a substance that has done so much harm?" The answer to this question may be found in the fact that the addict or alcoholic is not capable of remembering enough pain or suffering. Their inability to register enough emotional intense pain causes them to repeatedly fail to stay sober."

As bizarre as the next statement may sound, any addict or alcoholic knows it's absolute truth! That statement is "Addiction is not the problem it is the Solution." Drugs and alcohol are not a problem they are the answer to the problem. When people understand that the tremendous pleasurable feelings that any person will experience, regardless of whether they are an addict or alcoholic, is the fact that when they use a mood-altering substance it creates great pleasure and joy, then in no way can that be bad. How can anything be considered bad that makes a person automatically feel so good? Is it not a fact that almost two thirds of adults drink alcohol; is it just because it tastes so good or is it the guaranteed fact that it changes a person's feelings, usually in a very pleasant manner.

"Once you understand and accept these facts that SOMETHING that makes you feel so good can never be viewed as SOMETHING that is bad, enables you to understand the terrible dilemma of the addict or alcoholic. It becomes even more frightening when you understand that the VERY substance that is absolutely destroying the life and the lives of the family of the addict or alcoholic, is the VERY same thing that absolutely takes away the pain and suffering that it causes! The more they USE, the more they suffer, and the pain forces them to USE more to relieve the suffering, but the USE then creates more pain that needs more USE to manage and the merry–go-round spins and spins out of control!"

If I may be permitted to continue with this paradox, it may be found in the fact that "there is absolutely nothing wrong with using drugs or alcohol." How can there be anything wrong with manipulating a chemical or chemicals that guarantee that a person will absolutely experience maybe the greatest positive feelings they have ever known! No the problem is not the USE of the substances; it is the price that they have to pay for the right to USE the substances to get those spectacular feelings. In other words:

"The addict and alcoholic love what substances do FOR them but they cannot stand what substances do TO them!" Do to their families, Do to their health, Do to their finances, Do to their dream and hopes, Do to their self esteem, Do to their pride, Do to their sense of self, Do to their friends, Do to their freedom (arrests and going to jail), Do to their jobs and careers, Do to their school work, Do to their judgment, Do to their motivation and finally the devastation that substance abuse Does to their mental and emotional functioning."

Despite the incredible price that is paid for the right to use substances the addict and alcoholic are incapable of recognizing the fact it has become too costly and must be abandoned. The reason for this is that despite the

MASSIVE pain and suffering that is being caused by the USE of substances the alternative seems and FEELS much WORSE.

> "The addict and alcoholic are obsessed with the use and abuse of mood altering substances because their mind tells them that there is something terribly painful about NOT using them. In other words living in a clean and sober manner is NOT acceptable without access to a chemical filter. You can now see clearly how TWISTED their minds are and these PECULIAR perceptions, which are found in the Thought, Belief and Feelings of the addict or alcoholic ARE the driving forces of their madness!"

"To really hammer home how bizarre and peculiar the thinking of an addict or alcoholic are is to reflect on a sentence in the AA book on page 44 from Chapter Four, titled "We Agnostics" that states:

> "To be doomed to an alcoholic death or to live on a spiritual basis are not always easy alternatives to face!"

It will be helpful and informative to dissect this quote from page 44 that basically means that "to stop drinking or suffer death" are not easy "choices" to make. Now it would appear to be a "no brainer" that facing death or having to stop drinking should not be a very difficult decision to make, but for the addict or alcoholic quitting the USE of substances sometimes seems like DEATH itself. The concept of total abstinence may be a more frightening proposition than the fear of dying! The following will graphically express this paradox. The paradox that "Facing death or quitting drinking are not easy choices to make."

Lets analyze this quote—

> "To be doomed" means to be hopeless or condemned.

> "...to an alcoholic death" means to die a horrible, lonely agonizing miserable death; in which your body is severely deteriorated with open scabs and sores. You

are totally alone, despised and hated by most of your family and there are very few friends left.

"...or to live on a spiritual basis" means that you are living a life in which you are in good health and that you are a caring, productive, alert, sensitive, loving, kind person who has strong meaningful relationships with family and friends; as well as a strong connection to a "Higher Power." The last part of the quote is:

"...are not always easy alternatives to face" means that the addict or alcoholic suffers such severe mental illness, TWISTED and PECULIAR perceptions, that they struggle with the clear recognition that to live a productive happy, joyful and peaceful life; or die a lonely, decaying, empty shell of flesh are NOT easy "choices" to see."

To really REALLY drive home this very real bizarre contradiction of common sense I will state it one more time; but will do so with the full intent of making it as sarcastic as it can be; therefore when you read the next statement do so with an air of extreme sarcasm. In other words the person says to themselves:

"What SHOULD I do—Please tell me what SHOULD I do—I just don't KNOW the answer—"To die an alcoholic DEATH or to LIVE peacefully, productively and happily I just don't KNOW which one I should CHOOSE!!

As bizarre and unbelievable as this previous paragraph may sound, any addict or alcoholic would find full agreement; in the fact that they constantly will obsess on either the need or the desire to drink or drug due to the fact that when they are sober or clean, they are edgy, irritable, dissatisfied and discontented.

A simple metaphor to clarify this paradox may be found in the following. If a person was suffering a severe toothache and in fact the tooth had crumbled and the raw nerve was painfully exposed, but that person was on strong pain medication such as Percocet's or Vicodin; then that person would NOT be experiencing severe and overwhelming pain-and-suffering.

Now if that person were to be taken off of their pain medication, they would begin to experience INTENSE pain. In the case of the addict or alcoholic living life without access to filtering their experiences through a mood-altering chemical, is identical to the person suffering from an untreated severe toothache. "When you take away the pain medication the problem INTENSIFIES and cannot be ignored.

> "When you take away the mood altering substances from an addict or alcoholic the problem intensifies. The USE of mood altering substances provides a REAL answer to the addict and alcoholic and when you take away the substances it leaves them in a very PAINFULLY uncomfortable state."

> "This is the reason why so many people FAIL to succeed with long-term recovery. For many addicts and alcoholics the longer they go WITHOUT the use of a mood altering substance the more PROGRESSIVE becomes their discomfort, dissatisfaction, disillusionment, and their discontent."

As has been discussed earlier in this book the main reason that they experience such negative emotions instead of positive emotions is due to the fact that they have failed to emotionalize their achievements and their accomplishments. One of the best ways to demonstrate why an addict or an alcoholic will throw away recovery when they have worked so hard and have achieved so much; can only be understood in terms of how they value or fail to value those accomplishments.

The following will explain this. Imagine that you are a blue-collar worker and the job that you are doing requires you to work for 16 straight hours without a break. In the event that you were placing and finishing wet concrete, then you must work without a break, since you have to finish the job before the concrete dries. If you fail to finish the job and the concrete dries then you will have a major disaster on your hands and may have to get a jackhammer to fix the problem.

We will assume that the job was done correctly and now it came time for you to be paid for all your hard work and in return for your blood, sweat and tears, you were paid one penny per hour or $.16 for 16 hours of intense labor.

Now the question you would be asking yourself is "how could this happen, how could I get so Little when I did so Much, it's not fair." Now if I may play the devil's advocate the person chose to work and they were paid for their labor, so what is the real problem here?

It is quite obvious that the person was NOT properly compensated for the intensity and the degree of the work that they had to bring forth and as a result they would be experiencing much discomfort, dissatisfaction, disillusionment and discontent. It is in the same way that an addict or an alcoholic will work extremely hard to achieve and accomplish so many things that are earned as a direct result of staying clean and sober, but at the end of a certain period of time, they begin to evaluate and believe that ALL their Efforts were NOT properly compensated for.

"After some period of time the person begins to believe that things are not happening fast enough, good enough or even right enough. The reason that they Fail to acknowledge and register the value of their accomplishments and achievements, is due to the expectation that they Should get an emotional reward and when they Fail to get that reward they FEEL their efforts were done in vain, were meaningless and had LITTLE value."

When the person gets into this mindset it is easy for them to return to substance use and abuse. As was discussed throughout this book, it is absolutely necessary for the person to connect passionate emotion to each and every success, achievement, and accomplishment in order to establish enough value; that they would be willing to defend and fight and protect.

"Unfortunately the addict or alcoholic have the mistaken notion that they should experience an intense emotional reward equal to the experience they had when they were using and abusing mood altering substances."

"Since this is a mistaken belief they, will throw away their recovery due to NOT receiving the emotional reward or experience that they Expected."

Unless a person emotionalizes each day, every right action and decision and celebrate passionately those achievements, they will never FEEL that they have accomplished anything and therefore ALL the actions will seem meaningless as well as valueless due to those TWISTED and PECULIAR perceptions. I will refer the reader back to page 114 in the chapter titled "Desire How to Find the Fire" on how to build desire when none are present through the influence of incantations discussed in the chapter titled "Visualizing Victory."

To further understand addiction it may be helpful to recognize that when a person gets help to stop abusing or using drugs or alcohol it is usually due to having developed some degree of desperation. Now the question to ask is "Has the person STOPPED because it was a matter of life and death?" If it was NOT a fear of dying, then it may have been the Fear of experiencing the death or loss of a relationship, a job or something else of significant value.

I would like to emphasize here that when most people enter into treatment or recovery it is usually due to Desperation rather than motivation. It should also be noted that when a person is desperate enough to change their behavior, they are NOT doing it because they are motivated, they are doing it because they are in Great pain and discomfort.

> "Many times a person will enter into recovery with the belief that this decision will lead to relief. Unfortunately recovery requires radical changes in the way people Think, Believe, and Feel and this results in seemingly equal levels of pain and discomfort. This TWISTED view once again is due to their tendency to have PECULIAR perceptions."

The addict or alcoholic will enter into treatment or recovery with the strong belief that it will lead to freedom from or reduction of their pain and discomfort. What they Fail to realize is that continued use or abuse Will increase their pain and suffering, but what they totally Fail to understand is that there will be a great deal of PAIN and suffering when they STOP using.

In other words it is Pain for Pain. Since the alcoholic or addict expects relief they become easily disillusioned and disenchanted with the process of recovering. It should be noted at this time that there are two very distinct different types of pain. The following will define those distinct differences.

"Pain? Or Pain?" or to quote Shakespeare "To be or not to be? That is the question."

"The first pain is that of ongoing addiction and the second pain is related to recovery."

"The first pain is that of active addiction and will be described as Destructive, Nonproductive, Permanent but Controllable."

"The second pain is that of active recovery and is caused by all the changes that have to be made and in particular, the loss of the number one method of coping."

"This second type of pain may be described as Constructive, Productive, Temporary but Uncontrollable."

Now lets take a look at these descriptions from the perspective of, lets say once again, a person suffering a severe toothache. That person may be in severe agonizing pain, but they also have a dread and a great fear of going to a dentist and therefore they will be resistant from seeking help, even though they desperately need it. Now if their fear of going to the dentist is so strong and they never get treatment, what will happen to them? Will the toothache lead to severe complications such as infection spreading to the bone, into the blood or the person may stop eating?

Their fear could literally lead to their death. What I am illustrating here is that the first type or order of pain is the toothache and the second type or order of pain is the fear or pain of going to the dentist. As should be obvious going to the dentist may mean some additional pain, but that pain is absolutely Constructive as well as Productive and Temporary but it is not Controllable.

Now in the case of the addict or alcoholic who enter into recovery they will experience severe pain, which will be caused by grief and loss of a lifestyle including changing friends or even employment and the possibility of not seeing certain family members! Now since this is second order pain it is absolutely Constructive, Productive and Temporary but it is absolutely not Controllable.

The paradox is that active addiction and first order pain is absolutely Destructive, Nonproductive, and Permanent, but unfortunately it is perceived as very Controllable, at least as long as there is access to drugs and or alcohol. Why would I say that it is Controllable? It is due to the fact that as long as you

335

can stay intoxicated and under the influence you will be able to fully control the pain of active addiction.

What frustrates most recovering people is the fact that the pain of recovery is Temporary but NOT Controllable, and the fact that the pain of active addiction although it is Permanent, it is perceived as Controllable; so therefore the addict or alcoholic wants to be able to recover WITHOUT having to experience suffering.

It is due to this paradox that a person who is doing well in recovery as indicated by abstaining and being productive, may be experiencing severe pain and discomfort leading them to believe that "it is not working," and they will remember how quick relief can come by using alcohol or drugs.

It is therefore imperative, that there is a clear understanding that there are two very distinct types or orders of pain, and one will ABSOLUTELY set you free and the other can become a DEATH sentence. Always remember that the pain of active recovery is only Temporary and will absolutely pass but it may NOT be Controllable. A sponsor once stated, "You must be willing to walk a lonesome way for a little while and then I promise you things beyond your fondest dreams will happen; but you must be willing to take that lonesome walk for a little while!" We must stay painfully aware about NOT falling into the trap that is laid by the fact that the Pain of active addiction is perceived as Controllable and instead always remind ourselves that it is Permanent and will ONLY lead to Great losses.

"One last thought regarding the phenomenon of Pain or Pain. The addict or alcoholic who enters into recovery does so with the BELIEF that they will immediately experience relief from the pain of active addiction. They may state that they want to FEEL peace, happiness, relief, comfort, calmness, ease, contentment and even serenity, but instead they FEEL fear, worry, anxiety, stress, sadness, discontent and deep apprehension."

"All these negative painful emotions stack up on themselves and the person begins to BELIEVE that recovery is NOT good and it is TOO painful to continue to work. Due to the expectation that they should FEEL great relief they become disillusioned and become obsessed with seeking relief by returning to substance Use and Abuse."

It should always be remembered and never forgotten the saying that is heard quite frequently in the rooms of AA and NA.

> "Don't quit before the miracle happens!" What this means is that early on there are going to be many emotional and other challenges and if you stay on course then you will not only succeed, but you will also experience the meaning of being truly happy, joyous and free."

> "Remember that the pain of active recovery is only Temporary, and will absolutely pass if you "don't quit before the miracle happens."

One of the major things that lead to the destruction of a person's chances for long-term recovery is when they develop false self-confidence. It should be noted that in the book Twelve Steps and Twelve Traditions on page 22 it indicates:

> "...so far as alcohol is concerned self-confidence was no good whatever; in fact it was a total liability." (End of quote.)

> "Now one may ask how a concept such as self-confidence could be harmful or destructive as implied. To understand how this could be a liability is to recognize that when a person becomes confident they also become unteachable and unreachable."

Many people have noticed that when a person becomes confident they also tend to be less willing to take suggestions and recommendations. As a result of this resistance and the belief that they are strong enough, or they know enough, or they can do enough, is when they start to do less and less in regards to taking effective recovery actions. In other words they are now convinced they do not need to go to meetings, they do not need a sponsor or continue to speak to their sponsor, they do not need to avoid toxic friends and family and finally their confidence convinces them that they can safely be in unhealthy, high risk environments.

"As they follow the false FEELING of confidence they move further away from recovery and closer to a return to active substance use. Many times they begin to BELIEVE that since they can be in toxic environments and around substance abusers they begin to BELIEVE that they can do what they see and observe, and that is to use drugs and alcohol."

"Self-confidence is one of the most destructive and dangerous emotional states that an addict can develop in their recovery. Due to this false self-confidence they convince themselves that they are strong enough, capable enough and know enough and as result of this they are NOT willing or ready to take any direction or follow ANY suggestions."

To understand this is to recognize that most addicts and alcoholics when entering into recovery do so with a great deal of Desperation. It is this Desperation that they mistakenly BELIEVE is Motivation, but in reality it is Desperation and NOT Motivation. To understand this difference between Desperation and Motivation is to further recognize that people who are motivated demonstrate the ability to develop and complete goals, they have perseverance, determination and a strong sense of willingness to achieve their goals; whereas Desperation is strictly about running blindly from pain without ANY plan and without ANY direction.

"If a person had a flamethrower on the cheeks of their ass— would you say that they are Motivated or would you say that they are Desperate and are demonstrating Desperation to get away from that pain? It doesn't take planning to run from pain; in fact it is a natural instinctual response to experiencing suffering. Blindly running from pain NEVER takes Motivation it is just simply an act of Desperation."

The next example I will apologize for in advance, since it is about a burning building and the fact that so many people have directly as well as indirectly suffered so much trauma and horror in regards to burns from fire. If a person was on the roof of a burning building and they jumped off the roof would they do so knowing that they were going to die; did they plan and decide that dying was the best option or was it a sheer act of Desperation due to the fire was burning them. There is a clear difference between Motivation and Desperation! It should be further emphasized that a Motivated person never lets failure occur, they always find a way; whereas a person driven by Desperation can rapidly change decisions or directions due to there is no plan or determination to accomplish a specific goal.

Another simple example of the difference between Desperation and Motivation maybe found when a person is driving a car and they are speeding and they are not Motivated to follow the speed limit nor follow the traffic laws. Now if a police car was to appear with its lights flashing in the rearview mirror the person would probably become immediately Desperate not to suffer the consequences of their impulsive decision to violate traffic laws and they would immediately slowdown and behave and drive in a responsible manner. Now in the event that the police car was to pass by them, then how long would they continue to respect the traffic laws and drive in a responsible manner? Many of you know the answer to this, the Desperation that led to becoming a law abiding citizen would rapidly pass and the person would once again develop the CONFIDENCE that they can break the law and not suffer the consequences.

An interesting fact regarding the experience of Desperation may be found in the strange paradox that Desperation will always fade away. When people become desperate they rarely remain in a state of desperation and if they do remain in that state, it will usually lead to despair and depression. The most important thing to realize is that since desperation always fades away there is an important question to ask at this time. ""If desperation fades away what replaces it?" Understanding this next point is very vital in being able to develop and manage recovery.

"Most people in the early stages of recovery will be experiencing much desperation that leads them to be highly motivated to do things that are suggested and recommended. As the desperation fades away as it always will, what people do not realize…

"Is That Desperation Always Fades Into CONFIDENCE."

"In other words the less desperate someone becomes the more Confident they become."

A final example to clarify this very vital point regarding how Desperation will always fade into a form of false self-Confidence may be found in the following personal experience.

When I was a very young man I was working in a carpenter shop and they fabricated very fine cabinetry. As an apprentice I was not permitted to cut the expensive materials of Oak, Maple, Cherry or Mahogany and instead I was allowed to work with Pine or other less expensive materials. Before I was permitted to even cut inexpensive materials for the cabinet shop; they had to teach me how to use the large shop equipment. In particular there was an unshielded 12 inch table saw and I emphasis unshielded meaning there were no safety devices. This was a long time ago and OSHA safety requirements were non-existent, at least in this particular carpentry shop.

To train me on the big saw they gave me a truck load of 2"x 4"s, 1"x 2"s and lath material and since they had a contract with a large survey company, my job was to cut all this material into lengths and then cut points on every board. This was necessary due to the fact it was my job to cut all this raw material into survey stakes. I started at 7:00am and was given very clear-cut instructions with an emphasis on how to safely use and cut with the big saw.

Despite the big saw not being equipped with any safety devices, I was informed and clearly shown several safety rules. The first thing they told me was to stand firm and never reach and always position your feet in front of the saw, never lean or cut from the side of the saw! Next they gave me safety goggles and informed me never to take them off while cutting or when getting ready to cut! They stated that when cutting small edge cuts those slivers of wood will be hurled back into your face and could blind you! Finally they stated that as the cutting debris falls on the floor you must stop periodically and sweep it away from where you are standing due to the hazard of slipping on the chips and sawdust! Now you might be asking why is it necessary for all this detail about a life experience and how does it apply to CONFIDENCE and Desperation? Well then pay close attention to the following:

I began to cut at 7:00AM and I was absolutely very desperate to follow every rule because when they cranked up that big saw all I could see was that big 12" saw blade whirling and screaming that it wanted my fingers and hands! I began to cut with great caution keeping my hands way back almost to the point I could not control the cut due to the force of the blade pushing the material upwards so I had to move my hands and fingers closer to the blade for more control. You are probably by now getting bored with this story and my life so I will fast forward to make my point.

At 7:00AM I was a law-abiding citizen following every safety rule I was given but by 9:00AM, just two hours latter I was now cutting with a mass of debris on the floor and actually slipping and tripping as I was moving materials and cutting. Due to the sawdust and debris I was leaning and at times cutting from the sides of the saw. I was not wearing the eye protection due to the profuse sweat that was running in my eyes. Do you get the picture? Had I become very competent and capable in just two hours or just plain foolish and overly and falsely self-CONFIDENT?

Oh to mention one last thing, I was now cutting with my fingers so close to the blade I was getting a manicure. How was it possible for me to be so fearful and desperate to follow every rule and protect myself from injury, possible amputation as well as the threat of blindness at 7:00AM and within two hours had thrown away every precaution? Did I develop enough skill and expertise in that short time; had I become one of the most competent cutters in the shop or did I just lose all concern and desperation?

With out the driving force of fear and Desperation had I become careless and even more so very CONFIDENT that I was faster and quicker than the big saw? My desperation, which was my motivation to follow all the rules, had absolutely faded completely away when I began to believe I knew what I was doing, and the desperation to follow the rules was quickly forgotten because I had developed strong self-CONFIDENCE that I could not be hurt.

> "Lets state here emphatically that CONFIDENCE is only a feeling and when you believe that Feeling then it is absolutely misleading or false, it is false self CONFIDENCE and it is a total liability as well as being no good whatsoever as the AA literature stated long ago."

One last revelation regarding this long drawn out story-I am typing with both hands and with all my fingers-very fortunately I did not have to learn the hard way, at least with the big saw—But I did learn the hard way with drugs and alcohol!

> "Since desperation will always fade, It Is absolutely essential to replace it with a powerful and positive motivating force to offset the destructive tendencies that will result as false self-confidence develops. Since CONFIDENCE is a total liability then that emotional state CANNOT and should NOT be allowed to dominate a person's mind in early recovery. The

only solution is that while the person is in a state of desperation that they USE that driving force to develop strong recovery COMMITMENTS."

To clarify this, recognize that desperation and self-confidence are only emotional states and as stated numerous times throughout this book no recovering person should allow their emotions to dictate their actions. By developing, maintaining and fulfilling recovery COMMITMENTS enables the person to stay fully focused on their recovery and not to fall victim to the impulsivity that would be associated to allowing Desperation or CONFIDENCE to dominate their decision-making ability.

There are some additional concepts that we need to examine, which is the need to get a clear understanding of the radical differences between CONFIDENCE and COMPETENCE. Confidence is only an emotional state in which a person has developed a sense of certainty that they can accomplish and do some action or activity. As you may recall from the above story-I had a strong emotional feeling I could do what I want with the big saw, but I absolutely did not have any competency in operating the saw, which can only be earned through significant TIME and much PRACTICE.

Competency is when a person has a demonstrated ability or capability to accomplish or achieve something. The difference in these two concepts are very significant since they lead to very poor decisions that result in disasters and heart aches not only for the people in early recovery but can also sabotage a well established period of sobriety.

> "Confidence can develop almost instantaneously and this is why it is such a major liability as has been indicated in the early writings of Alcoholics Anonymous. Competency on the other hand requires TIME and PRACTICE. Whereas CONFIDENCE is only a feeling, COMPETENCY is a measure of former success and a high predictor of future success. The trouble with most addicts and alcoholics is that after a short period of time they begin to build CONFIDENCE, but that confidence is false because they have not had any time to develop COMPETENCY to back up that confidence."

A simple example of this may be found in thinking about a person who goes to see a plastic surgeon and he convinces the person that he is highly COMPETENT and the way he speaks creates a deep sense of CONFIDENCE in his ability to perform the surgery. Is it possible that the doctor may only be expressing a sincere CONFIDENCE, but after he performs the surgery the person finds himself or herself basically butchered. One could say that that although the Dr. was highly confident he was NOT very COMPETENT. Another example is the baseball player who demands from the coach that he be given a chance to play a certain position and he presents with such strong CONFIDENCE, the coaches then give that player the opportunity. Now the player has expressed incredible CONFIDENCE that he could handle the job he requested, but at the end of the game he basically failed to perform as well as he stated and personally believed.

In fact he lost the game and he was solely and totally responsible for that loss. As you can see from these two examples, just because somebody expresses or feels a deep sense of CONFIDENCE it does not necessarily mean that they are COMPETENT.

> "Once again CONFIDENCE is only a feeling and it measures absolutely nothing but it feels stupendously good. Since confidence is just a FEELING, I would like to remind the reader that feelings can really SCREW you over! After all, FEELINGS are only asinine sensations that we experience in our body and they have actually nothing to do with COMPETENCE, Capability, Ability or even Reality."

The addict or alcoholic who develops a high level of false self-confidence is at extreme risk to take chances that they really need to be more conservative about. When CONFIDENCE is allowed to dominate the psyche of the addict or alcoholic, they will BELIEVE, and even strongly desire to do many things that place them at great risk and serious harm. Examples of this would be: the person has the confidence to BELIEVE he can be around old friends, doing things that involve a drug or alcohol lifestyle, and BELIEVE that they will be able to manage and control not only those people, but the environment also.

It is precisely this type of false self-confidence that was cautioned against by the early alcoholics. Some of those writings indicated that if a person became complacent there was a great risk, due to the simple fact it means they have stopped working a plan of action or what is known as a program of recovery. The word complacent in this writer's view is not as clear in terms of what may trigger a recovery failure, as does the need to fully understand the implications of false self-confidence. It should also be noted that the person who develops false self-confidence is rarely, if ever aware that it is just a FEELING and has nothing to do with Capability, Ability, or just plain Reality; to that person it's not false CONFIDENCE, it IS confidence!

> "This perceptual error or what I have referred to earlier in the book as having PECULIAR perceptions explains how the addict or alcoholic BELIEVE that a FEELING—just a feeling gives them the power and ability to do anything or just what they want. The only counterforce that is available to address this perceptual error is for the addict or alcoholic to learn that while in a state of Desperation they must immediately begin to start their strong recovery COMMITMENTS. It is through developing and completing recovery COMMITMENTS that a person is able to control and manage dangerous IMPULSES and tendencies."

When a person develops a high degree of false self-confidence, is when they are at the greatest risk to act on Impulses of Belief or Thought. As stated earlier the most dangerous threat to a person's recovery is their tendency to be IMPULSIVE. Since Beliefs and Thoughts do not directly cause a person to take a physical action and it is FEELINGS that are the motivating and driving force for most, if not all actions that an addict or alcoholic take; then it is very necessary for IMPULSIVE tendencies to be eliminated or at least significantly controlled.

"The most powerful defense that an addict and alcoholic have is their ability to make and complete recovery COMMITMENTS. In other words a COMMITMENT protects the addict or alcoholic in the following way. Confidence and Desperation motivates a person to take many positive and not so positive actions, but they are only motivated by a FEELING and NOT by a plan of ACTION. Since the motivation may only be driven by FEELINGS; then as soon as those feelings shift the Motivation is lost. Whereas when a person develops, maintains and completes recovery COMMITMENTS, this has absolutely nothing to do with how they Feel, what they Feel or even if they have any FEELING whatsoever.

"A COMMITMENT is an on or off switch either you Do

it or you don't Do it. It is not negotiable, it is not flexible it is a contract and a promise to perform. That means it doesn't matter whether you're sick, tired, whether it is raining out, what you believe is necessary, whether you believe that it would harm you or somebody else, or not harm you or somebody else, it just does not matter what you THINK, what you BELIEVE, or what you FEEL. A COMMITMENT is an action that completely and totally overrules the IMPULSIVITY that is at the very core of the mental illness component of addiction."

"Since addiction is NOT a disease, but a Symptom of a very serious disease, and that disease is Mental Illness that manifests itself in a person's mind which is composed of everything they THINK, everything they BELIEVE, and everything they FEEL. The only thing that can overrule and overpower a diseased mind is the utilization of recovery COMMITMENTS."

"It should be especially noted that it is a virtual guarantee for any person who has ever developed and completed a COMMITMENT that they will always experience a high level of pride and an increase in healthy self-esteem."

Whether it is a commitment to make a bed or whether it's a commitment that literally puts the person's life on the line, when that commitment is completed that person WILL experience a boost in their self-esteem. Whereas any time a person has made and failed to follow through with completing a commitment, it is a guarantee that they WILL experience a significant negative impact to their self-esteem. Any time a person FAILS to follow through with a personal promise known as a COMMITMENT it will Always result in damage and reduction in their self-esteem.

It is necessary to understand the importance, the paramount importance of the previous paragraph. Since any addict and alcoholic that has been led to or forced to make a decision to stop drinking or drugging; has usually experienced some significant negative impacts to their sense of self-worth and self-esteem.

"It is only when a person begins to rebuild their sense of self and their self-esteem that they are able to better protect themselves against a return to substance abuse and use."

A recovery commitment can only occur when a person promises another person or group of people that they are going to do something or accomplish something in a certain exact manner and within a very specific time.

"If an action is taken and there is no regard for how it's done, or when it's done then that is not fulfilling a commitment; that is just an action driven by a mere good intention."

"It should also be noted that any action that a person promises to take that does not include another person is just not a commitment."

That type of action can only be referred to as engaging in or practicing self-discipline. As important as discipline is and as it was referred to in an earlier part of this book as one of the means of taking control and managing unmanageable emotions; or was referred to as Resisting the Resistance to Resist. The significant weakness of discipline as a major defense to protect recovery is that it is only a personal affair and there is no sense of consequence or accountability.

Failing to complete recovering commitments ALWAYS means that other people have been Affected and have Suffered consequences because of YOUR unreliability and irresponsibility. It is quite easier to rationalize, minimize or justify why you failed to follow through with an action that you promised yourself, than to be held accountable by others for that failure. In fact you can just simply wake up and have absolutely no desire to do whatever that personal discipline entailed.

"Therefore it can be clearly seen that COMMITMENTS are the only, and most powerful ways to manage the severity of your condition which is driven by a dysfunctional mind, that warps, twists and bends the truth, the best intentions and reality itself."

"Unless a person develops, lives by, completes recovery COMMITMENTS and then immediately develops, lives by and continues to complete recovery COMMITMENTS; there is or will be a very minimal chance for long-term sobriety or recovery."

It is through the concept of "commitment" that an addict or alcoholic finds freedom from the toughest part of their disease. They are put in a position of ACCOUNTABILITY that they cannot alibi themselves out of.

"Once the person learns to place COMMITMENTS ahead of their own selfish needs, they have gained extraordinary strength in their ability to resist temptation when it arises. Since it is tough making, maintaining and following through with COMMITMENTS the person learns that they do NOT have to be victimized by their sick "Thoughts, Beliefs and Feelings. In fact they can completely overrule all three by simply understanding the "Power of Commitments developed through the "Art of Accountability."

In the final analysis it comes down to this one concept, and that idea is that confidence vs. commitment has nothing to do with willingness, and in the end it all hinges on living, breathing and completing every recovery Commitment and any other Commitments, while ABSOLUTELY ignoring any Feelings or Emotions that would interfere with commitment completion efforts.

"One of the obstacles to fulfilling COMMITMENTS is the fact that the addict or alcoholic have "very good intentions," but my mother always preached to me " Jerry- Good Intentions Pave the Way Straight to Hell!"

In other words even though we know what to do, and have full intentions of doing it, for some mysterious reason, it does not get done or completed, and many times we don't even get started!"

The mystery may be explained by the following:

"Trying is Dying and Trying is Lying in that that Trying is a Feeling, yes another one of those dumb, stupid asinine sensations that enables us to BELIEVE our own "Bullshit." We believe because we have good intentions that gives us an excuse for being lazy, irresponsible or just procrastinating! Learn to take the committed action and completely ignore the FEELINGS. Therefore the best way to empower yourself is to make recovery Commitments, or in fact any Commitment, and just "do it"—not just TRY to do it!

To avoid and or overcome this dangerous obstacle that will interfere with the ability to follow through with necessary recovery commitments, it will be necessary to do the following:

Learn to become very alert and aware of your own speech. Develop the ability and the sensitivity to notice when and how you use the word "Trying" or "To Try." Once you become alert to your use of these words, learn to immediately repeat the statement that had these words in it, and leave those words completely out. In other words, an example of this would be when a person states "I am going to TRY to go to bed early tonight" or "I am going to TRY to eat healthier foods" or "I am going to TRY to stop smoking" or "I will TRY to apologize" or "I'm TRYING to do the best I can" or "I'm TRYING to change."

As you can see in these examples the word "Try and Trying" are actually setting up an excuse to fail. The reason that failure is highly probable is due to the fact that the word "Try and Trying" are the same as just having "good intentions."

The destructive and potentially deadly effect of freely using the word "Try and Trying" and not challenging yourself to remove them completely and totally from your vocabulary, will be found in the way these words, confuse and weakens a person's ability to plan a future action. These words create automatic indecision and doubt that the action can or will be accomplished. These words cause the person who uses them to immediately either consciously or unconsciously to create an excuse or to plan for failure.

If we return to the above statements that involve the word "trying and to try" and remove those words, those statements take on awesome power that is created through making a direct statement or plan, that is not diluted, but is expressed as a strong determination rather than an empty intention. This can be NOT only clearly seen, BUT emotionally experienced by removing those words, when the statement is verbalized Out Loud.

"I am GOING to go to bed early tonight" or "I am GOING to eat healthier foods" or "I am GOING to stop smoking" or "I WILL apologize" or "I'm DOING the best I can" or "I AM changing."

> "Through the rewriting of these sentences and leaving out those words and speaking those statements Out Loud you can SENSE a deep underlying power that WILL provide the drive to move you from having a Good Intention to having a strong DETERMINATION to get the action done!"

The following example will fully help you grasp the vital importance of understanding the fact that the words "trying, to try and try" are at the very least very self-defeating and at the very most potentially dangerous and deadly!

To demonstrate this all we need to do is observe that when someone begins a recovery lifestyle, they have usually been given numerous suggestions and recommendations of what TO do, as well as what NOT to do.

The addict in recovery would probably express acknowledgment of those ideas in the following manner: "Yes you are right, and I do need to go to more meeting and I will TRY." Or "I know I need a sponsor but I just keep TRYING and no one will help me." Or "I know that I need to TRY to read that book but as much as I TRY I can't find the time." Or "I will TRY to make it to that Home Group."

Now as I recommended any time you become aware of using any of the words, "trying, to try or try" then immediately remove it and restate the phrase. Notice how powerful the phrase becomes when these words are removed and stronger more direct words are chosen "Yes you are right, I do need to go to more meetings and I WILL." Or "I know I need a sponsor and I MUST find someone who will help me." Or "I will read that book and I WILL find the time." Or "I WILL make it to that Home Group."

> "Anytime you drop the words "try, trying or to try" and replace them with strong affirmative phrases and add words like "will, must, can, CREATES a strong emotional feeling that drives you to accomplish or complete what you said. In other words it turns a "good intention" into a "strong determination to get it done!"

Never forget that "Trying is Dying and Trying is Lying! And it directly causes us to fail due to it allows us to believe our own "Bullshit."

There is one last concept that needs to be discussed before we end this chapter and that is the need to provide a valuable tool to protect your recovery efforts. Since confidence is only a feeling and not a fact, then when an addict or alcoholic allows this feeling to develop they may begin to believe that feeling. This perceptual error gives them a belief that many times is false and misleading. It is this perceptual error that creates false self-confidence that can and will cause a person in recovery to place himself or herself in great danger by taking excessive and many times unnecessary risks.

"Before a person feels the absolute need to gamble with their hard won struggle for recovery, they need to recognize threats, triggers and the challenges that could absolutely destroy their recovery efforts.

"Lets emphatically restate what was previously mentioned and that is confidence is only a feeling and if you believe that feeling then it may absolutely be misleading or false, it is false self confidence and it is a total liability!"

"This feeling that they are strong and capable, this feeling that is really just false self-confidence leads the person to believe that they can do whatever they want, anywhere they want and at any time they want."

A strong recommendation I offer is to always discuss with a knowledgeable person who knows all about you, addiction and recovery, any situation in which alcohol or drug use may be present or available, and regardless of this danger, you believe you have an absolute obligation to attend.

Discuss the potential threats, triggers and challenges that may be encountered and then, with that person discuss the following strategy. If you do not want to talk to anybody for whatever stupid reason or belief that you have about the need to keep it a secret, then at least review the following strategy and consider fully implementing it to improve your chances. After all, it is about gambling with usually a very hard earned recovery and sobriety. When gambling you must ALWAYS weigh the Risks against the Rewards and then manipulate the Odds so they are in your favor.

"Every addict and alcoholic needs to understand the following concepts: RISK—Is the level of threat to recovery. REWARD—Is the level of joy or happiness, that makes it worth taking the RISK; and finally the importance of understanding how to improve the ODDS, and the absolute need to improve those ODDS, every time they gamble with jeopardizing their recovery."

Since life goes on with, or without us, we want to participate in and celebrate life, especially with others. For instance a family member or someone you know may invite you to a special occasion, such as a wedding, birthday party, retirement dinner, promotion party, house warming, holiday celebration or be a support at a funeral. Since there is Risk at these affairs due to the fact that there are people that may be drinking or doing drugs, you need to evaluate the dangers that could be a trigger or subject you to temptation.

When the addict or alcoholic has to consider gambling with their hard earned recovery; they need to consider asking the following questions.

"The first and most important question to ask is: What is the Reward or Rewards I expect as a result of taking this Risk? If the Reward or Rewards do not warrant taking the Risk, then the person should refrain from participating in the affair. There is always a possibility that the person's very life may depend on the right decision, and the person needs to be fully aware that the Risk they are taking matches or is worth the reward."

If a person can answer this question honestly, and they feel the need or obligation to attend a potentially threatening occasion or event, then the next thing that must be considered is; how can the Odds be improved to reduce the Risks? If the Reward is worth the Risk, then it is necessary to manipulate the Odds so they are in the favor of the addict.

To clarify this, we will use the example of someone invited to a family wedding. Since the person has decided that they must attend this family affair, and want to celebrate with their family, they feel the Reward of being a part of the family at this momentous occasion is absolutely worth the Risk. Having made the decision they can then make arrangements to have a sober or clean friend accompany them. If no sober supports can be found, then they can decide to just attend the church celebration and NOT attend the reception. They can make sure they have their own transportation and NOT allow themselves to become stranded, waiting on someone else to take them home. They also could plan to arrive late or leave early or DO both.

> "As can be seen from this example there are numerous ways that the Odds can always be improved to reduce the Risks anytime that a person believes or feels the Reward is worth the Risk of placing their recovery in jeopardy!"

*I Can do Everything through Him
who gives Me Strength.*

Philippians 4:13

Chapter Fifteen

Spirituality Defined And Understood

Spirituality may be viewed as the perpetual unending flowing power base that all people have access to. It needs to be emphasized that we can only exercise our power, or in fact any power, can only be used in the present. A simple way to understand this constantly flowing power is to think about the process of ocean surfing. In order to successfully surf or ride a wave the person needs to "catch" that wave. In other words if they try to catch it too soon they will be in front of the wave and depending on the size they could be crushed by the force of the breaking water. If they catch it too late they will miss the opportunity to ride that wave. There is only one place a person can surf and that is within the power stroke of the wave! Too late or too soon there is either too much or not enough energy to ride the wave!

> "Your personal power only occurs in the "breaking moment" and as that moment fades and passes, you have no power to create, change or complete anything in your life. You must act NOW and immediately whenever the need or opportunity to act on a decision presents itself."

There is absolutely no power to change the past or the future. Since the past has already been written and not one infinitesimal moment or fragment of the past can be adjusted or altered; the past is the past, and it is just the past. Despite the fact that many people believe that the past can influence their present as well as the future, they are very misinformed.

> "The future is completely unwritten so anybody can "write or right" their present life to create whatever future they choose. It is only in the now that we can control the future."

"You can't mow the lawn today with yesterdays gasoline and you cannot cut the lawn again today for next week- you do not have any power to address anything that has already occurred or has not yet occurred."

The past does not exist and if a person is focused on the past, all they are really focused on is the feelings associated to a past event, but not the event, because the event no longer exists. Whatever a person is focused on is what they will experience. As stated and described in various places in this book, anyone can change anything by just changing one of three things; what they focus on, what they say to themselves or the meaning they have assigned to an event or events and the way they position or move their body and the gestures they control or allow!

"It is absolutely unnecessary and senseless to have to rehash and review a past situation or event, when all that matters is that you take control and change one of those three things that drive current or present experiences. Spirituality is the vehicle for acceptance of the past and empowerment to create any future you desire."

The following vignettes and essays will better clarify this or these concepts.

In a film called the "Moses Code" it presented the idea that when Moses went up to the mountain to meet God, and was surprised and frightened by what he saw, "The burning bush that was not on fire." and he asked "Who are you to the voice he was hearing and the voice responded with "I am that I am." One of the movie commentators expressed that the "Code" to bring about all the good and greatness that a man or woman could ever want was a simple comma (,).

"In that by placing the comma after the word "that" the power of God becomes not only known, but fully accessible to anyone that understands a very simple and profound truth. "I Am that, I Am." Can be understood that God IS everything, and is IN everything, and EVERYTHING is God."

Another one of the commentators expressed that when he was searching for spirituality his teacher told him to spend the next sixty minutes walking down the street and to say "I am that" to everything he perceives around him. If he sees flowers state out loud "I am that". When looking at the sky and clouds state, "I am that." When witnessing violence state "I am that." When looking at handicapped or the underprivileged state "I am that."

Another commentator stated that he had a beautiful wife and the mother of his children, one night while he was away, two men broke into her residence where she was staying and murdered her. While the husband was taking calls his cell phone began to beep that the battery was dying, and when he tried to turn it off the picture of his wife appeared and the cell phone stayed on showing the picture. It was the only one in the phone or that he had at the time.

> "As he recalled that memorable moment he felt a very special connection after her death. He also stated that he felt incredible compassion for the men who murdered her, due to "what horrible things must have been done or happened to those men to make them want to or have to murder someone."

The incredible strength to not just accept the murder but to have compassion and concern for the murders can only come from the "Power of Spirituality" which in this case can also be defined as absolute unconditional love and to fully embrace the directive in the Bible to "love thy enemy."

> "The Moses Code reflected that we are all connected, and are all one, and other people may experience what one person does to another person, sometimes directly and sometimes indirectly. The film spoke about the need to learn to be humble and unselfish and in fact a "servant" of others. It is though the act of giving that we receive. It is through the "Art of Giving" that the "Power of Spirituality" is fully released."

A huge paradox is the fact that nobody can really give anything, for through the very act of giving; we also automatically receive, each and every time we give. It was once stated that the people who stay sick the longest are the people that know how to give, but they burn out because they don't know how to receive.

> "The only thing that blocks us from being able to receive is our Ego. It states that either "I am not worthy to receive or I just don't need anything from anyone. We must always be aware that when we do something and want something, and it is just for us, it is our Ego supplanting God or in other words EGO is "Easing God Out!"

It was strongly emphasized in the "Moses Code film that as you make a stronger and deeper connection to others and call out the name of God as "I am that, I am" then things will materialize from invisible sources. Resources will appear and opportunities and people will enter into your life to help you accomplish whatever you may desire. But this mostly happens when it is done for unselfish reasons.

One of the examples in the film showed a young man going through the rites of passage at his church in which it is traditional for the well wishers to give gifts of cash. When questioned what he was going to do to celebrate he stated, "I want to build a school in Africa and I am going to give away all my money I have received to do this." The commentator then showed the young man a few months later stating that he had received over five hundred responses, many from children who were willing to give all their money to help build that school.

The film also featured one of the first people to run to the World Trade Center, and assisted the rescue personnel by making them sandwiches and giving them drinks.

> "He shared the intense great sadness of the "first role call" at the disaster site. When out of the four hundred names that were called out, very few were present, due to the rest were buried or dead."

> "The hardened fireman and police officers broke down in tears and collapsed all around, when the reality and scope of the tragedy was known."

He stated that he was with the rescuers when they found the first body of a well-dressed man who was crushed under a fire truck. The commentator stated "I just can't wonder about how that man ran for the protection of what he believed to be total safety under a huge fire truck, but died when the truck got crushed.

Later that week while the commentator was on a couch in an abandoned apartment building getting some sleep he suddenly awoken to the sense that someone was behind him. He felt breathing on his neck and he visualized the dead man under the truck standing above and behind him. He then believed he heard the words "this could be your Viet Nam or ..." he stated he did not know what the "or ..." meant but he knew what he was witnessing could be the cause of severe PTSD in the future, unless he used it in some constructive manner.

So he immediately got up and left the apartment to resume helping with the rescue effort. He stated when he returned to "the Site" the place was ablaze with bright work lights and he saw all the rescuers appearing like spirits running all over the "Site." At that precise moment he began to envision all the possibilities of mankind, and...

> "He had a euphoric feeling of how all people can come together for the greater good of all, and he felt it very ironic that in the midst of this heart wrenching horrifying event, that he observed the greatest good, and the greatest possibilities for all people."

This truly is a demonstration of the "Power of Spirituality" being fully manifested though the genuine "Art of Giving." To get in touch with the power of God it was suggested to use breathing as a vehicle to accomplish this connection. Through the technique of meditation and deep breathing, it was suggested that a person should verbalize, "I am that" while they are exhaling and to say, "I am" while they are inhaling. In addition to this it was stated that we need to also know those five special words "I am that, I am." And through conscious active use or prayer with these words we will come to know that we are indeed one with the universe.

Another way to understand the concept of GOD is to use it for an acronym as G-is for Giving. O-is for Oneness, and D-is for Destiny. The film went on to describe that even in quantum physics it is now known that there is a single flow of all matter, and all of existence is on a single plane.

> "For indeed it may appear that things and people are separated entities, but when it is broken down to its smallest parts the entire world, and the people in the world are in a single stream of existence."

Once we really understand that we are a part of everything and we become willing to contribute without any regard for our safety or have any selfish motives, we then discover our true destiny. This can only occur when we eliminate all selfishness or desire for personal gain or glory. The question to ask yourself at this time,

> "What am I committed to-would have I ran to the "Site" or would I have run away or stayed away?" Of that event, and of that time we cannot, and never will know."

The following is this writer's experience at a sudden disaster scene.

While working on my Masters Degree, I was with several fellow students driving on a desolate and dark country back road, and we were on our way to help at a school for disturbed adolescents, when suddenly we came on the scene of a severe accident which involved a small pickup truck and a very large semi tractor and trailer. What I do know about myself is that at that one time, I was one of several people who arrived first to help at that horrendous traffic accident, in which the pickup truck and the semi tractor and trailer had collided head on.

The Semi was on its side in massive flames and the pickup had no front end and you literally could just lean into the cab from where the front engine compartment once was. Despite the threat of a massive gasoline fire engulfing me and the other rescuers, we all worked feverishly getting the two children and the mother out of the truck, but the grandmother was trapped and pinned in the wreckage. While we desperately tried to extricate her, the fire department and paramedics finally arrived taking control of the scene. As we were taking the woman out of the truck and placing her on the ground the paramedic yelled after shinning his flashlight in her eyes "Cover her! She is signal seven!"

I learned that "Signal Seven was the code for "dead." As I covered her with the blanket and they ran to help the other victims of the crash I was torn apart by sadness and confusion. I had spent what seemed an eternity to get the woman out of the truck and she was dead- it all seemed so unfair. I realized that we could have been burned to death if the gasoline all over road had been ignited, if even one ember had drifted over from the massive flames from the Semi, and it all would have been for nothing, for she was dead.

> "As I covered her very warm body, and that is strange

to say, because her body was very warm and yet she was very dead, and that just did not seem right."

While I was pulling her from the wreck I felt how wet she was and surmised that she had urinated and defecated on herself and that is what my bare unprotected arms and hands were feeling...

"But when I was covering her body after the "signal seven" statement made by the paramedic I noticed in the flashing light from the rescue vehicles that my hands and arms were soaked in her blood, and I just looked and looked and could not respond to what I was seeing."

It was several days later after several sleepless nights a friend helped me understand that somehow my mind had twisted the incident into being interpreted that, since I covered her body with the blanket that I intended to use for treating the woman for shock; was now instead of a blanket helping to preserve her life, it was now a "signal seven" symbol, and I was separating her from life.

"She could no longer see and the world could no longer see her, and I took responsibility for her death. It haunted me day and night, until my friend shared that because I had her "blood" literally on my hands, I suffered unwarranted guilt, and even shame that somehow I was responsible for her death."

Thank God for the brief friendship I had with this man, because I did not know him long, but he saved me from what may have been a very serious post traumatic stress condition—by alerting me to the way my mind made all the wrong connections during that intense emotional experience.

Whether I would ever endanger my life again, I may never know. But what I do know is that the mind during times of intense crisis can become very confused, and distort perceptions and reality. I also believe that if I did not have that brief friendship with that very insightful man that the events of that evening could have haunted me for many years. Even though the event would be long past, the memory of that event would create feelings that would have been so twisted that it could of created much emotional havoc, until the truth or clarity of what really happened was finally learned and accepted. Even though the event was over, the feelings that would be associated to the memories of the event would have been the cause of much unnecessary trauma and suffering.

> "The exchange between that man and myself I would call Spirituality, and the force that freed me from all that dreadful unwarranted guilt, I would refer to as the "Power of Spirituality which was fully demonstrated by this man's willingness to spend an entire night with me on his own time and without any compensation, other than the gift he in turn received through the "Art of Giving" manifested by freely giving so much of himself and his time to me."

> "As can be clearly observed by this mans example, it is not only limited to one addict helping another addict or alcoholic to recover; but it is the process of giving to anyone, anything that they may need or even want, that releases the "Power of Spirituality" through the "Art of Giving." The level of power released is directly associated to how freely and unconditionally the "giver" gives!"

One of the most profound prayers that exemplify this concept was included in the "Twelve Steps and Twelve Traditions" book that most members of AA own; and it is the "Prayer of St. Francis" found on page 99 of that book. The words of this prayer are so significant to understand the "Power of Spirituality" which can only be released through the "Art of Giving" that this author feels it should be stated in its entirety at this time.

If you are doubtful, judgmental, cynical, anti-religious or even an outright atheist, please excuse any references that St Francis made to any Spiritual entities, but do pay close attention to his clearly stated position regarding the concept of "giving."

The Prayer of St Francis

> "Lord, make me a channel of thy peace-that where there is hatred, I may bring love-that where there is wrong,

I may bring the spirit of forgiveness-that where there is discord, I may bring harmony-that where there is error, I may bring truth-that where there is doubt, I may bring faith-that where there is despair, I may bring hope-that where there are shadows, I may bring light-that where there is sadness, I may bring joy. Lord, grant that I may seek rather to comfort than to be comforted-to understand, than to be understood-to love, than to be loved. For it is by self-forgetting that one finds. It is by forgiving that one is forgiven. It is by dying that one awakens to eternal life. Amen."

When events happen in this world and whether we are responsible for them or whether we believe that we are responsible, the impact will be the same. Great suffering may be experienced by a person feeling responsible for some terrible situation or event, and that suffering can be relieved more readily and easily, when that person has a deeper sense of spirituality.

"Spirituality is the force and power that can effectively be used by a person to make sense of something that makes no sense."

In the event of some kind of tragedy, for instance the death of a child, the person may feel incredible fear, rage, confusion, and sadness or deep depression. Another person may have a strong sense of spirituality that may enable them to find real comfort in the belief that "all things work for the good of those who love God."

"In other words when a person is able to believe and accept "it was God's will" they have access to additional strength and resources, that enable them to "make sense of something that makes no sense." The ability to do this is truly the manifestation of the "Power of Spirituality."

The concept of spirituality needs to be fully explored, since it is constantly emphasized by many people in recovery, and by people with no interest in recovery. When people speak about Spirituality they have very specific ideas regarding this subject. A person's experience of Spirituality is always very unique, personal and special to them.

> "Although they may try to understand or perceive what another person's Spirituality is like, there is always a serious dilemma, and that dilemma is that no person will ever experience Spirituality in the same manner, simply because it is a very special and private experience."

Therefore for the purpose of gaining some understanding of this profound "Power of Spirituality," in which there is no possible or universal way to describe this concept; it will be necessary to discuss it in terms of...

> "What Ever Spirituality Is- It Has Characteristics That Others View And Judge As Spiritual In Their Nature."

What are these particular characteristics and how can they be categorized or are they just random behaviors or beliefs. A spiritual person recognizes specific behaviors, feelings and emotions as well as other less defined sensations. It is this combination of emotional psychological and even physical events in a spiritual person, which alerts others to the fact that they are in fact "Spiritual."

Can a person be Spiritual and not demonstrate it to others, but keep it a secret and known only to themselves? It is no more possible for a Spiritual person to hide their Spirituality than it would be to hide the sun or the moon.

> "Spiritual people have easily discernable traits that can be simply recognized by their beliefs that are manifested in a strong expression of a deep sense of confidence, not so much in themselves, for that would demonstrate arrogance or conceit, but by contrast their confidence lies in having a profound sense of FAITH and HOPE."

The Faith and Hope being discussed here should not be mistaken for how a religious person would describe it, for it is much more broad than a simple faith in God or a religion. In the context of Spirituality it should be noted that it is possible for very religious people to speak of having faith, but really lack spirituality. Therefore FAITH in the context of defining the characteristics of a Spiritual person needs to be viewed in the following manner:

"FAITH is a confident feeling and belief that no matter what is happening in the persons life they fully accept and Trust that they will effectively and successfully deal with the event."

Note that this is much more different than the belief that "God is in Charge" and or "It is Gods will and so I trust in God." While there is nothing wrong with a deep sense of trust and comfort in a belief in God, many people especially needing recovery are blocked off from the strength that comes from having such a belief in God. "Recovery FAITH does not require an acceptance of God, and instead it allows a person who believes they are cut off from God, to still benefit and develop a sense of HOPE. It is this form of HOPE that actually mobilizes the person to pursue actions and behaviors that will result in not only being able to solve a problem, but will enable them to develop strong healthy coping ability and behaviors.

"In other words they attain their goals, by having FAITH that they have the ability to achieve that goal, and then by utilizing HOPE they move towards that goal. They believe that they can resolve the issue, and the energy to take actions are manifested in their HOPE."

As in "I hope this will work-I hope I can find the answer- I hope it will hold together." Without this form of hope the person would be paralyzed and immobilized and fail to exert any effort or have any confidence that they would and could find the answers.

"In addition to "HOPE and FAITH" being a fingerprint of Spirituality so is Humility-Compassion-Sensitivity, or Any Mutually Beneficial Relationship Between Two Or More People That Is Non-Exploitative In Nature."

Anyway about this "SPIRITUALITY STUFF" –HERE GOES—"What is this thing that is referred to as Spirituality?" In AA and NA it is referenced all the time but what are THEY talking about? If you have read the AA book in the chapter "We Agnostics" it is mentioned about 30 times and connected to many other terms like "spiritually minded or spiritual experience or spiritual basis or spiritual matters or spiritual principles or spiritual approaches or spiritual things" this use of the word is used at least 30 times in combinations.

Since they wrote an entire chapter to educate and alert the alcoholic or addict to the importance of "spirituality" it could be very discouraging and even frightening when a person cannot understand or will not accept this need.

Having been one of those agnostic or atheist types in the past I was able to survive in the 12 Step Program by simple substitution and reframing the concept. I suggest for anybody who is adamantly resistant to the concept of "Spirituality" or has a strong opposition to the concept of believing in a "GOD" or "Higher Power." You need to just chill out and consider these suggestions---

"Forget the term completely regarding SPIRITUALITY and only view MY definition of the term Spirituality and—SEE IT—"As A Person Who Has The Ability To Practice Having "Faith And Hope"—

"Faith is defined as just having a "VISION" of the way something can be—that's all nothing more –just a vision of what may be possible –believing something that is desired can be acquired. In regards to "HOPE" see this term simply as the power steps to acquire the object of desire—in other words it is the ACTIONS you take –"as you walk or move toward the Vision. Each step of the way you may be saying, "I HOPE this works; I HOPE they can forgive me; I HOPE there is a solution."

Now regarding the term "GOD" there is a great and effective substitution that removes all prejudice, confusion, disillusionment or misunderstanding of this term. By taking the word GOD and turning it into an acronym, then…

> "The word "GOD " breaks down to "G" stands for Good and "O" stands for Orderly and "D" stands for Direction or "GOOD ORDERLY DIRECTION." Now no one in their right mind can oppose such a concept, regarding the need to have or get GOD into their life. Please tell me if there is something wrong with having GOOD ORDERLY DIRECTION in your life."

Is AA and NA or having a sponsor all "Higher Powers" in your life? As an addict if you are indeed powerless then do you need a" POWER GREATER THAN YOURSELF?" When a person is able to utilize the concept of God or learning to accept and live by "Good Orderly Direction," or have a strong sense of "Faith and Hope," then that person has great coping Ability and Capability. The following all true-life incidents, will demonstrate the "Power of Spirituality", but more in particular that of the "Art of Giving."

There was a documentary many years ago regarding a situation in which a truck driver was experiencing a murderous rage at his girlfriend, who was driving her own car while he was pursuing her in his fully loaded semi tractor and trailer. The incident took take place on a toll road when she approached the toll gate, and could not get away, her insane, homicidal boyfriend rammed her car from the rear and drove the front of her car into a small car in front of her, which resulted in a fiery explosion. Although the woman that was rammed from behind was not seriously injured, the car that she hit suffered horrendous damage. There was a small baby in the backseat of that car which was absolutely engulfed in flames, when the car the baby was riding in was hit from the rear.

> "Due to that insane moment that baby who was less than a year old suffered such severe burns to his body, that he required endless surgeries throughout his young life. By the time this child had reached the age of 19 or 20 his appearance was as follows: he had absolutely no ears, he virtually did not have a nose, his face was hideously scarred with layers and folds of twisted pink flesh. In addition to this he did not have many fingers;"

> "But despite all this at the age of 20 years old he was getting ready to graduate college and planning to marry the woman of his dreams."

Despite all his seeming handicaps he had accomplished and achieved tremendous success in not only his academic endeavors, but also, and even more importantly in his ability to form a meaningful and loving relationship. It should be noted that in viewing the woman who was planning to marry him, it was absolutely clear that the relationship was not one based upon pity, but instead admiration and deep respect. His future wife was extremely attractive and very intelligent.

> "What the above real-life story demonstrates is the power of Faith, Hope and unconditional Love, which

367

are clearly and obviously evidence for what is referred to as Spirituality."

To further demonstrate the deep depth of this man's Spirituality and his family's Spirituality, the next part of this man's and his family's story is absolutely unbelievable, and will now be presented.

While this man and his future bride were planning their wedding, and getting ready to celebrate his graduation from college, he and his family were both informed that the man that caused the accident over 19 years earlier had been apprehended. The perpetrator who attempted to murder his girlfriend and caused that fiery horrendous accident was now finally in jail for the attempted murder and fleeing the scene of the accident where he had caused serious injuries.

As you may observe the twist to the story, is that this man had been a fugitive for over 19 years; for after he had rammed his girlfriend's car he abandoned his truck and was able to successfully elude the criminal justice system for almost 20 years. It appeared that he had been living and working in Canada and on a routine traffic stop while he was back in the United States he was identified and promptly arrested. The family was notified by the prosecutor that they were being requested to come to the hearing since they were so severely victimized by this man's insane and homicidal behaviors almost 20 years before. As the family discussed their opportunity to finally see justice, the following discussion took place.

"They all realized that their testimony could and would result in extreme severe consequences and penalties for the former truck driver and although they felt anger and resentment towards the man, due to the terrible and horrible things that their child and they had to endure; they unanimously agreed not to press charges."

"As bizarre and strange as this may sound how the victims who finally could have their day in court, where they could see that justice is served; decided that it was best to forgive than to seek vengeance is a true demonstration of the "Power of Spirituality."

When they arrived at court they inform the judge and the prosecutor of their decision. They then stated that the family had to learn from almost the initial day of that fiery crash, that they could not allow their emotions to control their decisions and actions. It should be emphasized that throughout the almost 20 years that their child was undergoing horrible and painful reconstructive surgeries their child was so badly disfigured he looked like a creature from Hell.

> "Due to his hideous scarring and mutilation most people attacked, that child and as he was growing into becoming a man he had to emotionally and literally physically fight almost every day because people would torment, tease, judge and condemn him."

> "Now most people would conclude any human being who was attacked, hated and ridiculed every single day of his life would have developed a deep unforgiving hatred as well as profound self-pity."

Contrary to this conclusion if the reader was privileged to hear this man speak, despite his hideous appearance, he spoke calmly, articulately, with certainty and confidence. His voice was soft and even soothing.

> "This man's speech was absolutely and totally and completely incongruent not only with his hideous appearance, but even more so with regard to the horrible, abuse, ridicule, isolation, being excluded, banished, shunned and ostracized by cruel and insensitive peers throughout his life."

What the family and this man did express in court to the defendant was that they wanted him to know the horror and suffering that he had directly caused to their family. They also wanted him to know that...

> "In no way were they going to allow harsh and hateful vengeful feelings to destroy them or the family and therefore they informed him and the judge that they absolutely and totally forgave this man for the heinous monstrous harm he had caused them."

> "This man and his family demonstrate the profound "Power of Spirituality" and especially in the area of

forgiveness, which is truly manifested through the "Art of Giving," and in this incredible case the family "Gave their Forgiveness."

This next true story is that of a young woman who lost both her legs and yet with a deep deep sense of Faith and Hope she single-handedly caused the prosthetic revolution that is nothing less than a modern day miracle. Her story is as follows:

She was involved in a very serious car accident and while she was in the hospital she had to take an honest assessment of her assets and liabilities. The woman immediately recognized and accepted that she had no legs so therefore she must begin the process of building up her upper body. While in her hospital bed the woman used the traction apparatus and began to do pull-ups and chin-ups to accomplish the task of strengthening her upper body.

The woman continued to exhibit a profound and positive attitude and the hospital staff were shocked and amazed at this woman's resiliency and determination. A sudden and total reversal in her attitude shocked and surprised the staff when it came time for her to learn how to manage being a double amputee. When she heard the doctors, nurses and the physical therapist begin to speak about how she was going to have to make adjustments in regards to living in a wheelchair, she would NOT accept or LISTEN to what they were trying to TELL her.

"Despite the fact that she appeared to be so accepting and motivated, when she heard that she would be confined to a wheel chair for the rest of her life, she began to Loudly protest."

The medical staff became deeply concerned, when they realized what they thought to be extraordinary strength and resiliency in this courageous young woman, may have in fact, just been delusion or denial. This young woman was adamant and demanding that there was no way that she was going to accept having to live in a wheelchair and expressed in no uncertain terms that she had full intentions of walking again.

The medical staff believed that the woman was in need of significant psychiatric help. No matter what they told her, no matter what evidence they presented, no matter what they BELIEVED; she absolutely BELIEVED that she would walk again. In fact she stated, "When my family comes to visit me again, I am going to meet them standing up when they arrive at the airport."

"In an effort to Convince this woman that she was ABSOLUTELY handicapped and that she Must accept her fate to be in a wheelchair for the rest of her life, they made prosthetic legs for her and her physical therapist began to work with her. They all KNEW full well it would be to NO avail!"

The very first day while she was on the parallel handrails balanced on her new prosthetic legs and tried to take her first steps, she discovered she could NOT in any way use these prosthetics. She became frustrated and angry and continued to remain very adamant that she was GOING to walk again. She was so insistent and her physical therapist was so impacted by this woman's FAITH that they continued to work together, but absolutely to NO avail. No matter what techniques or methods they tried she could NOT even take one step.

"This is where the "Power of Spirituality" manifested itself through her very deep deep FAITH and indestructible HOPE and changed the reality of tens of thousands of amputees and their families."

Prior to this woman, when a person suffered the amputation of most of their leg, prosthetic replacement legs were rarely neither effective nor efficient. As Paul Harvey would pronounce, "here is the rest of the story."

"The woman's physical therapist happened to have a friend who was an engineer, and when he told his friend about this extraordinary incredible woman, and her almost insane FAITH and HOPE that she was going to walk again; something happened that defies logic."

It is important at this time to accept and understand that what many times is accepted as REALITY is actually just a mistaken BELIEF and a mass hallucination or delusion of other people. In other words "everybody Believed this young woman could never walk again" and that they claimed that it was "just reality." However this engineer that knew nothing about prosthetics never the less developed an alternative prosthetic leg design, and when they placed these devices on the woman's short stumps; everybody was shocked and amazed at what happened next, EXCEPT the woman.

> "When the woman positioned herself on the parallel rails she was ABLE to ambulate with the help of the rails. The physical therapist and other hospital staff had just witnessed a true marvel that was driven by a young woman's indestructible FAITH and unstoppable HOPE. Here truly was the full miraculous "Power of Spirituality.""

The woman did not seem as appreciative nor as excited as everyone else who witnessed for the first time a person with the severity of her amputations be out of a wheelchair; nonetheless be able to ambulate in a standing position. This had NEVER been done or SEEN before! The woman in a very nonchalant manner expressed thanks, but it was clear she was NOT surprised by what she had ACHIEVED with the help of the medical team.

What happens next is even more perplexing. Once the woman had demonstrated that these prostatic new devices were functioning better than anyone had expected or anticipated, and when the physical therapist informed her...

> "Let me take the legs back and fit them with skin so that they look like real legs." The woman then responded, "I don't know if you've noticed but I DON'T have real legs, all I WANT is to be able to walk, and I don't care what these things look like; they WORK and they DON'T need any improvements."

If you have not been able to glimmer the rest of the story, this woman has been responsible for the prostatic revolution that you have witnessed and observed on TV and possibly in real life, in which amputees are fitted with pogo stick like devices. You may have observed people snow skiing, water skiing or running marathons on these devices and in fact able-bodied people are NOT able to compete with these amputees who demonstrate an unfair advantage, and therefore the handicap MUST be handicapped in many competitions or it is not fair for the able-bodied person to compete against these devices.

> "As can be seen in this woman's true life story a person's spirit, which is manifested in their "Power of Spirituality" can and will overcome any obstacle. It is

only the limitations we place on others and ourselves that cause those limitations."

An afterthought regarding this prostatic revolution involves a man who attempted to climb a mountain possibly Mount Everest and he suffered a severe climbing accident. As a result of his injuries he lost both his legs and he vowed...

> "That mountain has NOT defeated me." A few years after that accident he went back to that mountain with no legs and climbed that mountain and CONQUERED that mountain. He used a modification of those revolutionary prosthetic devices in which he fitted them with mountain climbing modifications that ENABLED him to change rapidly from one type of climbing tool to another, almost like changing sockets on a ratchet wrench."

The next story has been exemplified and glorified through a Hollywood film titled "Apollo 13" in which the true life story of how three astronauts were Doomed to Death and through the efforts of one man directing an army of specialists was able to produce nothing short of an act of God. Every single person should view this film from its historical accuracy. I will summarize in a sentence or two this real-life drama.

Apollo 13 was a moonshot in which three astronauts were trained and were planning to land on the moon. Somewhere during their mission to the moon their vehicle suffered a severe accident. As a result of the accident they did not have the necessary navigation systems, life support systems nor enough electrical power to literally survive. The ship was on a possible course towards the sun, the oxygen supply was absolutely running out and they had NO way to change course or enough power to do so even if they could. Despite incredible and extraordinary odds against these three brave astronauts surviving they Were brought back to earth UNHARMED.

> "It is very important that as you continue to read that you pay particular attention to the concept of the "Power of Spirituality" manifesting itself through the human spirit and galvanized by FAITH and HOPE that anything and all things are ABSOLUTELY possible."

When Mission control was informed of the terrible accident that had befallen the astronauts there was great fear, terror, sadness and deep despair that virtually nothing could be done to save their lives.

> "The mission control director however had an entirely different scenario in his mind. He presented to his army of specialist and informed him "We ARE bringing them back and gentlemen FAILURE is not an option."

At this time he then got the best minds and engineers to work out every detail of how it would be possible to bring the craft back to earth.

Every person reading about this situation needs to view the Hollywood film and in that film they will see the small pittance of the things they had to work with to pull off this miracle. The engineers had to go into a room and place in that room all the accessible parts or pieces which may include things like duct tape and food wrappers and a piece of PVC pipe as well as a bundle of wires and figure out how to use each of these pieces to repair the navigation system, the electrical system and more importantly the life-support system.

> "Each detail was meticulously worked out and as a direct result the life-support system was restored, a method to navigate was determined and the formula was worked out in regards to almost nonexistent battery power that would have to be used to turn the ship around."

> "When you think about this extraordinary MIRACLE that happened against maybe more than a MILLION to one odds, once again demonstrates the "Power of Spirituality" manifested through bulletproof FAITH and unyielding determination and HOPE."

The next story that really exemplifies the human spirit may be found in the real life story of a woman who had no legs and traveled around on a skateboard.

> "This woman would leave her home on her skateboard and roll to a repair garage, where she would position herself near the bumper and then hoist herself into the

open engine compartment; at which time she would ask
that somebody "please hand me my tools."

This woman was a gainfully employed auto mechanic and when she leaves
her job and returns home an extraordinary loving man embraces her and lifts
her up and passionately kisses her. Now as extraordinary as this may seem
that this woman can be happily married and gainfully employed; despite the
fact of having absolutely nothing below the trunk of her body, and is still able
to function at such a high level; is nothing compared to the fact that she had
decided to have a baby. It should be strongly EMPHASIZED that this woman
intended to HAVE her baby, NOT adopt a baby.

> "Against all medical advice and caution this woman was
> determined to have a baby. She had deep deep FAITH
> to believe that she could get pregnant and deliver a
> healthy normal baby. Her doctors cautioned her that
> this could be extremely dangerous for not only her,
> but for the child, and she completely dismissed their
> concerns and fears due to the strength of her "Power of
> Spirituality."

When questioned regarding how she could possibly take care of the child
when she had no legs, she reported that at least for several years she and the
child would be on equal basis. This woman was able to give birth to a normal
child and her indestructible Faith and unyielding Hope defied all other
people's beliefs, expectations and perceived reality.

The next story concerns a family that was innocently driving down a
major interstate highway when a piece of steel flew off the truck that was in
front of them and when they hit the steel it ruptured the gas tank on their
minivan.

> "Instantaneously the minivan became a fireball and
> before they could pull the van over to the side of the
> road the couple from the front seat of the car watch
> their five children burning to death just inches from
> them. Although the couple made heroic efforts to get
> the children out and were badly burned in the process,
> they were only able to save their 13-year-old who

unfortunately died the next day of the extensive and severe burns she had suffered."

Although this may be an uncommon event, one must admit that car accidents cause horrible suffering for individuals and families involved in them. What makes this story extraordinarily Spiritual is the fact that it appeared on CNN news many years ago. When the man was seen on the TV screen both his arms were heavily bandaged and when he spoke he stated the following...

"I want the driver of the truck to know I do NOT harbor any anger towards him, for I KNOW it was an accident."

Now with most people you could never imagine they would be this calm, nonetheless so forgiving of a person who directly or indirectly was responsible for the death of their five children.

"What the man said next was even more astonishing and amazing and that was, "God tests our FAITH and we must remain faithful to Him."

How many people could demonstrate this level of acceptance, trust and Faith in God; when God seemingly destroyed their entire family? Where does anybody get the strength to accept the unacceptable, to believe the unbelievable and to remain faithful under such extraordinary conditions? In addition to this question a person needs to ask.

"Does this man have strength or is his blind acceptance a weakness?" Does this person exhibit extraordinary strength, or to have this kind of ability to accept and not condemn means that he is insane and crazy or that it means he is indeed an extraordinarily strong human being?"

Many times people suffer great injuries, wrong doings, injustices, cruelty and their response is "it was or is God's will." Are these people exhibiting strength or weakness when they can accept the unacceptable? It will always be a very personal belief of whether a person who can completely accept the unacceptable is either very very strong or just insane.

> "If you view their ability as strength then you must KNOW it is SPIRITUAL strength driven by ABSOLUTE unconditional love, unyielding FAITH and indomitable HOPE, which enables them to virtually DO the humanly impossible."

I describe it as humanly impossible because a human being who does not have a deep deep faith, hope and trust in their ability to manage the unmanageable, accept the unacceptable, forgive the unforgivable and to remain strong against insurmountable odds, could never accomplish these absolute impossibilities. Once again you can clearly see the "Power of Spirituality" manifesting itself in this person!

The last real life story, which I will keep very brief, is about the birth of my first daughter who suffered significant birth complications and then my second daughter when she was diagnosed with a possible malignant tumor. With the birth of my first daughter when we arrived at the hospital her mother immediately went into intense labor and everybody was expecting a quick and normal childbirth.

> "After several hours of false starts everybody began to realize that there were complications and this was NOT going to be a normal birth."

Due to the stress and my constant prayers I do not remember the time frames, but I do remember it was all night long my wife was experiencing intense labor until finally she could NOT deal with it anymore, and basically the labor pains subsided, which was NOT a good thing. We had prepared for a Lamaze birth, but the midwife realized that there were serious complications and had contacted the doctor.

> "It was discussed that a high forceps procedure would be necessary to deliver the baby. It was at that time hearing those words and waiting for the doctor to arrive that I prayed heavily and steadily without even knowing that I was praying and as the doctor arrived and had the

forceps in his hands, then suddenly my daughter was
born naturally."

It wasn't until several days later that the miracle that allowed her
normal birth was discovered. To the dismay of my wife she had undergone a
complication that only occurs once in 300,000 births. That complication was
responsible for my first daughter to be born naturally and without potential
injury and trauma. That complication or what I now know and we'll call a
miracle was the fact that her pelvis bones had separated and had this not
occurred this very large baby would've had to be pulled physically by her head
and only God truly knows what further complications my daughter could
have undergone and then been permanently affected by.

Referring to the situation regarding my second daughter the following
miracle occurred and this time I did consciously and diligently pray for
Faith and as well as Hope. At the age of four during a routine visit with her
pediatrician a small lump was located in her shoulder and her doctor expressed
great concern. Almost immediately she was admitted to a local hospital where
they basically removed and did a biopsy of that lump. The surgeon then
approached us, and informed us that he believed the tumor he had removed
had originated elsewhere in her body. This statement was extremely alarming
because it implied that what he had surgically removed was a metastasized
tumor from elsewhere in the body.

Although it was a long time ago, what I do remember of that conversation
with that physician was that he stated, "do not have a lot of hope." Now
whether I heard this accurately or it was my own fear that interpreted what
he said, I will never be sure. What I do know is that he stated the tumor
would be sent to the Bethesda Naval Hospital in Maryland and would be
more closely evaluated and it would take 8 to 10 weeks before a result could
be determined.

"The fear, terror, and worry when any parent is informed
that their child may in fact be terminally ill, can never be
accurately expressed or described. The potential despair
is overwhelming and emotionally crippling. Now before
I continue I just want to say that this daughter completed
college, and is now very happily married to a sailor.

Because at the time she had the surgery, there was no way of knowing
that she was in fact going to live, and we had to wait 8 to 10 weeks before we

would know the answer to the question, is my daughter going to be all right; is an agonizing lifetime of pending grief and mourning.

> "It should be noted that there have been several other deaths that I have gone through, that caused me to become very angry, disillusioned, and resentful at God." One of those deaths involved my six-year-old niece in which she was diagnosed with leukemia and I asked and prayed that she would live."

I was very young and I had just purchased my very first car that cost me personally $750 which I had earned myself at a rate of one dollar per hour. "As I prayed I offered this car in return for her life." She died within a month of the diagnosis and during that year my car was impounded for drug charges and sold at auction. As a result of this I became extremely angry and would actually try to attack other people who were demonstrating Faith and Hope. When I say I would attack, what I mean is I would try to destroy their sense of faith and hope. It should be noted that my sister the mother of my niece, fully accepted her daughter's death and stated, "it is God's will."

> "Within less than a year after the death of my niece, my best friend had received his orders to go to Vietnam."

Since many of the young men in the area had died-correct that-had been killed in Vietnam; we assumed he would soon be joining them! As a result of this belief we got high and drunk and celebrated life, knowing at least at that time, it was short.

> "Prior to leaving for Vietnam a miracle occurred that in some bizarre way turned into a worse nightmare. His new orders were to report to Germany and then maybe less than five months later, he was dead."

Whether it was true or not there was a rumor that he had been getting high and had died with three other soldiers when the armored personnel carrier that they were riding in careened off the side of a mountain. From what I know from military personnel stationed in Germany, the use of drugs and alcohol was very heavy. What I do know is that my best friend died, where and when he should never have died!

"The shock and surprise absolutely disillusioned angered and disgusted me in regards to the concepts of God, spirituality, nonetheless the concepts of faith and hope. The tragic sudden death of my six-year-old niece coupled with the impossible to have anticipated death of my best friend, caused me to abandon any belief in anything except, drugs and alcohol."

I regressed somewhat telling the story of my daughter, because I wanted you the reader to know, that I have deeply struggled with the concepts of God, spirituality and faith and hope. At the time my daughter was diagnosed with a tumor I was still deeply involved in confusion, ambivalence and anger regarding these concepts.

"It should also be noted that at the time my daughter was having the surgery the following situation and events were all occurring within an 18-month period. Both my mother and my brother were diagnosed with cancer and were dying side-by-side in my mother's home. My wife had collapsed and after some medical assessments they had indicated that she was seriously ill. My accountant, who was one of those very creative ones, was audited and therefore I was audited by the IRS. Also during this time I was having employment issues and within a month of burying my brother a few months after burying my mother, I was diagnosed with cancer. Now although it was a minor diagnosis of treatable skin cancer, the simple fact that cancer had killed many of my family members; caused me overwhelming fear and terror."

It should be noted that most people that would have some degree of faith and hope would feel a great sense of relief, when they were informed that the biopsy results showed positive results. Since I did not have much faith and hope when I got these results, the first thought I had, "How do I know they got every single cell and that one of them has not gotten away to start little families, villages and cities elsewhere in my body." Now this may sound somewhat humorous, and I do find it humorous now, but at that time it made me almost suicidal.

As you can see if you are a person, like I used to be, and I do emphasize "used to be" then it is essential that you grasp the need to learn how to use the "Power of Spirituality" and to do so immediately.

Returning to the story regarding my daughter and her tumor, I would like to relate how without the help of others during this time, in all probability I would have relapsed.

> "During that time I attended one or more meetings of AA on a daily basis and the people in those rooms had what I did not have. They demonstrated verbally and through their own experiences the "Power of Spirituality." They gave me great support, understanding and acceptance, regardless of what I said, felt or believed. As a result I was able to for the first time to develop a sense of Faith- that no matter what happened with my daughter-I would not relapse and I would not drink."

What I remember saying at one of those meetings was that "I will accept whatever happens and I will make it part of my story so that I may be an example to others." When I made this statement I had achieved a sense of Faith that would enable me to survive this very trying time. In addition to this—those people in those AA rooms gave me, what I could never get anywhere else, and that was a sense of Hope.

> "If you are reading this and you're struggling with the concept of spirituality, the "Power of Spirituality" or God, faith, belief or hope; then it is essential you realize that by yourself and of yourself you may never be able to overcome the challenge "of believing in nothing."

> "Therefore return to AA or NA or any other self-help group, or your church or your synagogue, or just listen to anyone that speaks with confidence certainty regarding their beliefs about spirituality, as demonstrated through their ability to effectively use faith and hope and teach it to you through the "Art of Giving" their experience, strength as well as their hope to you and for you."

One last astounding thing that I need to share with you in regards to not only the necessity of having a strong sense of spirituality, but the power of faith and hope to effectively use the "Power of Spirituality" will be found on page 43 in the book Alcoholics Anonymous. On the bottom of that page I will quote the last paragraph.

> "Once more: The alcoholic *and addict* at certain times has no effective mental defense against the first drink. Except in a few rare cases, neither he nor any other human being can provide such a defense. His defense must come from a Higher Power."

How this may apply to me personally will be revealed in the following story. If you remember during that 18 month period in which one of the events in my life was having my daughter diagnosed with a potentially terminal condition, my mother and my brother were actually dying of cancer.

My mother on one of her better days wanted to go to one of her favorite restaurants. Since she was in the mood for Chinese food we went to a place that we had been to numerous times before when she was healthy; and it appeared that by doing this would lift her spirits. The meal was served and was partially eaten when all of a sudden; I became obsessed with looking between my mother and my wife's heads, at the bar in the back of the restaurant.

> "Now it should be noted I was seven years clean and sober and yet, I was becoming obsessed with staring at the bar and wanting to drink. I never dreamed or believed that such a strong craving could engulf me and overwhelm me after such a long period of uninterrupted total abstinence from any drugs or alcohol. Yet there I was beginning to lose all control, of my ability to control myself."

Despite all the mental gymnastics and willpower I tried to summon, I still began to get up out of my chair to go drink. As if I was falling off the roof I grabbed the edge of the table to keep myself from standing up and that action did not stop me. This means as I got up since I was holding onto the table I lifted the table until the glasses fell over and the plates began to slide.

My wife and mother were shocked and astonished and my young daughter, who was with me, was laughing and giggling. Despite every bit of mental willpower and every fact I knew, nothing, and I mean nothing was working. It should be noted that I have always been a licensed professional mental health worker and active in working some sort of a recovery program. I fully grasped the magnitude of not being able to stop myself from relapse and knew that not only would I be giving up seven years of sobriety, but I'd be jeopardizing my very career. Not to mention the fact of the horror that my terminally ill mother and my loving wife were experiencing, yet none of this was a strong enough force to stop me from dropping the table and moving towards the bar.

That was one of the longest walks I have ever taken and it was one of the most terrifying moments of my life, when I knew "That there was no power on earth that was going to stop me from drinking." At the moment I reached the bar-I screamed out-"JESUS CHRIST-don't let me do this." It was at that moment I began to shake and I was able to run from the madness!

"By screaming out God's name was the only way I could break the magnetic hypnotic lock that had grabbed and seized my mind! For those who may be offended or misunderstand, please be aware that the choice I used to identify my higher power, does not have to be the same name that you may choose."

"But make no mistakes about it, one day you may be faced with a force so great that it will overwhelm or undermine every effort and desire you may have to stay clean and sober; and you must heed the warning that I quoted from page 43 in the AA book which I will repeat again."

"Once more: The alcoholic *and addict* at certain times has no effective mental defense against the first drink. Except in a few rare cases, neither he nor any other human being can provide such a defense. His defense must come from a Higher Power."

Deepak Chopra in one of his many books on Spirituality indicated in the chapter titled "Taking Jesus as Your Teacher" he offers 15 steps to God Consciousness by using Jesus teachings in which he asks us to consider the following:

1. The kingdom of heaven is within you.
2. Be in the world but not of it.
3. For my yoke is easy and my burden is light.
4. Ask and you will receive
5. Forgive us our trespasses, as we forgive those who trespass against us.
6. Be still and know that I am God.
7. As you sow, so shall you reap.
8. Resist not evil.
9. In my father's house are many mansions.
10. You must be born from above.
11. You are the light of the world.
12. So do not worry about tomorrow.
13. Abide in me, as I abide in you.
14. For where two or three are gathered in my name, I am among them.
15. What does it profit a man to gain the whole world and lose his soul.

These actual excerpts from the Bible are very deeply profound and even if you are not a Christian these statements will still have a profound effect when they are read out loud and used as a guide for daily living. In the event you are an atheist, then filter out the few that either offend or disturb you. But if you do find them disturbing then you may not be as much of an atheist as you think!

If the following offends some people then they will have to ask themselves how a few simple words from this author could have any power to do so. If you become irritated or even offended then you CHOOSE to allow this to happen to you. By now you must have gotten the message that "YOU are in control and YOU choose to feel, act and believe and if you are disturbed in any manner, then that is proof you are NOT so sure of what you believe or what you think you DON'T believe in.

By the way my belief about atheism is that:

> "An atheist is someone who has the deep belief that there is no God, but since it is only a belief and no one really knows, then an atheist is a person with deep faith in the concept that God does not exist. But since it requires deep deep faith to believe in nothing; then believing that deeply in nothing, is really deeply believing in

something and therefore they have a devout faith and that makes them very rigidly religious! If you really, and that strongly believe in nothing; is it not possible that really believing in nothing is really truly believing in something that some people and I prefer to call "God;" but you prefer to call "Nothing" and by believing that strongly in "Nothing" is really strongly believing in "Something;" therefore it follows you cannot be a true atheist for if you truly believed in nothing then this entire paragraph should mean absolutely nothing to you!" Either way it is not necessary to know or accept if God exists for the "Power of Spirituality" is never denied to any one. Any one has full access to this power regardless of what they believe, can't believe or don't believe!"

I hope this chapter on spirituality enabled you the reader to grasp the understanding and importance of the need of developing the "Power of Spirituality." I also hope that it is clear that we speak about spirituality in inclusive as well as exclusive ways in regards to any religious concepts.

In other words whether a person is devoutly religious, like my sister, who was able to use her Faith and Trust in God, to accept the unacceptable loss of her children. It should be noted here my sister also lost an infant prior to losing her six-year-old daughter. If you do not have a devout belief in any particular religion, then it is essential that you develop the ability to effectively use the concepts of and learn to implement "FAITH and HOPE" into your life. Let me just repeat the quote I wrote at the beginning of this chapter:

"FAITH is defined as just having a "VISION" of the way something can be—that's all nothing more –just a VISION of what may be possible –believing something that is desired can be acquired. In regards to "HOPE" see this term simply as the power steps to acquire the object of desire—in other words it is the ACTIONS you take –"as you walk or move toward the Vision. Each step of the way you may be saying, "I HOPE this works; I HOPE they can forgive me; I HOPE there is a solution."

"And what I HOPE most for you the reader, is that you do not remain as barren from FAITH for as long as I was, and live in "fear and worry" because you have not developed FAITH and HOPE! But most important of all do not be too shy or prejudiced when it comes time to ask God, and know that it does not matter whether you believe or do not believe—"JUST ASK!"

"The Power of Spirituality that is driven by the force of the human spirit and fully expressed through the "Art of Giving."

"Whether GOD is GOD or GOD is GOOD ORDERLY DIRECTION"—"ASK!"

Chapter Sixteen

Essays—Excerpts

Within the following pages you will find significant facts, ideas, suggestions and recommendations or what I refer to as Random Fact and Factors—that provide some additional insights and understanding of the—Application of "The Powers" and "The Arts" described and discussed through out this book.

I know that these thoughts are very important to further understand many of the concepts that I have been describing and discussing in this book. Some of this data is related to actual therapy sessions and other data I just found too valuable to leave on the cutting room floor. You may look at some of these "Essays and Excerpts" as simple outtakes; but each one played a vital part in giving me the clues I prayed for to be able to present these concepts in the most powerful and compelling manner that was possible.

My dream and fantasy and hope is that the information contained in this book will "Free the addict and alcoholic from their madness" and "relieve the, disgust, disillusionment, despair and depression that addiction and alcoholism has caused their families and loved ones to suffer." I will now present the ideas and observations that I feel were a vital part of the development of the concepts detailed through out this book.

"Reality"

Reality is what we create it is not something that we are subjected to as most people believe. Reality is made up of one thing "our beliefs." What we believe drives the forces that form and create the life we live. When we understand that a "problem" is just another word for "challenge"; we can immediately begin to employ our creativity to effectively resolve that problem. Since reality is strictly a "subjective affair" and not a condition that is forced upon us from some unknown outside power or force; we can learn to structure and change anything we desire.

> "It is most important to understand that the "subjectivity
> of reality" allows us to manipulate what we believe to
> be reality."

At this time it will be helpful to discuss and explore the roots of what we sense is reality. Many times people know that there are certain actions they can and should take, but they feel paralyzed to do so. An example of this is when a person is entering into recovery, and joining a 12 Step support group and they are told they need to select a sponsor. Unfortunately many people have much fear and apprehension when faced with this decision and it literally paralyzes them. It may seem so threateningly overwhelming that they leave the program, and this causes their chances for lasting recovery to be seriously reduced.

Why are so many people new to recovery so "blocked" from making literally life saving decisions? The answer may be found in their "twisted perceptions" discussed throughout this book. They assign way to high an importance on this process and have actually felt or believed, "It was like asking someone to marry you." Others have stated, "I just never have asked anyone for help." While some speculate "I just want to do it myself." They also have reported, "How do you trust someone when your own life depends on who you choose."

Whether it is fear, embarrassment or ego and pride the result is the same. Those people leave themselves in a very risky and vulnerable state due to the nature of their twisted and peculiar perceptions; they can make sense of something that can never make sense and that translates to getting high again when they can justify or rationalize to do so.

To alert someone to the fallacy of this thinking, it is only necessary to remind them that through out their lives they have turned to others for help and support. This occurred when they asked a store clerk for advice or directions, or when they were playing sports and there was a coach or a parent that gave advice that they followed. The question that is begging for an answer is why is it so different to ask for help or coaching when it comes to recovery? Why is it so seemingly different? I have found that rather than trying to unravel this riddle it is best to just recognize the following simple truth.

Every person has had to rely and depend on some other person numerous times in their lives and needing directions in recovery is not that different. In fact, the real fact is that when the addict or alcoholic reaches out to another person for assistance, they have actually helped to assure and improve the recovery chances of the person they are asking.

"Since "you cannot keep it unless you give it away"
as the cliché goes when you ask for help; contrary to
your twisted perception that you believe that you may
be disturbing or bothering someone you are actually
giving them a great gift, and thereby you have greatly
improved their chances for recovery and improved the
quality of their lives; by just simply asking for help."

As a therapist working with groups of addicts and alcoholics I would
attempt to teach effective ways to change attitudes and to manage these self
sabotaging emotions and feelings. I have found that the concept of learning
to "Resist the Resistance to Resist" had great appeal and novelty for the
members, and they would immediately begin the implementation of actions
regarding this personal challenge.

I would often ask clients to relate what actions they took today that they
preferred not to. Some of the clients stated they took a walk others stated that
they called their sponsor and still others stated they made their bed.

"As obscure and mundane as these actions may seem
the recovering person comes to understand that the
making of the bed is an act in which strong willpower
is required. This use of willpower allows the person to
exercise discipline in their life and it is the practicing
of this discipline that provides an effective protective
device that will help throughout the day."

It is by taking these simple actions that through the process of "Value
Exchange" all these ordinary and mundane activities take on great importance
simply due to the fact the person was able to resist their resistance or what I
have termed they are building "Resistance Muscle."

"The addict or alcoholic begins to sense there is value
in what they are forcing themselves to do and this in
turn leads to more effort to do even more; through
this process they change their reality, as in the same
way a person changes their body when that person
who is physically working out begins to take on more
challenges as they see the positive results of their efforts

in their bodies, and this creates value that leads to even more efforts to create desirable changes their body."

A person once told me that the "bullet was meant for him and not his friend." He stated for 10 years he had been drinking so he could sleep at night. He also expressed deep concern over the fact that he use to be very articulate, and had a huge vocabulary as well as a very good memory. Due to the heavy drinking he stated, "Now I have a hard time remembering names and can't spell the word "the." He further stated that he believes that by obsessing on the memory of his friend is the only way to continue to "Honor" that friend who "died in my place."

He was informed that his friend would not be honored by his obsessional guilt and by wasting his life due to having so much self-pity he is actually dishonoring the friend who gave his life so he could have a life, which he has been wasting due to drinking and self pity. Also informed the client that he may be punishing himself due to guilt and shame, and the vehicle he is utilizing is now obsessing on the damage he has done to his brain, and the fact that his cognitive functioning has been severely reduced from the level he believed he was once at.

In addition to this I expressed to him that since he feels so much shame he does not feel he deserves a better life or that he should have a good functioning mind. He expressed that he had a very sharp and clear functioning mind in the past, prior to his years of heavy drinking. He also expressed some confusion over the fact that when he watches "Jeopardy" on TV he is currently able to answer many of the questions very quickly. It was further explained to him that when he spends too much time contemplating something, that is when he experiences memory problems due to his anxiety and worry increase exponentially, but when he is more spontaneous such as when he watches "Jeopardy" and not trying to force his mind, allows it to work more effectively.

"In addition to this material also discussed with him how his PTSD occurs due to a very specific set of emotions and feelings and thoughts as well as current environmental cues, which all have to occur in a very specific manner that triggers the PTSD symptoms. By just simply adjusting or changing one of those factors can reduce the intensity or even eliminate the symptoms completely."

"Expressed to him how the "meaning "we assign to
things can be changed and therefore the memory and
the emotions triggered from that specific memory of
the experience can be changed even though the event
remains the same."

It is not the event that is the cause of the PTSD it is the meaning that the person has assigned to it and how they have defined themselves in relationship to it. He was informed that some people when feeling guilty or shame seek punishment as a means to reduce the emotional suffering from guilt and shame. He expressed that when he was wrong or did wrong he told on himself. "Confession being good for the soul" is an old saying, but it has a very deep and profound truth, and that is "keeping something secret is a massive burden that is immediately relieved through the sharing of the undisclosed behavior or action.

In the sense that there is relief in revealing the secret there is also relief in receiving punishment for the offensive behavior or action. Fear worry and anxiety and panic are all very emotionally punishing and in some very strange and twisted way, "We can create severe pain that actually is a cover up of pain." His first order of pain due to the death of this friend and the resulting "survivors guilt" has been unresolved for over ten years. To manage this pain he has created a defensive pain; that being the PTSD and Panic Disorder which is intense enough to distract him from experiencing the first order pain.

"It is a paradox that pain can be used to manage pain,
but if a person is totally preoccupied with suffering
from one condition they cannot suffer from a different
condition, due to the second order pain is an effective
distraction from having to deal with the grief and
sadness, and stops the healthy process of healing and
accepting that things happen and no one is to blame."

Expressed to him the metaphor of "Race Car Drivers." They love what they do and they love it enough to put their lives on the line for it. Sometimes they pay the ultimate price doing what they love and dying doing what you love to do is a good death. If you have to die. "Then it is the best way to die."

Informed him as a "warrior" and his friend being a "warrior" they both did what they loved to do being the best "professional soldiers" they could possibly be. He needs to accept that his friend died doing what he loved to do, and in fact gave his life for his FRIEND, and that should be celebrated and not regretted.

> "The life the friend saved should be lived in all the glory, compassion and greatness utilizing every living fiber and cell in the body to contribute to the world of the living their knowledge wisdom and love. In every way that is possible to be of Maximum Service and to avoid the trap of living in a life of reclusion, remorse and regret for that is the greatest tragedy of all

> "To waste the gift of the LIFE given for a LIFE."

To change a reality from one of guilt, shame and regret driven by a "survivors guilt" to one of appreciation and celebration of a life saved, it is helpful to use the example of the professional racecar driver who may have to give up his life doing what he loves. Despite the natural sadness of the loss and deep grief, many of his or her friends and family choose to celebrate that person's life, rather than obsess on their loss! They do not get caught in the remorse of endless grief—much like the Australian Steve Irwin who died doing what he loved. His passion was messing around with very dangerous animals and sea creatures-in his last action he got too close to a Stingray.

> "After his death everybody including his young daughter celebrated his life's work and publically demonstrated very minimal grief; for they knew he lived the life he loved and he died the only way he would have wanted to when it came for him to leave this life."

> "His family and friends choose the reality of celebration, instead of choosing a reality of lamentation (crying, weeping and mourning)!"

How we choose to create our reality, will always determine how and what we feel. How we feel is directly caused by the beliefs that we allow to dominate our mind after a particular situation has occurred. People's different realities may be seen in the following event. It concerns what may be termed a senseless death of a former client, who died on the same day she attended an Alumni function.

This event reminds us that life is very short and that it is not possible to predict when it is going to end. It should be noted that several staff, and some of the other Alumni believed the person was under the influence of some substance but nobody confronted her or asked her. Depending on how long and strong they allow the question of "Should we have intervened or confronted her?" last in their minds will determine what they experience as their reality. Whether they should or should not have done something; is totally irrelevant after the fact! What is very relevant is how they are going to define this event, and that will create their reality, which will determine how they will feel afterwards.

In a therapy group the next day the clients were asked if they knew anyone who had died as a result of addiction and several raised their hands, but no one was willing to share about this experience. Expressed to them that while this counselor was at that same Alumni event, there were two old clients talking about an intervention this counselor used in which each client is asked to "look deep into the eyes of another client to their right and then to look deep into the eyes of the client to the left."

This was usually accompanied with giggles and laughter, and then this counselor would state loudly and emphatically. "One of you just stared into the eyes of a corpse—for the odds of one person or more in this group, being dead from this disease is highly possible within the next six months." The same two alumni that reminded me of saying this also shared that on a daily basis when they contact each other they state "Fu-k Your Feelings Before They Fu-k You. "

"Every time I hear clients express these words, that I taught them and strongly encouraged them to speak loud, proud and frequently; always makes me a little uneasy if not real squeamish. I have to then remind myself that the boldness of this terminology was chosen as strictly a device to shatter the momentum of complacency that most recovering people fall victim to. Any other choices of words are just too ineffective and weak to break the hypnotic lock, once the addict or alcoholic fall victim to laziness and complacency."

"It is though the reality of these words that the addict or alcoholic can confront, shock and shatter instantly the

393

destructive addictive reality they allow to overwhelm them!"

It was explained in detail that the only reason people relapse is due to the fact that they allow their feelings to dictate their actions. When they no longer feel like going to a meeting they just quit and when they no longer feel like calling their sponsor they stop. If this pattern is not interrupted then following the same flow, when they feel like they want to get high, they just do. It was emphasized over and over that they have to learn to resist these types of feelings in which they allow themselves to stop taking effective recovery actions.

"What they choose to do should have nothing to do with the way they feel, but what they choose will definitely create very different realities, which will directly determine the feelings that they will experience! Our realities are really our choices!"

A very interesting paradox that needs to be clearly understood is how AA and NA are in "reality" perfectionistic programs. Despite the fact that in almost every meeting, when "How It Works" is read there is a sentence that states "We strive for Spiritual growth not perfection." The contradiction can be demonstrated by the fact that a person cannot celebrate time frames unless they correspond with the expectations of staying totally clean and sober for 30,60,90 days and then six months, nine months and increments of years.

Now if a person was clean up to the day before one of these time frames and smoked pot or had a beer, then they could not celebrate the fact that they were 89 days clean due to using on day 90. It was strongly emphasized that there are people who are able to stay clean most of the time, but they use prior to the moment of celebration and feel "shame and guilt and sometimes hopelessness."

A solution to this dilemma is to recognize that when a person takes more than one of the starter chips or key tags the act of taking this token for the third or more times may trigger a sense of failure. The repeated actions of taking the token can cause it to become associated with failure and therefore picking it up over and over represents failure, which can lead to additional failures.

"To avoid this potential negative association from forming it was strongly suggested that the person do not take a particular chip that represents a specific time more than three times. If the person has relapsed repeatedly, then they should not pick up a chip or a key tag until it is the first one they have achieved. In this way the celebration is associated with success instead of representing repeated failures. It was suggested that in "reality" that someone needs to openly recognize and celebrate any amount of clean time not just the designated time frames."

"Developing and Maintaining and Strengthening a Recovery Lifestyle"

In a discussion of how to integrate the 12 Steps into our lifestyles the question was asked. "Why have you chosen to put a lot of effort into keeping your apartments and personal space clean, neat and organized? The second question that was asked was. "How are you going to assure that you maintain a strong recovery momentum and continue to do the right things when you are discharged?

It was explained that too many times when people leave a treatment program they stop their disciplines and routines that they were practicing while in treatment. The third question asked was "Why do people fail to take the actions that would protect their investment they made when they came to treatment?"

"One of the clients expressed that it is a matter of "accountability" in which they fail to have anyone to stay accountable to, and that is why they get lazy and fail. The topic of accountability arose, and it was suggested that by making ourselves accountable is a very protective device that can be used to protect recovery."

The clients asked how can we do this and can God help us to follow through if we pray and believe that God is watching. Informed the group that believing that God is going to do this for them is really more of a disguised form of self-discipline, and most addicts do not do well with being disciplined. Ways to be more accountable was discussed and one client stated, "How do you force yourself to be motivated?

> It was suggested that by maintaining a written "to do list" is one of the most effective techniques that will enable completion of goals and tasks. It was explained that when things are written down they create an effect in the brain that facilitates a higher probability that the tasks written down will be completed."

Several clients stated that they agreed with this and in fact have done lists and know they help get things accomplished. One member complained that she writes exhausting lists and "It does not work, three days later I still have not done most of the things I wrote on that list." It was emphasized that if the list is over a day old the mind will not organize itself around getting the tasks done. It needs to be understood that, "A to do list is only effective for a day or two."

To learn how to begin to effectively use a "to do list" it was suggested that the person not write more than three things, and to do this on a daily basis. As the person succeeds with the easy three they can then expand on the list, but never list more than can be accomplished in any one day. In this manner the threat of becoming discouraged will be reduced if not just completely eliminated! Although some counselors tell people to write a weekly schedule, this is not as effective as writing a daily schedule every morning or evening.

In a different group a client expressed that he does real well when he is in treatment and even for a long time afterwards, but at some point he always feels or believes that he has completed all the tasks and tells himself there is no more to do and that is when he relapses. He was puzzled why he has a long history of doing this.

> "A person that has this pattern of recovery and relapse is referred to as the "Mountain Climber." This person gets his or her life "juice" from overcoming challenges, and once they achieve the goal they then begin to sabotage it. This is driven by the fact that the effort to achieve the goal, is more pleasurable than the achievement or reaching successful completion. Due to this tendency this person creates the circumstances to always be working to achieve rather that celebrating or appreciating their accomplishment or success. Many times substance abuse is the demolitions they use to destroy his or her accomplishments."

This counselor asked that client, "To what degree has this happened in which you have used substances to sabotage yourself?" He said every time and laughed even louder, once he recognized this was almost a predictable pattern driven by the failure to associate high enough value to all the efforts he has made over and over again. This is an example of what was discussed in the chapter on Values Exchange.

The story of the "World's Strongest Man" competition that is seen on T.V. was discussed in terms of how it is possible for a smaller athlete to be able to defeat his competitor that is at least one third larger and stronger. This show is about accomplishing great achievements in competitions that require massive strength and endurance.

The concept of deep focus and the importance of maintaining a strong steady momentum were reviewed. Many times if you look carefully at the competitor you can see in their eyes whether they will win the contest simply due to the intensity of their focus, as they begin the challenge. The "big" guy starts off with great strength and stamina as he walks the course pulling a bus full of cheerleaders. Before getting to the end he hesitates as he almost reaches the finish line, which costs him the competition simply due to the fact that he does not have the strength to lurch the bus back into motion.

In the meantime the smaller competitor maintains a "killer" focus and he pulls the same bus with the same cheerleaders across and even past the finish line. The question was asked, "What was the difference and how does this story have any relationship regarding recovery? It was explained that the big competitor allowed his feelings to dictate his actions in that he felt too tired; he thought he was too tired, therefore he believed he was too tired and could not push himself. Whereas the smaller athlete ignored any feeling that he could not succeed and he won.

Addicts fail because they allow "stupid' feelings to dictate their actions. It was emphasized that no one is powerless to stop himself or herself from acting on a feeling. In other words this is the concept described in the chapter titled "Turn Resistance into Resolution" or what I fondly refer to as "Fuck your feeling before they fuck you!"

Most people at one time or another may have thought about killing themselves or someone else and if they could not stop themselves from acting on that feeling they would not be alive today and a lot of people may not be alive also. It is a fact and quite obvious that feelings do not equal facts. Therefore the more a person learns to resist their feelings of avoidance and of failure to carry out some needed recovery action or plan, the stronger they are becoming. But if they give into their stupid, idiotic, asinine and self-defeating feelings, then they are practicing and building negative momentum that when they feel like getting high they will just succumb to it without any fight or resistance at all.

> "The way to begin to build "resistance muscle" is to learn through out each day to challenge the feelings of desire, for instance "while you may like a greasy cheeseburger it may be better for your body to eat dry Tuna and despite the fact that you "feel" like having the burger, you can resist the feeling, and have Tuna instead. As soon as this is done you have just strengthened yourself against a relapse."

> "Another simple exercise is to delay smoking a cigarette when you feel like one and instead look at a clock or a watch and delay lighting the cigarette for one to five minutes. Even though you are not resisting this dangerous deadly habit at least this teaches you to better control your feelings and impulses!" Learning to delay leads to control and control leads to decision and decision leads to new directions and new directions lead to new destinies!"

> "By practicing these actions in which you overrule what you want and desire to do, and instead do what is right or healthy, is the way you can build momentum that will allow you to successfully overcome that moment of truth when you feel like getting high."

It should be noted that no person calmly and cognitively calculates a relapse. Relapse is not something that is carefully thought out and intellectually weighed in the sense of a rational assessment of the "Pros and Cons." Most of the time a relapse is strictly driven by an emotional urge or impulse.

> "The more we learn to manage any feelings that cause us to do the wrong things or to procrastinate regarding taking or completing necessary recovery actions, the more we will be prepared, when a stupid "feeling" can

undermine and even destroy all the effort and hard work that a person has invested in their recovery."

A regular question that is frequently asked is "Why do most people bail out of AA or NA?" One of the responses were "It is because they are afraid and they have problems socializing." The importance and benefit of being in a recovery fellowship was emphasized as well as the absolute need for being involved in the recovery community, and how when people relapse they usually fail to maintain their associations with the twelve-step community.

"To drive home the point that community is vital to recovery the story of Jesus needing to hire 12 very ordinary people to give him a hand, and the true meaning of this was discussed. The chief question to ask is "Why would the son of God, being a God, himself need 12 uneducated men to give him a hand with his mission on earth."

"The message is that mankind is communal and we need each other and when we isolate or separate we do so at great peril and as strange as it sounds, even God asked for man's help."

"To try to stay clean and sober completely on your own. To refuse to ask for help from God, or his designee which is your fellow man, is actually the most inhumane thing you could do to yourself!"

The focus shifted onto the reason "Why are so many people resistant or are blocked from joining a recovery community?" The story of the little boy was told in which he falls down and is bleeding and what does he do? He runs for comfort from his mother or some care provider and if the care provided tells him "Shut up or I will give you something to cry about" then after numerous times and after years of trying to find relief or reassurance, the child learns that it is even more painful to run to someone for comfort, than the initial injury that caused them to seek comfort from another person in the first place.

"They are being taught and will follow the dysfunctional

rules, "don't talk-don't trust and don't feel." They have learned these rules, by the fact that they have been painfully taught that talking about feelings just leads to more pain, and because their feelings are responsible for forcing them to seek comfort that just led to more pain, they then learn to ignore the feelings and deny their existence. They also will no longer be able to trust themselves or anybody else due to the confusion and pain."

Therefore, it is not easy to enter a room full of strangers, and start 'talking about feelings and trusting that they will not regret it or even be hurt. They have no trust due to their family experience and it is impossible to trust a total stranger when you could not trust your own "blood" family.

"It was strongly emphasized that each person in the group needs to learn to share their feelings and any time they feel that others don't care or are judging them they need to tell that stupid "feeling" to go Fuck itself."

Explained that the word "Fuck" is a powerful mood altering word and can force an instant change in focus, mood and mental states by simply being willing to use that word with passion and in the exact context that I teach. This concept can be a powerful tool to protect them from allowing feelings to dictate foolish and or self-defeating actions.

Utilizing Transformational Communication Through Transformational Vocabulary

When working with depressed, anxious or even chronic pain sufferers, I would immediately challenge them to change the words that they were using to describe their condition or symptoms. I would instruct them to choose different words than the ones that they were currently using to describe what they were experiencing.

When a client would state, "I don't know what to do I have always suffered from deep depression?" Or they would state, "I have an intense anxiety condition and I frequently have severe panic attacks and I need medication or I feel like I may kill myself!" Or another client may state, "Two years ago I suffered a devastating car accident and my back and neck are permanently severely damaged and there's no way I can function even one day without drugs-without my pain medication!" And in still another case the client may state, "I have tried getting help numerous times and there is nothing anybody can do for me I will just never understand and I will never change, being here is just a waste of time!"

Upon hearing a client state these discouraging and disempowering comments and beliefs about themselves, I would challenge them to state in depth and detail exactly what they had just previously expressed, but to do so without using the disempowering and discouraging words that they were choosing to use. Many times the client would become frustrated and express their complaint in exactly the same words, and it would take much prompting or even provoking to force them to search for other words to describe a condition.

Take for example the client who stated, "I have always suffered from deep depression." I would instruct that person to repeat that statement, but to do so without using the words "always suffered" and to not use the term or words "deep depression."

> "Upon hearing this the client would be come somewhat confused, disoriented and even extremely frustrated because it would be the first time that they would be forced to THINK about what they were saying rather than just saying what they were feeling without any THOUGHT whatsoever."

What I have witnessed every time a client has taken on this challenge is their surprise in regards to how their reality reorients itself just because they chose different words to describe what they thought they could only feel, which was the degree, depth and discouragement regarding their situation or symptoms. Now returning to the example of the person who stated, "I have always suffered from deep depression." They changed the words to "I have experienced much sadness" or they change the words to "I have felt lost" or another variation of words chosen "I just don't really know what I'm feeling." Although it may be difficult for you the reader to fully understand how this process works.

> "It is through the use and choice of words that all of life that we experience is measured and brought to our attention. In other words when people are experiencing "something" until they describe that "something" that "something" does not exist."

It is only when we bring it into our reality by choosing words to describe the event the situation or even symptoms, is when we become aware that any of this even exists.

> "Everybody has experienced times when they may have had a severe headache, felt overwhelmed by some situation, or was actually very physically sick; but when they became distracted or preoccupied regarding some other totally different experience, the headache, the overwhelming situation, and the physical sickness mysteriously vanished, until they remembered those symptoms and pains once again."

In the example where the person stated, "I have an intense anxiety condition and I frequently have severe panic attacks and I need medication or I feel like I may kill myself!" that person was confronted with the need to restate their feelings in depth and detail, but to repeat it without using the following words, "intense anxiety" or "frequent panic attacks" or "kill myself." When the person attempted to share the feelings that they clearly stated in the above statement without having access to the words I prohibited them to use, they then experienced a very bizarre and strange change in their previously believed perception of their reality.

They expressed the following, "I am just real nervous and get real shaky and I just don't know how to stop it." As you can see when you compare these two statements there is a massive change in the way these words will create or impact in a very positive way their feelings and emotions.

In fact not only is there a significant reduction in the sense of helplessness and hopelessness but there is an immediate shift in how they are thinking about their situation or condition.

> "This new choice of words unleash a large degree of new self empowerment and awareness of a larger number of options available as a direct result of using the "Power of Transformational Communication" through the "Art of Word Selection."

To strengthen these new resources I instructed this person to repeat once again the statement they last made to describe in depth and detail exactly what they were feeling, but this time I prohibited them from using the words "real nervous" and "real shaky" and "don't know." When they reconstructed that statement it was presented as "There is something wrong and I have to stop it." This third statement was the most bizarre reversal of a previously stated belief that the person believed that they were absolutely helpless and hopeless in regards to this situation or condition.

> "As can be seen in these two examples when a person chooses to change discouraging, discounting, depreciating, debilitating or disturbing words they can and will completely alter what they perceive to be their reality."

In the next example in which the person stated "Two years ago I suffered a devastating car accident and my back and neck are permanently severely damaged and there's no way I can function even one day without drugs-without my pain medication!" I challenge this person to repeat exactly what they are feeling in as much depth and detail as was humanly possible, but prohibited them from using the following words and terms, "suffered" or "devastating" or "permanently severely damaged" or "there's no way."

The rapid extraordinary change in their affect or facial expression was absolutely astounding when they rephrased their feelings in the following manner. "Two years ago there was an accident and I hurt my back and neck and I function with pain medication." Although this statement may seem similar to the first statement the change in this person's face showed that an extraordinary shift had occurred and their reality was indeed reoriented. The reason for this will be clearly seen and how the choice of words created a new sense of hope and a different belief than the one in which they were suffering a hopeless condition in which they were helpless to change or manage.

> "By removing the absolute words "suffering, devastating, permanently, severely, damaged and no way," enables a person to develop a completely different perspective, which enables them to redefine the experience and therefore to change that previous held belief or reality."

In the last example in which the person states "I have tried getting help numerous times and there is nothing anybody can do for me- I will just never understand and I will never change, being here is just a waste of time!" Upon hearing this statement I challenged that client to restate how they felt, but I prohibited them from using the following words and terms, "tried" or "numerous" or "nothing" or "just never" or "we'll never" and "waste of time."

The client after much arguing and prompting and feeble attempts to change this statement finally was able to construct the following statement, "I have gotten help several times and they couldn't help me." As you can see from this second statement it is significantly different than the first statement, and by choosing to change the words this person now has a new sense of possibilities.

By removing the words that measured absolute conditions, enables the person to begin to recognize other possible options. Although the second statement sounds almost as fatalistic as the first, it absolutely does not have the same impact or negative intensity on the person and therefore changes some of the disempowering beliefs they had about themselves.

> "As I did in the previous example I also challenged this client to polish up the statement by prohibiting them from using the additional terms, "several" and "couldn't." They formulated the following statement, "I have gotten help and sometimes it helped." As you can clearly see in this third and last reconstructed sentence or statement, that this person has experienced a complete reversal in their initial sense of helplessness and hopelessness!"

All this power to completely alter your negative realities are at your disposal within a heartbeat moment. Therefore it is unnecessary and needless to suffer, when you have the ability, and so much power to shift things in an instant.

> "Learn to be aware and very sensitive to what your thoughts are but even more particularly to what you speak out loud. The words you choose to speak out loud creates the reality of what you will experience; as can be clearly seen in the four previous examples, that they absolutely demonstrate the "Art of Word Selection" when you CHOOSE to engage the "Power of Transformational Communication"

> "Taking control of your own mind and directing it

to what ever means or ends you desire is instantly
possible and will work faster than any drug you have
ever done!"

In another group members indicated what actions they were taking that
demonstrated they were changing their behaviors. One client expressed that
he is now talking about things from his childhood that he had kept secret
for all these years, and by sharing his experience he is finding some relief and
release from his hate and anger and resentment he has towards the people
who hurt him.

Using his sharing as a means to jumpstart the discussion I expressed to the
group that in AA and NA there is a saying that "We are as sick as our secrets."
The response by some of the clients was as follows: "If I have secrets and I
tell lies this may cause me to use drugs again." Lies are the same as having
secrets in that the person being told does not know the lie and therefore your
knowledge of lying is the secret that is being kept.

Another client asked if you tell one other person a secret is it still a secret.
Informed that person that the book Alcoholics Anonymous states, "We must
tell our entire life story to someone." The benefits of self disclosure was
explored in that the person who reveals things about their life to another gains
a sense of relief and freedom providing that they do not experience shame
and or embarrassment. It was emphasized that no one should be ashamed
of things that were done to them or happened to them, due to the fact that
they did not plan or ask for those negative and painful experiences to occur
in their lives.

It was emphasized that the best way to enhance recovery is to take control
and take full responsibility for their emotional as well as mental states and
demonstrated methods to control focus and states by clarifying the language
they were using. Confronted the clients that they need to identify something
that they do not want to do, but by doing it would enhance their recovery.

"Explained to them that most of the things that they will
do for recovery will not count because—they are just
doing what they always did –"Just What They Wanted
To Do" – but the real test is when they no longer have
motivation to do the right things, then will they be able
to Force themselves to do the right things?"

Some of the clients stated that they are doing their assignments and
reading and they don't want to. One woman stated, "I will finish my reading

assignments" expressed to her that she needs to clarify "what assignments" and when she stated her Relapse book and her AA book I asked her "and when are you going to complete the assignments" and she stated "I will finish my AA and Relapse book reading assignments today."

Emphasized to her and the group that by using the "Art of Word Selection" and then by using Words that describe something in very measurable and definite terms creates a much higher probability of actually getting the task done. Another client stated that she writes lists to get things done and then when it is done she crosses it off and "I <u>feel</u> like I accomplished something." Confronted her to change her language and leave out the word "<u>feel</u>" and restate it. She then said, "I cross out something and I <u>know</u> I have accomplished something." Emphasized to her and the group that the word "feel" in the context she was using it was detracting and reducing her sense of "accomplishment, since it has nothing to do with how she "feels"— she "COMPLETED THE TASK(S)" and now "NEEDS TO CELEBRATE THAT FACT."

Another client stated that he intends to take recovery seriously by finishing his goals and doing what is necessary. Suggested to him that he change his words to be more specific and less generalized. He stated, "I will get a sponsor and work the steps" confronted him about "When are you going to get the sponsor and what specific steps are you going to work." He replied "This week I will get the sponsor and begin the steps." Expressed to him that he needs to be even more specific and state what day or night he intends to ask someone to sponsor him. He replied, "By Thursday night I will ask someone to be my sponsor."

> "Once again reinforced the concept that the more specific and measurable the statement the higher the probability of accomplishing the task."

> "Explained that the mind works with specific details and very specific words must be used-Ones that have the Power to Organize the Mind."

> "Once time frames are stated the mind begins to organize itself around accomplishing the task. Without clear stated time frames the mind does not know when or where to make this a priority. Therefore the task will not be done and it is only a "good Intention" but has no chance of being carried out."

Another client stated, "You Have to do the right thing whether you want to or not!" but mumbled these words.

Challenged him to say them out loud and verbalize with much physical energy and suggested he move his body rapidly and swing his arm in a gesture of excitement. With much reluctance he did this after being prompted several times, and when asked what he experienced he stated that there was a significant and positive change in the way he was feeling regarding the comment.

> "Emphasized to the group the more Animated and Loud and Energized you are when you say things the more Appreciative and Excited you WILL! Absolutely Will!—Get over what you are saying. It should be noted that the first time the client made the statement it was expressed with much apathy and an almost sarcastic air of judgment.

> "It is only when you fully emotionalize a word or statement that it is given value, and only what we value will we do and pursue!"

"Demonstrating the Power of Commitment"

An extremely interesting exercise I have used with groups is to utilize a dry erase board and then do the following: (SEE THE CHART THAT DESCRIBES THIS EXERCISE AT THE END OF THIS SECTION) Each member of the group would be asked to state the longest sobriety period of time they had ever achieved. The time frames were then written on the board from top to bottom on the extreme left side of the board. This first column was labeled "Sobriety or Clean Time." Once each of the members had stated their individual time; they were then informed that they needed to identify the specific actions that they had taken that directly led to the achieved time of sobriety. This next list was labeled "Recovery Actions" and was written in the column right next to the first column marked "Clean Time."

The following list will be partial to what was actually reported, but it will enable the reader to gain a glimpse of the process. The clients reported the following actions: Physical exercise, traveling out of town regularly, being in jail, working the 12 step program, having a sponsor and sponsoring others, going to school, reading recovery literature or other spiritual material, attending church or doing other religious activities, being employed, having two or more jobs, time with family, being pregnant, attending 12 step meetings, hobbies, keeping a journal, calling a sponsor or other people in recovery, praying, reading the Bible, staying compliant with needed medications, meditation, yoga and virtually any other actions that they engaged in while sober that they could attribute to helping them achieve sobriety time.

Once this list was exhausted they were then asked to state the feelings or emotions that would have to be present in order for them to take the actions they just described. This next list was written just to the right side of the second list. Once again a partial list will be sufficient to understand the overall process of this exercise. The third list was labeled "Motivational Emotions" and it consisted of the following: Determination, commitment, fear, desperation, dedication, love, compliance, discipline, defiance, hate, surrender, willingness, open-mindedness, gratitude, loneliness, compassion, honesty, willpower, spite, appreciation, and as can be observed any emotion or emotional state can be a catalyst for motivation to take affirmative actions that result in establishing and maintaining sobriety.

This list demonstrates why negative as well as positive emotions can be utilized to maintain recovery momentum. The last part of this exercise was to demonstrate to the group what the most effective Motivational Emotions to utilize are, and to help them understand why most of the motivations we have will fail at times.

To better understand this the following concepts were presented. The question of whether the condition they have is a "Disease or a Choice" was explored. The members were asked, "Who believes that addiction in a disease? Who believes that addiction is a choice?" The words "disease" and "choice" were then written on the board, and under the word "Disease" was written the word "Powerless," and under the word "Choice" was written the word "Power."

The members were asked which concept is associated to each of the words. It was expressed that when you have a disease it is actually a physical condition and therefore you cannot choose not to have it. Whereas when you believe that the problem is a matter of choice then that implies the person has power and therefore does not suffer from a disease.

Next the members were informed that "addiction" is not a disease but actually a "symptom" of a disease. The next question asked was "If it is a disease and since all diseases have a location in the body where is this one located?" The group expressed in the brain and the body and so the counselor expressed that it is in the "Mind and Body." If it is in the mind and body then where is it strongest in the mind or the body? The members stated that it was more in the mind than the body. The counselor next expressed. "So when a person enters into treatment which of these two responds the fastest in treatment?" The clients responded that the body did. They were then informed that as soon as someone's body improves they start to feel what? They then express this by saying something like "I am feeling better now." Just because they say they are feeling better or are in fact actually feeling better; does that mean they are "better?"

Since it is mostly a mind disease, then one has to accept that they are suffering from a mental illness and that addiction is the proof that they are in fact mentally ill. At this juncture most clients feel some offense being called mentally ill; so it is helpful to explain this fact.

If someone is schizophrenic and believes they are Napoleon and tries to convince others, that in fact they are Napoleon, then without hesitation you would know the person is in fact mentally ill, because they believe something that is absolutely not true. In the same sense the addict or alcoholic believe something that is absolutely untrue and what they believe and is actually almost hardwired into their brain or at least into their belief system that "Some how, some way and someday I can use a substance and get away."- Meaning using without consequences.

It was finally expressed that since we suffer from a mental disorder, then it is helpful to define the "mind" as a trilogy composed of everything a person "thinks, believes and feels." If this were true then it would follow that at times their "thoughts, beliefs and emotions" cannot be trusted. To drive home this point the counselor expressed that everyone in the room has experienced doing something they have regretted and then had to ask himself or herself "What was I thinking." The mere fact that they could act on a thought meant that they must have had a "belief" that allowed them or encouraged them to act out on that "thought." After the regretful action they then ask themselves. "What made me believe that I could do that or could of gotten away with that." The final part of this trilogy is the "emotions" and the question asked was "is it the thoughts or the beliefs that trigger a person to take an action or are most actions driven by "acting on feelings."

It was further explained that when a person acts out on emotions they are referred to as being "impulsive." The question of whether a person can be successful with their recovery if they are impulsive was asked and most of the group recognized that it would not be possible to stay clean and sober if they remained "impulsive."

Once the group under stood these concepts it was then presented that the only solution to the problem must incorporate a "Mind + Body "solution. At this point each of the "Motivational Emotions" were discussed to determine which ones were of strictly the "Mind" type and which ones were of the "Body" type, and which ones were a combination of both "Mind and Body."

It was emphasized that the ones that were a combination of both were the ones that would have the most power and influence. Otherwise the ones that were one or the other were too fragile to be trusted as long-term "Motivational Emotions" that would consistently remain an effective catalyst that would trigger on going right actions that would protect and provide for long term sobriety.

As each "Motivational Emotion" was discussed most were ruled out as not being able to address the "Mind" ("M") as well as the "Body" ("B") problem. The only "Motivational Emotions" that were a full solution (M+B) in the end were the only ones that fit the solution were "Fear" which is both a serious emotional or physical "Body" experience as well as "Mind." The other one was "Commitment" which entails both the "Mind and the Body." In other words, if you take the list of "Motivational Emotions" and ask the question regarding whether each one is strictly a change in what you do with your body, or whether each one is strictly an attitude in your mind; determines how they are labeled either as (M) for mind only or (B) for body only. If there is one that is a combination it is labeled as (M+B).

To clarify this the following examples will help: Determination is an attitude and therefore it is only a (M), commitment is a mind and body process and is therefore labeled (M+B), fear is in the mind and felt in the body therefore it is (M+B), desperation is really only a mental construct and therefore it is strictly a, (M) experience; dedication, defiance, love, hate, surrender, willingness, open mindedness, gratitude, loneliness, compassion, honesty, will power, spite and appreciation are only mental states or attitudes and can only be labeled (M). Compliance, discipline are strictly body (B), events in that the person forces their body to take certain actions that their mind would rather not do. Some people may believe that discipline is a mental thing but it is actually only seen in the actions that someone demonstrates. You cannot see mental discipline.

What this exercise demonstrates is that most of the forces that a person needs to stay motivated are located only in their mind (M) and that means that most of the driving forces inside a person to stay sober and take recovery actions; could vanish in a heartbeat! A person may get bad news or wake up on the wrong side of the bed and "just not feel any dedication, defiance, love, hate, surrender, willingness, open mindedness, gratitude, loneliness, compassion, honesty, will power, spite or appreciation. If these were the only "Motivational Emotions" then all the motivation washes away as the motivating feelings wash away.

Keep in mind that good and bad emotions could motivate and do motivate; but any emotion that is relied upon to create recovery actions is simply very fragile due to the reason it is just a feeling, sometimes a "dumb ass feeling" and sometimes a very "Nobel feeling." But either way they are just feelings and can vanish in a twinkling of an eye!

The only real protection and the only real solution is to embrace the "Motivational Emotions" that have the complete solution of (M+B) and there were only two. One was "Fear" and the other was "Commitment." If we were to use fear then it would only work for a short time due to the pain and suffering associated with using fear as a motivator. Fear becomes too much to bear and to escape the pain relapse is highly probable. You can just force yourself to do something due to fear for just so long, before it becomes intolerable! The reason for the huge failure of every other "Motivational Emotion" to protect a person's recovery lifestyle has to do with the fact that addiction is a mental disorder and since the mind is the cause for addiction, then the person must find a way to function "Out side of their mind."

THE FOLLOWING CHART DEMONSTRATES THE ABOVE EXERCISE

Sobriety/ Clean Time	Recovery Action Taken	Emotional Motivators	M	B	M+B
11 months 8 months 2 years 17 months 21 months 4 days 4 ½ years 88 days 6 months 7 ½ years	Physical exercise, traveling out of town regularly, being in jail, working the 12 step program, having a sponsor and sponsoring others, going to school, reading recovery literature spiritual material, attending church, being employed, having two or more jobs, time with family, being pregnant, attending 12 step meetings, hobbies, keeping a journal, calling a sponsor or other people in recovery, praying, reading the Bible, staying compliant with needed medications, meditation, yoga	Determination Commitment	M		M+B
		Fear Desperation	M		M+B
		Dedication Love	M M		
		Compliance Discipline		B B	
		Defiance Hate	M M		
		Surrender Willingness	M M		
		Open-mindedness Gratitude	M M		
		Loneliness Compassion	M M		
		Honesty Willpower	M M		
		Spite	M		

"Is it a disease or is it a choice?

If it is a Choice then it is all about having the ability to exercise personal power and choose between options!

If it is a Disease then it is about powerlessness and there is no power to choose!

> "As strange as the following concept sounds keep in mind that the "MIND" is made up of the trilogy of "Thoughts, Feelings and Beliefs" and therefore the disease lives in the mind. It lives in the Thoughts, Feelings and Beliefs!"

> "Unless a person can find a way to get "OUT OF THEIR MIND" they will not be able to stay clean or sober! Commitments solve this impossible challenge because, commitments have absolutely nothing to do with what a person "Thinks, Believes or Feels."

> "Therefore a commitment is the only force that you can use to protect yourself from your diseased "Thoughts, Beliefs and Feelings."

When "Commitment" is utilized, as the "Motivational Emotion" then there is a major positive result, due to the fact that when a person makes and lives by commitments this will always result in a constant and steady increase in self worth as well as self-esteem!

The following story will clarify the "Power of Commitment through the "Art of Accountability." When a person takes on the "coffee commitment" for a 12 step group, then it is of little importance of how they Think, Believe or Feel, for the commitment rules out these three mental states and they have no relevance in regards to whether someone is going to prepare the coffee or not.

The AA or NA group does not care a "rats ass" if that person "feels" sick or they don't "believe" anything bad will happen to them or the group simply due to not showing up to make the coffee. No! The group could not care less what the assigned coffee maker was "Thinking, Feeling or Believing;" all they expected was someone to be there to make the coffee as they had promised, or at least of had the common courtesy to have called some one else to come in their place. It should be further noted that just as when a person completes a commitment they always will experience an increase in their self-esteem; failing to fulfill a commitment will always result in lowering self-esteem.

"The Power of Commitment is found in the way it forces action regardless of the what a person "Thinks, Believes or Feels" and it is through this power that a person is not just able to do right, but to feel right!"

"Self-Defeating Attitudes and Behaviors"

Clients have asked and adamantly expressed "Do I have to go to those meetings the rest of my life?" "I don't need no sponsor?" "Will I ever be able to smoke "Pot" or drink again?" "I don't believe in this spirituality stuff?" "Why do I have to do the steps?" "I have more problems than substance abuse, I am depressed and anxious and I'm just not motivated to recover, what should I do?" "I just don't feel like stopping." "I can't stop the cravings?" "I don't want to give up my friends that drink and my partner drinks what should I do?"

"All questions always trigger thoughts, therefore the wrong questions trigger the wrong thoughts, which will always lead to unhealthy actions and disempowerment, which results in a progressive loss or decrease in self-esteem as well as self-worth!

"Conversely the right questions trigger the right thoughts, which will always lead to healthier actions and empowerment, which results in a progressive gain or increase in self-esteem as well as self-worth!"

Every day we're moving in one of two directions-either towards "Recovery" or towards "Relapse"-to determine which direction the following words will describe in detail as well as measure that direction. If a person is in "Recovery" then they are fully living in "Commitment" and the following words would accurately describe this state of mind. Dedicated, devoted, determined, desire, discipline, delighted and dependable.

If a person is moving in the direction of "Relapse" then they are living in just mere "Compliance" and the following words would accurately described that state of mind. Disgruntled, disgusted, dissatisfied, disillusioned, defiant, detached and despair. It is very important to be fully aware of the difference between "Compliance" and "Commitment." By learning to recognize the distinct differences between these attitudes will enable the addict or alcoholic to clearly see their daily recovery status. Depending on the amount of words that they can select out of the above mentioned lists will determine the recovery strength and will help measure how far away or how close they are to either "Relapse" or "Recovery."

The following diagram explains this concept:

DAILY MOTIVATOR		ATTITUDE		DAILY STATUS
COMMITMENT	=	Dedicated Devoted Determined Desire Discipline Delighted Dependable	=	RECOVERY
OR				
COMPLIANCE	=	Disgruntled Disgusted Dissatisfied Disillusioned Defiant Detached Despair	=	RELAPSE

Depending on the question or questions that a person asks themselves will always determine the way any particular incident or situation will be experienced as well as understood. Therefore the bad things that you believe that are happening to you may actually be good things. When things go badly you get dissatisfied and this provides for you an opportunity to search for, find and use effective coping skills.

"Daily living frequently provides for "Life-Changing" moments that occur in a microsecond but can permanently lead to both positive and negative changes in a person's destiny."

"The best example of one of these "Microsecond Moments" was the first time a person uses alcohol or a drug. From that simple act of ingesting a mood altering substance it triggered an instantaneous change in the way they will "Think," "Believe" and "Feel" for the rest of their lives!"

Therefore it is essential for an addict and alcoholic to be willing to engage in new behaviors and to be aware of opportunities that are presented through the suggestions and recommendations of other people.

"Just as the life of an addict or alcoholic was radically "Negatively" changed the instant they ingested a mood altering substance; then trying new recovery action or behaviors may provide an opportunity to seize a "Positive Microsecond Moment" that could instantaneously reverse the damage done from the "Negative Microsecond Moment" that led to the destruction of a healthier lifestyle!

State Dependent Learning

To better grasp how the mind becomes so totally wired in a matter of one heart beat moment; it is helpful to understand the phenomenon of "State Dependent Learning." By appreciating how "State Dependent Learning" leads to or even creates self-defeating as well as self-destructive behaviors, will enable the reader to fully recognize this potentially deadly negative force on a person's chance to have a lasting recovery.

The simplest way to define this phenomenon is to basically understand that when a very positive experience happens to a person, then there are associated environmental things that become attached to that experience. Some people referred to these phenomena as "Triggers" and an example of this would be, when a particular article of clothing or a specific song occurs it "Triggers" a desire to engage in the activity or behaviors that were associated to those related things.

The following story will clearly demonstrate this concept. It takes place on the back of an ocean cruise ship in which a husband and a wife were standing on the very back or stern of the ship and gazing out into the distance and observing the horizon, the wake of the ship as well as the sun setting. It was at that moment the husband reached up and began to search his upper shirt or breast pocket and his wife observed his fingers frantically searching that pocket.

When she inquired of her husband why his hand was searching his empty pocket, he became very puzzled and even somewhat alarmed. He could not explain his behavior nor at least for the moment stop his frantic search with his fingers through his empty breast pocket. All of a sudden his hand and fingers stopped moving and he blurted out "OH Shit!"

He turned to his wife and stated with a shocked affect "I am looking for a cigarette." His wife now had an even greater look of shock than the husband did, and she stated "Honey you haven't smoked in over 20 years-why do you want to start now!" He immediately expressed to her, "The last thing I want to do is smoke a cigarette but that's not stopping me from looking for one now!" They both stared at each other in deep confusion and great bewilderment regarding the conversation they were having due to his bizarre behaviors and gestures due to looking for a cigarette he did not-and I emphasize absolutely did not want to smoke!

The mystery of his bizarre behavior suddenly resolved itself when he recognized and told his wife, "You know I used to smoke on the back of the Destroyer when I was in the Navy, and many times at the end of the day when the sun was setting on the horizon I would smoke just peacefully watching the white wake behind the ship."

As you can observe from the story the power of "State Dependent Learning" is an awesome force to be reckoned with or even control. In the case of an addict or an alcoholic virtually anything that has become associated to their use of drugs or alcohol may have become a "State Dependent Learning" connected experience, event or thing. This means that in a heart beat moment or a "Microsecond Moment" the actions that a person is making or intends to make could be radically and instantaneously changed.

It is due to "State Dependent Learning" that many recovering addicts and alcoholics can and will lose their recovery due to being unprepared for how to manage this probable and potential threat to recovery in their lives. Throughout this book I have expressed the need for the addict or alcoholic to learn to teach themselves to be stronger and more powerful than their asinine stupid feelings that are the cause of decisions that lead to deep despair, disgust, disillusionment, bafflement and bewilderment.

It is through and only through preparing for that moment, and to absolutely know exactly how to respond to that overwhelmingly instinctual like force. It will be at that precise moment that all the past effort and training to use the "Power to Resist the Resistance" will provide the force and strength to overcome those or any "Self Defeating Feelings, Attitudes or Behaviors!"

Self-Defeating Feelings, Attitudes or Behaviors

In exploring common self-defeating attitudes and behaviors the following discussion examined several. The issue of "Meeting the expectations of others while sacrificing one's own needs and desires" was studied in some depth. One client shared that he went to the Naval Academy due to his family's expectations.

When he really did not want to continue with his studies, and he felt that he was forced by his family to stay in school and complete is studies, he turned to drugs to sabotage his education and dropped out. The client expressed that all his life he did what his family wanted, and this eventually led to strong resentments and drug use to deal with those feelings. The client expressed that he now wants to begin to set some boundaries and stop living the life his family desires for him, and design the life he wants!

The story of an attorney was told who was about the age of 39 who had a great life. He had the dream car, the perfect family, the most beautiful house and an incredibly successful practice. His life was absolutely the manifestation of the "American Dream." At least that is how others viewed it, but he was very unfulfilled and even depressed because he never wanted to be an attorney.

He loved building things and always wanted to go into the trades and be a carpenter. He then realized he had lived half his life, and it was the life that his family wanted him to live, but not the one he would have chosen for himself. If he did not feel such strong obligations to live up to the standards and expectations of his father, he would have been living an entirely different life and would have had a completely different destiny.

> "The danger of surrendering your dreams and hopes for yourself is that you then live another person's life and not your own. For an alcoholic or an addict this can lead to a deep state of despair or even resentment that triggers the use of chemicals, to cope with the horrible feelings of having failed to fulfill their own destiny or dreams."

Several other clients shared how they had been trying to live up to the expectations of others. When questioned why or how they have allowed this to happen and what stopped them from pursuing their own dreams and needs? The response was "I did not want to get into a confrontation" or "I did not want to disappoint or hurt them."

> "The discussion continued regarding how tragic it is to never have lived the life that you wanted due to these fears. It was emphasized that while the motivation to live up to others expectations is designed to reduce conflict and disappointment; in reality it causes much turmoil and despair in the person making the sacrifice."

If a person is too fearful to set boundaries due to it may disturb others, this will usually lead, to disregarding their own beliefs and values. This neglect is experienced as a lowered sense of personal worth and this invites the use of drugs and alcohol.

Another self defeating issue was explored in terms of "Why is it that when great or good things happen in life the addict or alcoholic, finds or believes that it is never satisfying enough, and they want to artificially induce an even more intense and greater feeling?" The question is why "is GOOD not GOOD enough"

To illustrate this the following example was given: Why is it that something as wondrous and fantastic and extraordinary as having a son or daughter, is not in itself absolutely and totally the best most powerful peak emotional experience that a person can have? When a mother or father who have just had a child needs to drink or do drugs to "celebrate," there is something horribly wrong with that person in their ability to recognize this is the ultimate of all emotional experiences. Instead they believe that it would be even better to enhance this natural peak experience even more.

What is terribly wrong with a person, when the most powerful emotional experience that could be possibly experienced "just is not good enough?" One of the factors that may contribute to this twisted perception that blinds so many people to recognizing and enjoying the most special moments in life, without having to resort to substances, may be partially caused by their early use of drugs or alcohol.

Young adults have to learn the coping methods and skills they will need for the rest of their lives, and if they discover the fact that substance use and abuse can be used as a means of coping, then they will fail to develop the ability to deal with life issues without a chemical filter. It is this tendency to have to use chemicals to deal with the feelings that occur when challenges need to be met that also cheats the person from recognizing all the good feelings that happen when the person is successful. Since they have learned to use chemicals to enhance good feelings as well as use substances to deal with the bad feelings, they then begin to use chemicals when they are experiencing any feelings. Whether it is a good or a bad feeling the use of substances becomes a normal part of the way they have to process these or almost any emotions.

"To further understand this tendency to rely on a chemical filter when experiencing emotions it is helpful to understand that, "There is nothing wrong with the use of drugs and alcohol."

"As this may sound like the ravings of a madman let me take a moment to explain this brash and outlandish sounding statement? Just for a moment clear your mind of any prejudice or negative past memories regarding drugs and alcohol."

Now that I have your attention, listen to the following facts: When a person puts a mood altering drug or substance into their body they feel a positive mental or emotional state almost 100% of the time. Nobody takes drugs or drinks alcohol because they hope it will ruin their day or cause incredible pain. No in contrast they take substances because they are counting on it creating a very desirable emotional and mental state. Despite the fact that their use may be accompanied by severe consequences they are counting on the fact that they will feel "better or even great" as a direct result of ingesting the chemicals.

"No one can argue with the fact that if something is put in the body and it can create a feeling state that is more pleasurable and more powerful in a positive way than any previous actions or things could produce; then the person can easily rationalize or even justify the continued use of the substance."

"It is also helpful to realize, "No one has ever picked up drugs and or alcohol to feel bad- and in fact the use of a substance initially is always almost 100% of the time a very positive experience."

"Now you may want to argue with this, but first consider the fact that even in the deepest depths of agonizing withdrawal, the addict absolutely can rely and count on the fact that getting a fix will absolutely make them feel better, in fact much better! In fact it is an absolute guarantee!"

Why is it that a person has the inability to connect the consequences of use with the pleasure of the use, so that they can reach a point and acknowledge that "My continued use of this substance has become too costly and I need to stop?"

It was explained that the mind is split into two parts and many times one part cannot effectively communicate or influence the other part. Now if one part completely understands and acknowledges the problems and consequences of using substances, but it cannot effectively convey this to the other part, then this breakdown results in the perception that "There is nothing wrong with the use of substances."

Now the other part of the brain interprets the experience of using drugs and alcohol as exceptionally positive and pleasant and therefore interprets the use of substances as being that, "There is nothing wrong with the use of substances." This breakdown of communication between the two halves of the mind results in the inability to stop or even want to stop even when extreme suffering accompanies the use of substances.

"When an addict or alcoholic is in the pain of withdrawal they almost instinctively know that ingesting chemicals will reduce or even eliminate the discomfort. It is necessary to recognize that the addict or alcoholic is not taking substances to feel good or to celebrate, they are using substances to JUST feel normal or at least to reduce pain."

"Anything that reduces discomfort and pain will be perceived as very valuable and desirable even though it is the very thing that is causing the suffering."

"Since it takes away the pain, then it can never clearly be seen as something bad, or even something that should be avoided. Instead it is seen as something to defend and protect."

Turning Desire into Disgust

Another group focused on feelings and why we allow them to dominate what we do. The discussion started by simply asking this question. "Why do we allow feelings or what is it about feelings that undermine recovery efforts." There were many responses from "It just is that way" to "I can't control my feelings and emotions and that is why I use drugs." The tendency for some addicts to glorify their past addictive exploits was brought into question by two of the group's members who emphatically stated "I want nothing to do with drinking or drugs. At one time I did but no more." They expressed that they attend 12 step meetings and no one including themselves talk about drug use in any kind of favorable light. Since they were so passionate about their disgust for drinking or drug use; they were challenged to step back and identify the specific thoughts and physiology that is associated to their disgust with substances.

The clients were instructed to search for the individual ways in which the perception of disgust is being formed and created. They were asked to do this so they would have a technique that they could use at any time to trigger this "disgusted state" as a method to deal with uninvited thoughts or feelings regarding returning to drug or alcohol use or glorifying their past using history.

"The clients struggled with identifying the specific ways that were causing the disgusted feelings. It was strongly emphasized that they need to become more aware of the fact that if they are feeling disgusted, then that feeling is specifically related to clearly identifiable behaviors such as posture, breathing and focus. It was pointed out to them that each of them spoke in a strong articulate manner regarding how they loath substances and at the same time they made a facial expression that clearly connoted that of disgust and they spoke negatively about the substance use and the harm it has done to them."

When this formula is used by these two clients it will automatically trigger substance use disgust. In this manner each client can become more empowered to manage their risks by simply knowing how to consciously respond to any "cravings and or unwanted interests or desires to use alcohol or drugs."

Resistance in Action—Ability to Force Yourself

Discussed a "Laughter Therapy Group" and demonstrated all the strange and bizarre forms and types of laughing that you would hear in that group. Emphasized to them that by laughing they instantaneously change their mood and in fact the easiest way to change a feeling or mood is to just Force Yourself to move any muscle in the face and demonstrated that even a small tiny change in the distance you raise your head immediately changes the way you feel and even think. Once again at the end of the group I challenged someone to do something they did not want to do but would be good for their recovery.

When other group members who had not shared refused to verbalize anything I confronted them and challenged them to simply say their name, since they obviously did not want to share and they should share, and in this way they could take on the challenge to share when they don't want to speak. Talking when you don't want to talk creates a powerful Paradox!

Slowly some of them did speak up and say their name and when they did, I prompted the entire group to loudly applaud them. Each one was asked after the applause how they felt with getting all the cheering, and they stated it felt good. Utilizing this experience reminded the group that many times people go to AA or NA and they are too shy or afraid to share and just sit, and listen and cheat themselves, because they don't FORCE themselves to interact which would result in experiencing a wonderful recognition like we just gave to these few clients. They now realize the true "Power of Paradox" through the "Art of Resistance in Action!"

Reasoning over Emotions or R/ E = Sanity & E/R = Insanity

A client asked "Convince me that something terrible will happen if I just smoke a joint at some point in the future." The client also asked "What is wrong with picking up women who drink at a bar and act hot and inviting." Another client asked "What's wrong with going to the Hookah Bar?" "What about smoking cigars when you use to make them into Blunts?" Also one client related that she went to the dentist and refused any pain medications after having a tooth extracted.

It was discussed how the formula of R/E which stands for "Reasoning" over "Emotions" can be quickly inverted when a person uses a mood altering substance. It does not matter whether a dealer or bartender or doctor gives the substance the impact to the brain is the same. The reversal occurs due to the substance is filtered through the emotional state and causes the person to become excited when emotions rise to a position of high influence and control over our behavior, and the "Reasoning Center" is pushed below the "Emotions" and the inverted formula looks like E/R so what has happened is that the original formula of R/E which represents "sound rational thought is compromised and "Emotional Logic" takes over and "Emotional Logic" has been described as a state of thinking and feeling in which the belief and emotion gives the direction that "What feels Good is Good and more is even better!" The way this can be illustrated is as follows: R/E +(drug) = E/R. E/R is the representation for "Emotional Logic."

Once again it needs to be emphasized that "Just because something feels Good does not necessarily mean it is Good! Emotional Logic is the epitome of warped, twisted and "Peculiar Perceptions." It is "Emotional Logic" that is the cause of an addict or alcoholic relapsing because through it they "Make sense out of something that could never make sense" and that is returning or continuing to use mind altering substances, just because drugs and alcohol makes them "Feel Good!"

To assist the client in understanding the danger of drinking beer when a person has a problem with Heroin or the danger of a Cocaine addict smoking Pot or having a drink of alcohol is that there is a tendency to become disappointed and dissatisfied, in the feeling that the lesser harmful drug creates, and this use of a substitute only "teases" the person.

> "The lesser drug creates longing or need for a level of "high" that they desire and have expectations to experience. So not only does the initial use of the substance reverse their logic it also mechanically creates a sense of disappointment. It is this feeling of being let down coupled with the "rational thoughts" being inverted to "Emotional Logic" triggers the need to ramp up the experience by searching for a more intense and rewarding "high."

The issue of the need to maintain a "Zero" baseline as the best protection from relapse and to remain absolutely free on a daily basis from any potentially dangerous mood altering substance(s) was strongly emphasized. The concept of "Long Term Loss of Control" was explored and the need for caution; since a relapse or any return to drug abuse may lead back to drug dependency and there is always the danger that once the person has returned to drug use or abuse, it may be years or even possibly decades before they are forced to stop or even try to stop.

> "In one unguarded moment the addict or alcoholic may create severe consequences that may totally ROB them of many years of their lives. That unguarded moment could result in CAUSING them a LIFETIME of suffering legal, family, job and economic as well as physical problems and deterioration."

It was strongly emphasized that there is great danger in considering the use of a lesser harmful substance and there is even greater danger in believing that a medication prescribed by a physician is safe such as pain medications or certain antianxiety medications.

The following myth will demonstrate the danger of failing to change "Self Defeating Feelings, Attitudes and Behaviors!"

To illustrate this it can be represented by "RIP Van Winkle" who was the mythical character who went out to the woods one day and fell asleep and did not wake up for twenty years and some say he went to sleep for a hundred years. Either way it speaks reams of truth that...

> "If you take a nap during your recovery it may be literally many years before you get a chance to return to recovery and for some they never will get the chance again. It is too critical to ever let up on the necessary momentum that enables long lasting recovery."

> "Also the name "RIP" is an acronym for "REST IN PEACE" which happens to many people due to complacency and believing that they can rest and take a nap or sabbatical from their daily recovery efforts."

The issue of "Picking up women at bars who drink and are hot and inviting" was discussed in the context of "Is spirituality needed for a person to recover and if it is, then how does taking advantage of impaired women strengthen recovery or does that attitude and behavior detract from building a spiritual foundation?" The AA book relates a story of a man who relapsed due to he "Failed to enlarge his spiritual experience." The group expressed various views including one young lady who strongly confronted the client with the idea that "No one should just consider women as a sperm receptacle."

Doing things you don't want to do
—but are good for recovery.

I stated to the group "Everything that you need to do for recovery you will not want to do." Some of the clients argued strongly that there are many things they want to do, and they know it is good for their recovery. Such as prayer and meditation, taking walks, calling on the phone, doing assignments, as well as journaling, doing the workbook exercises, going to the gym, eating healthy, dancing or attending certain groups and meetings.

> "Since the clients were able to strongly assert themselves, in regards to doing all the positive things that they do, and want to do, to enhance recovery; they were challenged to express how they know, or would know, if the things they do, are really that beneficial and will protect them from risk. There are many things, that clients do, that they want to do, that are good for their recovery; but the real test and the greatest strength for recovery occurs when they paradoxically understand the significant benefit; that is received from the process of doing the things they don't want to do; but are good for their recovery."

Attributes vs. Conditions or Choices—Being
the Problem vs. Having a Problem

In another therapy session one of the clients expressed that "I am an introvert and I could never talk to people and I am just a loner." I confronted that person and helped them understand strongly, that no person should limit their power by believing in personal limitations, and emphasized that making a statement such as "I am an introvert" and "I am a loner" creates the belief that "It is what I am" rather than "It is a condition that I have."

The difference between these two phrases is extremely huge; in that the first statement indicates an attribute and attributes can never be changed because they are unchangeable characteristics of a person. We must know the difference between characteristics, behaviors and attributes. Hair color and eye color and especially height and weight are all attributes and cannot be easily or automatically changed in an instant; but despite popular beliefs and myths anybody can change in an instant what they believe or the way they behave.

To clarify these concepts just simply observe the following: If a 6' tall angry Chinese man came in the office and received treatment for his anger and left without anger; he would still be Chinese and 6' tall—his anger was not an attribute and was resolved or removed; but his height and race are attributes. He came in with them and he is leaving with them.

When a person identifies himself or herself as the "problem" rather than having the "problem" they immediately limit their power and resources to make an immediate change or adjustment. They fall victim to the myth that their condition is an attribute and due to that they believe "It will take a long time to make changes." In reality any change can be done instantly, unless it is an attribute.

No addict or alcoholic should ever identify himself or herself as an addict or alcoholic; as in when we state, "Hi I am Jerry and I am an alcoholic." The reason for the need to change this is three fold.

First, the admission of identifying myself as the problem makes me begin to believe it is an attribute instead of a condition and it also does nothing to build self-esteem or self worth.

Second, by identifying myself as the problem significantly reduces my ability to view myself in a more empowering manner.

Third, every human being on earth should never identify himself or herself as the condition that they have. In other words you are more than the condition that you have; you are a million other possibilities and probabilities.

If all you constantly do is focus on "I am an addict or I am an alcoholic" this will reduce your options to search for and find a fabulous and passionate life. Even though you believe that you must state, "I am an alcoholic" in AA meetings; the preamble of the AA program clearly states, "The only requirement for membership is "a desire to stop drinking;" which means you are NOT required to admit you are an alcoholic.

It is my contention that no one should have to admit they are an alcoholic or an addict within the first several months of attending AA or NA meetings. There is a time when to admit this, becomes empowering, in that a person carries this designation, in the same way a soldier proudly wears their campaign badges; but early on this admission can create even greater despair as well as a sense of helplessness and hopelessness that could undermine any chances for recovery.

Even if they feel compelled or even comfortable in the AA or NA meeting to state "I am….." Then outside of the meetings they should refer to themselves as "I am … and I am a miracle" or "I am … and I am a college graduate" even if you don't even have your GED at this time. Developing strong positive compelling visions of a spectacular successful future is what drives success.

Unfortunately most addicts and alcoholics take the weakened position of "Just holding back" or "Holding on" instead of pushing forward and leaving addiction behind them. Life is about growth and any one who just tries to hold the line will always fall backwards. They must be challenging themselves and through that vision of future change and strength they will be pulled forward instead of trying to hold back.

> "I really want to emphasize this universal truth, and that no one should ever express or have beliefs that limit them. No one is an introvert, no one is a loner, no one is an addict and no one is an alcoholic. They are just behaviors or conditions acquired or learned and they absolutely are not attributes."

Hopefully you are still reading because there is more to the story. What I am stating here is not that there is no such thing as an addict or alcoholic; and I am not denying these are serious life threatening conditions, as Cancer and Diabetes are very serious conditions.

> "But the person is not the disease. They have the condition but they are not the condition that they have; they are so much more and should not limit themselves to this designation."

While it sort of flows off the tongue to refer to oneself who has a Diabetic condition as a "Diabetic" or for a person who has an addictive condition to refer to themselves as an "addict" or "alcoholic;" there is a clear distinction in these terms.

> "While the "Diabetic" terminology refers to a specific problem with processing sugar; the designation of being an "Addict" or being an "Alcoholic" does not stop at the point that this individual has a specific problem with the way they process certain substances. It goes far deeper

than having a serious medical or physical problem as does the "Diabetic;" it smacks of deep spiritual and personality deficiency and flaws as well as significant stigma."

It is this designation that degrades and discourages most addicts and alcoholics from staying in and benefiting from a Twelve Step program; and it is believed by this writer, that this is the main reason AA and NA have had such minimum impact on substance dependency.

After all, it has been over 75 years, and statistics inform us there are 18 million alcoholics and 5 million people addicted to other substances and the total membership in both AA and NA are just over two million; despite the fact that over 700 thousand people are in some form of treatment on any given day and they hear the strong suggestion or mandate to attend AA and or NA.

"Despite all this exposure the great majority of substance abusers have not found answers in these programs. It is only hoped that they have found other solutions and that most are not actively using and dying in madness and leaving the legacy of massive suffering and agony for their families and loved ones to continue to endure. Once again my purpose of this book is to:

"Free the substance abuser from their madness and end the needless suffering of their families and loved ones."

"Why Best Efforts Fail?"

In the previous section of this chapter I referred to the breakdown of communication between the two halves of the mind. This bizarre mental disconnect was described in the book Alcoholics Anonymous as "a strange mental blank spot."

This is related to the fact that substance use almost always produces a positive and pleasant feeling. The "strange mental blank spot" is related to the failure to recognize the fiction or nonsense to believe that it is safe and there are no consequences. The following story will fully demonstrate the really nasty nature of this split or outright "madness."

Unlike the rest of the references and stories of addicts and alcoholics told through out this book the following is in regards to a "shopaholic." This particular gentleman really was obsessed and enjoyed buying and trading electronics including computers and stereos and the various components and accessories that are utilized to enhance the pleasure and use of these products. His obsession with "Having to buy and own every new gadget and accessory caused him to experience severe financial trouble."

His problem was severe enough for him to seek professional help with a counselor with some expertise in this area. The counselor instructed him to get rid of all but one of his credit cards. The card he was left with, was suppose to be for "emergencies" only. To assure that the card would only be used for emergencies the counselor had the shopaholic take red ribbon and wrap the card completely and then put tape over the ribbon. In this way it would take much effort to cut the tape and unwrap the ribbon that was protecting the card from being damaged by the tape.

A few days latter he walked into a Best Buy store and became completely engrossed in the new technologies and after a long conversation with the sales woman, he knew that he had to have this latest product to improve the performance of his already fully blown out sound system.

As he was closing the deal he took the card out of this wallet and despite the fact that it had red ribbon and tape on it, he did not connect that the card was for emergencies only. He had no memory at that moment that the ribbon was there as a failsafe to remind him and stop him from frivolous spending! The "Madness" was upon him and despite all the clues that he was not suppose to be engaging in this transaction he completed it any way.

It should be noted that the sales woman did look a little perplexed over the card as he unwrapped it and she inquired, "Is that card any good, why do you have it wrapped in ribbon." At which point he assured her the card was good and asked her for a knife or scissors to cut the tape and continued to reassure her the card was valid and closed the deal. Once the process of completing the sale was over, he was more bewildered than he had ever been in his life, over how he failed to manage his shopaholic condition.

"The explanation for this is found in the way that certain minds have a tendency to have a disconnect, so that when a person is trying to teach themselves how to manage a condition like addiction, there is "that strange mental blank spot" or "Peculiar Perception" or "Emotional Logic" that sabotages the effort or determination; because there is another part of the mind, that just does not register those efforts."

"In fact when there are strong emotions such as desire and excitement it is this part of the mind that responds; since the positive thoughts have less emotional impact and therefore less influence in controlling the decision-making processes."

Regarding the concept of "Can you force yourself to like something that you do not like," and contrasting it with the concept that it is easier to "Do something that you need to do but don't want to do than to force yourself to like something that you dislike." The idea that relapse is caused by feelings and not something that is carefully planned or thought out was explored. The following example was presented:

Does a person who is actively injecting drugs, just one day wakes up in the morning and decides that, "You know I am just NOT going to do Heroin today; instead I am going to the beach and just SKIP drugs today." In the same context that a recovering person does not wake up and state "My life is going so good I think I will just do drugs and maybe I will even be arrested and put in jail by tonight; boy today is going to be great."

"No what happens to people is that "a stupid feeling gets in the way" an asinine sensation that they cannot resist and completely changes everything that the person is doing for their recovery. They respond to the ridiculous self defeating feeling and verbalize "I don't feel like going to a meeting" or "I don't feel like calling my sponsor" or "I don't feel I need to go to a halfway house" or "I don't feel it is a problem to sell drugs or being around my friend and family that drink and do drugs."

"The best defense against this danger is to learn to resist acting on feelings and to practice right behaviors and actions regardless of whether you want to or not or whether you feel like it or not."

"Every time a person allows their feelings to dictate an action; whether it is a good action or a bad action, they are STILL setting themselves up for acting impulsive and this tendency is disastrous and always leads to relapse.

Once again it cannot be over emphasized that each person is capable of changing their states or those stupid asinine sensations or feeling by just simply moving their body physically and staying alert to what they focus on. By just changing the depth and rhythm of breathing will shift a mood or state.

By viewing an actual photo in your hand or just creating a mental image in your mind of your child or loved one will immediately change the focus on wanting to get high or drink. Staring at that picture enables you to speak to the loved ones and this also will shift that asinine self-defeating behavior, before you do something that you will absolutely deeply regret, and feel that disgust probably within minutes of ingesting alcohol or drugs.

"It was strongly emphasized that since an addict is very selfish and self-centered, they need to focus on caring and having concern for others, and this new focus will take them out of themselves."

"The change in focus provides protection, by enabling them to be driven by concepts, such as, placing other people's needs ahead of their own wants and desires."

"It is by having this new purpose and vision that will provide significant protection against relapse behaviors."

A person related and indicated that "I can't do this or I have never done this" and their choice of words was carefully examined and the theme of "language" was explored. The need to stay aware and alert to disempowering words was emphasized to this person. The words that people use actually creates the feelings as well as the reality that they live in. When a person says disempowering things about themselves; then they limit their ability to access personal and other resources, that they need and could use to change their circumstances. If they state they are powerless, then they are powerless; that is why in an early chapter I went into great depth to explain the difference between admitting being powerless and the need to understand the constructive force of "Practicing Powerlessness" not just admitting it but practicing it enables the person to gain power over what they previously were powerless over.

The discussion went into detail regarding the fact that when a person takes the right actions it increase their sense of self-esteem, and conversely if a person continues to get away with low standards and bad behaviors will lower their self-esteem. One client reflected that when he gets away with stuff it increases his self esteem in that his EGO gets a boost "Yea I got away with it." At this point discussed the nature of people who have "antisocial traits" in that they cannot learn from their past mistakes and they also do not want to change themselves. They just want others to leave them alone, and or do what they say and want.

Emphasized the danger of being diagnosed with "antisocial traits" and how this person cannot learn from their past mistakes. Reflected to the group that this designation also fully applies to the clients in the group. Despite all the past problems and suffering they have repeatedly exercised the same bad judgment and behaviors especially in regards to addiction.

It was emphasized that addiction is not the condition or the disease; but it is the symptom of the disease which really is chronic mental illness. It was further illustrated that the degree or severity of the mental illness is reflected in the addicts or alcoholics behavior. A parallel disease such as Diabetes was presented to demonstrate that even though a person may manage this condition carefully and live a very healthy lifestyle it does not cure them of the Diabetic condition. In the same manner an alcoholic or addict are never cured and they must monitor and manage their behaviors and attitudes to insure long lasting recovery. The issue of inquiring from the group of how many of the clients have done the proverbial 90/90 only two clients indicated they had done this and both admitted that at the end of the 90 days they stopped attending meeting regularly and both relapsed within three weeks. It does seem like some people cannot learn from their past mistakes!

The concept of how people in recovery build false self-confidence and how this false self-confidence is what erodes away their previous efforts for recovery was investigated. It was explained that when a person feels confident, they are more inclined to stop taking the necessary actions. The very things they were doing, to do better, and feel better, were abandoned once they felt that things were improving for them. They then stopped practicing these behaviors, and in a short time they regressed significantly enough to fail.

It was explained that as soon as a person starts to change and dictate how they believe they should work a recovery program it is at that time they give themselves permission to drop more and more of the recovery actions and activities. As soon as they drop one thing it becomes that much easier to drop another thing until they drop everything.

"It was emphasized further that the only protection from allowing this false confidence to dictate recovery behaviors is to make and maintain commitments and to never reduce any of the momentum that you have developed in taking actions; unless you first discuss it with someone else, like a counselor or your sponsor and they agree that it is time for a change."

It should be noted that one young lady expressed that she intends to do the 90/90 but she is going to take every Saturday off due to "I need to have quiet time and be by myself and not feel all this pressure to perform." Confronted her that she is lying to herself and even though she wants private time she cannot claim she has done or is doing the 90/90 because that would be a boldface lie.

Expressed to her that she can do it her way but she has to describe it as "I go to meeting six days a week but I take Saturdays off. Another client confronted her and stated, "You could go to meetings seven days a week; it is not that much of a burden and it is not going to interfere with anything that you are doing."

Emphasized to the client that when in active addiction she did not take time off and in active recovery she needs to maintain daily momentum.

"Sex, Drugs, Rock and Roll"

Reasons that one night stands are dangerous and destructive to chances for recovery!

"Sexual Behavior is a problem due to the fact that if it is just PURE SEX without any emotional component attached, then the following occurs: You have to be detached, distant, cold, uncaring, a user and an abuser of others, as well as manipulative, have a business like attitude, remain unemotional, insensitive, selfish, self centered, indifferent disconnected, and completely detached."

Now if you are a person who believes that developing a Spiritual foundation is necessary for recovery; then does engaging in pure sexual lust for no other purpose but to experience Organism, build or destroy Spirituality? Are these the emotional states necessary for the development of Spirituality?

Even If you are not the predatorily motivated type as defined as:

"Being greedily destructive; relating to predators; and ruthlessly aggressive."

In other words, a person who does not give a rat's ass about any human being. You may in fact believe that you are caring and concerned and "In Love" and you only want the best for the person that you "ARE" pursuing. That you may actually "BELIEVE" that you are not the type of person that would just simply "USE" another person like a condom and "THROW" them away when you are through with them. If you think that you are a caring and concerned person in regards to your romantic infatuation with another person then you better read with a very open mind the following statement and then definitely pay attention to the short vignettes thereafter!

"Since most addicts or alcoholics are "childish, self centered, grandiose, oversensitive, emotionally immature and highly critical. Then it follows that these are obviously not the traits that are the foundation for a fruitful constructive and productive happy relationship."

"The dangers of forming relationships in early recovery are a topic that frequently appears. One of the female group members, wanted information presented in a very graphic manner so that she hoped she would have a better chance to internalize the information since hooking up with guys was a steady and serious problem for her."

"She expressed the need for help and hoped a graphic understanding of these dangers would significantly improve her chances to stay out of relationships, and to stay focused on her recovery."

The question was asked, "How does the AA or NA programs respond in regards to this matter of relationships in early recovery." One of the group members stated that he had heard numerous times that, "Relationships should be avoided in the first year." In regards to this admonition to avoid these interactions the following question was asked. "Is there any danger and or what is dangerous regarding these relationships." One of the clients expressed that if you are dishonest or deceitful with the person, that behavior could be a threat to your recovery." Another client asked "What is wrong with two informed consenting adults doing it." The group was asked, "Is the subject on having a relationship or just having sex?"

It was pointed out that in AA's early days they confronted this issue regarding sex in the AA book on page 69.

(You have to realize that suggestions regarding sexual behavior starting on page 69, definitely proves the author had a twisted sense of humor, since he put the only sexual comments in the AA book, on page 69.)

Page 69 states clearly that first of all

"We do not want to be the arbiter of anyone's sex conduct-everyone has sex problems and we would hardly be human if we didn't."

It should be noted just a few paragraphs latter it expresses the opinion

"If we are not sorry and our conduct continues to hurt others we are quite sure to drink. We are not theorizing. These are facts out of our experience."

In the next paragraph they warn us that if we cannot control our selves,

"If sex is very troublesome, we throw ourselves the harder into helping others. We think of their needs and work for them. This takes us out of ourselves. It quiets the impervious urge, went to yield would mean heartache." (End of quote)

"The discussion regarding sexual behavior then focused on attitudes, beliefs, experiences and ideas of the various ways that a person could be hurt and how this could trigger the guilty party into relapsing. Some of the clients expressed that when two people are in a relationship very early in their recovery, there is a high probability one is going to rapidly outgrow the other in those first few months and this could be experienced as a devastating blow that could cause relapse."

Recognizing that if in the first year of recovery a person does not actually start to change their feelings towards whom they are attracted to, then that would be a sign of an absolute failure to grow.

"Therefore the natural evolution is that one of the two people in the early relationship would change and have no further interest in their partner. If they have been actively involved with the recovery program, their tastes, views and interests will drastically change, causing them to become incompatible with the other person."

"In addition for the natural tendency for one person to outgrow the other person, there is an additional danger, and that is frequently in early recovery it is highly probable that one of the people in the relationship will relapse, and this may cause their partner to join them in that relapse."

To drive home the point that engaging in relationships with peers, whether in a treatment center or even in an AA or NA meeting is inappropriate at the least and at the most down right dangerous to one or both of the people; it was dramatized that being in a relationship with someone with less than a year of clean time or sobriety was no different than having sex with your brother or sister.

"It was strongly emphasized that anyone in their first year of recovery needs to accept and recognize that they or another person with this short amount of recovery time, need to view themselves as family members."

"Every man and woman who first begins their recovery needs to maintain a very strong focus on recovery, and an equally strong focus of finding out who they are, what their values are, and what they are going to value more, now that they have stopped the use of substances."

"It was emphasized strongly that in the first year of recovery each man and woman has to respect each other and view each other as siblings as brother and or sister and when a brother or sister have sex together it is called –"incest." Incest is not good for families and it is certainly not good for AA or NA members or for their chances for a lasting recovery."

To clarify these ideas it was presented that each person must understand

and accept that the risk of developing confused priorities could lead to death, not just relapse. Due to the very real danger of relapse or even death. It was expressed strongly that any person who develops a close caring and even loving relationship with another person in early recovery, needs to cease and desist any and all further contact with that person. Failure to be willing to sacrifice having a relationship with the person indicates that there is total selfishness and the person is only interested in using the other person for their personal emotional and physical pleasure.

The need to recognize the danger of falling in love or falling into lust and how these runaway emotions could threaten a person's sobriety and even their life was emphatically stated over and over. The goal of this presentation was to break the sense of complacency that "casual sex" or even relationships between peers in recovery is not only reprehensible; but too many times someone pays a terrible price, because one or both of them are not aware of their priorities.

> "If a person really cares for another person then they should care more about the welfare of that person, and be willing to accept that by being involved with that person they are potentially going to do them great harm."

> "It is just a cold hard fact that two people in recovery early on do not have the maturity, the emotional strength, or the capacity to deal with the rollercoaster of emotions that will erupt during the times of their interactions and this could trigger a relapse."

> "Since they know only one way of how to cope with the confusion and frustration that absolutely will occur anytime people are in or form intimate relationships."

Since one of the group members asked for this to be a "graphic" presentation the following description was expressed in vivid and great detail. If you still don't understand the magnitude of danger and even if you do understand that there is great danger to both people, then the following may help to shatter the almost hypnotic trance that people fall into when they become deeply attracted to each other.

When people in early recovery (defined as the first 12 months) hook up and get together, they need to view this behavior on the same level as when kissing or having sex with their partner, to additionally see it as if they were really involved with their sister or brother. To clearly visualize that they are

437

actually "sticking their wet tongue into their brothers or sisters ear and then licking their cheek as they move their tongue deep into their sisters mouth and she sucks hard on her brothers tongue and then picture the brother and sister naked together having unrestrained hot wet sex.

"As disturbing an image as this may be there is no difference if the people in early recovery do this because it is harmful at the very least, since it is a major distraction from working a recovery program, or spending time with peers doing recovery things, or working with your sponsor and at the very most could cause relapse and death for one or both."

"If someone cares about someone in early recovery and they have strong feelings towards them, then they should cease and desist any further involvement. Failure to do this places them in the same role as that of a child molester who takes advantage of a mentally ill child! For a child is too weak to resist their own passionate emotional desires and therefore that child needs to be protected not exploited."

In the years I have been a counselor I have seen numerous couples die or kill themselves! One young lady when dropped by her rehab romance gentleman after two months, went home to her mothers house and shot herself in the upstairs bathroom due to rejection, despair and depression over the loss.

In another rehab romance the young lady came home to their apartment to find him dead with a needle sticking out of his arm. She then promptly followed him, but fortunately did not die from the overdose.

Still another romance that was developed in the fertile rooms of NA that led to both relapsing, since one could not stand to be without the other, and their undying love of less than three months led to a double suicide at the side of the road with the help of Heroin and a garden hose from the exhaust to the closed windows.

"They committed suicide after neither his nor her parents would help any more and there was no insurance and no resources and they were too proud to go to a free or county program, even when they had the offer."

"They wanted everything or they wanted nothing and they settled for death as their everything."

In still another case of the warm fuzzes the man could not take it when his lover left and he jumped in front of a police car committing "death by cop car!"

Another beautiful and I mean beautiful young lady (actually a professional model) hooked up and let a man new to recovery move in with her and she bought him things and took care of him and when he went back on "Crack" and when she tried to refuse to buy him any more; he went outside and brought in a concrete cement block-not a small brick-but a large grey concrete block and proceeded to cave her face in, and then he took her money for more "Crack." He was arrested and fortunately for him she lived but unfortunately for her, due to what he had done she will never model again or ever look the same!

Hopefully this information was as graphic as requested and may have a useful impact in alerting people to be caring and cautious and be willing to end a relationship before it begins and be mature enough to sacrifice having the relationship for the benefit and safety of the person they re attracted to or even have come to believe they actually have fallen in love with..

"My final admonition in regards to early relationships is to strongly and emphatically state, "Anyone who has sex with someone in their first year of recovery is a LOW LIFE SLIMY PREDATOR who cares nothing for the person and is only interested in using that person to meet their own animal selfish and self-serving emotional desires and physical needs."

"For if a person really cares and knows and accepts the danger of an early recovery romance, they should be willing to protect the person they supposedly care about by immediately ending that early relationship with them, and not exploit them even when the other person is too weak to resist their own misplaced needs, desires and feelings."

It has been stated that, "Having sex with someone in early recovery is tantamount to molesting a child due to both do not have the capacity to understand the ramifications and consequences of their actions, and indeed both are being exploited by the person who does know as you clearly NOW know! If you have honestly read this entire discussion on early recovery romances!

"Relapse Victims and Manipulation"

One of the clients was upset and crying and stated that "My brother died because no one cared enough to help him and so my heart always goes out to the suffering addict and I don't get mad when they relapse." The issue of anger towards another client who had relapsed twice in a short time became a very controversial topic. Some clients were angry as well as judgmental and this counselor confronted them about where their anger was coming from. Some realized they were mad at the addiction and others at the addict due to causing them to lose hope that recovery is possible. Other clients stated that they could see themselves in that person and this disgusted them and yet still others were able to recognize as well as admit they were jealous and wanted to drink or use drugs!

This counselor expanded this topic to include clients significant others and the dynamic of trust and hope. The focus was on exploring how to manage or deal with situations in which when confronted by an old drug using friend or a drug dealer, they need to be aware of the risk or danger that exists any time they engage or are involved with these old friends or associates.

One of the clients indicated that they ran into their old drug dealer/friend and they talked about old times. Other clients shared that they did not see anything wrong with doing this and believed that due to having completed treatment that they are strong enough to resist. One of the clients expressed that being around or seeing a drinking former associate would make them feel disgusted and want to throw up. This person remembered the way they use to be and found the idea that if they were around anyone who drinks they would be revolted by it.

Another female client shared that her mother told her that the stepfather who is an alcoholic was passing out in his food, fell off the toilet, crapping on himself, and fell down several times severely hurting himself. The mother then stated. "He reminds me of the way you use to be." The client felt disgusted and became tearful when she related that her mother would always remember her in her worst alcoholic behavior.

She shared that she has much compassion for the stepfather due to his alcoholism she knows that he is a victim as much as her own mother, who is suffering due to his bad behaviors. Another male client shared how his girlfriends family has been deeply hurt and disillusioned when they found out that he was a "drug addict" once they heard about the "needles and heroin" they are pressuring the girlfriend to leave him.

Another group focused on discussing the weekend relapses and asked the clients for their feelings and thoughts on why eight people relapsed. The people in the group showed much compassion and concern for their relapsed peers. When the inquiry was presented regarding if any of the clients in the group had observed any behaviors that would have signaled that relapse was eminent; some indicated that they were totally surprised and others felt they could see that the person was failing in their recovery efforts. One of the roommates of the relapsed client stated that he had just arrived and he could tell by looking at them and their speech that they were using substances. He was grateful they never offered it to him because he is not sure if he could have resisted the temptation.

Another client reported that she thought her roommate was drinking but she could not smell any alcohol; but the person was groggy and their head kept drooping and the next day they were drooling and totally nodding out. One other client stated that one of the women that relapsed was craving in the detox facility and actually going through the ceiling tiles hoping someone before her had stuck a stash up there.

This counselor discussed the correlation between room cleanliness and organization with the predictability of a relapse and the clients shared the following regarding this theme. When the inquiry was presented that how does room care and organization become a measure of recovery or relapse potential; some of the clients shared: "I got up today and felt bad and angry, but I began to clean my room and make my bed and went for the walk and now I feel really good."

"Emphasized to this client that by taking control of his state and forcing himself to take positive actions he was able to manage the underlying negativity and replace it with positive feelings."

"As a result of this he felt a boost to his self-esteem. Inquired of the group if being held to a very high standard of room care and organization felt like harassment or overkill and they replied, "If you did not have a standard then we would try to see what else we could get away with."

Also during this group the issue of "Remembering the good times and how nice it was when doing drugs or drinking" came up. To help demonstrate the concept of "remembering the good times" the model of the "Highline" was utilized. This model consists of taking the concept of a persons "Lifeline" and converting it to a "Highline."

The Highline

------/----/----/----/----/----/----/----/----/----/----/----/----/----/----/----/----/----/--

"The "Highline can be represented by drawing a line as shown above and then placing small intersecting "Hash" marks along that line. Each of those short vertical hash marks represents a negative event along the persons "Highline." They signify negative events that have occurred as a direct use of alcohol or drugs.

They may symbolize things such as: an embarrassing moment due to drinking, a hurtful word or action against someone, an arrest, a threat or ultimatum from a family member or employer, a physical injury due to being drunk or falling due to being high, an emergency room admission or admission to detox, damage done to a car or other property due to intoxication or impairment, loss of money or possessions due to careless spending or just plain stupidity, shame, fear, disgust, guilt and worry, or virtually anything that causes the addict or alcoholic a major or even minor conflict with their own value system. By showing all the negative events that have accumulated through all the years of drinking and getting high by representing them on the person's "Highline;" graphically demonstrates the damage and destruction addiction has done to not only the person but their family or significant others as well.

> "It should be noted that no matter how crowded the "Highline" becomes, no matter how close each little "Hash Mark" is, or how much suffering and damage has been done; the addict or alcoholic only remembers the "Euphoria" of using. It is this "Euphoric Recall" that blinds the person from registering at a deep emotional level all the misery that they are experiencing or are causing their loved ones to suffer!"

This can be represented by making one small infinitesimal pencil "Dot" under the "Highline" so that a dramatic comparison can be immediately recognized between that small miserable "Dot" and the extensive length of the line and the dozens of "Hash Marks" symbolizing all the heartbreak and agony!

This may be diagramed as:

------/----/----/----/----/----/----/----/----/----/----/----/----/----/----/----/----/--

"."

This Dot (".") Represents All The Good Times In Comparison To All The Bad Times

"That dot represents all the "Good Times" in comparison to all the sorrow, grief and unhappiness that has been endured. When it comes to remembering the pain or the pleasure the addict always obsesses on the pleasure; the "Euphoric Recall!" –That ridiculous infinitesimal small Dot (".")

"The memory of the "Good Times" overwhelm any memory of the "Bad Times" in fact it should be common sense that when the addict or alcoholic accumulates a huge history of negative events; it should deter them from any further use."

"In other words the massive accumulation of disasters in their lives should cause them to refrain and stop any further use; but the addict or alcoholic is literally incapable of experiencing at a deep emotional level the pain that would force a person to stop using."

"This is caused by the strong intense feelings related to the "Euphoric Recall" that block any ability to feel the suffering caused by the accumulation of all the consequences of using alcohol and drugs!"

It is just an unfortunate fact that "Euphoric Recall" is stronger than any memories of all the agony and suffering caused by the drugs and alcohol.

"Euphoric Recall" embeds itself into our memory and therefore the history of suffering and loss is not consciously available to deter us from future use.

This perception was described as a component of the mental illness model in which the serious perceptual errors that addicts suffer can be precisely compared to the Schizophrenic who has a delusion of being Napoleon. In this manner the Schizophrenic is no sicker than the addict that is hard wired with "Euphoric Recall" which is the buried belief that "some how some way someday I will be able to use and get away," without consequences "I will be able to use and control my use."

It was expressed that this is a very serious delusion, which is as bad as schizophrenia. In this way "Euphoric Recall" is a delusional system that "Blocks" the addict or alcoholic from feeling the necessary pain and suffering that would enable them or force to clearly recognize the need to cease any further use of mood altering substances.

One last point during this group was to alert the clients to be more sensitive to how their families suffer. It was emphasized to be sensitive to the fact that in the same way the client, felt deep emotional pain over seeing treatment or recovery friends fail; they need to compare that pain to what their own loved ones have repeatedly had to endure.

Informed those clients that they now know firsthand what their families have felt over their relapses or failed attempts to stop or control their own drinking or drug use. While their recovery buddy or roommate or peer is a total stranger and they feel so much pain regarding that person's relapse it was especially emphasized that their strong feelings for their roommates who are literally total strangers is nothing in comparison to how much more is the pain compounded for their significant others when they hurt or disappoint their loved ones.

"The DISEASE IS CHRONIC PROGRESSIVE AND OFTEN FATAL—"as soon as you think you are OK that is when you are not OK!!—We suffer from PECULIAR perceptions and as the AA book states, "strange mental blank spots" which causes us to be somewhat hopeless, but we can protect ourselves by frequently and actively engaging the "Power of Practicing Powerlessness" through the "Art of Turning Resistance into Resolution" as well as the "Power of Resisting Resistance" through the "Art of Self Defiance" and fully engaging the "Power of Commitment" through the "Art of Accountability!"

Chapter Seventeen

Service Sacrifice—Satisfying Sensations

A very interesting phenomenon that I have observed in almost every human being I have ever encountered, whether they are actively in their addiction or in recovery. Whether they are people who have never had a drink or a problem with a drug, or whether they have never drank or drugged in their entire lives; is the fact that there is a built in tendency to want to help others and to get some satisfaction from that action. In other words the activities of "Service and Sacrifice" create very "Satisfying Sensations!"

"There is one thing all people have in common, and that is when anyone any where helps another human being it gives them a guaranteed feel good sensation."

The only exception to this may be the full-blown sociopath, who has no conscience and therefore no compassion for others.

By utilizing this universal principle the recovering person can begin to build very strong resistance against relapse by forcing himself or herself to do these "help other actions." It is highly recommended that the following list of activities from the website "Random Acts of Kindness" be carefully reviewed and at least three on a daily basis be selected as a "Worthy Challenge." (Remember worthy challenge from the chapter on the "Power of Positive Pressure" through the "Art of Controlling Click."

"By doing these Random Acts of Kindness on a daily basis, you will be able to utilize the "Power of Right Action" through the development of the "Art of Service and Sacrifice" to jump start into a super good feeling— the right type of feelings!" Service and Sacrifice are the true paths to "Safe Satisfying Sensations" instead of those experienced by using "Deadly and Dangerous Destructive Drugs!"

The following is a list of positive actions that are beneficial to others—i.e.: picking up your Cigarette butt after throwing it on the ground; enables you to implement the concept of the "Art of Service and Sacrifice" What will dramatically increase your "Power of Right Action" is when you force yourself through the "Power of Resisting the Resistance" by engaging in the "Art of Self Defiance to pick up cigarette butt(s) that are not yours; asking someone if they need an item, since you are going to the store; using phrases such as "please" and "thank you" and "excuse me" so you are more polite with anyone you are involved with in getting something or getting your needs met; being aware and alert to your choice of words and reducing or eliminating vulgar language; when at a register or check out in a store allow someone to get in front of you if they have less items than you do; let others choose activities and do them regardless of how you feel about them, let them watch the show they want to watch or view the movie they want to see; make someone else's bed or if you want to acquire even far greater Power-clean someone else's bathroom; invite someone to join you in an activity that you rather do alone, but would be appropriate for others to join in; pray for someone at least one time-to gain greater Power pray regularly or daily for that person; the greatest Power unleashed is when you pray by name for multiple people regularly or daily; and the way to tap the greatest strength is to pray for some one you dislike; hate or even despise, and to pray they get all the good things you want for yourself and to do this on a daily basis. The Prayer of St. Francis found in an earlier chapter in this book is a great guide regarding this. And absolutely fully demonstrates the principle of the "Art of Service and Sacrifice!"

The following is a partial list of actions that can change your life especially if you do not want to do them and you can practice your personal power to make them happen-it will give you a rush and the ride of your life. These ideas were found on the internet at the following website--

www.actsofkindness.org. The following paragraph is from that website:

"Welcome to the Kindness Movement! We hope you find in these pages a wealth of ideas to help you encourage and promote Random Acts of Kindness (RAK) in your community! Whether you choose to implement these particular ideas or allow them to stimulate ideas of your own, we hope that your brainstorming and planning is both exciting and inspiring for you. We call our volunteers Kindness Coordinators, and they come from all walks of life, ages, and professions. We hope you will decide to join our tens of thousands of participants and become a Kindness Coordinator in your area. Everything you do to share and promote kindness helps make the world a better place. Please use our website to print our free resources. This "Ideas for Individuals and Groups" document provides a wealth of kindness ideas..."

Please look this site up and make yourself knowledgeable of the hundreds and hundreds of ideas to how to practice and spread kindness. As a recovering person you must maintain a unselfish state of living and this is a fool proof and never get bored method to find lots and lots of things that are kind, and you may absolutely do not want to do. In case there are many that you do want to do-feel free to splurge; engage and exploit all you care to binge upon. According to the site "These Activity ideas for Individuals and Groups provide a wealth of kindness ideas for people, organizations, communities and groups who want to do kindness in their area. Feel free to add to these and adapt these ideas to your own"

IDEAS FOR KINDNESS

Collect goods for a food bank.

Make floral arrangements for senior centers, nursing homes, hospitals, police stations, or shut-ins.

Volunteer

Extend a hand to someone in need.

Give your full attention and simply listen.

Sing at a nursing home.

Offer a couple of hours of baby-sitting to parents.

Remember the bereaved with phone calls, cards, plants, and food.

Pay a compliment at least once a day.

Call or visit a homebound person.

Transport someone who can't drive.

Mow a neighbor's grass.

Say something nice to everyone you meet today.

Volunteer at an agency that needs help.

Wipe rainwater off shopping carts or hold umbrellas for shoppers on the way to their cars.

Give the gift of your smile.

Adopt a homeless pet from the humane society.

Organize a scout troop or service club to help people with packages at the mall or grocery.

Offer to answer the phone for the school secretary for ten minutes.

Write notes of appreciation and bring flowers or goodies to teachers or other important people, such as the principal, nurse, custodian, and secretary.

> "In addition to the above GREAT ideas or what you may perceive as Worthy Challenges then there are many more Fantastic things that you can Choose to do!"

Give a hug to a friend.

Tell your children why you love them.

Write a note to your mother/father and tell them why they are special.

Write a thank-you note to a mentor or someone who has influenced your life in a positive way.

Give blood.

Visit hospitals with smiles, treats, and friendly conversation for patients.

Stop by a nursing home, and visit a resident with no family nearby.

Give another driver your parking spot.

Tell a bus or taxi driver how much you appreciate their driving.

Leave an extra big tip for the waitperson.

Open the door for another person.

Pay for the meal of the person behind you in the drive-through.

Leave a bouquet of flowers on the desk of a colleague at work with whom you don't care for.

Call an estranged family member.

Pay for the person behind you in the movie line.

Give flowers to be delivered with meal delivery programs.

Give toys to the children at the shelter or safe house.

For one week, act on every single thought of generosity that arises spontaneously in your heart, and notice what happens as a consequence.

Let the person behind you in the grocery store go ahead of you in line.

When drivers try to merge into your lane, let them in with a wave and a smile.

Buy cold drinks for the people next to you at a ball game.

Give a bag of groceries to a homeless person.

Laugh out loud often and share your smile generously.

Plant a tree in your neighborhood

As you go about your day, pick up trash.

Send a letter to some former teachers, letting them know the difference they made in your life.

Buy books for a day care or school.

Slip a $20 bill to a person who you know is having financial difficulty.

This is not just a list of suggestions for addicts and alcoholics but for all human beings. Doing these suggestions at any age would greatly benefit anyone who would choose to do them.

> "The addict and alcoholic needs to seriously consider taking these actions, simply due to the fact that these actions probably do not have much appeal to them and for the addict or alcoholic these actions may be a matter of life and death. The reason for this is that several forces

drive addiction and the strongest force is that of the need or tendency to be very selfish."

"The best protection from this selfishness threat is to fully develop and utilize the "Power of Right Action" by developing the "Art of Service and Sacrifice" and begin to experience those "Safe Satisfying Sensations!"

In regards to the addicts or alcoholics tendency to be very selfish and this selfishness being a serious threat to the chance for a long lasting recovery; it should be noted that even when it appears a person is altruistically engaged in an activity, it may be more motivated by the fact that the addict or alcoholic experiences a good feeling or sensation from the action, rather than the action is being done purely for the other persons joy or comfort.

As disturbing as this may sound it is nonetheless true. For instance the person may be observed deeply involved with their children or family, or they may be involved in ministries at their church, or they may be actively involved in some type of a community service organization or community activity, especially such as Alcoholics Anonymous, Narcotics Anonymous, Gamblers Anonymous or any of a hundred or more such organizations, and yet despite appearances the main motivation for all this effort and contribution to others is driven by "Pure Selfishness!"

"Addicts and alcoholics whether by nature or simply due to the habitual use of a substance have become very self-centered, self focused, self obsessed as well as self directed and when they are so consumed with only thoughts about themselves it is not possible to recover."

"If a person can place one other persons needs genuinely before their own needs then that person will not relapse."

"Relapse always occurs because the person is self obsessed and only cares about his or her own feelings. By learning to sacrifice for others they engage and have access to the "Power of Right Action" through the "Art of Service and Sacrifice" which changes this negative tendency,

and strengthens their ability to resist an opportunity or
offer to drink or do drugs."

Once again simply stated, addicts and alcoholics will never relapse unless
they are in a selfish, self-centered, self-obsessed, self-consumed and self-directed
emotional state. By the simple act of reading this short list of "Random Acts of
Kindness" on a daily basis the positive energy and feelings will begin to flow
into the person. A slow, but strong desire to do these activities will develop;
as that healthy desire begins to pour into the addict or alcoholic it will begin
to wash away the self-centeredness thus significantly changing the attitudes
and behavior that drive the desire to use drugs and alcohol.

As stated numerous times through out this book, taking actions whether
you want to or not does not matter, all that matters is that you take the actions
and suggestions regardless of how you feel towards taking or not taking those
actions!

"Actions that are taken when a person feels a resistance
towards taking those actions always strengthens their
Resistance Muscle and it is through the Power of Right
Action" that helps develop the ability to develop the
"Art of Service and Sacrifice" for others, that results in
building strong self esteem."

We can describe the concept of "Resistance Muscle" through comparing
these efforts to that of weightlifting. If a person was interested in reaching a
goal of being able to Bench Press 450lbs and for several years they were very
committed to doing their weightlifting routines and worked consistently
hard, could they or would they be able to get the result that they originally
desired?

Before you answer this question, you need to know that the person never
lifted more than a pink three-pound weight for the years that they were
working out. Now if you were to place a 450lbs weight in to their hands while
they were lying down on a bench with their arms straight up, what would
happen? My guess is that they would be either crushed or even killed!

When an addict or alcoholic chooses to stay in their comfort zone
and only take actions that they feel like taking, then all their effort and
work is as useless as the weightlifter who limited his or her workout to no
more resistance than a pink three-pound weight. In the same way that the
weightlifter would never reach the goal of Bench Pressing 450lbs due to not
progressively increasing the weights; the addict or alcoholic will never be able

to develop the strength to resist the offer, interest, opportunity or cravings that they will encounter.

It will be the same result as suddenly dropping 450lbs of weight on someone who has only been lifting pink three-pound weights. When the addict or alcoholic are confronted with a risk or temptation, that sudden load will crush the addict or alcoholic due to they have not built up their strength though progressively working with greater and greater levels of resistance.

Once again it needs to be clarified that the only way an addict or alcoholic can possible build up their ability to resist an offer or opportunity to drink or use drugs is by preparing before that moment of truth. What they need to fully understand, and which has been frequently mentioned through out this book, is the fact that they have to learn to resist their own desires.

> "Desires are what lead to returning to "Deadly Dangerous Destructive Drugs." Desire has to be challenged and when the person does things that—"they do not desire to do," that is when "Resistance Muscle" is being built."

> "By engaging in as many as possible of these suggested "Random Acts of Kindness" will provide enough healthy resistance that will significantly improve a person's chances for long term recovery success through the development of " Safe Satisfying Sensations" through "Service and Sacrifice!"

After all in the book Alcoholics Anonymous on page 20 it clearly states this in the following quote…

> "Our very lives, as ex-problem drinkers, depend upon our constant thought of others and how we may help meet their needs."

In addition to this it states on page 86 the concept of the need to maintain an unselfish way of life and is exemplified in the following quote…

> "Were we thinking about ourselves most of the time? Or were we thinking of what we could do for others, of what we could pack into the stream of life?"

Now Faith is the Substance of things Hoped for, the Evidence of things not Seen.

Hebrews 11:1

Chapter Eighteen

Breathe Right—Feel Right

One of the most powerfully effective methods for taking control and being able to manage any undesirable feelings, sensations or emotions; is through the use of breath management. In this chapter you will learn the power and gain the ability of Centering—Connecting—Comprehending the "Power of Breathing" through the "Art of Breath Management!"

Addicts and alcoholics have a tendency to be oversensitive, which causes them to be over reactive. They need to learn how to control and redirect their negative feelings and emotions. When a person becomes overwhelmed with undesirable and destructive thoughts and emotions, they lose all perspective in regards to the potential consequences and price that they will pay, if they act out on these unhealthy perceptions.

It may be helpful at this time to recognize that any time a person may experience what they perceive to be an unpleasant, undesirable, unwanted or uninvited emotional sensation, it is always driven by a very particular pattern of breathing. The best way to describe how a pattern of breathing is directly related to a pattern of feeling is to show a clear connection.

Whenever a person is experiencing anxiety, tension, worry, fear, concern, apprehension or any other emotion that creates a feeling of stress, those feelings will always be associated to a pattern of high, rapid, shallow breathing. In other words the person is taking rapid short breaths, high in their chest.

The following exercise will demonstrate the clear connection between the way a person feels is directly related to how a person breathes. I want you to now think about a problem or concern that causes you much worry and stress, and I want you to focus on allowing yourself to not just feel, but to deeply experience those emotions. Once you notice that you are actually not just thinking about a specific thing, that you are worried or concerned about, but also actually feeling apprehension deep in your body; then and only then will you be ready to do the second part of this exercise.

"Once you have been able to really "Center" the tension and stress in your body, not as just a superficial or random thought, but as a deep sense of nervous discomfort then you will be ready to fully "Comprehend" how feelings, emotions and your breath are intricately "Connected" and interrelated."

"When you have reached the point in which you are actually "Centering" on feeling the emotional distress, then "Comprehending" how emotions and patterns of breathing are intricately woven together will be easier to recognize."

"By just simply understanding how "Connecting" the pattern of breathing with a particular feeling or emotion; will give you total and absolute control over any and all unpleasant and undesirable emotional states."

This connection will be demonstrated to you by challenging you to do the following. Clearly identify the level of distress and discomfort that is being experienced due to the worry and concern about the problem that you have been concentrating and focusing on. To gain the maximum benefit from this exercise it will be helpful to place a rating on the level of distress that you are experiencing and to increase it. For instance if you were to use a scale between 1 and 5 and 1 represented a very low level of stress and 5 represented extreme sleepless anxiety; I want you to increase your perceived distress to at least 3 or 4. If you are struggling with accomplishing this then you are just not trying hard enough!

"A sure way to succeed in reaching the higher numbers is to take control of your breathing and begin to breathe in a rapid, short and shallow manner or pattern. Notice what immediately happens—yes you begin to feel more anxious; so you can see even before we continue with this interesting exercise you have already gained some power over your moods and feelings!"

Now while in that intense state of stress and worry notice that as you inhale the unpleasantness and the uncomfortable feelings will actually intensify.

Once you have maximally inhaled your breath, prior to exhaling, challenge yourself to maintain the same high intense level of emotional discomfort that you had while you were inhaling. Using the 1 to 5 rating scale; try to maintain the same high number on the exhaled breath as you found was so easily to do on the inhaled breath.

To review the instructions for this exercise or challenge take the worry and concern you are experiencing in your mind as well as in your body, and while you are inhaling give it a score of 1 to 5. One on this scale being a feeling that is hardly even noticeable and five being so incredibly uncomfortable that you would do anything to change it. I want you to not just try this four or five times, but do it four or five times. As you are thinking about the thing that is causing you stress, increase that stress as you are inhaling and then challenge yourself to maintain that high level of discomfort as you are exhaling. As stated do this three or four more times.

What you will notice will please and shock you, and that is…

> "It is impossible to maintain the exact same high level of stress and discomfort when you're exhaling as what you experience when you're inhaling. The reason for this is that it requires a high degree of tension throughout the body to inhale and conversely tension throughout the body must be relaxed in order to be able to exhale. This is the reason why tension and stress are clearly experienced more on the inhale and far less on the exhale."

Once you prove this to yourself then the way you can use this vital fact is to manipulate your own pattern of breathing to take complete control of any emotional state. As an addict or an alcoholic the ability to change states rapidly and effectively is absolutely necessary to protect recovery. When a person drinks or drugs they usually do so because they cannot tolerate the emotional state that they were currently experiencing prior to returning to drug or alcohol use. Through the utilization of breath management or the "Power of Breathing" through the "Art of Breath Management" the person is empowered and protected from the need to have to use mood-altering substances.

This method of breath management can effectively be utilized to control and manage any unpleasant feelings, sensations, as well as cravings, by just simply being aware of the pattern of breath that is associated to these emotional states. In other words if a person was to experience strong cravings, those feelings of craving can only occur when the person is in a pattern of "high rapid shallow breathing."

> "Therefore by changing their breath pattern they can completely change the undesirable or destructive emotional state that could cause them to resort to drugs or alcohol to gain relief. In the same sense by learning to breathe "Low, Deep and Slow" they can remove or reduce any cravings."

> "By learning to utilize breath management and to become more aware of the need to engage in a conscious effort to breathe in a "Low, Deep and Slow" manner the addict or alcoholic reduces the need to rely upon drugs or alcohol."

When you gain full understanding of the "Power of Breathing" through the "Art of Breath Management" by actually doing the above exercise, then you will need to learn the most effective and healthiest method of breathing. The following method will teach you how to "breathe right-feel right."

The type of breathing that is most effective in reducing and eliminating negative emotional sensations and feelings is what is referred to as diaphragmatic breathing. The following instructions will clearly show you how to engage in this type of breathing.

To breathe diaphragmatically it is necessary to recognize that most people tend to breathe in a shallow and fast manner. Take a moment and notice the difference between the two following methods or patterns of breathing. In the first pattern, take a deep breath and as you do so expand your upper chest and notice how your shoulders rise and tend to move backwards as does your neck and head follow the shoulders.

Now generally most people refer to this pattern of breathing as "deep breathing" but in actuality it is really "shallow breathing." Many times when a person is told to take a deep breath, this would be the pattern that they would engage in. The reason I referred to this breathing as "shallow breathing" is due to the fact that when you breathe high in your lungs, there is less capacity for the exchange of oxygen in the upper lung due to the fact that there are less oxygen exchange structures in that area of the lungs.

Now take a moment and follow the directions to engage in the second pattern of breathing and notice how radically different they feel. The second pattern I will instruct you in is that of "diaphragmatic breathing." This pattern of breathing is referred to as a yoga style of breathing and is the most effective method in moving the greatest quantity of oxygen from the lungs into the bloodstream. To engage in diaphragmatic breathing, it is necessary to recognize the clear difference, "between a high shallow breath" and a "Low Deep Breath." As discussed previously a "high shallow breath" will occur when a person moves their chest and shoulders up and back. Whereas a "Low Deep Breath" can only be accomplished when a person consciously pushes their lower abdomen out deliberately and forcefully.

To engage in the second pattern of yoga style breathing, imagine that your lungs are empty plastic bags and instead of filling them with oxygen, fill them with water. As you imagine filling your lungs with water that is in form of the oxygen you are pouring into your lungs with one long deep breath. Now push your abdomen out as if it is filling like those plastic bags that are now expanding and bulging and pushing your stomach out.

It may be helpful to understand that as you follow this instruction you have learned to engage your diaphragm and therefore are now breathing diaphragmatically. The reason your lower abdomen expands outwards is due to your conscious control of your diaphragm muscle is forcing your lower organs to be pushed out. Don't be alarmed your organs are well connected and attached and all that is happening is the diaphragm is now being used to maximally inflate your lungs, and in this manner the greatest quantity of oxygen can more efficiently as well as effectively be inhaled into your lungs and into your blood system.

Once you fully understand the second pattern of breathing, this "diaphragmatic breathing" you should practice it many times each day, until it becomes your first pattern of breathing. Any time you notice tension or stress either in your mind or in your body by engaging in this pattern of breathing will immediately reduce if not completely eliminate that tension or stress.

The reason various methods of meditation that involve breath management is so effective is that it triggers something in the mind and the body that was referred to as "The Relaxation Response" and in actuality what this will do; will allow you to take some control over what you experience as negative feelings or sensations and emotions. With practice this technique could actually give you the ability to take full control over unpleasant or undesirable feelings.

In his book, first published in 1976 by the same title "The Relaxation Response" Dr. Herbert Benson indicated that his research demonstrated significant emotional as well as physical improvements and reductions in related symptoms that are related to or caused by stress. He stated on the first page of his book the following:

"There are 10 reasons to learn the relaxation response (1) relieves fatigue and helps you cope with your anxieties. (2) Relieves the stress that can lead to high blood pressure, hardening of the arteries, heart attack and stroke. (3) Reduces the tendency to smoke, drink, "turn on" with drugs. (4) Can be used to help you sleep. (5) Conserves the body store of energy. (6) Makes you more alert, so you can focus on what's really important. (7) Reaffirms the value of meditation and prayer in daily life. (8) Can be learned without classes and lectures, in your own home. (9) Can be used anywhere, even on the way to work. (10) Has no dangerous side effects.

Dr. Benson indicated in that book that the "Relaxation Response" occurs in context of religious teachings and he stated that religious prayers and related mental techniques have measurable, definable physiologic effects on the body. He also goes into great depth and understanding of the "fight or flight" responses in the body whenever a person is or feels threatened. It is this "fight or flight" response in regards to stress that has been scientifically linked to significant physiological diseases. These physiological changes have been linked to the causes of hypertension, hardening of the arteries, heart attack and stroke.

Even though this book was written 35 years ago and the relationship between stress and these diseases was just beginning to be understood, we can see how accurate his research was, when we compare it to our understanding of this relationship between the Mind, the Body and the emotional Spirit at the present time.

The addict and alcoholic will not only benefit from learning to control unpleasant and undesirable as well as an invited negative emotional and mental states through the practice of engaging the "relaxation response" but they will also be able to protect and improve not only their recovery but there emotional, mental as well as physical health.

The relaxation response has been more commonly known as "meditation." The benefits of meditation have clearly been described elsewhere in this book in regards to the chapter "Visualizing Victory." No matter which method of meditation you choose to practice, and there are countless types that you can study, there is however four (4) very basic elements. Following these four suggestions will maximally improve the ability to meditate and therefore improve all the benefits that will be gained through this practice.

Those four elements are:

1. The need for a quiet environment-you have to be able to disconnect from not only internal stimuli but also any external distractions. Find a quiet room, or just being outside completely with nature, without any man made sounds or distractions.

2. Use a very specific object or word to deeply focus upon-this could be a favorite prayer or phrase, such as from a Bible or some other religious work, or from a poem.

3. It is essential to learn how to empty all thoughts and distractions from one's mind. This is not difficult to do when the "Power of Breathing" is implemented through the "Art of Breath Management" and diaphragmatic breathing techniques are fully utilized!

4. Find a comfortable position. It is suggested that a seating position is most effective and it should be noted, that if you engage in the techniques to create the Relaxation Response while you're in a laying down position, such as being in bed, these techniques will cause sleep.

Even though a person may desire to use these techniques to learn to fall asleep more easily; falling asleep is not the same as meditation. The benefits of falling asleep although are great, sleeping will never compare to the massive benefit received from regular meditation.

In his book Dr. Benson relates that meditation is not a form of sleep nor can it be used as a substitute for sleep. Meditation does create some of the same physiological effects of sleep, but the two are not in any way interchangeable, nor is one a substitute for the other.

In the 12 step programs the 11th Step states "Through prayer and meditation we improve our conscious contact with God as we understand Him." The early alcoholics, who contributed to this conclusion, recognized the need and benefit of prayer and meditation to improve their chances of a lasting recovery. It is therefore strongly recommended that any addict or alcoholic learn the practice of meditation

It should be clearly stated that although it's absolutely necessary to engage in meditation if not some form of prayer it is not essential to do it in any particular manner or way. The reader is free to choose any means or method they care to, but they must consider the necessity to do this minimally once a day and preferably more than a dozen times a day.

"It is through learning to control and manage your emotions and your feelings that will enable the addict or alcoholic to gain the ability to change any feeling, sensation or emotion instantly and at will."

"It is through this learning that the person will develop the ability and capability to take full responsibility for the management of any undesirable or unpleasant feeling, without the need to even consider the use of a mood altering substance."

For addicts and alcoholics that are religious there is a powerfully effective technique of meditation and deep breathing that is focused on experiencing a feeling of connection and closeness to God.

"The method is to verbalize, "I am that" while you are exhaling and to say, "I am" while you are inhaling. By deeply focusing on those five special spiritual words "I am, that I am" and concentrating on the above pattern of breathing while not just stating those words. But through the conscious active use of these words you WILL experience a really DEEPER feeling that WILL begin to enable you to KNOW that we are indeed ONE with the universe."

As you may recall in the chapter titled "Visualizing Victory" the benefits of mediation are fully explained.

Epilogue

Is It Really Over And Completed?

Whether you liked it or not—It is definitely quite a testament—for a man who ABSOLUTELY has detested and hated writing my entire life and who was forced to learn to use a computer in the late after hours into the late night due to "Jerry no one can read a single word that you write and we cannot stay in business or continue to help people without legible documentation—you must learn to print!" What they did not know was that I was already printing as clearly and as fast as I could!

The final question I am asking myself is how do you end a book that is composed of a lifetime of observation and experience?

You don't end it –it is Life and it never ends and we and I will be adding chapter after chapter—none the less written and unwritten in this life and the next and others will write written and unwritten necessary chapters for themselves and the ones they love and love them!

I have had the privilege and honor to write what already existed but was unwritten!

I give the deepest humblest gratitude and appreciation for what God has done through me and through having had the opportunity and privilege to be an instrument of His Peace and deeply care for, treat and learn from so many of His Children!

If you know me by now—You Know That You Don't Know—and if by now you have actually read every word and you are still that egotistical to be offended by any reference to God—then for you alone I resubmit the proposal that GOD is an accurate acronym for having GOD in your life "G" for Good "O" for Orderly and "D" for Direction! No human being can deny the need to have Good Orderly Direction in their life—it is so much easier to just Resist the Resistance to Resist and state whether you want to or not—build that "Resistance Muscle" and verbalize LOUD and PROUD "I NEED GOD IN MY LIFE."

After all "What do you have to loose?!"

Bibliography

How To Sell Anything to Anybody by Joe Girard, Published by Warner Books 1979

The Relaxation Response by Herbert Benson, M.D. Published by Avon Books 1976

Awaken the Giant Within by Anthony Robbins, Published by Free Press 2003

Think & Grow Rich Action Pack by Napoleon Hill, Published Hawthorn Books, Inc. 1972

Alcoholics Anonymous, World Services, Inc. 2003

Twelve Steps and Twelve Traditions, World Services, Inc. 2003

Sermon on the Mount by Emmett Fox, Harper Collins Publishers Inc. 1989

Holy Bible (King James) Version